It Is not Death to Die

A New Biography of Hudson Taylor

James Hudson Taylor in middle life

It Is not Death to Die

A New Biography of Hudson Taylor

Jim Cromarty

CHRISTIAN
FOCUS

Dedication

To my three faithful critics whose manuscript reading
and the subsequent suggestions for improvements,
have been greatly appreciated:
my wife, Valerie;
my sister-in-law, Elizabeth; and
my Pastor's wife, Lindy.
And special thanks must go to Charlotte Hails
of Overseas Missionary Fellowship International, London
for answering all my questions and the help she has given in sorting
out the use of research material.
To these four ladies I give my sincere thanks.

© Jim Cromarty
ISBN 978-1 84550-367-3

10 9 8 7 6 5 4 3 2 1

Published in 2001
Reprinted 2008
by
Christian Focus Publications,
Geanies House, Fearn, Ross-shire,
IV20 1TW, Great Britain

www.christianfocus.com

Copyright material is used by permission of OMF International
Cover design by Daniel Van Straaten
Printed by CPD Wales

Contents

Contents

Introduction

In 1874, when facing great difficulties, feeling forgotten by the Christian world and confined to bed Hudson Taylor wrote:

If God has called you to be really like Jesus in your spirit, He will draw you into a life of crucifixion and humility, and put on you such demands of obedience that *He will not allow you to follow other Christians*; and in many ways He will seem to let other good people do things that He will not let you do. Other Christians and ministers who seem very religious and useful may push themselves, pull wires and work schemes to carry out their schemes, but you cannot do it; and if you attempt it, you will meet with such failure and rebuke from the Lord as to make you sorely penitent. Others may brag on themselves, on their work, on their success, on their writings, but the Holy Spirit will not allow you to do any such thing; and if you begin it, He will lead you into some deep mortification that will make you despise yourself and all your good works.

Others may be allowed to succeed in making money, but it is likely that God will keep you poor, because He wants you to have something far better than gold, and that is a helpless dependence upon Him, that He may have the privilege (the right) of supplying your needs day by day out of an unseen treasury. The Lord will let others be honoured and put forward, and keep you hidden away in obscurity, because He wants some choice fragrant fruit for His coming glory which can only be produced in the shade. He will let others do a work for Him and get the credit for it, but He will let you work and toil on without knowing how much you are doing; and then to make your work still more precious, He will let others get the credit for the work you have done, and this will make your reward ten times greater when Jesus comes.

The Holy Spirit will put a watch over you, with a jealous love, and will rebuke you for little words and feelings or for wasting your time, over which other Christians never seem distressed. So make up your mind that God is an infinite Sovereign, and has the right to do as He pleases with His own, and He may not explain to you a thousand things which may puzzle your reason in His dealings with you. He will take you at your word and if you absolutely sell yourself to be His slave, He will wrap you up in a jealous love and let other people say and do many things which He will not let you say or do.

Settle it for ever that you are to deal directly with the Holy Spirit, and that He is to have the privilege of tying your tongue, or chaining your hand, or closing your eyes, in ways that He does not deal with others. Now when you are so possessed with the Living God, that you are in your secret heart pleased and delighted over the peculiar, personal, private, jealous guardianship of the Holy Spirit over your life, you will have found the vestibule of heaven.

These were the thoughts of a man who walked closely with his God, and who, when deserted by the world, knew that his Lord was near by, giving him the strength and wisdom to carry out His purposes.

Hudson's life was based upon the teaching of God's Word which he knew to be the infallible, inspired word of the Sovereign Ruler of the universe who was to be obeyed at all times.

His philosophy was simple:

> There is a living God.
> He has spoken in the Bible.
> He means what He says,
> and will do all that He has promised.

Hudson Taylor's life is one that should encourage Christians to step out in faith to fulfil the commands of God. His life's work was motivated by love of God and a love of his fellow man. His heart's desire was to see Christ glorified in the salvation of sinners, particularly the Chinese.

1

Heirs of Life Together

The Royston Anglican church was a hive of activity as two popular locals were to be married. The bell ringers were hard at work ringing out the announcement that it was time for the bridal party to arrive. However all was not well. Betty Johnson the lovely bride was ready, but the groom, James Taylor, a local stone mason, was nowhere to be seen.

The bell ringers played on as they anxiously gazed down the road hoping to see their friend appear.

However, events were taking place that would forever change the character of the man who would be the great grandfather of James Hudson Taylor, the founder of the China Inland Mission. That day God was establishing his covenant with a sinner who was about to enter the Kingdom of God.

James Taylor believed himself to be an upstanding Christian; after all he was a member of the Staincross Ridge Anglican Church choir, and one who with others rang the church bells each Lord's Day to announce the time for public worship.

James, always the life of the party, was a very popular young man, who enjoyed dancing and musical activities.

In 1776 the Church of England was spiritually dead. Many of the men who occupied the pulpits did so because the ministry was a life of security and ease. The great doctrines of grace were largely forgotten, resulting in a marked decline in the morality of society. Drunkenness, with all its associated evils was widespread, and many godly men and women saw the nation's only hope to be in a spiritual revival!

God in his mercy had raised up a group of men to preach the great Biblical doctrines of salvation in a risen Christ, through the new birth and the subsequent godly living.

George Whitefield and John and Charles Wesley commenced a vibrant ministry throughout the United Kingdom and America which resulted in hundreds of thousands of men, women, boys and girls coming to faith in Christ.

When those great evangelists were rejected by the established Church of England, they preached Christ in the open fields. Thousands came to hear the gospel preached with the result that society was changed. The Spirit of Christ touched sinners' hearts and many began to live righteous lives.

With the kingdom of Satan under attack its members rose up in anger to oppose those who dared preach a risen Christ.

John Wesley had visited the Barnsley area where James Taylor lived with the result that some locals were won to Christ. His next door neighbours, Joseph and Elizabeth Shaw, had been converted and were now members of the new Methodist faith. Elizabeth, who suffered from rheumatic problems, had been a cripple for a long time, but when she and her husband attended a meeting of a visiting Methodist preacher, not only did they come to faith in Christ, but Elizabeth was miraculously healed of her physical disability. Now, instead of the groans of a sick woman next door, James heard songs of praise. He also noticed that the Shaws met with farmer Cooper and his family to study the Scriptures and worship God.

This way of life was not for James. He had a slight understanding of the Bible, but was unconverted and wanted nothing to do with the 'Bible Bashers' who were considered by the locals to be religious extremists.

It was not just in Barnsley that the Methodists were treated with contempt, but wherever the fearless preachers warned of God's wrath upon sinners and the coming judgment when Christ returned, violence and persecution followed.

The courageous preaching of the evangelists was accompanied by the power of God and revival began to sweep through the countryside.

In 1760 a Wesleyan preacher had visited the Barnsley area where he was confronted by the godless young locals who shouted out their curses upon both God and the evangelist. When they had finished their mocking they took out the rotten eggs and manure they were carrying and took aim. In this way they made the preacher's work a misery. But what more could be expected in an age where duelling, immorality, adultery, drunkenness, fornication, gambling, swearing and Sabbath-breaking were commonplace.

Despite the opposition and persecution, Christ was faithfully preached by the Wesleyan ministers who lived godly lives and cared for their converts.

John Wesley himself had visited the area staying overnight with the Shaws where he found a small group of Wesleyans worshipping God.

James was really unconcerned about the Methodists as his great joy was to be found in the fact that he was to marry his beloved Betty Johnson of Royston.

It was the morning of his wedding day but his mind was in turmoil. As he carried in some bundles of corn, the seed from which he would make flour for his new wife to bake bread, a passage of Scripture filled his mind. He simply couldn't get the words out of his mind. He had no idea where he had read or heard the words, but it was possible that he'd heard them from John Wesley himself: 'As for me and my house, we will serve the Lord.'

That very day—his wedding day—the Holy Spirit commenced a work of grace in James' heart that would produce fruit, a thousand fold through his witness and that of his descendants, especially James Hudson Taylor, his great-grandson and founder of the China Inland Mission.

For a time, all thoughts of his wedding were blotted out with more weightier matters, concerning his eternal welfare.

In the barn where the sheaves of wheat were being stacked, James dropped to his knees in prayer as his heart was overcome by thoughts of sin and judgment.

Kneeling upon the straw floor, the love of God flooded his heart and he surrendered his life to Christ. The words of Scripture: 'As for me and my house we will serve the Lord' which had so troubled his mind were now part of his life. Then and there, not only did he dedicate his life to Christ, but he also promised that his family would serve the Lord.

Suddenly James realised that the hours had flown. For a time eternity had reached down and invaded time, but now there was a wedding to be attended!

The sun was high in the sky, the bell-ringers were at their post and the bridal party was ready, but the groom was still missing!

Hurriedly James dressed and set off to catch up with the wedding party, while the bell ringers played a little longer, giving him the extra minutes he needed.

There in the old church at Royston, on 1 February, 1776 James and Betty were married, but Betty soon found out that the man she married was not the same one who had courted her. He was now a new creation and the servant of the Lord Jesus Christ.

As he escorted Betty to their home he told her everything that had taken place that morning. Gone now were the days of dancing and other worldly activities that they both once loved.

Betty was shocked by what she heard. This was not the man to whom she had been engaged. Yet in his face she could see the change and in surprise exclaimed, 'Surely I have not married one of those Methodists!'

Soon Betty found out that married life was not all she had expected with the once fun-loving, worldly James. He was now mixing with the Shaws and Coopers and others who were members of the *Staincross Society* which met in the Shaw's home.

Frivolity and worldliness were no longer part of his life. Gone were the times when he entertained the crowds at the local fairs with his fiddle and singing. Now he used all of his gifts in the service of his Lord and Saviour. With his fiddle and lovely singing voice he now glorified the Lord Jesus Christ.

After their first evening meal together James took out his Bible and announced that in future 'family worship' would be conducted in the Taylor house. Betty, however, had made up her mind that she would have nothing to do with her new husband's extremist ways.

No! She wasn't going to take part in family worship, even though she felt that what he was doing was right.

When the Bible was brought out, Betty made herself busy with the household chores giving James a tongue lashing about his new way of life. She was unwilling to follow her new husband's spiritual life and suffer the mocking of her friends!

Each night James read the Scriptures and prayed aloud, making sure that Betty heard every word spoken.

Betty continued to voice her complaints about her husband's spiritual life until he could stand it no longer.

One night, he picked her up in his strong arms and carried her upstairs to their bedroom. Sitting her down, he knelt in front of her and confessed the deep feelings of his heart. Then, bowing his head and closing his eyes he prayed that God might touch Betty's heart and save her from her sins by giving her a saving faith in the Lord Jesus Christ.

How he praised God when his prayer was answered, because the very next day Betty was deeply convicted of her sins. That night when the Bible was brought out for family worship, she knelt beside her husband while he prayed.

Now, the two young lovers were forever united in their love of God. They had become heirs of life together in the Lord Jesus Christ!

2

A Dirty Frying Pan

James and Betty knew what it was to suffer persecution for Christ's sake. Daily they took up their cross to follow the Lord Jesus. At Staincross Ridge, they opened their home for meetings of the despised Methodists.

However, a serious accident meant that James was unable to continue the heavy work associated with being a stone mason. The only other work available in the country area was heavy manual labour so the family was obliged to pack their meagre belongings and look for employment in a larger town.

Nearby Barnsley was a manufacturing centre and it was there that James found work in a linen warehouse owned by the local magistrate, Joseph Beckett. There he earned thirteen shillings and six pence a week out of which he paid rent on a four roomed cottage in Old Mill Lane, as well as the usual government taxes.

With two sons and three daughters James and Betty found it difficult to make ends meet, particularly as the cost of living was much higher in Barnsley than in the country.

Before spending any money, they sacrificially tithed, putting aside one shilling and six pence for the work of the gospel and the help of the poor and needy. This sacred giving was put into a cup set aside for that holy offering to the Lord.

The citizens of Barnsley were spiritually dead as the Church of England and the nonconformist churches failed to preach Christ.

This state of affairs upset the Taylor family, who continually heard the name of Christ blasphemed. Consequently Betty and James commenced spiritual meetings in their own home, where Christ was glorified in song and teaching. Soon this group became an official Methodist Society consisting of seven members. In time James proved his worth and was appointed the group leader.

Opposition to these meetings was so intense that often some of the local trouble makers gathered outside the Taylor home and did all they could to disrupt proceedings. They banged on pans and kettles and anything else on which they could lay their hands.

When attempts were made to set the front door alight, members of the congregation were pelted with 'the foulest filth' as they extinguished the flames.

Another practice was to cover the chimney with clumps of grass and dirt, causing the meeting room to be filled with clouds of smoke.

Loving Christ meant that James stood firm for spiritual truth. He preached in the streets and suffered the assaults of an ungodly community. Often he was the target of the local hoodlums who pelted him with stones and garbage. On other occasions he was dragged from his preaching place and rolled in the filthy mud.

But he was strong in faith and believed the encouraging words of Christ: 'Blessed are you when they revile and persecute you, and say all kinds of evil against you falsely for My sake. Rejoice and be exceedingly glad, for great is your reward in heaven...' (Matt. 5:11, 12).

He considered it an honour to be knocked down in the market place, dragged through the streets and covered with stinking garbage. Each time, when he was rescued from the angry mob, he stood up and again fearlessly preached the gospel.

At times he faced very violent opposition. Once he was met by several men who pretended friendliness, but they were determined to cause trouble. While he was talking to one of the men the other rubbed a mixture of glass and mud into his face. He was saved from serious injury when Joseph Beckett appeared on the scene and the men escaped.

James refused to take any action against them because he was willing to suffer for the sake of his Saviour, telling Mr Beckett: 'No, the Lord is well able to deal with them. I would rather leave it in his hands.'

When the injuries meant that he was unable to work for seven weeks his friend and employer, Mr Beckett decided he would take action through the courts on James' behalf.

When the charges against one guilty man were read out he denied all knowledge of the assault and in an oath called upon God to strike him with blindness if he were lying.

Soon after he became blind and for the remainder of his life was forced to use a guide dog to get around. His accomplice felt the rod of God's anger and never prospered in his work or life.

At Eastgate a godless woman saw James walking down the street wearing his good coat and having a dirty frying pan in her hand attacked him by rubbing the soot and fat over the back of his coat. Instead of rebuking the woman, he turned around and invited her to do the same to the front of his clothes.

Betty and James suffered greatly for the cause of Christ, but eventually much of the opposition ceased when the locals saw their gentleness, faithfulness and godliness.

They had the privilege of entertaining the great evangelist, John Wesley overnight—an honour the family never forgot. We can only imagine the joy and honour they felt when the great and godly leader of the Methodists sat at their table.

John Wesley recorded his visit to Barnsley in his diary: 'Friday, June 30, 1786: I turned aside to Barnsley, formerly famous for all manner of wickedness. They were then ready to tear any Methodist preacher in pieces. Now not a dog wagged its tongue. I preached near the Market Place to a very large congregation, and I believe the truth sank into many hearts.'

James, who was thirty-seven years old when John Wesley visited his home, died nine years later.

It was then that his eldest son, John, assumed his father's mantle, becoming the class leader of the Barnsley Methodist congregation.

This meant work!

Class leaders were expected to visit each member at least once each week to encourage, rebuke, counsel and receive gifts to be used helping the poor in the community. Leaders were to meet with the Minister to discuss local problems and make sure that stipends were paid.

John, who spent many hours distributing tracts, the Scriptures and other spiritual material, preached each night. This work was in addition to his normal daily trade.

He married Mary Shepherd and together they opened their home in the service of the Lord. Like John's mother, Mary became a class leader.

Opposition to the Methodist movement was gradually dying out, but John suffered for his Saviour. On one occasion as he walked along the street an angry man ran to him and punched him.

'Take that for Jesus Christ's sake!' his attacker shouted.

John calmly looked at his attacker and quietly replied, 'I do take it for Jesus Christ's sake.'

John and Mary Taylor were grandparents of Hudson Taylor, missionary to China.

3

Growing Up

John and Mary's son James, wanted to study medicine, but despite his father's successful business producing 'reeds and stays' for the linen looms, the family situation made this impossible. He was one of eight children so he commenced the study of pharmacy, little realising that he would become a well-to-do Barnsley chemist. He was apprenticed to a Rotherham pharmacist which meant he spent seven years away from his family. He loved his Saviour and spent many hours before an open Bible because the study of theology was his delight.

He was an inventive person who developed a shorthand scheme which proved very useful in his studies and later in sermon preparation.

When he was young his parents moved to a new home across the street which meant they were living very close to Benjamin Hudson, the Wesleyan minister. As a result the two families became close friends—especially James and Amelia. Many happy hours were spent worshipping, singing and playing together. It was said of John Taylor that he had 'a very beautiful voice and a perfect musical ear'; and of Amelia, that she had the voice of a 'nightingale'.

She was fifteen years old when her family moved to Barnsley but because of family financial difficulties she commenced work a year later as the governess of three youngsters—the children of a wealthy farmer at Castle Donnington.

During her holidays with her family at Barnsley everyone noticed that James Taylor also made his way home. After all it was only a ten mile walk to visit his parents—and the girl he loved!

There was great joy in both families when James and Amelia announced their engagement—he being twenty-two years of age and she just sixteen.

James studied hard, but always spent a lot of time bearing witness to the Lord he loved. Every Sunday, when he had the opportunity, he visited the surrounding villages preaching salvation in the Lord Jesus Christ. The church leaders, recognizing his spiritual gifts, appointed him as one of the Barnsley preachers when he was just nineteen.

Following his successful apprenticeship he leased a pharmacy at 21 Cheapside, Barnsley. Then with financial help from his father and elder brother, he purchased the property.

He proved to be a good businessman who was totally honest in his dealings with other people. He worked in the pharmacy six days a week and devoted the Lord's day to preaching and other spiritual activities. After several years he repaid his debt to his father and brother. As he was financially secure, on 5 April, 1831, he and Amelia were married.

Amelia had a pleasant, quiet personality and soon proved her worth in the family and the church, teaching a girls' class where she was greatly loved and respected. She also gave valuable assistance to her husband in his work as a class leader of about fifty young men and boys.

It was during those early years that James developed a prayerful interest in China where he longed to do missionary work, if it ever proved possible.

Together he and Amelia conducted family worship, reading the Word, praying and praising God in song. They longed for a child, praying that God might give them a son who would take the gospel to the Chinese people.

The word spoken to Moses and recorded in Exodus 13:2 made such a deep impression upon their hearts that they covenanted to obey what their Lord had commanded his ancient people: 'Sanctify [set apart] to Me all the firstborn,…both of man and animal; it is mine.' Before their baby was born, they knelt down and gave him back to the Lord.

When James Hudson Taylor was born on 21 May, 1832, he was dedicated to the Lord who accepted their offering and set him apart

Hudson's father, James Taylor, later in life

to take the good news concerning Christ to the Chinese. Hudson knew nothing of this until he had spent many years as a missionary in China.

James Hudson Taylor was named after both parents, yet soon was called Hudson by everyone.

Two years after his birth another son, William, was born, but he only lived seven years.

Next came a sister, who became his dearest friend. She was named Amelia, after her mother. Another brother arrived, but he died when he was young. When Hudson was eight years old Louisa was born.

Hudson's father was in some ways a strange man, who was extremely shy, even with his friends. He didn't talk much and often went out of his way to avoid meeting people who visited his shop or home.

Yet he was a most efficient chemist who was sought out by people from all social classes, seeking his advice for their medical problems. He was widely read and proved very capable in the diagnosis and treatment of illnesses.

James loved his Lord and visited the surrounding villages preaching the gospel. He and Amelia opened their home to their Christian friends especially those from the outlying districts. Many of these people had welcomed him into their homes when he visited their locality. Together they would sit down to a meal, and when time permitted they sang hymns of praise to Christ. Then the Scriptures would be read followed by prayer to the God and Father of the Lord Jesus.

James was known for his honesty and his debts were always paid on time. He said, 'If I let it stand over a week, I defraud my creditor of interest, if only a small sum.'

He enjoyed mathematics and served for twenty two-years as manager of the local Building Society which had been established by the Methodist Church to provide finance to people who otherwise would never have been able to purchase a home.

To ensure accuracy of loan repayments he worked out interest payments to four or five decimal places.

He was a generous man, always ready to help those in need. He refused to take anyone to court to recover a debt and often returned the payment to those who couldn't really afford the cost of his services. His usual comment to such people was, 'It's all right ....We'll send that bill up to heaven and settle it there.' To others who needed help he often said, 'Come again, come again. Bring the bottle back when the medicine is done and I will gladly fill it.' Of course this was done free of charge!

However James, who was at times quick tempered, was very careful with the use of money. Wanting to make sure that his family would be left well-off when he died he bought property, making every effort to pay off the debt as quickly as possible. Consequently Amelia found it a struggle to make ends meet with her household allowance.

Only plain foods were eaten by the Taylor family with breakfast consisting of porridge and bread and butter. Again there was bread or toast and butter for the evening meal. Meat was on the table for one meal each day. Although cakes and puddings were a rarity Mother provided some delicacies at times—fruit, nuts and raisins.

To save money James decided that his children should receive home teaching.

He taught them self control by having them say no to things they wanted. This was practised sometimes at meals when he asked, 'Who will see if they can do without something to-day?'

He also expected his children to eat all that was set before them and there were times when their father's punishments seemed very severe. Amelia was sent to her room one Sunday evening when she left a tiny piece of food on her plate.

James, who knew he was responsible for teaching his children to be obedient, respectful and submissive to God, often spoke of Eli who failed in his parental duty and lived to see his adult children bring shame upon the name of Jehovah and himself.

Sometimes Hudson objected to his father's strictness, but his mother, always the peacemaker, warned him with the words, 'My dear, he is your father. Not a word! Remember, "Honour your father".'

James demanded punctuality at all times, reasoning that if everyone was just one minute late for a meal, many minutes would be wasted each day and over a year the wasted time would amount to hours and even days.

Mother called the children from bed no later than 7 a.m. and everyone had to be seated at the breakfast table at 8 a.m.. The midday meal was at 12:30 p.m. and the evening meal at 4:30 p.m..

The family wasted no time, even when dressing!

Mother on the other hand was loving and kind in every way, with a good sense of humour which Hudson inherited. She worked hard to make sure that the family was well fed and educated.

With her husband she worked to promote the glory of Christ in the local community, and taught her children of their need of Christ as Saviour and Lord. It was their mother who had the greatest influence upon the growing children making sure they had a sound understanding of English and music.

She encouraged the children to investigate the world about them with the result that Hudson developed an avid interest in nature, collecting specimens all over the world.

Their father taught mathematics, French and Latin.

Both parents found home schooling very time consuming but they enjoyed each other's company. Being at home most of the time the growing children frequently mixed with adult company. When Hudson heard them discussing Christianity and missionary work in distant heathen lands he often said, 'When I am a man, I mean to be a missionary and go to China.'

The Taylor home at 21 Cheapside was an exciting, four storey home for the young family. The basement was the kitchen and the storehouse for the pharmacy chemicals.

Above the basement was the pharmacy and the dining room which became the family room. It was used for schoolwork, meals, lessons, sewing and play. As their father used the dining room as a consulting room, it always had to be kept clean and tidy.

In this room there was a couch along one wall, a fireplace and a cabinet containing the family crockery. Above the couch was a window through which the family could see into the shop and out through the front door to the Market Place.

A clean, well scrubbed wooden table and chairs could be seen in the middle of the room.

There were four doors in the room—one leading into the shop, another to the stairs leading to the upper storey, one opening on the backyard and yet another to the kitchen below.

A chest of drawers and a bookcase were hidden by a lovely crimson curtain which hung from the ceiling to the floor.

On the bookshelves were sewing material, needles and threads, children's books and plenty of adult reading material as well as the pots, pans, cutlery and crockery which their mother used when preparing meals.

Hudson's mother, Amelia, when Hudson was a child

The lower bookcase shelves, which were usually empty, were used to quickly hide anything unsightly when an emergency arose. It was also ready for the children to pack away whatever they were using when the table was needed for meals.

Everything in the room was always kept well dusted and tidy in keeping with their mother's motto: 'A place for everything and everything in its place.'

Above the dining room was a spacious sitting room beside Mum and Dad's bedroom. On the top floor there were bedrooms for the children and servants. The assistant who worked in the pharmacy shared Hudson's room.

Later in life Hudson recalled many incidents of his young days. He remembered the family pew beside the pulpit and the time spent learning the Hebrew alphabet on his father's knee. His first essay, written when just four years of age was about a sinful old man of eighty who had never repented of his sins.

He found it hard work printing all the words in large letters but he only wrote one chapter which he said was not very long.

One upsetting incident that remained vividly in his memory all his life, was the day when his grandfather (John Taylor) died.

John and Mary Taylor always sat in the Church pew behind Hudson's parents. On many occasions he was allowed to sit on his grandfather's knee during the closing part of the worship service. He loved his grandfather's smile and kind words of encouragement which always thrilled him. But the day came when Grandfather Taylor died. Hudson's parents took him to the bed where grandfather's body lay and there he was made to touch the dead body which he found to be so cold and still.

Hudson was a bright, intelligent boy who loved life. Although he had a pale appearance he was a healthy, active youngster, who suffered no serious illness until his late teenage years.

Both parents decided that their children should be taught the value of money so they did many jobs about the home and shop to earn a penny. When eleven pennies had been saved a twelfth was given as a reward. They always found the bright new shilling coin something to be treasured.

On one occasion when a fair came to town, Hudson, wanting to visit the display of birds and animals, was very disappointed to be told there was a two pence entry fee. Having just one penny left he bargained with the animal owner trying to gain admittance. Despite his efforts the gate remained closed.

Running home with tears in his eyes he poured out his heart to his mother who was always ready to listen to her children. She reasoned with him in a kindly voice explaining that the man was only doing his job by insisting that everyone pay the entrance fee to see the lovely birds and animals. Then handing him the penny he needed because he had been such a good help to her lately she said, 'Run off again, now, and the man will be glad to let you in.'

Seventy years later he still remembered his mother's kind words and the gift of the much needed penny.

Sometimes a game called 'Still' was played with a small coin as the prize. The game required the children to sit quietly for a set length of time—between five and ten minutes.

But the game that Hudson really enjoyed was playing minister where he stood on a chair pretending he was the pastor at the Sunday evening service. He would act the part of the brave Wesleyan preachers who had suffered so much for Christ. No doubt he had heard stories of his great grandfather and the abuse he suffered for the sake of Christ.

All the children were taught the truths of Scripture, their father keeping a record of the daily Bible readings. Each day after breakfast and the evening meal, the family gathered for worship where the Scriptures were read and explained, songs of praise sung and prayer offered to God.

The children were taught to pray and when Amelia was just three years old she could pray, 'O Lord, take away my naughty temper and give me a new heart.'

At bedtime their father gathered his children to his side and together as they knelt beside the bed he prayed for each one by name. The constant seeking of God's face in prayer had a marked effect upon them all. Both parents longed to see the covenant promises fulfilled in their children and many times Hudson heard his father call upon God to fulfil those precious promises.

'He cannot deny Himself. He would not be God if He could,' he heard his father say.

Sundays were special days in the Taylor household, when dressed in their Sunday clothes they accompanied their parents to the worship service.

Mother made it a special day in many ways. It was the day when the most enjoyable toys came out and the most colourful picture books were read. Often the family gathered around the piano to sing great hymns of praise to God. The wonderful stories of Scripture were read and discussed and often their mother read passages from *Pilgrim's Progress*. In the afternoon she would hand around some fruit, much to everyone's enjoyment.

As children were expected to be seen and not heard in that day and age, they sat at the table waiting until they were served. They were not to ask for things at the table. On one occasion Mother forgot to serve Hudson. After waiting patiently he quietly asked for the salt to be passed. This request was considered by his parents to be reasonable, but the person sitting beside him, noticing his empty plate asked, 'And what do you want the salt for?'

Quietly Hudson replied, 'Oh, I want to be ready. Mamma will give me something to eat by-and-by.'

Another incident he remembered late in life was when his plate of sweets was overlooked. 'Mamma,' he asked gently, 'do you think apple-pie is good for little boys?'

The family rules were few in number, but the children were expected to be obedient. They loved their mother and were obedient, although sometimes Hudson tried to have his own way.

He loved reading, but when he was put to bed this was not possible, because there was no light. All the leftover candle ends were kept for use in the cellar or the kitchen. Once he decided to take some of the small leftover pieces to light his bedroom and read a story he was enjoying. Realizing that it would soon be bedtime he went to the cellar and quietly took some of the forbidden candles. He knew what he was doing was wrong, but how he wanted to complete that book!

As he walked through the sitting room with the candle ends hidden in his pocket, a visitor took him by the hand, sat him on his knee and started to tell him a story. As much as Hudson enjoyed stories he knew he was sitting too close to the fire because he could feel the heat melting the stolen candle ends.

Quietly, but urgently he made an excuse to leave, but by the time he reached his bedroom his pocket was a mess of melted tallow. When his mother entered the room she found him crying. He confessed what he had done and his mother, seeing genuine repentance, let the matter pass without any punishment.

All was not study and strict discipline. Hudson and his sister Amelia became the best of friends and Saturday afternoons were times of games with friends, or searching the nearby paddocks for butterflies and other insects.

Early in life Hudson learned to protect all of God's creatures, always making sure that butterflies and other insects were not treated cruelly. When a specimen was wanted for his collection, the little creature had to be killed using chloroform.

His father warned him, 'What you sow in this way, you will certainly reap. You will be made to suffer for all the suffering you inflict, as God is God and knows everything.'

Often their walks through the countryside were made more enjoyable because Dad, who knew so much about the butterflies and flowers accompanied them.

When fairs were held on the village green there were many side-shows for those who could afford the entrance fee. The family enjoyed the merry-go-rounds, stalls of every kind and the displays of everything imaginable.

Each year they stayed at 'Grandmamma' Shepherd's home during the Christmas period. She had a lovely home surrounded by many interesting gardens where her grandchildren enjoyed themselves for hours on end.

Growing up was a stimulating time for young Hudson. Because he often mixed with adults he became very mature in his thinking. Home was where his character was shaped—a character that God would sanctify for his service, when finally he set foot upon the shores of China.

4

The Chinese Story

The Protestant faith entered China much later than Roman Catholicism.

Roman Catholic Mission to China

In the early years of the thirteenth century John of Monte Corvino reached Cathay where he preached to the Chinese. Towards the end of his life he wrote of his isolated missionary work: 'It is now twelve years since I have heard any news from the West. I am become old and grey-headed, but it is rather through labours and tribulations than through age...I have learned the Tartar language and literature, into which I have translated the whole New Testament and the Psalms of David, and have caused them to be transcribed with the utmost care. I write, read, and preach, openly and freely, the testimony of the law of CHRIST.'

In 1601 Matthew Ricci gained the Emperor's approval to recommence the mission work which had suffered many setbacks because of bitter persecution. As a Jesuit he combined his missionary work with other activities that won the admiration of the Imperial Court. He and his Jesuit priests, dressed in the Chinese clothing of a scholar, won the respect of the people.

The Jesuits taught mathematics, prepared a calendar which was a great benefit to the farming population and were proficient in repairing European clocks which had become popular with the Chinese. Others were artists and architects who gave valuable assistance to the Emperor's building programme. Some were competent cartographers who mapped much of the land.

In 1644 the new Manchu dynasty overthrew the existing Chinese Imperial Court, and approved of the Jesuits' continued presence. However, in Rome the Dominicans complained to the Pope of the Jesuits' toleration of the Chinese converts continuing their custom of honouring their ancestors in what appeared to be the worship of the dead. The Emperor Kang Xi sided with the Jesuits in the dispute, but when the Pope decided against the practice he felt deeply insulted and issued an edict forbidding the propagation of foreign religions. Persecution now became part and parcel of life for the Chinese converts to Catholicism.

The First British Protestant Missionary to China

Robert Morrison offered to become a missionary, working for the newly formed London Missionary Society, which in 1805 was considering opening a work in China.

While in London he commenced studying Chinese, using some old manuscripts held by the British Museum.

Missionaries were not welcome in China so the East India Company which had a trade monopoly in Canton refused to allow Morrison to travel on their vessels. Consequently he went to the United States of America where an American business gave him passage to China on one of their ships.

As foreigners were not permitted to rent accommodation from the Chinese, Morrison was allowed to occupy two rooms owned by the company that had met his travel costs to mainland China. He was also given a minor job which permitted him to freely move about in Canton. This was made easier as he wore Chinese clothes, ate Chinese food with chopsticks and improved his use of the local language.

His was a very lonely work because the additional missionaries sent out to help him were forced to leave.

One missionary, William Milne, who finally settled in Malacca became involved in the translation of the Bible into Chinese. Morrison followed this with the translation of the Shorter Catechism, a section of the Church of England Prayer Book and a six volume, four thousand five hundred page Chinese-English dictionary.

In 1809 the East India Company had a change of heart towards Morrison, employing him as their official interpreter. In that capacity he had freedom of movement and the right to live in Canton, even visiting Peking in 1816.

He still had time for missionary work although this had to be done without being observed by the Chinese authorities. Occasionally he travelled about the city carrying a pair of shoes, pretending to be a shoemaker. In dangerous times he carried a vial of poison which he intended to use if taken prisoner. In 1814 his first convert was secretly baptized, and in 1824 he ordained Liang his first native Chinese evangelist.

Worn out by the effects of work and the climate, he died on 1 August, 1834 and was buried at Macao.

Missionary work and the fledgling Chinese Christian Church were at a very low ebb at that time.

Gutzlaff

This missionary-minded man was born in Prussian Pomerania in 1803, and following his conversion offered his services to the Netherlands Missionary Society which appointed him to work in the East Indies. He sailed for this region in 1827.

Following the study of Chinese at Bangkok he commenced a series of journeys along the Chinese coast, reaching Tianjin in the north.

On those trips he distributed Christian literature to anyone who was willing to take it. This was a very dangerous practice, but Dr Gutzlaff, dressed in Chinese clothing, freely mixed amongst the native people.

Owing to his work 'The Chinese Union' was formed to take written material into many regions of China where foreigners were forbidden to travel. The one hundred and thirty men who were involved in the distribution of the literature claimed that 3,000 Chinese had confessed their faith in Christ and had been baptized.

The regular, glowing reports to Europe and Great Britain of his missionary activities created a lot of interest. Hudson Taylor was one of those who willingly supported this God-honouring work.

However, many of Gutzlaff's 'helpers' were thieves and swindlers. Only a few were teaching the truth concerning Christ while the majority were spending their time and Gutzlaff's money in the opium dens. The Christian literature they were supposedly distributing was sold to the printers who in turn resold them to Gutzlaff.

When he discovered what was happening he was brokenhearted, believing his missionary endeavour was a failure.

Events in China

In the middle of the 18th century some British ships visited several Chinese ports, but it was Canton alone that was open to trade with foreigners. There foreign merchants had to deal through the licensed Chinese merchants: the 'Thirteen Hongs' (Thirteen firms).

Foreigners were not permitted to live in the city limits and during autumn and winter had to move to Macao. Foreign women were banned from Canton, and it was a crime for any Chinese to teach their language to foreigners, or sell Chinese books to the western traders.

These traders were confined to a small area of land where foreign law was to be used. If a Chinese citizen was involved in legal action, Chinese law applied and this resulted in several foreigners being executed for the accidental killing of a local citizen.

Trade with China had become important to the British as the industrial revolution created a need for markets. The huge population seemed to be a ready market for their products, but the Chinese, a proud people, let it be known that they had no need or interest in the products of the foreign barbarians.

In 1793 the British Government, taking advantage of Emperor Qian Long's eightieth birthday, sent Lord Macartney, loaded with gifts, to Peking to convey the best wishes of the British Government.

All Britain really wanted was the exchange of ambassadors, and the opening up of more ports for trade and commerce. When Lord Macartney arrived he was viewed as the representative of an inferior race and was compelled to *ketou*[1] to the Emperor who told him that China had all the products it needed and thus there was no need of trade with barbarians. Then came the 'but'– but foreigners were welcome to buy Chinese products through Canton, according to Chinese regulations.

The British Government, desperate for increased trade to pay for the large quantities of tea being imported from China in 1816, sent Lord Amherst to negotiate trading rights, but when he visited Peking, the new Emperor refused to meet him.

It was then that the issue of opium began to make itself felt. In 1750, four hundred chests of opium had been sold to the Chinese for medical purposes.

The East India Company which had a trading monopoly in the far East, saw China as a huge market for the opium grown in Bengal. As more opium was smuggled into China, addiction grew, especially amongst the educated, ruling classes.

In 1821 five thousand chests of opium found their way into China. In 1839 it had risen to forty thousand chests as China had in excess of two million opium addicts. Now it was China's turn to experience economic problems because the imports of opium exceeded the value of her exports, with the result that silver was used to meet her foreign debt.

Peking forbade the imports of opium, but open smuggling continued. Some Chinese suggested the problem could be controlled by taxing opium imports while others suggested that China commence growing her own.

However, the Emperor refused to agree to either proposal. He was very concerned about the well being of his people and issued edicts forbidding the import of opium.

Commissioner Lin who was sent to enforce the Emperor's edict arrived in Canton in March, 1839 where he blockaded the foreign traders' storehouses, demanding that all opium be handed over. The British Captain, Charles Elliot, took charge of the situation for the merchants and issued receipts for all the illegal opium which he then handed over to Commissioner Lin.

Lin took the twenty thousand chests of opium valued at eleven million dollars and after mixing it with quicklime, salt and water, spent twenty three days washing it into the ocean.

The result was the arrival of the British fleet demanding compensation and freedom of trade. The Emperor agreed to pay compensation and permit an extension of the opium trade, but when the British demanded the territory of Hong Kong, the Emperor refused.

1841 saw some British warships capturing the coastal forts below Canton and when the Emperor decided to fight, the British shelled Canton defeating the Imperial Manchu army.

In May of the same year six million dollars was paid to Great Britain to ransom Canton from their forces. The British Government was not satisfied, and so demanded more concessions which the Chinese refused.

In a new show of force, the British navy in 1842 shelled Shanghai, killing many citizens. When the naval force moved towards Nanking the Chinese made peace.

In August, 1842 the Treaty of Nanking was signed with additional sections added in 1843. This treaty humiliated the people because:

1. The Island of Hong Kong became British property;
2. Five ports were opened to foreign trade and residence—Canton, Amoy, Fuzhou, Ningbo and Shanghai;
3. Foreigners were subject to the law of their own nation except where Chinese citizens were involved. In such situations they could have their own legal advisors present;
4. The Chinese language could now be studied by foreigners without fear of arrest;
5. Foreigners were confined to the five Treaty Ports and were not to travel beyond the thirty mile limit; and
6. Foreigners were permitted to establish hospitals, schools, places of worship and homes.

Nothing was included in the legislation concerning the rights of missionaries or the status of the opium trade, but soon afterwards edicts were issued giving missionaries the right to operate in the five Treaty Ports.

In Shanghai the British purchased land outside the city walls where the Foreign Settlement grew. Soon missionaries made their way to the Treaty Ports, especially Shanghai, and it was there that Hudson Taylor first set foot on Chinese soil.

By 1844 approximately forty Protestant missionaries had made their way to China, many of whom were involved in medical work.

The Taiping Rebellion

This rebellion which commenced in 1851 continued for fourteen years. China was experiencing great social unrest due to the effects of the opium trade and trade generally. The importation of cheap nails and needles put many out of work while the sailors on the junks couldn't compete with the efficient foreign ships.

In 1841 and 1843 great floods in the Yangtze River destroyed crops which resulted in the deaths of hundreds of thousands of people. During the same period many crops were destroyed by pests.

Hong Xiu-quan, the son of a Cantonese farmer, was born in 1814. He received an education which prepared him for the public service.

Once when visiting Canton he was handed a Bible, which he took home and put aside.

Falling ill for forty days he hallucinated, believing he was in heaven where he met an aged man and his own elder brother with whom he fought demons.

Recovering from his illness he commenced reading the book given him years before. He believed he had been in heaven where he met God the Father and his elder brother, Jesus. It was with Jesus that he fought demons which he believed were the idols found throughout the land.

Using the Bible as a source for doctrine he formed 'The Society of God' and with the help of faithful adherents, some of whom claimed to speak for God, he soon had many followers known as the Taiping rebels. However, the organization was only part Christian, adhering to the teaching of the ten commandments. Grace was said before meals, prayers were made to God and images destroyed wherever they were found. The Taiping rebels were also violently opposed to the use of opium. They cut off their pigtails and refused to wear Ming Dynasty clothing. Hong was known as 'The Heavenly Prince'; the society as 'The Kingdom of Heaven'; while Taiping meant 'great peace' and 'equality'.

By 1850 the rebels were in open conflict with the Chinese authorities and when confronted by the militia they fought and won. Outright war was declared against the Emperor on 11 January, 1851.

Fierce fighting followed and soon their soldiers captured Nanking which became their headquarters and was renamed 'The Heavenly Capital'.

These rebels created the impression that they were a Christian force, which encouraged foreign missionary societies to make extra efforts to send missionaries to China. In 1853 Sir George Bonham, the British Governor of Hong Kong visited Nanking and reported that the rebels were Christian and it appeared that God had providentially opened China's door to Christianity.

That same year Shanghai fell to local rebels, the 'Red Turbans', who claimed an association with the Taiping Rebels. The Taiping leaders however refused to acknowledge the Triad rebels of Amoy and Shanghai as followers.

During the next decade the Taiping uprising disintegrated and by 1865 it was drawing to an end, Hong having taken poison in 1864. By 1868 the rebellion was over.

The Second Opium War

In 1856 the Chinese officials at Canton seized the Hong Kong registered vessel, 'Arrow', which had a British captain, flew a British flag and was manned by a Chinese crew. The crew was arrested and charged with smuggling.

The British decided to make an issue of the incident in order to gain more concessions from China. The crew was returned, but as there was no formal apology from any high ranking Chinese official, Britain sent three battleships to Canton and shelled the city. The wall was breached and for a time British forces entered the city. In retaliation the Cantonese attacked the foreign business area which brought France into the dispute.

In 1857 Anglo-French troops assembled in Hong Kong demanding that the treaties with China be revised.

On 28 December Canton was again bombarded all day, resulting in the deaths of many thousands of her citizens. The London press was very critical of this cruel action and one paper commented: 'A more horrible or revolting crime than this bombardment of Canton has never been committed in the worst ages of barbarian darkness'.

The British forces sailed north to Shanghai and then on to Taku which was bombarded on 20 May 1858. Eleven days later Tianjin was invaded and within a short time the flags of Britain and France flew over the city. Both nations then dictated terms of peace.

The outcome was the British—Chinese Treaty of Tianjin signed on 26 June, 1858 which opened more ports to trade, and granted freedom of movement to all foreigners who wished to travel throughout the country. Britain was paid compensation of four million dollars and an equality of diplomatic representation with Peking.

Missionaries, with a guarantee of safety, were assured of their right to travel throughout the nation preaching Christ.

They all rejoiced for now China was open to the proclamation of the gospel.

5

A Useful Tract

With many Methodists visiting the Taylor home for Sunday lunch the children spent much time with adults. Many years later Amelia wrote of those days: 'I used to love to hear them talk—those local preachers gathered round our table for high tea. Theology, sermons, politics, the Lord's work at home and abroad—all were discussed with so much earnestness and intelligence. It made a great impression upon us as children.'

1839, the 'Centenary Jubilee' of the outbreak of the great revivals of the previous century, was remembered with much time being devoted to prayer. Support for missions increased with the result that great blessings were poured out upon the church.

Consequently, missionary effort grew in India, but China was overlooked, much to the disappointment of the Taylor family.

As a result they devoted more time than ever to prayer that God might lead Hudson to become involved in mission work in mainland China.

Life in the Taylor family revolved around the gospel!

When he was just seven years of age Hudson enjoyed accompanying his father on his preaching engagements. This was a time of spiritual revival and following the worship service it was customary to hold a prayer meeting for the conversion of the sinners present at the service. Often the meeting was attended by people under deep conviction of sin, who were there pointed to Christ, 'the Lamb of God who takes away the sin of the world.'

Many people commented upon Hudson's spiritual earnestness and when he saw sinners confessing their sins and trusting in Christ for salvation his voice could be heard with the congregation praising God with the words: 'Praise God, from whom all blessings flow.'

His home schooling continued until 1843 when it was decided that he should attend a day school which was opened by Mr Laycock in the reed-making factory once used by Hudson's grandfather. For two years he attended the school, but a change of teacher resulted in his withdrawal and recommencing home schooling. During this time his spiritual life suffered a setback.

In 1844 he attended a 'Camp Meeting' at Leeds. While the camp was for older people, the talks made a deep impression upon his attentive mind and for a time his spiritual life blossomed.

The guest speaker was an Australian—Mr Henry Reed from Launceston, Tasmania, who told the sad story of a criminal by the name of Gardener, who had been executed for the murder of a friend and workmate with whom he shared a small hut.

Gardener, in his younger days had no desire to become a Christian, but one day he heard a voice speaking, 'Gardener, give me your heart!'

However, he had sinful ambitions. He wanted to make money and believed Christianity would frustrate his plans. Putting the thought of repentance and faith in Christ out of his mind, he believed that he would give himself to Christ at a more convenient time—after he had made his fortune.

When he saw his partner counting the small amount of money he had saved, temptation filled his heart—he had to have that money for himself! As he sat looking greedily at it a thought filled his mind, 'Kill the man and all his money will be mine!'

The speaker stressed that just a few hours before Gardener committed his terrible crime, he had been considering God's call to turn to Christ. He had rejected that call and now temptation overwhelmed his heart as his eyes gazed on the small pile of money on the table. Waiting his time, he killed his partner.

Mr Reed had spoken with Gardener and five others for several hours before they faced the executioner's rope.

That story made a deep impression upon Hudson's heart especially his words, 'My son, give me your heart.'

But formal school days were over and at thirteen years of age, dressed in a white apron he started work in his father's pharmacy.

Home lessons continued, but now he was expected to spend more time with his father, grinding and pounding chemicals, mixing medicines and wrapping the customers' orders.

Again and again he tried to make himself a Christian, but failed. He continued reading the many books his father treasured, but became tired of the strict religious atmosphere in the family home.

He was beginning to find it uncomfortable living with a Methodist lay preacher father and a mother who was a 'Class' leader.

After his fifteenth birthday, James decided that his son would benefit from work in a local bank. He needed to gain some experience in the outside world, as well as skills in business principles, book-keeping, the writing of correspondence and general administrative work.

Later in life Hudson thanked his father for this experience, which proved to be very useful in his missionary work. However, at the time he found bank work to be most unsettling.

For the first time he faced the mocking of ungodly workmates who ridiculed his Christian background. They laughed when he was unable to answer their arguments.

Hudson was shocked when he heard people swearing and blaspheming, and was very surprised when he noticed the size of the bank accounts of people who professed to be Christians. Some of those people had not repaid loans on time, a matter that upset him. Others had accumulated great wealth while Christian work languished in the areas where they lived.

Hudson's spiritual life slowly began to die as he ceased praying and reading his Bible. From all he had been taught at home he knew that Christianity meant a total commitment to Christ. If this was not possible then he decided he might as well live for himself and the world.

Later he wrote of his days at the bank: 'I well remember how I used to wish for money and a fine horse and house when I was in the Bank…my whole heart was set on this world's pleasures, and I longed to go hunting as some did who were about me.'

He knew that the love of the world was filling his heart and he was neglecting his spiritual duties. However, God had a special work for Hudson and soon a spiritual change took place.

With all the close mathematical work and poor lighting his eyes were affected. After nine months work at the Bank he later said, 'My eyes gave out at balancing time...very fortunately for me or I might have been swamped.'

Soon he was wearing spectacles, but now he was again working with his father in the pharmacy.

This was a difficult time for him. He was spiritually bankrupt, downhearted, aware of his spiritual backsliding and tired of his father's strictness. He had become a quick-tempered, rebellious, unhappy sixteen year old adolescent.

His father tried to help his downcast son, but became very impatient, which distressed Hudson more than ever. However, his mother was more understanding and gentle, showing him great kindness. She spent many hours in prayer for the son she and her husband had dedicated to the service of their Lord and Saviour, Jesus Christ.

It was at that time that thirteen year old Amelia covenanted to pray for Hudson's conversion three times every day, until the Holy Spirit brought about the new birth. Hudson later wrote that God answered those prayers in a wonderful way.

It was in June, 1849 when he was seventeen years of age, spiritually downcast and the object of the prayers of Amelia and the other family members, that he found himself at home alone. He took a tray of tracts from his father's bookshelf and looked through them hoping to find one that would be worth reading.

The one he picked up and read was about an ungodly coalman, who, with his wife, lived in a very poor suburb of Somerset. While his wife carted bags of coal to customers he was at home dying of consumption. So filthy was their home that the visiting doctor refused to enter their rooms.

Some faithful, local Christians continued to visit and pray for the sick man and his wife. One day after reading the story of the sick woman who was healed when she touched the hem of Christ's clothes, the man exclaimed, 'Oh that I could reach Him!'

When he heard the words, 'Who his own self bore our sins in his own body on the tree' he said, 'Then it's done!'

Hudson was only interested in the story and had decided to put down the tract before he read the spiritual application. He had no intention of 'becoming serious' as conversion was called.

Unknown to him, at that very time his mother, who was absent from home, was praying that he might be converted that very day. And she had decided to continue praying until she knew that he was born again.

Amelia Hudson Taylor

Locking the door to her room, for some hours she pleaded with God to save her ungodly son, until she could pray no more. Suddenly she felt the urge to praise God for Hudson's salvation, which she did in the full assurance that God had answered her cries.

Meanwhile Hudson, coming to the words, 'The finished work of Christ,' asked himself, 'Why does the author use this expression? Why not say the atoning or propitiatory work of Christ?'

He asked himself, 'What is finished?' Then he answered his question with, 'A full and perfect atonement and satisfaction for sin: the debt

41

was paid by the Substitute; Christ died for our sins, and not for ours only, but also for the sins of the whole world.'

Suddenly the truth burst upon his heart and he asked himself, 'If the whole work is finished and the whole debt paid, what is there left for me to do?'

Led by the Holy Spirit, he fell to his knees and accepted Christ as his Saviour, promising to praise him for ever.

Later he found out that while his mother was praising God many miles away, he was doing the same in the warehouse where he was reading the tract.

Rejoicing, he ran to Amelia to tell her what had taken place. She was overjoyed when she heard her brother's words, but was sworn to secrecy as he wanted to be the one to tell his mother of God's gracious work in his heart.

All his life Hudson called that day in June, 1849 the day of his being born again.

Later when his mother returned from her holiday he met her at the door ready to announce the exciting news. However, she put her arms about his neck and hugged him tight saying, 'I know, my boy; I have been rejoicing for a fortnight in the glad tidings you have to tell me.'

At this Hudson asked, 'Why, has Amelia broken her promise? She said she would tell no one!'

When he heard his mother's explanation of all that had happened he then knew the power of prayer in the life of God's people.

Later, accidentally, he picked up and opened Amelia's diary where he read of her pledge to pray for his conversion.

He noted that it was just one month after the entry in the diary, that the Holy Spirit had changed his heart and he had been turned from 'darkness to light.'

It was then that Amelia and Hudson became spiritual soulmates.

6

Studying to Become a Doctor

Hudson was overjoyed when he realised he'd been forgiven and united to Christ. He was saved! The years that followed were growing times, when daily he grew closer to the God he loved.

However, some changes took place which disappointed him. It was decided that Amelia would continue her education at Aunt Hodson's school in Barton where she'd live in the family home. It was there she became very close friends with two teachers—Marianne Vaughan and Elizabeth Sissons.

At that time, needing extra help, Hudson's father invited his nephew, John Hodson to become his apprentice. This meant that Hudson had to share his room with an ungodly young man who became a hindrance to his spiritual growth. John was an energetic, flippant young person who had no real interest in spiritual matters, while Hudson wanted peace and quietness in order to pray and study the Scriptures.

His parents had taught him what the Christian life meant, but now he rejoiced that his life was motivated, not just out of respect for his parents, but because he loved the Lord Jesus.

He longed to be holy and prayed for the sanctifying work of the Spirit to conform him to the character of his Saviour.

This longing, reflecting the theology of John Wesley, was expressed in a letter he wrote on Sunday, 2 December, 1849, to his sister, Amelia:

Pray for me dear Amelia. Pray for me. I am seeking for entire sanctification.…My heart longs for this perfect holiness.…What a happy state it must be.

> Oh! for a heart to praise my God,
>   A heart from sin set free…
> A heart in every thought renewed…
>   Perfect, and right, and pure, and good,
>   A copy, Lord, of thine…'

Hudson now longed to become a missionary and it was the thought of China that captured his imagination. He still worked in his father's pharmacy, but in his spare time he served the Lord in every way possible. Each Sunday morning he attended the worship service with his Christian brothers and sisters, and soon he became a Sunday School teacher which he considered to be a good training ground for the work to which the Lord called him.

Not long after his conversion he decided to spend some special time in prayer seeking God's direction for his life's work. Of that afternoon he wrote:

> Well do I remember that occasion. How in the gladness of my heart I poured out my soul before God; and again and again confessing my grateful love to Him who had done everything for me—who had saved me when I had given up all hope and even desire of salvation—I begged him to give me some work to do for Him, as an outlet for love and gratitude; some self-denying service…that I might do for Him who had done so much for me. Well do I remember, as in unreserved consecration I put myself, my life, my friends, my all, upon the altar, the deep solemnity that came over my soul with the assurance that my offering was accepted. The presence of God became unutterably real and blessed; and…I remember stretching myself on the ground, and lying there silent before Him with unspeakable awe and unspeakable joy.
>
> For what service I was accepted I knew not; but a deep consciousness that I was no longer my own took possession of me, which has never since been effaced.…

Hudson was convinced that God had a special work for him to do, but what it was he was not sure.

Each Sunday afternoon he was involved in outreach activities amongst the ungodly, poor citizens of Barnsley. He distributed tracts, spoke to people about Christ and took every opportunity to help those in need. Often Amelia accompanied him when he ventured into the poorest part of the town. What disappointed him more than ever was the spiritual deadness that he found amongst the people he met.

So he set himself to pray for revival.

There were times when he was downcast and felt spiritually worn-out. This greatly upset him as he longed to be Christlike. He feasted on the Word of God wanting to know everything that was expected of him. When he read of tithing he began to set aside a minimum of one tenth of his income for the Lord's work.

Hudson, a new creature in Christ, knew that he was called to a special work so he prayed that God might reveal his plan. There upon his knees he wrestled with God in prayer, determined to pray until God answered. The answer came—it was as if God gave the command: 'Then go for me to China!'

Of this decision Hudson wrote: 'It was in China the Lord wanted me. It seemed to me highly probable that the work to which I was thus called might cost my life.'

On 25 April, 1851 he wrote to George Pearse of the Chinese Evangelization Society (CES) of his momentous decision:

> Never shall I forget the feeling that came over me. Words can never describe it. I felt I was in the presence of God, entering into a covenant with the Almighty. I felt as though I wished to withdraw my promise, but could not. Something seemed to say, "Your prayer is answered, your conditions are accepted." And from that time the conviction never left me that I was called to China.

There was no more doubting in Hudson's mind. God had called and he had answered. His life was now to be directed to the one great end— serving God in China. His life now had purpose as his mother later wrote: '...from that hour his mind was made up. His pursuits and studies were all engaged in with reference to this object, and whatever difficulties presented themselves his purpose never wavered.'

He began reading his father's books—Parley's *China*, Gutzlaff's *Journal of Three Voyages*, Hall's *Voyages* and Davies' *Spiritual Claims*.

Searching for more information he was told that the Barnsley Congregational minister had a large library amongst which was a copy of Medhurst's book about China. He decided to visit the man and borrow the book.

When the minister asked him why he wanted to read the lengthy book Hudson told him that God had called him to spend his life as a missionary in China.

'And how do you propose to go there?' he inquired.

His reply was that he didn't know, but just as Christ had sent his disciples out without 'money bag or sack', relying on God to supply their needs, so God would do for him.

The minister gently placed his hand on Hudson's shoulder and replied, 'Ah, my boy, as you grow older you will get wiser than that. Such an idea would do very well in the days when Christ Himself was on earth, but not now.'

As he studied Medhurst's book he realised that a knowledge of medicine would be a great advantage to him in that far distant land. It was then that he began to give serious consideration to studying medicine.

Visiting a friend, who had contact with the British and Foreign Bible Society Hudson discovered that he had a copy of Luke's gospel and the Book of Acts written in the Chinese Mandarin language.

To learn more of China Hudson subscribed to *The Gleaner in the Missionary Field*, the magazine of the Chinese Society, which contained a wealth of material about missionary activities, especially in mainland China.

Faced with their son's decision to offer himself for missionary work in China, his parents rejoiced, but it would be many years before they told him how they had dedicated him to the Lord's work.

They decided they wouldn't exert any pressure on their son as to the pathway he should follow. However being concerned about his health and knowing he would face times of physical need and poverty they urged him to take care of both body and mind. Hudson then decided to make a real effort to get himself into the best possible physical condition, and to learn all he could about China.

Out went the feather bed mattress and in its place he put a more solid one. Many of the comforts of home were sacrificed as he began his physical training for the Lord's service.

He also began learning to read and write the Chinese language. He had no teacher and couldn't afford the very costly textbooks—but as he had the gospel of Mark and the Book of Acts each written in Mandarin he was determined that with those books he would teach himself the language.

With the help of his cousin, John Hodson, he began the process of comparing the English Bible with the Chinese Bible and within a short time had discovered the meaning of well over five hundred Chinese words.

They wrote down a dozen or so Bible verses having the one English word in common. Finding the same verses in the Mandarin Bible they were able to discover the Chinese character that matched the English word.

After writing the Chinese word on a slip of paper they searched the Chinese gospel for the same word, which they then checked to see if it matched with the word in the English Bible. When they were sure of the English equivalent the words were written in ink in their dictionary. The work was slow at first, but over time they became more proficient and soon had a list of over four hundred Chinese words with their English equivalents.

Of those days Hudson wrote:

> I have begun to get up at five in the morning, and so find it necessary
> to go to bed early at night. I must study if I mean to go to China.
> I am fully decided to go, and am making every preparation I can.
> I intend to rub up my Latin, to learn Greek and the rudiments of
> Hebrew, and to get as much general information as possible. I need
> all your prayers.

He was very concerned that his own Methodist Church had no missionary work in China, while other Churches had commenced gospel work in the five 'Treaty of Nanking' ports of Canton, Amoy, Fuzhou, Ningbo and Shanghai. As a result of the opium war those cities were opened to foreigners, including missionaries.

The treaty meant that the inland areas remained out of bounds to foreigners, although the Roman Catholic Church had successfully penetrated inland provinces.

When Dr Gutzlaff visited Europe he spoke optimistically of the openness of China to the gospel and of the work being done. His words encouraged Hudson and others who were concerned about the spiritual need of the people. Dr Gutzlaff had made seven trips along the coast of China during the years 1831–35, risking his life to bear witness to the saving work of Christ. Dressed in Chinese clothes he was able to freely mix with the people.

The society reported on the devoted work being carried out by the one hundred and thirty native Christians who supposedly preached the gospel and distributed Christian literature. They had reported that several thousand Chinese had been baptized upon their confession of faith in Christ.

Hudson wrote to Mr Pearse, the Secretary of the 'Chinese Association' expressing his support of all involved in missionary work, and indicated that he was ready to devote his life to work in China. In the meantime he asked for whatever information was available which he could use to introduce others to the work of the 'Chinese Association'.

He also wanted to forward any money he collected to the Chinese Union, and being careful with the monetary gifts he decided to forward them through the Bank instead of by postal order. In this way he saved three or four pence of the Lord's money.

Sad to say however, Gutzlaff's Chinese workers were largely swindlers and thieves, who instead of promoting Christ, had spent their time enjoying themselves in the opium dens. Their glowing reports were just the dreams of opium addicts. When this became known, Gutzlaff was heartbroken. He believed his work was a failure, but was convinced that God answered prayer, and that the day would come when Christ would be worshipped by millions of Chinese.

Support for his work dwindled when it became known that he had been swindled.

However, Hudson did not lose heart and was more determined than ever to devote his life to preaching the gospel to the Chinese people. Later he recognized Dr Gutzlaff as 'in a very real sense the father' of the China Inland Mission.

He contacted Mr Pearse suggesting that Gutzlaff's work be reorganized in such a way that never again could the society be cheated by unscrupulous people.

Hudson devoted his activities to preparation for life in China, reading each issue of *The Gleaner* with a true missionary zeal. He saw great value in Dr Gutzlaff's missionary methods believing that foreign missionaries should identify themselves with the people and mix freely with them. He was convinced that each missionary should adopt Chinese dress, before making his way into inland China— '...as far as possible, [he should] become Chinese that he may win the Chinese.'

The more he read of missionary work in that great land the greater was his desire to leave home and begin his life's work. However, he knew that more study was needed before he could leave England.

He was convinced that medical knowledge would be a great advantage to him in China and writing to Amelia he outlined his use of his time when he was not working in the pharmacy: 'Up at 6 am; on Monday—Latin; Tuesday—theology; Wednesday—Chinese; Thursday—pharmacology; Friday—"the science of disorders" and physiology; Saturday—Chinese…I go into the warehouse or stable or anywhere for private prayer, and some most blessed seasons I had.'

Consequently he began seeking employment with a doctor in order to learn the trade. He needed to be somewhere where he had access to medical books.

As a result of correspondence with Mr Pearse an offer was made by the Chinese Society to help meet the costs involved in studying medicine, which would necessitate moving to London.

On 25 April, 1851, he wrote to Mr Pearse thanking his committee for their kindness, but stating that he had no way of supporting himself, and if he had a full time job he would have no time left to study at the hospital.

He continued, 'My age will be nineteen on 21st of May, 1851. Of course I am unmarried. As to the general state of my health, I have never had any serious illness, but cannot be called robust. I have never been better than at present….'

He outlined his educational qualifications explaining that he was working in his father's chemist shop. Finally he indicated that he and his family had resigned from the Methodists because of doctrinal differences.

Hudson was ready for a move and when he received the offer of work as assistant to Dr Robert Hardey, a surgeon at Hull, he was overjoyed to say, 'Yes'.

This well known doctor was the brother-in-law of his Aunt Hannah.

Then there was his sweetheart Marianne Vaughan! In correspondence with Amelia he wrote, 'Give my best love to my dear Marianne.'

He was unsure whether Marianne would marry and accompany him to China. He questioned whether she felt called to such a work, telling her that missionary life would be very demanding and urged her to pray for guidance from God.

The last couple of weeks before leaving Barnsley proved to be a very busy time. He preached his first sermon to a group of Christians in a home, as well as speaking to crowds who had gathered to hear him. This was followed by a round of farewell meetings.

In a letter to Amelia he wrote: 'At night we crammed about five hundred in the room and at least as many went away without being able to get in…Afterwards we had a glorious prayer meeting and twelve adults and five children came to the penitent form and were saved. There were five or six others I know of who were under deep conviction but they would not come up. Oh! it was a glorious time.'

He was now ready to commence the next stage in his preparation for missionary work in China. He praised God for his continuing goodness, but found leaving home to be a difficult break with people he loved and respected.

7

A Change of Address

It was on 21 May, 1851, that nineteen year old Hudson reported for work with the well known surgeon, Dr Robert Hardey who lived and had his surgery in a well-to-do part of Hull. His upper class patients were treated in his home, while those from the working classes found their surgery at the bottom of the back yard. Many of his patients were poor Irish workers who had been forced out of Ireland because of famine. They were rough men and women and often the local priest had to be called to read the riot act to his violent parishioners.

The area had such a terrible reputation for crime, immorality and violence that very few police dared venture into the suburbs alone. Hudson, however, who soon became known as Dr Hardey's assistant, found he could safely move about amongst the poor, underprivileged people.

When he visited patients who needed treatment, he took the opportunity to distribute tracts, and was often able to preach the gospel to small groups who gladly gathered to hear him speak. This evangelistic work proved to be a good preparation for China.

Dr Hardey, a highly respected surgeon at the Royal Infirmatory, lectured in obstetrics and gynaecology at the medical school. He and his wife opened their home to Hudson and soon he was settled into a very comfortable room. Mrs Hardey, however, was an unfriendly person with a very cultured personality.

Dr Hardey on the other hand was a very kind, cheerful man who was loved and respected by his patients. His good sense of humour appealed to Hudson and as a very devout Christian, and member of the Methodist Church it wasn't long before they bowed together in prayer, seeking God's blessing upon their labour and witness amongst their patients.

Hudson's first day at work didn't end until late at night, and it was almost midnight before he found the time to write to Amelia. Life now was greatly different to that at home in Barnsley. At first he felt very uneasy in his new surroundings, but was confident that he would enjoy his work. He was also aware that now he would have more opportunities to see Amelia and Marianne as they were living reasonably close. In fact he thought he could use his one hour lunch break each day to visit the ones he loved. However, his mother warned Amelia not to take advantage of the situation and spend too much time with him, because the day would come when they would be separated, maybe permanently.

Hudson soon found that he had plenty of work, as Dr Hardey's practice involved the care of the many local factory workers who were involved in workplace accidents. To begin with, Hudson dispensed medicines and dressed wounds, but he also accompanied Dr Hardey when he was called out to deal with midwifery cases.

When the doctor found out that he was experienced in book-keeping, he was given the additional job of looking after the financial accounts.

Despite all the extra work, he attended medical lectures for intending doctors.

George Müller

Hudson used every spare moment to study the Scriptures and pray in preparation for his future work in China. He joined a Brethren congregation pastored by Andrew Jukes where he heard the Word of God faithfully preached and made lifelong friends with a devoted group of Christians.

It was there that he and the congregation were kept informed of George Müller whose life and work was lived in total dependence upon the providential blessings of God.

George Müller was one Christian who proved God's faithfulness as promised in Philippians 4:19—'And my God shall supply all your need according to His riches in glory by Christ Jesus.'

Hudson and others were encouraged when they heard reports of God's faithful provision of Müller's needs in the work he carried out in Christ's name.

In February, 1834 Müller established a missionary organisation—'The Scriptural Knowledge Institution for Home and Abroad'—which had five aims:

1. To assist with the establishment, and provide assistance for all types of schools—Sunday Schools, Day Schools and Adult Schools;
2. To provide copies of the Old and New Testaments and complete Bibles to all who wanted a copy. They were to be provided free of charge to the poor;
3. To give financial assistance to freelance missionaries;
4. To provide tracts in the many languages of the world; and
5. To provide homes for orphans.

Müller spoke of his work, but never asked for financial help. As a result many stories circulated of the miraculous ways in which God answered his prayers.

A story that encouraged Hudson, was of the time when there was no food on the breakfast table for the orphan children being cared for by Müller.

The tables were set, but the plates were empty and there was no money to buy food. With the children seated and waiting for their meal, Müller lifted his hands heavenward and prayed a prayer of thanksgiving for the food the Lord was about to provide. No sooner had he finished praying than there was a knock on the door and there stood the local baker with an armful of loaves of bread. He explained that he couldn't sleep that night as he was concerned that the children were without food. As a result, he rose early in the morning and baked some fresh bread for the orphanage.

A few minutes later there was a second knock on the door and the local milkman announced that he had cans of fresh milk for the children. His milk cart had broken down outside the orphanage and as he had to unload the milk to make repairs, they could have it all.

The God of grace had come to Müller's aid when his need was greatest, answering his prayer of faith. George Müller became known as 'the man who gets things from God.'

Hudson's own faith in God was strengthened when he heard the reports of God's answer to Müller's prayers.

He believed that the God who did the impossible for George Müller, had called him to missionary work in China and would do the same for him. He began to believe more than ever before that God honoured his promises. One promise that came to mind as he heard of Müller's successes through prayer, was that found in James (5:16b): 'The effective, fervent prayer of a righteous man avails much.'

This encouraged him to trust himself more than ever to the goodness of God. He was convinced that if God called a person to a special work he would also provide all that was needed to make the work prosper.

A broken heart

In the midst of his studies and growing confidence in the power of God, his relationship with Marianne began to cause him much heartache. Although he loved Marianne, his love for Christ was stronger and he was willing to sacrifice everything for the Lord who loved him and had saved him from his sins.

His letters home were saturated with Biblical expressions and displayed a willingness to sacrifice everything he possessed for God.

Writing to his mother he said that although it appeared that he and Marianne would part, he lovingly accepted the will of God, who only did what was right.

Marianne didn't believe she was called to be a missionary's wife, working in China.

'Must you go to China?' she often argued, believing Hudson could faithfully and effectively serve the Lord in Great Britain. Hudson continued to pray that God might change her attitude and call her to be his life partner in his missionary endeavour, but that was not to be. Like the missionary Henry Martyn, he would sacrifice the love of a woman for the sake of faithfulness to his heavenly calling.

Months later the break came when Marianne finally said, 'No' to becoming his wife. Her father also objected to his daughter becoming involved in such a sacrificial work.

Hudson's love for Marianne did not immediately die, but periodically his thoughts of her caused him much emotional distress. Later when he moved to Drainside he wept with sorrow over his loss of her.

In December, 1851, alone in the surgery he was tempted by Satan to abandon his plans for China, marry Marianne and commence some comfortable, Christian work in England. He wrote to his mother of that night:

> Alone in the surgery I had a melting season. I was thoroughly softened and humbled and had a wonderful manifestation of the love of God. "A broken and contrite heart" He did not despise, but answered my cry for blessing...Oh may I be filled with His Spirit, and grow in grace until I reach "the measure of the stature of the fullness of Christ". I am happy: not without trial, anxiety or care, but by the grace of God I no longer bear it all myself. "The Lord gave, and the Lord has taken away." ...Trusting God does not deprive one of feelings or deaden our natural sensibilities, but it enables us to compare our trials with our mercies and to say, "Yet not withstanding, I will rejoice in the Lord, I will joy in the God of my salvation."

He was now assured that, just as God had sustained him through that difficult time, God would strengthen him in whatever lay before him.

He was then convinced that his relationship with Marianne was finished.

A meeting with William Lobscheid

Still living with the Hardeys, Hudson heard of the impending visit to Great Britain of William Lobscheid, a fellow worker with Dr Gutzlaff. He decided he would like to meet the man whose story had been told in *The Gleaner*, which now devoted the majority of its pages to overseas missionary work, especially work in China. Hudson was challenged by what he read and closely studied the way the gospel was penetrating China.

In June the headline of one article announced: 'China Open! How Far can This be said?'

The article spoke of the many years of prayer that had ascended to God pleading with him to open the door so the gospel could penetrate mainland China. The writer then said that God had answered the prayers of his people through the results of war and the Treaty of Nanking: '...in return for the evils which have been rendered to the people by the poisonous opium drug, it seems to be demanded of us to give them the antidote to their misery—the glorious gospel.'

This was followed by an explanation of the way the gospel work had been carried out. Hudson rejoiced when he read: 'To one who possesses the knowledge of surgery and medicine, there appears an unlimited opening of usefulness on the mainland…China is far more open to the labours, even of foreign missionaries, than they are prepared to take advantage of.'

Efforts were being made to select missionaries with medical knowledge to go to China. As Lobscheid was expected in England in August, 1852, Hudson wrote to his mother seeking advice: 'Do you think I would be justified in going to London and expending…money at a time when I need it to attend lectures? If it was only for my own pleasure, I could soon decide…but sometimes I think Lobscheid might give me some information worth going for.'

As well as meeting Lobscheid, a trip to London would give him the opportunity to visit Prince Albert's Crystal Palace Exhibition which was serviced by cheap train fares. As Amelia was ready to leave school, a trip to London was an opportunity to celebrate her sixteenth birthday. Their parents came to the rescue with financial help, Dr Hardey gave Hudson a week's leave and an uncle booked rooms in Soho for them both. On 17 September they set out for a short stay in London.

Amelia was overjoyed to be spending time with her brother as well as visiting the Crystal Palace. Hudson on the other hand was more interested in finding out all he could about missionary work in China.

When they met Mr Pearse of the Chinese Evangelization Society they found he was unable to spend time talking during his working hours at the bank and Stock Exchange. Arrangements were then made for them both to spend Sunday at his home in Hackney where he would have time to answer Hudson's many questions. While they were there Mr Pearse took the opportunity of taking Hudson to Tottenham to meet many members of the Chinese Society who became his lifelong friends. Amongst those kindly Quaker people a Miss Stacey opened her home to Hudson. He found her home and garden places of peace and tranquillity when the stress of work weighed heavily upon him. Many of the Quaker ladies were already supporting missionaries in China.

Mr Pearse introduced Hudson as a future Chinese missionary and despite his pale appearance, they soon realised that he had qualities that suited him for such a work.

Years later in China, he said that his friends in Tottenham who supported him in prayer and finances were very special to him.

Hudson met Mr Lobscheid, who after spending some time with him concluded: 'Why, you would never do for China,' he exclaimed, drawing attention to Hudson's fair hair and blue-grey eyes. 'They call me "Red-haired Devil", but would run from you in terror! You could never get them to listen at all.'

'And yet,' replied Hudson Taylor quietly, 'it is God who has called me, and He knows all about the colour of my hair and eyes.'

A Move To Drainside

Soon Hudson's brief holiday was over, and back with Dr Hardey he rejoiced and praised God for the encouragement he had received from the Tottenham Christians. When Dr Hardey informed him that the room in which he lived was needed, he moved to a very comfortable room at Aunt Hannah's. This change of address proved to be very convenient as Dr Hardey's surgery was only a couple of minutes walk away and the medical school where he attended lectures was just across the road. Dr Hardey increased his salary so that the cost of his board and lodgings would be exactly covered. This arrangement created a problem for Hudson who faithfully tithed his income, including his living allowance. Now he had insufficient funds to cover his additional living expenses.

Growing uneasy about his comfortable way of life he realised that this was not good training for one who hoped to commence missionary work in the inland provinces of China. He knew he needed to live an austere life.

As was his customary practice, he took the matter to the Lord in prayer. Later he made the decision to leave his aunt's comfortable home and rent a small bed-sitting room owned by Captain Finch and his wife at 30 Cottingham Terrace, Drainside. That move made it possible for him to tithe out of the whole of his income. Now he would have more time available to study the Word of God and visit the poor. He would also be able to carry out more evangelistic work than he had done before.

He came to meet and help many poor people who were suffering financial and spiritual distress, and with careful budgeting he found he had more spare money than ever.

The Drainside neighbourhood was a marshy area drained by channels in which many water birds lived. Herons caught the fish in the drains while the farmers used the marshy area in which to keep their milk cool. Cans of milk were sunk into the marshy ground and this preserved the milk for lengthy periods.

As Captain Finch was a sailor who spent long periods away from home, his wife was delighted to have a young medical apprentice living downstairs. For three shillings a week rent Hudson had a room measuring about four yards by four yards to himself. His basic furniture consisted of a bed, table, chair and a fireplace.

Drainside was really a suburb of two rows of houses facing each other across a drain into which the residents threw their rubbish. Hudson was surrounded by poverty which suited his purposes. Now, however, he had a long walk to Dr Hardey's surgery, through an area where crime was prevalent. As the marshy area of drains and holes meant walking was dangerous, Hudson's mother made him promise he would only walk in the safe areas where there was some street lighting, despite the fact that it took an extra fifteen minutes to walk to his workplace.

He found life lonely, but now he made his own decisions how he would spend his spare time and what he would eat. It was there, during the period of November, 1851, till September, 1852, that Hudson, really matured because he was thrown upon his own resources.

He often wandered across the marshy areas praying God's blessing upon his preparations for the future.

With more spare time for spiritual work amongst the underprivileged Drainside people he visited the docks where he distributed tracts and spoke of his wonderful Saviour. To the crowds that gathered he read from the Scriptures and preached the glorious saving grace of God in Christ. Some of the people mocked him, throwing nut shells at him, while others wanted to hear more. When he was moved on by a policeman he commented that when there had been a fight in the area the police had not interfered.

A Concerned Family

Hudson economised more than ever before and found he had extra money to help the poor. Later he wrote:

> I soon found that I could live upon very much less than I had previously thought possible. Butter, milk and other such luxuries I soon ceased to use;…I found that by living mainly on oatmeal and rice, with occasional variations, a very small sum was sufficient for my needs. In this way I had more than two-thirds of my income available for other purposes, and my experience was that the less

I spent on myself and the more I gave away, the fuller of happiness
and blessing did my soul become.

Christmas time was a lonely time for him at Drainside. Thinking of
the family at home, enjoying one another's company and eating the
foods that usually graced the Christmas table he went for a walk and
bought a special treat for himself—'some treacle parkin' at fourpence
a pound' which he shared with the Finch family. He allowed himself
a luxury and bought a shortbread biscuit which he ate with a glass of
raspberry vinegar and water.

When his mother received news that he was not looking well
and appeared to be losing weight, she wrote to him expressing her
concern.

Was he eating sufficient good food to keep him fit and healthy? To
put everyone's mind at ease he wrote to Amelia explaining what he
usually ate: 'I take as much good, plain, substantial food as I need,' he
wrote, 'but waste nothing in luxuries.'

His breakfast consisted of brown-bread biscuits and herring. For
lunch he ate prune and apple pie and on occasions roast potato and
tongue. Sometimes he had peas in place of the potatoes. In the evening
it was biscuit and apples. He varied his diet to include cheese, fish,
rhubarb, pickled cabbage and lettuce.

Concerning his reported loss of weight, he explained that he was
wearing a large coat. No, he had not lost weight, but the coat was big
and he had a cold. That was why he wore the thick, oversized coat. In
his letter he reassured his mother that all was well: 'I eat like a horse,
sleep like a top and have the spirits of a lark.'

Spiritual Growth

Hudson was making tremendous spiritual strides. He appreciated
Mr Jukes' preaching, and living in the expectation of the immediate
return of the Lord Jesus Christ he gave away his unwanted clothing
and material possessions. He urged his friends and relatives to be ready
for Christ's return 'with oil in our vessels and our lamps trimmed.'

During those days he was baptized upon his confession of faith and
soon after he baptized Amelia by immersion in a local stream.

He was extremely zealous in his faith and this caused his mother
some concern. His letters home flowed with Biblical language. He
studied everything he could about China and rejoiced when he read of
the need of missionaries with medical knowledge to work on foreign

fields. His love for Christ grew stronger and his desire to glorify and serve God became more evident to all who knew him.

He frequently meditated upon the words of John 3:16- 'For God so loved the world that he gave his only begotten Son, that whosoever believes in him should not perish but have everlasting life.'

He was continually amazed at God's great gift to save sinners—He gave his Son! He then reasoned that if God gave such a wonderful gift he would give everything, even his life if necessary, in making known to the Chinese the riches of salvation in Christ.

He wanted to get on with his work as he knew that millions of Chinese were passing into a lost eternity because they had no saving knowledge of Christ.

On one occasion he wrote to his mother: 'Oh! mother, I cannot tell you...I cannot describe how I long to be a missionary—to preach the Gospel to poor sinners—to spend and be spent for Him who died for me. I feel as if for this I could give up all, everything, every idol, however dear.' Yes, Hudson was willing to sacrifice everything for his Lord and Saviour, Jesus Christ!

His medical studies were progressing well. He studied anatomy, analysed blood, cut up a cat, assisted Dr Hardey with patients and kept the accounts and surgery records up to date.

And all the time he had his heart set upon China. He considered his Spartan life, motivated by the desire to serve Christ as a medical missionary, to be a good preparation for what he expected on foreign soil.

His prayers ascended to God, seeking his continued blessings upon all his labours. More and more he cast himself upon the mercy of Jehovah to provide his daily needs. He knew that when he reached his destination his only security would be found in Christ, and from experience he knew that God would not let him down.

One issue that caused him some concern was that he still had no academic qualifications nor was he ordained to the ministry. However when he read of others without such qualifications taking the gospel to foreign lands and receiving God's richest blessing, he felt assured that he could do the same.

8

Putting God to the Test

Two passages of Scripture were imprinted upon Hudson's mind. The first was one that Mr Lobscheid found so comforting: 'And my God shall supply all your need according to His riches in glory by Christ Jesus' (Phil. 4:19); and the second was also from Paul's writing to the Philippians (3:7-12):

> But what things were gain to me, those I have counted loss for Christ. But indeed I also count all things loss for the excellence of the knowledge of Christ Jesus my Lord, for whom I have suffered the loss of all things, and count them as rubbish, that I may gain Christ and be found in Him, not having my own righteousness, which is from the law, but that which is through faith in Christ, the righteousness which is from God by faith; that I may know Him and the power of His resurrection, and the fellowship of His sufferings, being conformed to His death, if, by any means, I may attain to the resurrection from the dead. Not that I have already attained, or am already perfected; but I press on, that I may lay hold of that for which Christ Jesus has also laid hold of me.

Hudson was willing to sacrifice everything, even life itself for the Saviour who loved him, yet later he wrote, 'I never made a sacrifice.'

He knew that God could satisfy all of his needs. Time and again he had seen the providential working of God in his life and realised that his Lord did answer the prayer of faith.

But he wanted to be assured of this great practical truth while he was still in England and decided to put God to the test.

He knew that when he reached China he would be beyond the help of his relatives and friends and then it would be God alone who would provide his daily needs. From the Scriptures he knew that God would not let him down, but wanted to experience this truth before he left England's shores. He wrote:

> There was no doubt that if faith did not fail, God would not fail; but, then, what if one's faith should prove insufficient? I had not at that time learned that even "if we believe not, he abides faithful, he cannot deny himself"; and it was consequently a very serious question to my mind, not whether He was faithful, but whether I had enough faith to warrant my embarking on the enterprise set before me.
>
> I thought to myself, "When I get out to China, I shall have no claim on anyone for anything; my only claim will be on God. How important, therefore, to learn before leaving England to move man, through God, by prayer alone!"

The ever busy Dr Hardey asked him to remind him whenever his salary fell due, which was every three months. Hudson, however, decided that he would not ask the doctor for his pay, but would, through prayer, have God bring the matter to his attention. In this way he would prove that God heard and answered the prayer of faith.

On one occasion his pay was due but Dr Hardey had obviously forgotten. Hudson kept praying till one Saturday, after paying all of his accounts he was left with just one coin—a half-crown.

Following the Sunday worship service he set off to visit boarding houses in the poorest part of town. This work was a great spiritual joy to Hudson who thought of it as not just preparation for missionary life in China, but as a small portion of heaven itself.

That night at ten o'clock he met a man from a slum area, who pleaded with him to come and visit his dying wife. He agreed, but realising that the man was an Irishman, asked why he hadn't sent for the priest. The distressed man replied that when he had asked the priest to come he had demanded a payment of one shilling and six pence. The man didn't have the money as his family was at the point of starvation.

Hudson knew that he would have to assist them with some financial help, but he only had one coin and that was the last of his money. He had enough food for his night meal and breakfast, but that was all. When he reminded the man that he should have gone to the 'relieving officer' to obtain some help, he was told that he had done this, but was advised to come back the next morning. He believed his wife would be dead by then.

Hudson's immediate thought was of the coin in his pocket. If he only had some change he would have willingly given the family a one shilling piece.

Later he said: '...the real truth of the matter simply was that I could trust in God *plus one-and-sixpence*, but was not yet prepared to trust Him only, without any money at all in my pocket.'

He went to the man's home which was in a district where he had been assaulted on a previous visit. In fact the locals had warned him to never again come that way.

Soon he found himself in a room where there were four or five starving children and the man's wife, lying on a filthy mattress, with a newly born baby at her side. The poor woman was moaning and appeared to be close to death.

'Ah!' thought Hudson, 'if I only had two shillings and a six pence instead of half a crown, how gladly should they have one and six pence of it!'

He found it difficult to comfort the man and his wife when he reminded them that there was a kind, loving God who would see them through their troubles. Then the thought flashed into his mind, 'You hypocrite! Telling these unconverted people about a kind and loving Father in Heaven, and not prepared yourself to trust Him without half a crown!'

He was greatly distressed, but knew he could pray. He loved prayer and as he knelt beside the dying woman he closed his eyes and began: 'Our Father who art in heaven...' But again his mind troubled him: 'Dare you mock God? Dare you kneel down and call Him Father with that half crown in your pocket?'

He continued, stammering out a prayer for the family. When the prayer was finished he stood up and heard the plea of the distressed husband: 'You see what a terrible state we are in, sir; if you can help us, for God's sake, do!'

It was as if Christ had spoken to him at that very moment: 'Give to him who asks of you!'

He put his hand into his pocket and took out his only coin. As he handed it to the man he told him it was the last of his money, but he was reasonably well off and God would care for him.

Suddenly Hudson's heart was flooded with heavenly joy. He felt free to speak as he had before he had entered the home. He was again at peace with his Lord.

He wrote of that moment: 'Not only was the poor woman's life saved, but I realised that my life was saved too!'

That night he returned home with a song of praise on his lips. 'My heart was as light as my pocket,' he later wrote.

After eating his meal he knelt by his bed and reminded God of the promise of Scripture 'that He who gives to the poor lends to the Lord.' He asked God to please repay the loan quickly as he had no dinner the next day. Then with a peaceful heart he committed himself to the loving care of God and slept well.

The next morning as he sat down to eat the last of his food he heard a knock at the front door followed by a knock on his door. Mrs Finch handed him a small packet which had come in the mail. This surprised Hudson as he usually didn't receive any mail on Monday. Opening the parcel he found a pair of kid gloves and out of one glove fell half a sovereign.

'Praise the Lord!' he exclaimed. 'Four hundred percent for twelve hours investment; that is good interest. How glad the merchants of Hull would be if they could lend their money at such a rate!'

Hudson said that that particular incident was a great encouragement when in the future he faced what appeared to be insurmountable difficulties: 'If we are faithful to God in little things,' he said, 'we shall gain experience and strength that will be helpful to us in the more serious trials of life.'

But still he had not been paid his wages and the ten shillings he now had wouldn't last very long.

Upon his knees he asked God to remind Dr Hardey that his pay was now overdue. Hudson wasn't troubled by a shortage of money, as his ten shillings lasted for several more weeks, but he began to face the problem of unanswered prayer.

'Can I go to China?' he asked, 'or will my want of faith and power with God prove to be so serious an obstacle as to preclude my entering upon this much-prized service?'

He would soon have to pay the rent to his Christian landlady who depended upon the regular payments. Should he ask Dr Hardey for his pay? He then began spending his spare time in prayer, pleading with God to bring to the attention of Dr Hardey that his salary was not just due, but overdue.

After almost a week of constant prayer he was unsure of what to do. Should he ask for his salary or simply wait on God's timing?

He concluded that he should pray on and wait for God to act as he saw fit and in his own time.

At five o'clock on Saturday evening as the doctor put down his pen after writing a prescription he looked at Hudson and asked, 'By the bye, Taylor, isn't your salary due again?'

Hudson was surprised by the words he heard, and while thanking God silently for answering his prayers he reminded Dr Hardey that his pay was well overdue. Almost at once his joy turned to a feeling of 'revulsion' when Dr Hardey replied, 'Oh, I am so sorry you did not remind me! You know how busy I am; I wish I had thought of it a little sooner, for only this afternoon I sent all the money I had to the bank, otherwise I would pay you at once!'

Hudson returned to his small workroom, upset by what had happened. Soon, however, he was on his knees thanking God for reminding the doctor of his obligation to pay his wages. He was still confident that God could and would provide the money he needed.

So with a confident spirit he spent time preparing for Sunday worship. He read the Scriptures, prayed and prepared his talk for the time he would spend in the slum areas.

Finally he put on his coat, turned off the gas and as he prepared to leave he heard Dr Hardey walking towards the backyard surgery. As he was laughing Hudson wondered what could be so amusing at that time of night. Dr Hardey entered to tell him that a rich patient had just called to pay his account, something that was very unusual. The doctor was amazed that such a person would come to pay an account at ten o'clock at night.

He had immediately come to Hudson, wanting to make an entry in the financial ledger indicating that the account had been paid. Then as he was about to leave the surgery he handed Hudson some banknotes with the words, 'By the way, Taylor, you might as well take these notes; I don't have any change, but can give you the balance next week.'

Soon Hudson was praising God for his goodness and faithfulness. Later he wrote: 'To me the incident was not a trivial one; and to recall it sometimes, in circumstances of great difficulty, in China or elsewhere, has proved no small comfort and strength.'

During his time at Drainside, he grew closer to God. Now he was certain that the God who had saved him and called him to service in China could be depended upon at all times. He longed for the day when he would leave English soil for China where he could preach the unsearchable riches of Christ to a people who lived in spiritual darkness.

He spent many hours each day reading and meditating upon the Word of God and rejoicing in the promises he found—promises that stirred his heart, assuring him of God's presence and support in everything that lay ahead. And as he read, he prayed that the Holy Spirit would continue the wonderful work of sanctification in his life. He longed to have a Christlike character and continually sought the prayers of others that God would humble him and make him more like his Saviour.

9

A Move to London

Hudson's desire to go to China, coupled with the stories he heard about missionaries already there preaching the gospel unsettled him. Articles by Lobscheid and others, calling for more missionaries, produced a feeling that his time in Hull should end.

One particular story that encouraged the unordained Hudson was that of George Piercy. Believing God had called him to missionary work in mainland China, he saved enough money to support himself for two years work and left on a Chinese manned vessel. During the five months journey he was taught their language.

Upon reaching Hong Kong, Piercy was welcomed by Dr James Legge and after some time visiting hospitals and the army barracks he commenced a Wesleyan work. Hudson saw that Piercy's venture was a success—and what really encouraged him was that he was not a highly educated man, nor was he ordained.

His enthusiasm to follow George Piercy's example became stronger when he read in *The Gleaner* the uplifting reports of evangelistic work in many parts of the world, particularly China. He just wanted to pack his bags and start the work to which he was called.

To Amelia he wrote on 1 March, 1852:

> I feel I have not long to stay in this country now. I do not know what turn Providence is about to take, but I think some change is coming...But if my Saviour calls, shall I not obey? If he has left

his throne in glory to come and bleed and die for us, shall we not all, *all*, follow Him? If I stay here another two years and save fifty or sixty pounds to pay my expenses to China, I shall land there no better off than if I go at once and work my passage out. In two years there will die in that land at least twenty-four million people....if I could instruct in the truths of the Gospel one poor sinner, and the Spirit accompanied the word with power to his soul and he were saved—to all eternity he would be happy, praising the Redeemer.'

Likewise he wrote to his mother, expressing his love of Christ and desire to get on with the work of fulfilling God's call.

As he couldn't afford the fare to China he discussed the matter with Captain Finch, who was on leave. He wanted to find out all he could about travel to that part of the world and how he could obtain a cheap passage.

When he indicated he was willing to work as an assistant to a ship's surgeon, or if need be, to work his passage to the Far East as a sailor, Captain Finch warned him of the physical and spiritual dangers of such a scheme. After telling him that the journey would take about five months he went on to explain a sailor's work, suggesting he would never survive the hardship of the mariner's life at sea.

He said that most sailors were godless men, and not ideal companions to anyone who loved the Lord. However, Hudson simply saw this as another aspect of suffering for the Lord he loved. He also thought of the opportunity such a trip would present to confess Christ to the sailors.

His letters to Amelia and his mother were filled with outbursts of love for Christ and his desire to be on his way to China. Often he wrote of Christ's amazing sacrifice for sinners, and his desire to thank God for his salvation by the faithful proclamation of the good news to the Chinese. He often tenderly wrote of his mother's sacrifice of her son to Christ, her Lord, when he finally left England.

In the midst of all his plans he received advice from relatives and Christian friends—people whose counsel he valued. He had been praying for guidance concerning his future and decided that God would use their counsel in reaching a final decision. His friends suggested that it was not yet time for him to leave England, as he was still a young man who had studies to complete.

The result was that he saw the hand of God in the advice given and while disappointed decided to remain at Hull for another year.

In April 1852 he went home to spend a week with his family. This was a time of physical refreshment for a tired young man. He appreciated the companionship of his parents, particularly his mother with whom he was very close. Life at home was so restful compared to his busy, rough life at Drainside!

All too soon his short holiday came to an end and he was back in his small room with the Finch family. He found it difficult to settle down to his old way of life, but soon he was hard at work in the surgery as well as the spiritual activities in the community.

For exercise and to help Mrs Finch, he dug up a vegetable garden between the front of the house and the drain. Mrs Finch was able to pick fresh vegetables, and he had a more enjoyable view from his window.

His devotional times became more lengthy, claiming that he accomplished more in the day after one hour with the Lord.

His fervour to fulfil God's call became stronger when he read in *The Gleaner* of their intention to send twenty-three missionaries to China, Mr Lobscheid being the first of that projected number.

Previously the Chinese Society had only supported missionary endeavour, but now there was a change in policy and a change in name. In future the organization was to be known as *The Chinese Evangelization Society* (CES).

The June and July *Gleaner* contained information from Mr Lobscheid's journals, especially the news that there was freedom in China to preach Christ. The theme of the magazine was: 'China is ripe for the gospel, but if it is to be reaped we must go amongst the people.'

When he read, 'We trust it may please God to raise up another European medical missionary,' his heart rejoiced.

He was now twenty years of age and understood the value of extending his medical education, which would better equip him for his life amongst the Chinese. He had a growing conviction that his time with Dr Hardey should be terminated, which would enable him to move to London to continue his medical education.

Dr Hardey however had other plans!

He saw in Hudson a godly young man of integrity and ability; a man he would like as his apprentice. Hudson however came to the conclusion that to bind himself to Dr Hardey for a lengthy period could well create problems in the future. What if God opened the door for him to begin his missionary work and he was still under contract to the doctor?

Turning down the proposal he suggested that his cousin John, who was still working in Barnsley with his father, might be a fine replacement. John was now a converted young man who wanted to commence medical studies.

In the midst of his mental turmoil Hudson received a request from his father, through Amelia, that caused him much heartache.

He wanted his son to return home and take over the management of the pharmacy. Their father was just forty-five years of age and had become very unsettled with his life. He still longed to become involved in missionary work, but that was not all. He wanted to visit relatives in Australia and then possibly start a new life with his family in Canada or the USA, which would mean an expansion of his business and greater security for his family.

Just at that time Hudson was considering travelling to China with Lobscheid, and to agree to his father's proposal would mean a postponement of his plans.

This he could not do, unless he knew his father's resolve was to sail to China and there preach the gospel. If this was his father's plan he would return home for several years and manage the family business.

He wrote to his mother expressing his concern, but her reply was to accuse him of being an ungrateful son, considering all that his father had done for him. She reminded him of the fifth commandment and his obligation to obey God's decree. She told him not to mention Australia in any letters home.

Hudson took his mother's rebuke to heart and wrote to his father expressing repentance for his ungodly attitude: 'I…write to say in the language of the prodigal, "I have sinned against heaven and in your sight, and am no more worthy to be called your son." Conscience has often troubled me about the answer I sent to your enquiry as to whether I was willing to come home for two years, should you go abroad, and I can no longer rest without…entreating your forgiveness.'

He continued, outlining the many sacrifices he knew his father had made for him and begged his forgiveness.

Then he said he would willingly return home and manage the pharmacy for two years, just as his father had requested. After that he would commence his God-given work in China. His letter was signed, '…your affectionate son, James Hudson Taylor.'

Within a short time however, his father had changed his mind and again became deeply involved in his chemist shop and spiritual obligations in Barnsley.

It was in this letter that Hudson made special mention of his first effort to amputate a finger. What made this so special was that he did it alone.

During the days that followed, his faith was strengthened. To his mother he wrote of the promises of Psalm 37 which thrilled him: 'Trust in the Lord and do good, so shall you dwell in the land and verily you shall be fed. Delight yourself also in the Lord, and He shall give you the desires of your heart. Commit your ways unto the Lord, trust also in Him, and He shall bring it to pass...Rest in the Lord and wait patiently for Him...'

Matters were coming to a head as far as Hudson's future was concerned. He had been offered financial help from both the CES and his father, but decided to decline both offers and put himself totally at the mercy of God for financial support. His efforts to obtain work proved fruitless, although full time work would have interfered with his attendance at the medical lectures and practical hospital experience. He saw this as another trial of faith—trusting God to meet his every need.

He had been reading of George Müller's life of dependence upon God, and the words he had inscribed on his orphanage window: 'Jehovah-Jireh—the Lord will provide', were burned into his heart and became his war-cry. Now he was confident that what God had done for Müller, he would also do for himself concluding that he would never borrow from any person, but by the grace of God make himself totally dependent upon Jehovah for the provision of his every need.

Having received a letter from Mr Pearse concerning the imminent departure of Mr Lobscheid for China, he decided to travel to London. This trip was at the expense of the CES and brought him to the point of making a firm decision concerning his future. He returned to Hull determined to leave Dr Hardey and move to London. When the CES renewed its offer to meet his hospital training fees he gratefully accepted.

Friends gave him the names of London Christians who would be a help, while his mother's brother, Uncle Benjamin Hudson, arranged accommodation for him in Soho Square, at Ruffles Boarding House.

On 25 September, 1852 Hudson boarded a steamer and left Hull for the next step in his preparations to fulfil God's call.

10

A Very Busy Student Life

Hudson travelled the cheap, second class fare to London, providing his own food of brown bread and pickled herrings.

When the steamer reached its destination he made his way to his uncle's apartment at Ruffles Boarding House in Soho Square.

He quickly settled into his new surroundings, but found that his cousin Tom often called in. He lived in a room around the corner from Uncle Benjamin but soon arrangements were made for Hudson to share his accommodation. This was a real saving for Hudson because he had no income and his meagre savings were quickly dwindling.

Living with Tom was difficult because he lived for worldly pleasures and spent much time discussing politics and business affairs with Uncle Benjamin. Neither were interested in spiritual matters and Hudson found it difficult to get away for his times of meditation and prayer. They couldn't understand why a person would live in total dependence upon God and Tom often went out of his way to try and involve Hudson in worldly activities. Even his father often thought his son had become extreme in his religious practices.

Hudson, however, began to pray for Tom's conversion, and in the following months he became interested in spiritual matters. Before the end of the year Hudson's prayers were answered and Tom confessed his faith in Christ and began to live a life of witness to the one who was now his Lord and Saviour.

Hudson's uncle, who had a wide circle of influential friends, including some doctors, wanted to introduce him to them in the hope that he would get work as an apprentice. However, Hudson didn't want this, as he needed his time for studies and was convinced that God would provide all he needed as he prepared himself for overseas missionary work.

No one seemed to understand his attitude; even the CES was unconcerned about his situation. He then decided he should seek counsel from Mr Pearse, the Foreign Secretary of the CES.

Leaving home early one morning, he set out to visit Mr Pearse before he left for work, but because of his work commitments, he didn't have the time to speak to him. However, he invited him to visit him at Hackney the following Sunday when they could discuss his plans.

Mr Pearse told him that as the offer to meet his medical training expenses was dependent upon the CES accepting him as a prospective missionary he was required to submit a formal application, with references concerning his character and suitability for mission work. This disappointed Hudson as he believed a firm offer of support had already been made.

This was the first time he faced 'red tape', but his formal application was altered to require just several letters of reference relating to his suitability to serve as an overseas missionary. His mother was also invited to submit one reference. Hudson was then told that the Society meetings were not called to deal with special business, but only met on a regular basis. This meant his application would not be considered for some weeks and his money was in short supply.

In the middle of his difficulties he received an invitation from his father to return home to the family business. His father, who couldn't understand God's dealing with his son and the poverty of life he lived, was of the opinion he should have a permanent job.

Hudson's reply wasn't given to his father as his mother knew he would be offended by the sentiments—'Thank Father for his kind offer of a home, but tell him, *those who trust in the Lord* always have something to depend on.'

With little money, no work, the dithering attitude of the CES and the fact that lectures were about to commence at London Hospital, Hudson prayed on, assured that God would provide for his every need.

His spiritual life suffered a setback when he started worshipping with an exclusive Brethren group. He enjoyed the company of three or four hundred worshippers each Lord's Day, but realising that they were cultish he commenced worshipping with an independent Baptist group which he found more to his liking.

A month after arriving in London, he received word from the CES that his medical fees would be met and he could commence his studies on 25 October, 1852.

This meant a long four mile walk each way from his accommodation as he couldn't meet the cost of a cab or a horse-drawn bus.

Then he decided to really strengthen his body by living a Spartan life. He survived by daily buying a loaf of brown bread as he walked home. The evening meal consisted of half the bread. The remainder was for breakfast which he usually ate as he walked to hospital, or while taking a short rest along the way. For lunch he ate several apples. He was very satisfied with his life and thanked God that he had a roof over his head, clothes on his back, food on the table, was studying medicine and had still a little savings. His life was one of self-denial and helping others.

Except in the suburbs where the rich lived, London was little more than a great slum. Unemployment was rife, the street girls plied their trade and drunkenness was found everywhere. The open sewerage which flowed beside the streets was ideal for the spread of disease and in 1848 sixteen thousand Londoners died from cholera. This plague broke out again in 1853 and 1854.

Hospital conditions were terrible. Nurses at the London Hospital were a mixture of prostitutes and more respectable women, who were motivated by a love for Christ or a desire to comfort the sick and needy.

Each huge ward was normally allocated seven candles a week and unless a surgeon ordered more, when they were finished the ward was left in darkness.

Anaesthetics were not used by surgeons, who prepared patients for surgery with a swig or two from the whisky flask. It was some years before doctors regularly used Simpson's chloroform. Without antiseptics or any real understanding of medical hygiene the surgeons, in their blood and pus splattered coats, carried out their excruciatingly painful work.

Patients were held down or strapped onto the operating table before the surgeon commenced his operation. If help was needed to further restrain the patient, a bell was rung, calling more strong men to hold the screaming, struggling person. The smell of putrefying flesh, dried blood and gangrene greeted everyone who visited London Hospital. Much of Hudson's time was spent preparing patients for surgery.

Despite the fact that he had to mix with a rowdy group of godless, blasphemous medical students, his faith grew stronger. His love of Christ intensified as did his desire to leave for China and there preach the gospel.

In November, 1852 he wrote home telling his family of his very busy life:

> I begin the morning [by having] to be at the Hospital at 8 am, before which time I have a short walk...I get my breakfast on the way to rest me a little.

8 am—9 am	ward rounds with M.Ds;
9 am—10 am	lecture on surgical anatomy;
10 am—10:30 am	dissecting room or library;
10:30 am—11:30 am	chemistry or dissecting demonstrations;
11:30 am—1 pm	dissecting room, museum, library or dressings and operations in outpatients. Then lunch.
1 pm—3 pm	operations and rounds with surgeons;
3 pm—4 pm	lectures on surgery or physiological anatomy and once a week an exam.
4 pm—5 pm	'medicinal lecture'.

> On Saturdays 7 am—8 am a lecture on dental physiology and surgery. (Then I walk home and) if possible read up on some subject, transcribe notes, answer letters and then [use any] spare time with eating and sleeping....Sometimes I have been so tired I was forced to ride part of the way home...all but about half a mile for three pence for a mile and a half for one penny...[With two or three weeks' vacation at Christmas] I...thought of popping down if there were any cheap trains, and I could save by getting any "grub" out of you....

Hudson's life was certainly very busy!

11

Staring Death in the Face

Hudson continued to depend upon God for all he needed, but he soon faced several trials which strengthened his faith even more than ever.

He had been helping his Drainside landlady by collecting her husband's half pay and forwarding it to her, thus saving the bank costs which ate into the pay packet.

He received a note from Mrs Finch asking him to forward the next payment on time as it was urgently needed to meet expenses. This presented no difficulty, but as he was facing an examination which he hoped would result in a study grant, he decided to send her his own money which would be replaced when he collected what was owing to Mrs Finch.

As the London Hospital Medical School was closed due to the Duke of Wellington's public funeral, he took the opportunity to visit the offices of the shipping company which employed Captain Finch. To his dismay, he was told there was no money available, as Captain Finch had absconded to seek his fortune overseas on the goldfields.

Despite his explanation of what he had done, the clerk assured him that there was nothing he could do to help him. At first Hudson was very upset by what had happened—he also needed money—but soon recovered his confidence remembering that Jehovah ruled the universe. God's resources were unlimited so it would be no difficulty for Him to come to his rescue.

He remembered the time at Drainside when he gave away his last half crown only to be repaid with four hundred percent interest. He never found out how this came about, but knew that God controlled the affairs of the universe for the well-being of the saints and for his own glory. His uneasy feeling disappeared as he meditated upon the God he loved and served.

All the time he was seeking the latest news about overseas missionary activities. Mr and Mrs Lobscheid had sailed for China as CES missionaries, and this event resulted in an increase in giving for missionary work in that part of the world. Then came the appeal for Christians to pray for China every time they drank a cup of tea—after all, tea came from China!

Encouraging information had reached the CES concerning the followers of Hong Xiu-quan, the leader of the Worshippers of Shangdi, who were demanding freedom of religion in China. They were the founders of the Taiping rebels who claimed to be Christian. The movement was alive and progressing slowly—certainly not dead and buried as had been reported.

Promising reports were also received concerning Mrs Gutzlaff, who was carrying on the work her husband had started in Hong Kong. These reports excited Hudson who believed that as a medical missionary he would have a part to play in God's purposes of establishing the church in China.

It was on 14 December, 1852 that he pricked his finger while sewing pages together to make a booklet. The incident didn't bother him at the time, but the following day he was involved in the dissection of a rather gruesome body.

Everyone took special precautions knowing that it was very easy to become infected from such a body. Before the morning was over he was forced to go outside as he felt very sick. This was unusual for him, as he usually had a strong stomach for such work. He was violently ill, but after a drink of water went back to work, dissecting the body.

In the afternoon he became increasingly unwell, having such severe pain in his side and arm that he couldn't hold his pencil to take notes.

Realising that he couldn't continue, he explained to the lecturer what had happened. The surgeon told him he must have become infected by the decaying body and that he should get home as quickly as possible, even hiring a hansom cab.

His words shocked Hudson when the lecturer continued, 'For you're a dead man.'

Despite feeling so unwell he replied, 'Unless I am greatly mistaken, I have work to do in China, and shall not die.' He was fully convinced that nothing would frustrate God's plans for him.

To this the surgeon replied, 'That is all very well, but you go and get a hansom and drive home as fast as you can. You have no time to lose, for you will soon be incapable of winding up your affairs.'

Hudson didn't have the money to hire a cab so he set out walking. But before long he could go no further and was forced to finish the journey on the bus.

Staggering through the front door he asked a servant for some boiling water and before going to his room he urged the woman to accept Christ then and there, as her Lord and Saviour. As he began to bathe his infected hand he fell unconscious and woke to find himself on his own bed.

Uncle Benjamin soon arrived on the scene and told him that he'd asked his own doctor to visit him—and he would pay the account.

After the doctor heard Hudson's story he gave what proved to be sound advice: 'Well, if you have been living moderately, you may pull through; but if you have been going in for beer and that sort of thing, there is no…chance for you.'

Hudson explained his Spartan life style, to which the doctor replied, 'But now you must keep up your strength, for it will be a pretty hard struggle.'

The prescription? A bottle of port wine each day and as many chops as he could eat. Hudson had no money to buy such luxuries, but Uncle Benjamin came to the rescue and provided all that he required.

Not wanting to worry his parents, he had his Uncle and Tom promise to keep his sickness a secret from them all. At home his parents were unconcerned at the lack of news from their son—after all they believed he was hard at work studying for his examinations.

Several weeks passed before Hudson was well enough to go outside his room and when he did he received news of two other students who had lost their lives from infection when dissecting a body. Again he saw the hand of God in the preservation of his life.

When the doctor next visited him, he advised a holiday in the countryside. Even though Hudson knew his parents would have welcomed him home and helped him meet the expenses, he decided to remain where he was.

Then, remembering the shipping company and Captain Finch's lost wages, he decided to visit their office to ask if there was any change in the situation. Before setting out on the two mile walk he prayed that God would give him the necessary strength to last the distance. In this way Christ would be glorified as the one who alone could strengthen the weak.

He found the going difficult, stopping every few steps to regain his strength. Arriving at his destination he faced the difficult walk upstairs. Every couple of steps he was forced to sit down and rest for several minutes.

When he finally faced the clerk with whom he had had dealings, he praised God as he heard him say, 'Oh, I am so glad you have come, for it turns out that it was an able seaman of the same name that ran away. The mate is still on board; the ship has just reached Gravesend, and will be up very soon. I shall be glad to give you the half-pay up to date, for doubtless it will reach his wife more safely through you. We all know what temptations beset the men when they arrive home after a voyage.'

Then, noticing that Hudson was most unwell, the clerk insisted that he come inside, sit down and share his lunch before returning. Hudson was happy to accept the invitation before he set out for his room. On the way home he bought a money order for the money that was still owing to Mrs Finch and before reaching his room posted it to her.

The next morning, feeling much better, he set off to visit Uncle Benjamin's doctor to pay his account even though his Uncle said he would meet the expense. The doctor refused to have a medical student make any payment, but accepted the cost of the quinine he had prescribed.

Hudson then took the opportunity to tell him of God's goodness to him over many years.

After he told him of his walk to the shipping company, the doctor replied 'Impossible! Why I left you lying there more like a ghost than a man.'

Hudson explained that God had given him the strength to undertake the long walk. As he paid the doctor the money owing to him, he told him of the accounts he still had to pay and showed him all that was left—sufficient to return home on the bus and to buy food along the way. This story so affected the doctor that tears swelled in his eyes as he said, 'I would give all the world for a faith like yours.'

Hudson, who never again met the doctor, reminded him that such a faith was there for the taking, without money and without price.

The doctor soon afterwards had a stroke and died.

The next day Hudson went home for a restful three weeks of mother's care.

When he returned to London, his parents made him promise to accept the help that others offered him and not to be so extreme in his total dependence upon God to provide for his every need by some unexpected providence.

Hudson was certain that those weeks of testing proved that he had the physical, mental and spiritual stamina to cope with the hardships of life away from Western civilization.

It was during this time of convalescence that he again met Marianne.

12

Hudson's Prayer-Answering God

While at home Hudson's family and friends became more fully aware of the sacrifices he was undertaking in his preparation for life in China. Then a visit from Marianne revived the flames of love. With her father's blessing they became engaged and began preparing for life together on the mission field.

All too soon his stay at home came to an end and he returned to London where he found Tom with a severe case of 'rheumatic fever'. Tom didn't have the money to obtain the services of a good doctor so Hudson made himself responsible for the diagnosis and treatment of the disease—strong mustard and vinegar plasters did the job, and soon Tom was recovering.

The time Hudson spent with his Tottenham Christian friends proved to be valuable in strengthening him both physically and spiritually. Miss Stacey frequently had the young doctor in her home where she made sure he had nutritious meals and a quiet time. Often he stayed over the weekend, returning to the London Hospital on Monday morning. Other friends also opened their homes and hearts to the overworked and tired, young, prospective missionary. Later in life he remembered with love the kindnesses of his Tottenham friends. However, at that time no one really knew the total extent of the sacrifices he was making for his Lord and Saviour.

During those days a Ladies' Association of the CES was formed to pray for God's blessing upon the missionary endeavours being made on the Chinese mainland. Many prayers were offered for Mr Lobscheid and the others associated with this work.

Spiritually Hudson was growing closer to God as he saw His gracious hand in everything that was taking place. Yet, he continually sought God's guidance as he made his plans for the future.

Then his relationship with Marianne took a turn for the worse. In a letter to Amelia, he confided that Marianne was being advised by her friends that the proposed marriage was a great mistake. Her father also had second thoughts about his daughter's intention to leave England for a difficult life on a foreign mission field. Hudson detected a cooling in her attitude towards him as she always seemed to have an excuse ready when he suggested an outing together.

In addition to this heartache he was again short of money. He was unwilling to ask anyone for a loan, but waited upon God for an answer which came in the form of an offer of work and accommodation from Dr Brown of Bishopsgate. His responsibility was to work for the doctor in the late afternoon and evening, leaving time for his studies at London Hospital.

By the end of March, 1853 he had moved his few belongings to Dr Brown's home resulting in regular, nutritious meals and a soft bed on which to sleep.

He had no contract with Dr Brown as he was unwilling to commit himself, not knowing when he might pack his bags and sail for China.

He was also concerned that a continuation of his studies for a medical degree required he swear an oath to uphold the good name of the Royal College. This Hudson wouldn't do as he believed the Scriptures prevented the taking of such an oath (Matt. 5:33-37).

The CES was ready to meet the one hundred pounds educational expenses involved in obtaining his degree, but Hudson saw this as placing him under an obligation to use medicine as a base for missionary endeavour. He believed this would restrict his missionary activities.

Everyone who served with the CES was obliged to sign an agreement binding them to do as requested. One regulation stated: 'Every person...shall hold himself ready to go to such a place and at such a time as the Board shall decide upon.'

Hudson saw this as signing away 'liberty and conscience'. He was confident that as God had honoured the travelling preachers of the past, so he would do with him. He was fully assured that God had called him to preach the gospel—not to build hospitals.

Again he sought God's guidance before making a decision concerning his future. Then in the midst of this intense time of prayer, his relationship with Marianne caused more anguish.

Her mother had become seriously ill and this, with her father's refusal to bless their life together as missionaries, resulted in the decision to end their relationship. They knew that to disobey the expressed wish of her father dishonoured him. Both Hudson and Marianne wrote to Mr Vaughan, again seeking his blessing upon their forthcoming marriage, but his refusal meant that the engagement should be ended. This greatly upset Hudson, who for over three years had loved Marianne.

The early months of 1853 saw many very encouraging missionary reports in *The Gleaner*. More than ever he interpreted them as God opening the door for him. At the same time, Mr Pearse and other CES members encouraged him to settle down to study and obtain his medical degree.

With qualifications from the London College of Surgeons they saw Hudson as being suitably qualified to commence a medical, missionary work in China. The money was available to meet the costs involved, but he was fearful that if he accepted their support, his time would be largely devoted to medical work, with preaching attached. The usual pattern for such missionary endeavour was for a hospital or school to be established in a missionary compound. Then, as funds became available, they would be used for a church building and printing equipment. He saw his call to an itinerant preaching ministry, not to some preaching attached to hospital work. However, he knew that a medical degree would gain him work as a doctor on a ship bound for China which would mean a considerable financial saving.

Meanwhile, London Hospital, trying to find a way to accommodate his refusal to take an oath came up with the acceptable suggestion that he could make a 'declaration'.

Life was extremely busy for Hudson. He had to be in attendance at London Hospital between the hours of 8 am and 3 pm and then return to Dr Brown's surgery where after a meal, he visited patients, dispensed medicines and kept the accounts.

Each Sunday his Tottenham friends saw a very tired young man. They opened their hearts and homes to him, but had no idea of the spiritual guidance for which he prayed.

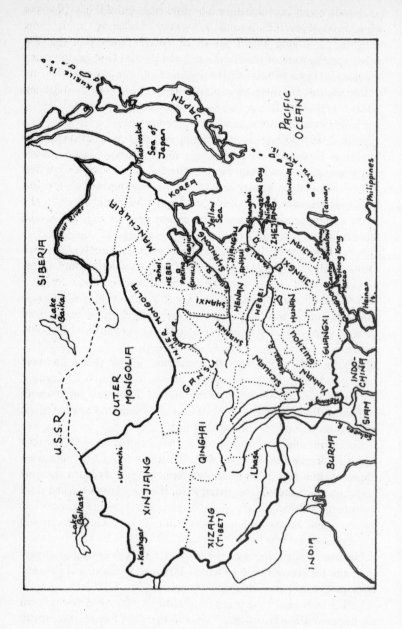

China: Borders, Provinces and main Rivers

Despite a very busy schedule he found time to fulfil his Christian obligations of love. His great desire was to be used by God to bring sinners to a saving knowledge of Christ. He knew that the new birth was the work of the Holy Spirit and praised God for the many people who came to know Christ as their Lord and Saviour in secure circumstances. However, he wanted to witness the power of God when he preached Christ in 'unpromising circumstances'.

He was soon to witness such a conversion!

He had the unpleasant duty of daily visiting a man suffering from gangrene. He dressed the foot of the patient who was not fully aware of the seriousness of his condition. The man lived with a Christian family, but said he was an atheist, completely opposed to religion. The local minister had visited him, hoping he would listen to the Scriptures being read, but the response was a violent outburst as well as being spat upon.

When Hudson visited him he decided to say nothing of his Christian faith. After a couple of times carefully and tenderly dressing his wound, the man showed some appreciation for what he was doing.

Hudson then took the opportunity to speak to him of his love of Christ, which was his motivation for everything he did. Instead of abusing him, the man simply turned away on his bed and said nothing.

He then took the matter to the Lord, praying that God would save the ill man before he died. At each visit, and after carefully dressing the man's wounds, Hudson quietly and with compassion spoke of Christ to the dying man. Each time the patient, looking annoyed, turned away from him and said nothing.

After many efforts, the day came when following the dressing of the man's leg, he decided to leave without mentioning Christ. The man looked at him with surprise on his face. Hudson returned the look and then overcome with compassion for the man, burst into tears and went to his bedside.

'My friend,' he said, 'whether you will hear it or whether you will not, I must deliver *my* soul.'

He then pleaded with the man, saying how much he wanted to pray with and for him—if only he would agree. To Hudson's surprise the man quietly answered, 'If it will be a relief to you, all right.'

Falling to his knees he prayed that God would save the dying man. He believed it was at that very moment that the Holy Spirit renewed his heart, because from that day onwards the man rejoiced to hear the Word of God read and to unite in prayer with his 'Amens.' Several days later the dying man confessed his saving faith in Christ.

He told Hudson that he had not entered a church for forty years. He'd been married in a church building, but had refused to enter the church from which his wife had been buried.

The conversion of that hard-hearted man encouraged Hudson to persevere when he faced the opposition of other antagonistic, cold-hearted men and women. He realised that Christians needed to be more intense in their prayers for the conversion of sinners. When this happened, he knew that God would bless their witness. Faith in the saving power of God was essential for winning sinners to Christ.

China was at that time experiencing political and social turmoil. The May, 1853 edition of *The Gleaner* devoted many pages to the annual report of the CES. Sections dealt with the growing income being given by concerned Christians, as well as the apparent success of gospel preaching throughout Asia. One article also mentioned two young men who were then being trained by the CES for overseas missionary work. Hudson was one of those men!

The Taiping rebellion was again in the news after a period during which it appeared that the rebellion had come to nothing. The rebels, led by Hong Xiu-quan had bound themselves to a code of belief and conduct that mirrored the Christian faith. They fought to overthrow the Manchu dynasty, destroy idol worship and eradicate the cursed opium trade. Their soldiers believed the Bible to be the Word of God and as a consequence obeyed the ten commandments, observed Saturday as the Lord's Day and in their worship services glorified the Triune God of Scripture. The troops obeyed a strict moral code of behaviour, making every effort to care for the poor. They were expected to respect private property and pray before meals.

Any soldier involved in rape, adultery, opium and tobacco smoking, suffered the death penalty by whipping with the bamboo cane. Women and children captured in battle were treated with respect and kindness.

Reports of the activities and successes of the rebels were a great encouragement to European Christians who saw the events as God's providential way of opening the nation to a concentrated missionary effort.

The Taiping forces divided the nation in two sections as they continued their offensive towards the coast, along the Yangtze River. By March, 1853 they had successfully captured the ancient city of Nanking, and there they consolidated their position. Idols were destroyed and the population indoctrinated in the teachings of Hong Xiu-quan.

The British closely watched the progress of the Taiping forces, making regular reports to the Home Office in London. They were assured by the rebels that the Shanghai Foreign Settlement would not be touched when the city was invaded.

Sir George Bonham, representing the British Government, met with some Taiping leaders and won their approval with his reply to the question whether he worshipped 'God the Heavenly Father.'

When his reply included the repetition of the ten commandments, the two groups exchanged written material and Bonham left with high hopes for future contacts with rebel held China. However, some of the written material circulated by the Taiping soldiers contained doctrinal statements that caused concern amongst Christians. All was not orthodox Christianity.

In Shanghai and the surrounding countryside the Chinese officials considered Christians as supporters of the rebels and consequently Roman Catholic priests and church members were persecuted.

The news of the Taiping successes reached Europe, causing great excitement among all who were interested in Chinese missionary endeavour. Hudson read the reports with great excitement believing he should immediately leave for China and commence preaching the gospel.

In May a group of Triads known as the Short Swords captured Amoy in the name of the Taiping rebels, but as they advocated loose living, the worship of idols and the use of opium they were disowned by the Taiping leadership.

At that time, foreign governments began to supply the opposing forces with arms. Soldiers of fortune offered their services to all parties with the result that the Taiping forces found their strongly held ideals becoming adulterated. However, this period was the glory period for the rebels.

In June the Taiping army moved northward, crossing the Yellow River and invaded the Shanxi province.

All of these momentous events stirred Hudson to action. The CES now wanted him to immediately leave for China under their banner. Mr Bird, the Home Secretary, suggested he pack his bags at once and set sail before September, thus avoiding the normal autumn gales. To Hudson this was an answer to his prayers and he immediately asked for the CES application form.

This required a detailed statement of his theological position that highlighted some areas where Hudson held beliefs which were contrary to what would have been considered mainstream theology. He objected to the division of the church into two sections—Clergy and laity, strongly believing that all Christians had the right to preach the gospel and administer the sacraments.

Instead of waiting for a reply from the CES he stepped out in faith and tendered his resignation to Dr Brown. His employer didn't want to lose him, so offered him encouragements to stay on for another year and obtain his medical qualifications. However, Hudson knew that his call was to preach Christ to the Chinese.

On 9 July, 1853 he wrote to his mother: 'I have just received a note from Mr Bird informing me that I am accepted by the Committee and that as soon as I can make arrangements for going out, they are prepared to send me...How long would you like me to be at home?'

Now he found that his time was in short supply. Friends and relatives had to be farewelled, and supplies, equipment and drugs were to be purchased. Very soon he would set sail for China, and to all his friends and relatives this meant they might never see him again in this life.

13

Farewell England!

Much had to be done in the few weeks before the *Dumfries* was due to sail from the Liverpool docks on 12 September, 1853. Dr Brown, despite the fact that Hudson had resigned from his service, allowed him to use his home as a base for his comings and goings.

So Hudson set about buying the surgical equipment he thought he'd need in China. He purchased what was necessary to carry out amputations, bleeding, dental work, and instruments to be used in obstetrics. He also bought chemicals he thought would be useful in pharmaceutical work.

Next there were the endless visits to be made. He spent some time at home in Barnsley with his family and friends and during that time he gave his two pet squirrels to Amelia and Louisa.

Returning to London he was visited by many friends and interested people. His close friend, Benjamin Broomhall came up from Barnsley and presented him with a book. Arrangements were made for him to speak to the congregation at Tottenham where he outlined the great work that lay before him. Many of those people were close friends who supported him in prayer and finance during his many years of missionary endeavour. Miss Stacey, who was a very close friend, told him to purchase a warm dressing gown and send the account to her.

On Friday, 9 September, he met with officers of the CES at their London offices where a service was held, setting him apart for missionary service in China. Prayer was offered to God seeking His protective care and blessing upon the new missionary.

He was formally given his instructions concerning the service he was to give the CES. When he reached mainland China he was to set out for Nanking which at that time was the headquarters of the Taiping rebels. This seemed to be the ideal place for him to commence work, as the Taiping soldiers were believed to be Christians. He was assured of financial and spiritual support while serving the CES.

During his last weeks in London, he became very much aware of his unmarried status as he believed that he would never find a suitable wife in China and wanted a good prospect before he sailed. As his relationship with Marianne was over he turned his attention to Elizabeth Sissons who was also Amelia's close friend. Once she had expressed her love for him, but at that time it was Marianne who had his attention. He wrote to Elizabeth's father seeking his permission to correspond with her in the future. She had shown a lot of interest in overseas missionary work and he knew that she subscribed to *The Gleaner*. Everything he knew about Elizabeth encouraged him to get to know her more.

But little did he know that at that very time Maria Dyer, the girl he would marry, was already in China. Her father had been a missionary, serving with the London Missionary Society in Singapore. Both of her parents had died years before and their three daughters had returned to live with their grandparents in England.

When Miss Aldersey, the mistress of the Ningbo school for Chinese girls, invited Burella Dyer to take up a teaching position, Maria decided to accompany her. In September, 1852 they set sail with Rev. and Mrs Cobbold, Maria being just fifteen years of age.

As the time for Hudson's departure drew near he made his way to Liverpool in order to pack all his equipment in his newly painted ship's cabin. His parents also came to farewell their beloved son.

Hudson's mother arrived first and settled into the Owens Hotel and soon his father arrived with Aunt Hannah Hardey. This was an exciting time for Hudson, who was overjoyed to be leaving England to commence his God-given life's work. Much time was spent in prayer, seeking the blessing of God upon each family member—after all his mother and father were sacrificing their son in the Lord's work.

Owing to the extended delays to the ship's sailing, his father returned home as he'd been away from his business for a long period. Hudson and his mother accompanied his father to the railway station and there a sorrowful farewell took place between father and son.

As the train gathered speed Hudson ran along the platform holding his father's hand until all too soon he could run no further. Their parting was sorrowful, but there was rejoicing because now his son would be doing a work that he would have loved to have done. As the train disappeared down the track both father and son wondered if they would ever again see each other this side of eternity.

During the short time remaining he wrote letters to those he loved and in a letter to Amelia he enclosed a brooch for Elizabeth Sissons. His letters also showed a deep concern for the spiritual wellbeing of his sister Louisa, and he promised to pray for her conversion wherever he might be. He also had time to write to his father:

> My soul rejoices in the Lord and I feel very happy...Perhaps I shall see (England) and you no more in the body—but I know we shall meet to part no more....The God of Peace bless you...and use you more than ever in bringing sinners to Jesus...I...can only conclude by hoping you will forgive me in every respect in which I have acted improperly towards you.

The night before the *Dumfries* expected to depart from the Liverpool wharves on Monday, 19 September Hudson and his mother met for the final time in his hotel room. Tears flowed as he read John chapter 14 and then prayed that lost sinners might find Christ. After heartfelt prayers for his friends and family the time came to part. Tears again flowed freely, but his mother rejoiced that Hudson was about to embark on what was obedience to the call of the God they loved.

Monday arrived—it was almost time for the *Dumfries* to set sail. His mother, accompanied by George Pearse of the CES and some godly friends, met in his cabin to again commend Hudson to God. There was a deep sense of the presence of the Holy Spirit as together they sang the beautiful hymn: 'How sweet the name of Jesus sounds'; followed by the reading and singing of several psalms.

When the ship's bell rang they all knew it was time to separate and Hudson's mother wept and had to be helped ashore. Years later, he wrote of his last hours with his mother:

> My beloved, now sainted, mother, had come to see me off from Liverpool. Never shall I forget that day, nor how she went with me into the little cabin that was to be my home for nearly six long

months. With a mother's loving hand she smoothed the little bed. She sat by my side, and joined me in the last hymn that we should sing together before the long parting. We knelt down, and she prayed—the last mother's prayer I was to hear before starting for China. Then notice was given that we must separate, and we had to say good-bye, never expecting to meet on earth again.

For my sake she restrained her feelings as much as possible. We parted; and she went on shore, giving me her blessing; I stood alone on deck, and she followed the ship as we moved toward the dock gates. As we passed through the gates, and the separation really began, I shall never forget the cry of anguish wrung from that mother's heart. It went through me like a knife. I never knew so fully, until then, what "God so loved the world" meant. And I am quite sure that my precious mother learned more of the love of God to the perishing in that hour than in all her life before.

As the small group stood on the dock saying their last goodbyes, Hudson ran to his cabin and returning with a small pocket Bible, tossed it to his mother. On the fly leaf he had written: 'The love of God which passes knowledge.'

As the ship moved away from the dock the waving continued. Then he climbed the ship's rigging, from where he continued to wave to his mother, until at last he could see her no more.

A short time after leaving the wharves it was discovered that one sailor was missing which meant the ship came to a standstill while a search was made. With the ship safely at anchor, Hudson and the captain returned to Liverpool by boat.

At first he thought he should meet his mother but realised that this would mean another heartbreaking farewell so he returned to the ship. By the time the man was found it was too late to catch the tide. When the time arrived to weigh the anchor the pilot was found to be too drunk to carry out his duties which meant another wait till morning light.

Finally the ship made its way into the bay and the long trip to China commenced. Hudson found the rocking motion of the ship very unsettling and feeling sick he went to his cabin, took a creosote pill and slept soundly for some hours.

The *Dumfries*, a three masted sailing ship weighing four hundred and sixty eight tons, was manned by a crew of a captain, two mates, the bosun, a cook, a steward, a carpenter, eleven seamen, two boys and two apprentices. In addition the ship carried three pigs, three dozen fowls, two dozen ducks, two cats and two dogs.

Hudson began organizing his cabin for the long trip awaiting him, realising that now he was totally reliant upon God for his every need.

Another reason to remember the 19 September, 1853 when he sailed from England was that on that day the British and Foreign Bible Society decided to raise fifty thousand pounds to publish and distribute a million New Testaments in the Chinese language.

14

A Safe Arrival in China

Hudson soon discovered that shipboard life was not all relaxation. During the five and a half months at sea he had much time for prayer, study and meditation, but the first twelve days proved to be a testing time.

Rough weather greeted the *Dumfries* and several times the ship was in danger of being wrecked. Of those frightening days he wrote:

> Our voyage had a rough beginning...We had scarcely left the Mersey when a violent...gale caught us, and for twelve days we were beating backwards and forwards in the Irish Channel, unable to get out to sea.
>
> The barometer was still falling, and the wind increased until it was a perfect hurricane. The Captain and Mate said they had never seen a wilder sea. Between two and three in the afternoon I managed to get on deck, though the pitching made it difficult.... The scene I shall never forget....The sea, lashing itself into fury, was white with foam....The waves, like hills on either side, seemed as if they might swamp us at any moment...we were making little or no headway, and the wind being from the west we were drifting quickly, irresistibly, toward a lee-shore.
>
> "Unless God help us," said the Captain, "there is no hope."
>
> I asked how far we might be from the Welsh coast.
>
> "Fifteen to sixteen miles," was his reply. "We can do nothing but carry all possible sail. The more we carry the less we drift...God grant the timbers may bear it."...

> It was a fearful time. The wind was blowing terrifically, and we were tearing along at a frightful rate—one moment high in the air, and the next plunging head foremost into the trough of the sea as if about to go to the bottom. The windward side of the ship was fearfully elevated, the lee side being as much depressed; indeed the sea at times poured over her lee bulwarks.
>
> Thus the sun set....

During the cold night with waves crashing over the ship everyone was wet through from foam and spray.

Hudson, realising that he and the crew faced the prospect of drowning, spent much of his waking time in prayer—not just for the safety of the crew and himself, but for the blessing of God upon his family and the ungodly Chinese.

He was also concerned about the spiritual state of the sailors if they should drown. He was unconcerned about his own eternal security and didn't fear death—but there was something about drowning in a raging sea that terrified him.

In his journal he recorded the events of those frightening hours:

> I went below, read a hymn or two, some Psalms and John Chapters 13 to 15, and...fell asleep and slept for an hour. We then looked at the barometer and found it rising....I asked the Captain whether we could clear Holyhead or not.
>
> "If we make no lee-way," he replied, "we may just do it. But if we drift, God help us!"
>
> And we did drift!
>
> Our fate now seemed sealed. I asked if we were sure of two more hours. The Captain could not say we were....I thought of my dear father and mother, sisters and special friends...and the tears would start....The Captain was calm and courageous, trusting in the Lord for his soul's salvation. The steward said that he knew that he was nothing, but Christ was all. I felt thankful for them, but I did pray earnestly that God would have mercy on us and spare us for the sake of the unconverted crew...as well as for His own glory as the God who hears and answers prayers. This passage was then brought to my mind: "Call upon Me in the day of trouble; I will deliver you, and you shall glorify Me": and very earnestly I pleaded the promise, in submission to His will.

It was a clear moonlight night, but Hudson, understanding the danger they all faced, went to his cabin where he took out his pocket book and in it wrote his name and address which could be used to identify his body if the ship went down and he drowned. Then he made a package of his belongings that might float and prepared for the worst. He commended his soul to God, prayed for the unconverted sailors and then asked God, if it were his will, to save the ship.

Returning to the deck he asked the captain if it was possible to build a raft of some sort from the spars. The captain's reply was that there was not sufficient time to carry out the suggestion saying, 'We cannot live half an hour now; what of your call to labour for the Lord in China?'

Hudson's confidence in God was strong and he replied that he expected to reach China, but if he drowned he would die obeying the command of his Saviour.

The captain decided to turn the ship and tack through the mountainous seas in a last attempt to clear the headland. After several tacks through the foaming waves a cheer went up as the ship cleared the rocks by just two boat lengths and made her way out of the bay.

Hudson then praised God for his providential care with the words of Scripture: 'Oh that men would praise the Lord for His goodness and for His wonderful works to the children of men.'

Later he remembered his mother's advice to put on a life jacket ('swimming belt') if the situation demanded it. However, he believed that this was unnecessary as he had committed himself to God's keeping. He argued that to wear a life jacket was to trust in it and not God.

In the midst of the danger he took off the jacket and committed his keeping to God alone. Later he realised the inconsistency of what he had done, because while refusing to use the life jacket he had gathered together some bits and pieces in the hope they would keep him afloat if he ended up in the ocean. Then he wisely wrote:

> The use of means ought not to lessen our faith in God; and our faith in God ought not to hinder our using whatever means He has given us for the accomplishment of His own purposes.
>
> For years after this I always took a swimming belt with me, and never had any trouble about it; the question was settled for me, through the prayerful study of the Scriptures ....When in medical or surgical charge of any case, I have never thought of neglecting to ask God's guidance and blessing in the use of appropriate means... to me it would appear as presumptuous and wrong to neglect the use of those measures which He Himself has put within our reach, as to neglect to take daily food, and suppose that life and health might be maintained by prayer alone.

The only injury during that violent storm was one sailor who received a badly bruised arm.

At last all on board settled down to a more peaceful time, although the *Dumfries* found the going difficult in the Bay of Biscay when a violent storm blew up.

Much to his joy, Hudson found out that the Captain and the steward were good Methodists, the steward having been a Bible class leader. The Swedish carpenter was also a soundly converted man. This small group regularly met together for a time of worship—reading the Scriptures and praying to their Heavenly Father.

The Captain gave Hudson permission to conduct weekly services with the crew, and while some showed a real interest in spiritual matters, he was disappointed that none were converted. During the times of worship he read *Pilgrim's Progress* to them.

He was also given permission to hold nightly meetings in his cabin for any of the crew who wanted to attend. At those meetings the Scriptures were read, psalms and hymns were sung and prayer made for God's care of the crew and the ship.

With time on his hands he studied the Bible, read theological books and prayed for the people at home. He praised God for watching over the ship as it made its way down the African coast.

He also reread his books about China, mathematics, astronomy, medicine, chemistry and magnetism. When the Swedish carpenter needed his eyebrow stitched Hudson rejoiced that he was able to practise his medical skills. Several of the crew had abscesses lanced and the steward had a tooth extracted.

Taking every opportunity to practise his dissecting skills the ship's cat ended up on his table when it died. Then he turned his surgical interest to sea creatures and birds.

Finding himself in a new part of the world, he saw stars that were unknown to those who lived in England and he glorified his Creator as he watched the colourful tropical sunsets.

'Nothing can be more lovely,' he wrote of the tropical nights. 'The calm quiet, only interrupted by the flapping of the sails, and the murmur of the waters as they wash up the sides of the vessel. The clear blue sky and few light clouds. The occasional illumination from sheet lightning, and here and there the splash of the bonito or albicore, and the leap after the…flying fish.'

In his spare time he helped the Captain with his algebra and taught him how to play the concertina. The second mate played the flute so

Hudson gave him some tuition. Often he helped the crew with their work but usually had plenty of time to enjoy their companionship, relax and prepare for the future. When the crew launched a rowing boat he took the opportunity to enjoy himself swimming while the crew kept a watch for sharks.

The ship made good progress—some days covering almost two hundred miles—and all the time he was more fully aware that he would soon be in the land to which he was called.

In the Indian Ocean, Christmas was celebrated, but in a way so different to the family at home in Barnsley—a pig had been slaughtered for Christmas dinner!

During this time he praised God for his providential care over many years. He thanked God for his many praying friends and relatives in Great Britain, and again prayed for the conversion of his sister, Louisa.

When the *Dumfries* reached South East Asia her guns were loaded as the region was well known for the many pirates who sailed amongst the thousands of islands dotted over the area.

There were times when the ship was becalmed and strong ocean currents swept her near hidden reefs. During those days the sails flapped gently, waiting for the stronger breezes which sprang up at nightfall. The temperatures were very warm which made life uncomfortable for all on board.

Hudson continued with his weekly worship services which were reasonably well attended, but after one long morning service, as punishment, no one turned up for the evening service. He was often the butt of good natured comments because of his sincere faith in the Lord Jesus Christ.

The sailors blamed him for the storms, the lack of wind and the currents that slowed the ship's progress, yet he became a close friend of the Swedish carpenter who rounded up the crew for services. Often at night they sat together on the bowsprit, in the bright moonlight, singing the praises of God. Together they prayed and meditated upon the majesty and glory of their Lord.

Passing close to many islands, Hudson grieved for the natives who lived without Christ. He prayed that God would raise up men and women to take the gospel to those pagan people.

His faith in the preserving power of the prayer answering God, who controlled heaven and earth, was displayed time and time again.

He wrote of an incident when the ship was becalmed:

...we were in dangerous proximity to the north of New Guinea. Saturday night had brought us to a point some thirty miles off the land; but during the Sunday morning service, which was held on deck, I could not fail to notice that the Captain looked troubled, and frequently went over to the side of the ship. When the service was ended, I learned from him the cause—a four-knot current was carrying us rapidly toward some sunken reefs, and we were already so near that it seemed improbable that we should get through the afternoon in safety. After dinner the long-boat was put out, and all hands endeavoured, without success, to turn the ship's head from the shore.

After standing together on the deck for some time in silence, the Captain said to me, "Well, we have done everything that can be done; we can only await the result."

A thought occurred to me, and I replied, "No, there is one thing we have not done yet."

"What is it?" he queried.

"Four of us on board are Christians," I answered..."let us each retire to his own cabin, and in agreed prayer ask the Lord to give us immediately a breeze. He can as easily send it now as at sunset."

'The captain complied with this proposal. I went and spoke to the other two men, and after prayer with the carpenter we all four retired to wait upon God. I...then felt so satisfied that our request was granted that I could not continue asking, and very soon went up again on deck. The first officer, a godless man, was in charge. I went over and asked him to let down the...corners of the mainsail, which had been drawn up.

He answered, "What would be the good of that?"

I told him we had been asking a wind from God, that it was coming immediately, and we were so near the reef by this time that there was not a minute to lose.

With a look of incredulity and contempt, he said with an oath that he would rather see a wind than hear of it! But while he was speaking I watched his eye,...and there, sure enough, the corner of the sail was beginning to tremble in the coming breeze.

"Don't you see the wind is coming? Look at the royal!" I exclaimed.

"No, it is only a cat's paw," he rejoined (a mere puff of wind).

"Cat's paw or not," I cried, "pray let down the mainsail, and let us have the benefit!"

The noise of the crew at work brought the captain up on deck. Within a couple of minutes the breeze had strengthened and the ship was moving through the water at six or seven knots. Soon the captain announced that the ship was out of danger.

Of God's answer to prayer on that occasion Hudson wrote: 'Thus God encouraged me, ere landing on China's shores, to bring every variety of need to Him in prayer, and to expect that He would honour the name of the Lord Jesus, and give the help which each emergency required.'

With the shores of China getting closer each day, an excited Hudson began sorting and repacking his equipment. On 15 February, 1854 the *Dumfries* passed near Taiwan, leaving another seven hundred miles before Shanghai was reached.

As the ship approached mainland China his mind was filled with so many differing emotions. He was overjoyed to be so close to the people he longed to tell of the Lord Jesus Christ, yet he was somewhat apprehensive knowing that he'd soon be standing on foreign soil, knowing no one and facing the unknown. All he had were three letters of introduction to men he hoped would give him guidance. However, the words of God filled his heart with comfort: 'I will never leave you...Lo! I am with you always....'

The final stages of the long journey were rough seas and freezing weather. On 22, 23 February, he saw some junks sailing by and knew his long journey was soon to end. When he was told that the island near which they dropped anchor was Gutzlaff's Island he realised they were at the entrance to the Yangtze River!

Soon a British pilot arrived to guide the ship to her berth. He was full of news for the crew.

The situation in Shanghai had changed. The rebels—a faction of the feared Triads—occupied the city and there was a possibility of their forces invading Peking. Outside the old walls the Imperial Army was poised ready to attack the rebels masquerading under the name of the Taiping forces.

On Wednesday, 1 March, Hudson first saw Shanghai and the Huangpu River, a tributary of the Yangtze River. He caught a passing pilot boat, and after sailing through junks and European ships of all sizes, at 5 pm he stepped onto Chinese soil for the first time and was surrounded by citizens of all classes and occupations. He found it strange to be surrounded by many new sounds and smells and a babble of foreign voices. The ornate oriental buildings impressed this young Englishman, but his heart wept for the citizens of the city who had little saving knowledge of the Lord Jesus.

Praising God for his safe passage, he made his way to the consular office where he hoped to collect some mail from home, and maybe a letter from Mr Sissons.

Much to his disappointment he found the office closed and was told it would not open till the next morning. Then he discovered that two of the men to whom he had letters of introduction were no longer in Shanghai.

One had passed away five months previously and the second had returned to the USA. His best advice was to visit the compound belonging to the London Missionary Society where he would find Dr Walter Medhurst. This meant a walk through the narrow streets of Shanghai as well as trudging through the muddy tracks beside the Huangpu River.

Arriving at the compound entrance he couldn't help noticing a name which when translated meant, 'Medhurst Family Enclosure'.

Following a knock on the front door he was greeted by a Chinese servant who couldn't speak English, but after some time gesticulating, he worked out that Dr Medhurst was not home.

The arrival of Joseph Edkins, a junior missionary, resolved Hudson's problems. He was told that the Medhursts had left the compound, which was too close to the fighting, for the protection of the British Consulate. Dr William Lockhart was still living at the Settlement and while he was being found, Mr Edkins invited the newcomer to meet some of the other missionaries.

Hudson was now alone in a foreign land, without ready money and having nowhere to live. However, Dr Lockhart graciously opened his house to the stranded young Englishman.

15

Difficult Days

Hudson found himself alone and totally dependent upon the good will of other Shanghai missionaries for the necessities of life. When Dr Lockhart of the London Missionary Society (LMS) offered him a spare room there was nothing he could do but gratefully accept as he had nowhere else to go! During the next couple of days he was introduced to most of the missionaries in the area and began to familiarize himself with the city, visiting the hospital where he heard Dr Medhurst preaching to the waiting patients with their relatives and friends.

Mr and Mrs Burdon of the Church Missionary Society (CMS) invited him to the evening meal and this family became close friends for many years.

The day after his arrival he walked to the Consulate to collect his mail. He'd heard nothing from home or the CES for many months, but all that awaited him was a letter from his parents and two copies of *The Gleaner* for which he had to pay two shillings postage before he was given the long awaited package. He was delighted to receive the letter, but very disappointed that there was only one.

There was nothing from the CES. He had been given no money when he left England but expected a letter of credit waiting for him in Shanghai. As it had not arrived he was very concerned but arranged for some coolies to collect his belongings from the *Dumfries* and carry them to his room where he unpacked. There he sadly discovered that some of his things had been ruined by the salt water.

As the local missionaries advised him to commence his language studies immediately, he employed a teacher who instructed him for five or six hours each day.

He soon realised that he was in a war ravaged city, the Triads (Red Turbans) having captured Shanghai. This criminal group thought they would have been supported by the Taiping rebels, but when this didn't eventuate, the Triads, who were totally lacking any Christian conscience, made money by selling opium.

The Chinese Imperial forces having arrived, set up camp about the city walls and daily battles were common. Following some trade between the local farmers and the Triads, the Imperial army took cruel action against the locals, cutting off their ears and then beheading them.

Hudson wrote to Amelia graphically describing the situation:

> You have never seen a city in a state of siege…God grant you never may! We walked some distance round the wall and sad it was to see the wreck of rows upon rows of houses near the city. Burnt down, blown down, battered to pieces—in all stages of ruin they were! And the misery of those who once inhabited them….
>
> A little further on we met some men bringing in a small cannon they had captured, and following them were others dragging along by their tails (queues) five wretched prisoners. The poor fellows cried piteously to us to save them, as they were hurried by, but, alas, we could do nothing!…It makes one sad indeed to be surrounded by so much misery; to see poor creatures so suffering and distressed, and not be able to relieve them or tell them of Jesus and His love. I can only pray for them.

From his window, Hudson could see wounded men and dead bodies lying about, the result of the battles taking place day and night outside the city wall.

Often when Dr Medhurst went out preaching, Hudson accompanied him, longing for the day when he'd do the same. Soon he was able to walk about the city with Mr Wylie of the LMS, distributing tracts.

Then there was the cold weather! Writing to his parents he said, 'It is so cold that I can hardly think or hold the pen.'

In a letter to Mr Pearse he expressed his utter disappointment in failing to receive letters from the very ones who had encouraged him to go to China and promised support. He outlined the cost of living, his lack of finances and the real danger of trying to live in the city area which suffered continual bombardment from the Imperial Army.

For some time the battles had been drawing closer and now they were near enough to the foreign Settlement to cause some concern. An attempt was made by some soldiers to break into a British warehouse and steal goods, but when the owner shot and killed two of them, the rest fled. This was followed by several savage attacks upon foreigners.

Hudson wrote home describing the times when cannon 'balls' landed in the Settlement area:

> ...early in the morning, I had joined one of the missionaries on his verandah to watch the battle proceeding, at a distance of perhaps three-quarters of a mile, when suddenly a spent ball passed between us and buried itself in the verandah wall. Another day my friend Mr Wylie left a book on the table after luncheon, and returning for it about five minutes later found the arm of the chair on which he had been sitting shot clean away. But in the midst of these and other dangers God protected us.

The Consuls seeing the danger to the Europeans demanded that the Imperial soldiers fall back or face western forces. The outcome was that a platoon of about three hundred Anglo-American soldiers, supported by about one hundred local residents, attacked the fifty thousand Chinese soldiers in the Battle of Muddy Flat, which resulted in the withdrawal of the Chinese forces. The superior firing power of the European soldiers won the battle. Now the Chinese knew that the Settlement was out of bounds for warfare. The humiliated, retreating Chinese soldiers then took out their frustration upon the local Chinese population, killing and maiming many.

Seeing the terrible suffering of the Chinese, Hudson wanted to live in their midst in order to help them and to tell them of Christ, but he knew it was not safe to venture outside the Settlement for any length of time.

'I have great fear,' he wrote. 'Turning to the right hand I fear the Rebels, and on the left the Mandarin soldiers fill me with alarm. Truly these are hard times to live in.'

Soon he felt like an intruder in the Settlement, as he had no academic qualifications and was not an ordained minister. The CES failed in their obligation of support and with the lack of mail and money he began to feel very lonely. He was almost totally dependent upon the goodwill of the LMS to survive.

Sadly he realised that some of the missionaries were not doing their job, but spent much time in their social activities.

This was not what he wanted—he wanted to learn the language and get on with the work to which he had been called. He wanted to see sinners being won into the kingdom of God.

With warmer weather he found he suffered from prickly heat, headaches, kidney stones and renal colic. Times were hard!

Yet, in the midst of all his difficulties he began his insect collection. He saw his first huge butterfly—'To-day,' he wrote to his mother, 'I caught sight of a large black butterfly with swallow-tail wings, the largest living butterfly I have seen....At first I thought it must be a small bird.'

Most evenings he spent alone as he didn't want to impose on the Burdons. With his money in short supply and personal mail not arriving he suffered loneliness and great embarrassment.

On one occasion he walked a mile and a half to the consulate, then waited for several hours only to discover that there was no mail for himself, but plenty for the rest at the Settlement. He was thoroughly upset, particularly as it was six weeks before the next mail was expected to arrive.

In another letter home he pleaded for news: 'Do please write. I have no letters, no *Gleaners*—no papers—no companions...You would (write by every mail)...if you saw how disappointed I am when a mail comes and no letter.'

Indirectly he heard of the imminent arrival of the Scotch physician, Dr William Parker and his wife, who expected to be supported by the CES. Hudson had not received any formal advice from the CES, nor had he received any money in order to prepare for their arrival. In fact very little mail arrived from anyone, and it was a disappointment that his father never wrote to him.

He was dependent upon the LMS for so much, but now, even though suffering from heat and dysentery, he knew he had to find some other accommodation for himself and the Parkers. He was too embarrassed to confide in other missionaries about his problems, but soon everyone knew of the Parkers' impending arrival.

Hudson wrote to Mr Pearse explaining that no accommodation was available to rent in the Settlement, and urged the CES to consider buying property for use as a base from which to launch into the interior.

He began looking for a house in the Chinese section of the city, but it seemed an impossible task and in a letter to Amelia expressed his confidence that God would provide: 'I have been puzzling my brains about a house, etc., but to no effect. So I have made it a matter of prayer, and have given it entirely into the Lord's hands, and now I feel quite at peace about it. He will provide and be my Guide in this and every other perplexing matter.'

Not long after he was offered a twelve room house which needed a lot of repairs. Despite the fact that it was in a dangerous part of the city, he employed some Chinese workers to whitewash the rooms, clean out the rubbish and put on doors to make the place habitable. He soon understood that he had to closely watch the men otherwise they sat down and did nothing.

Hudson was lonely, but at least he could commence some missionary activity. Joseph Edkins suggested that he establish a school with Mr Si as the teacher. The class of ten boys and five girls commenced and concluded the day with prayer and readings from the Scriptures.

In the meantime he spent many hours at his language studies. He organized family worship, carried out some medical work and when he had the opportunity accompanied Mr Edkins distributing tracts and copies of the Scriptures. The Bible Society had given him three thousand copies of the Testaments to distribute.

With Mr Quarterman and Mr Edkins he visited sailors on their junks where they were received graciously.

When his money was almost depleted he cashed a letter of credit which was to be used in crisis situations, only to be told by the CES that emergency bills to the value of forty pounds would be honoured each quarter. Still no money arrived to allow him to prepare for the arrival of the Parkers.

When Mrs Burdon fell ill Hudson helped as he had been greatly assisted by the kind lady in setting up his home. Nevertheless, she passed away soon after.

The weather was growing cold and Hudson was feeling very uncomfortable. His clothes had worn so thin that he began to feel embarrassed when mixing with the cultured, well-dressed missionary community. His thin blankets didn't keep him warm in his house where draughts blew through the many cracks. With almost no money left he couldn't afford new, warm clothing. On 2 October, confronted by the danger of daily battles, he wrote home:

> As to my position, it certainly is one of great peril. On two successive
> nights, recently, bullets have struck the roof over my head. How
> a little difference in the direction of the gun might have rendered

them fatal to me. But "as the mountains are round about Jerusalem" so the Lord is on every side to protect and support me and to supply all my need...I can truly say my trust is in Him. When I hear guns fired near me and the whizz of the balls as they pass the house, I do feel alarmed sometimes; but a sweet, still voice says inwardly, "Oh you of little faith, why did you doubt?"

Awakened suddenly in the darkness by the thundering report of guns from the North Gate which shake the house, and hearing gongs and firearms discharging close at hand I have felt lonely, and my heart has palpitated painfully at times, not knowing whether my own house might not be the object of attack.

During his walks he met a kind local who gave him a pet singing cricket with the instructions that he was to be fed daily with two grains of boiled rice.

He was relieved when he heard that a LMS house in the Settlement was to become available as John Burdon had decided to move following the death of his wife.

But Hudson had no available money! He was renting the house in the Chinese section of the city and certainly couldn't afford to pay the rent on a second house for the Parkers.

Again he wrote to the CES pleading for instructions concerning the Parkers and for money to make arrangements for their arrival, but still he heard nothing.

When a four or five pound cannon ball hit the roof of his home and landed very close to Mr Si's son who was in the courtyard Hudson wondered what he should do.

He was becoming depressed with the situation. His letters to the CES criticized their failure to provide the necessary support, and he was disappointed with the easy-going life he found among the missionaries, concluding that only the LMS was doing a good work.

Then he discovered that the house next door to his at the North Gate had been set on fire hoping to scare him away. Fortunately the fire didn't harm his property, but again he saw the danger of living in that section of the city.

Finally the day arrived when he had to make a decision concerning the LMS house which was only available until a new missionary, Griffith John and his wife reached Shanghai. After prayer, Hudson drew twenty pounds from his credit and paid the first period of rent on the house.

When he discovered that the Jenkins family was in need of accommodation he sublet half the house to them which meant that he was responsible for only half the rent. But what was he to do when the Parkers arrived—there were only three rooms left for them all?

He then closed his school and said goodbye to Mr Si. As he was packing his goods together to return to the Settlement he received word that the Parkers had landed.

Fortunately they were tough Scots who did their best in the difficult situation. There was little in the way of furniture, no stoves, no warm clothes, no heating fuel, no cupboards and for several days no beds. Together they had very little money and although the Parkers had been assured of a Letter of Credit, it had not arrived.

In their difficult situation the other missionaries began to gossip about Hudson's apparent failure to make suitable preparations for the arrival of his CES missionary partners.

Humbly Dr Parker and Hudson approached the company which dealt with their letters of credit and when they were told nothing was at hand the manager kindly gave them an advance of twenty pounds in anticipation of the credit bill arriving. This was most humiliating for the two men, but with the money they were able to buy some essentials—beds, heating fuel and warm clothing—and food! Because of the cramped living quarters, Hudson made every effort to take Dr Parker on trips about the city, distributing tracts and other material and speaking as best he could to the poor Chinese. Both men also kept up their language studies.

He was becoming very concerned about the continuing failure of the CES to provide for the necessities of life, and its failure to understand the desperate situation in which the Parkers and he were placed. He was also critical of their decision to dishonour any credit letter which exceeded their set limit. He explained the poor financial situation the Parkers found themselves in when they reached Shanghai, and went on to describe how cold it was, pleading with the CES to urgently do something to alleviate their hardship.

Towards the end of 1854 Hudson was again humiliated by an article in *The Gleaner* which was very critical of the missions in Shanghai, especially the London Missionary Society, whose workers had helped him many times. There was no doubt that the officers of the CES in England had no idea of the situation their missionaries faced in China.

When the Chinese warfare became more intense, the French (later helped by the British and the Americans) assisted the Imperial Army against the Triads who had become a danger to the Europeans. The fighting went on for several days resulting in the death of sixty-four French and in excess of a thousand from the Imperial army.

Life in Shanghai was very dangerous!

16

Inland Adventures

First journey

On Saturday, 16 December, 1854, Hudson set out on his first expedition with Joseph Edkins of the LMS who had hired a boat. Their aim was to preach the gospel and distribute copies of the New Testament and tracts. He felt sure he would have opportunities to practise his medical skill and so went prepared.

For this journey he packed clothes, bedding, medical instruments, drugs, food, books and tracts. After their careful preparations, the British flag was hoisted and they set out up the Huangpu River, hoping to reach Jiaxing.

The single masted sailing boat, manned by a Chinese crew, was forty feet in length with one fairly comfortable cabin.

The following day, Sunday, they had arrived at the ancient city of Sonjiang. Knowing that crowds were sure to be found at the temples they set out, dressed in European clothes, which attracted much attention. Arriving at a temple, Joseph preached while Hudson distributed tracts and copies of the New Testament which he carried in a carpetbag. They took the opportunity to speak to a temple hermit who had spent many lonely years living in a bricked-in cell. He was very pleased to accept the Christian literature.

SHANGHAI HINTERLAND
The immediate 'interior'

While walking back towards the wharf where the boat was moored they were surrounded by a crowd of inquisitive, boisterous Chinese youths, who began to cause trouble. Quickly Hudson and Joseph escaped through some gates which they believed led to their boat, only to find themselves on a privately owned wharf.

Realising that escape was urgent, Hudson shouted to some passing sailors to come to their rescue. When they ignored him he jumped onto a junk and had the crew move it to a spot where Joseph could clamber aboard. Later they were off loaded and left to find their way back to their own boat. Again the unruly crowd found them but the missionaries were saved by a local teacher who had taught Hudson Chinese. The man spoke to the crowd and quietened them, while the two missionaries returned safely to their boat.

They restocked and again entered the city only this time they walked quickly, handing out literature, but not stopping to talk. In this way crowds were not given the opportunity to gather.

The journey to the city of Jiaxing was dangerous as it meant passing through an unsafe border region where criminals lived and plied their trade.

Arriving unharmed both men received a warm welcome from the city officials who ensured their safety. In fact they were given an official escort into Jiaxing where once again curious crowds gathered, anxious to obtain some Christian literature from the strangers.

Jiaxing, a beautiful city surrounded by a solid wall and moat, was well known for its trade in cotton, silk, copper goods and books. Outside the city area mulberry plantations were in abundance, the leaves of which were used to feed silkworms.

Having achieved their goal, Hudson and Joseph returned to Shanghai, rejoicing that they had safely travelled beyond the thirty mile, Treaty Port limit, set for foreigners. They praised God that they had been able to distribute such a large amount of Christian literature, including copies of the New Testament.

Both men now realised the need to avoid attracting big crowds, which could be manipulated by local trouble makers to cause problems.

The journey had taken eight days and when they reported to the government officials that they had ventured beyond the thirty mile limit, no one seemed concerned. This was an encouragement for future inland excursions.

Hudson, understanding where his future work lay, purchased an old boat with all of its equipment for the princely sum of twelve pounds.

He continued his study of the Shanghai dialect and Mandarin but difficulties were at hand. The LMS indicated they needed the house in which he was living. Consequently he wrote to the CES outlining the desperate need of permanent headquarters in Shanghai, which he believed necessary before making any move into the inland provinces. He suggested the need of a compound consisting of a doctor's house, hospital, school, dispensary, living quarters and eventually a chapel which would cost several thousand pounds. While waiting for the reply, he and Dr Parker spent much time in prayer pleading with God to prepare the hearts of the people to receive the gospel.

It was winter time and so cold—twenty-five degrees Fahrenheit at night—and the cost of heating fuel was so expensive that Hudson sailed inland where he could buy cheaper wood. In order to get a warm night's rest he made a mixture of charcoal and salt-petre which was added to burning wood ashes contained in a brass pan with a tightly fitting lid. With two such 'fires' in his bed he was kept reasonably warm during the freezing nights.

Mrs Parker used the available money with great care which was important as the CES still failed to send the much needed finance. As a result Hudson was forced to accept a ninety pounds advance from the firm that cashed his letters of credit. Writing to his parents he said: 'If they [the CES] make any nonsense with [Parker], he will resign…It is shameful to send a man and his family here, and tho' promising, not to send any credit to him, and now…do not send us funds to carry on our work…If we three retired the Society would be ruined, and to prevent this we daily make it a matter of prayer that we and they may be directed aright.'

During the Christmas period the war raged, resulting in the deaths of many Chinese citizens—men, women and children—who were beheaded by the Imperial soldiers. The French soldiers in turn killed the Chinese soldiers involved in the cruel slaughter of defenceless people.

But it was Christmas and Mrs Parker baked a cake into which, much to Hudson's amazement, she put some peppermint. She repaired his worn out trousers, but ruined the distinctive fringe around the bottom of each pair.

Now Hudson commenced a series of journeys setting a lifetime pattern.

Second Journey

Using his own boat with a Chinese crew, he set out in freezing weather on 25 January, 1855 to visit Chuansha, Nanhui and Zhapu where he distributed literature and preached. He also wanted to see the Chinese reaction when they met a lone European in Western dress.

In Chuansha he distributed literature to those who were able to read, but refused to give books to the illiterate who were known to use the book pages to line their shoes. During this stopover he treated twelve patients.

Approaching Nanhui, the city officials heard that he was coming and closed the east gate to prevent his entrance. He made his way to the west gate and was soon preaching and distributing literature in the city. When the city official who had ordered the closure of the gate met him, he gratefully accepted a copy of the New Testament, particularly when he understood that Hudson was only preaching and handing out literature.

In the temple area he was privileged to preach to a crowd of four or five hundred people. He also visited a man's sick wife and advised that she be admitted to hospital. Now he realised that medicine was one way to win the attention of the people.

In Zhapu he again preached, handed out literature, and as food was cheap he stocked up his supplies before returning to Shanghai, rejoicing at the success of his solo expedition.

Back in Shanghai the cannon balls were still flying about, some even landing in the foreign Settlement. The Chinese feared an attack by the Imperial forces and starvation was widespread. In parts of the city every animal had been killed and eaten—cats, dogs, horses, frogs, mice and insects. Then the starving people began eating the grass and weeds that remained.

Hudson and Dr Parker continued to visit the Chinese sections of Shanghai, preaching and giving whatever physical help they could.

Third Journey

This time Hudson was accompanied by John Burdon of the Church Missionary Society and Alexander Wylie of the LMS. They left Shanghai on 16 February for Qingpu and Songjiang where they freely preached and distributed literature.

From the hills about Songjiang they looked towards Shanghai, and to their horror saw clouds of smoke rising from the city area. The

Imperial forces had attacked the rebels, who had set fire to many parts
of the city before fleeing. When the missionaries heard this news from
some who had escaped they decided to return to Shanghai at once.

Arriving home they found the Chinese suburbs had been
devastated by the escaping Triads. Hudson wrote home of the terrible
destruction:

> Here such a scene of desolation met my eyes, as I never before
> witnessed...the city itself was a mass of smoking ruins. I...saw
> bodies without heads, ripped open...broken coffins (that the
> corpses might be beheaded)...places with which I had been most
> familiar were so altered I was unable to recognise them. I returned
> home quite sick of the sight.

In another place they found evidence of cannibalism as many Chinese
believed that by eating the heart, and liver (and other body parts) they
somehow gained the characteristics of the person being eaten.

Dr Parker was also horrified by the scene of death that lay before
him. On one occasion he saw some soldiers dragging a prisoner to his
execution. He looked to Dr Parker for help, but that was impossible.
As he watched 'they had him down by his face, hacking at his head
with a sword like a butcher's knife, and after much ado the head was
severed from the body.'

Dr Parker and Hudson were dismayed by the revolting cruelty of the
ruthless Chinese. They knew their only hope was to be found in Christ.

The Chinese however were a resilient people and soon the city began
to return to normal.

When the CES again failed to forward money, Hudson wrote to
his mother: 'I wish some wealthy friend would send us a thousand
pounds to put up our hospital, school and other premises ....Do you
think a Bazaar could be got up anywhere to assist us in the purchase
of ground and erection of suitable buildings? If you could get the
ladies interested, it would be sure to succeed.'

He had decided they should get things going themselves, as they
couldn't depend upon the CES for support.

Fourth Journey

This time Hudson, accompanied by Dr Parker set off on 19 March
for Jiading where they preached the gospel and distributed Christian
literature to those who could read. Crowds gathered to see the

Europeans dressed in their strange clothing. By this time Hudson was quite proficient in Mandarin and the local dialect which allowed him to speak quite freely.

Dr Parker gave medical help to the sick, but this ended when his surgical equipment was stolen.

At Qingpu they again carried on their Christian work and on this occasion found support from a man who agreed that idols were useless, dead and had no feeling. The man took a stick and proved his point by hitting a nearby idol.

Upon their return to Shanghai they received an offer of fifty dollars towards the cost of building a hospital. As a result Hudson again appealed to the CES for help. Meanwhile Dr Parker helped John Burdon, who was experiencing difficulties in attracting people to his chapel services. He opened a clinic, and before long the numbers attending services increased greatly.

Then the offer of fifty dollars towards the building of Dr Parker's hospital was doubled, in the hope of attracting more donations.

Fifth Journey

Money was in short supply as the CES had failed to transfer funds to their missionaries. Hudson and Dr Parker constantly complained, but the society was experiencing a marked drop in giving which meant the missionaries went without. However, the godly William Berger regularly forwarded gifts for use by the two men.

Hudson dearly wanted a wife. He was lonely and again wrote to Elizabeth Sissons proposing marriage, and another letter to her father, begging him to allow his daughter to sail to China and become his wife.

On 17 April, Hudson, John Burdon and two Chinese teachers, set out on two hired junks to visit several islands in the Yangtze River estuary. Hudson's boat was too small for the thirty mile journey across what at times was very rough water.

The missionaries knew that temple areas were the best places to find crowds of people. In the city of Chongming, Hudson mounted a huge incense urn to preach to a crowd of five or six hundred. Often they were jostled by the people wanting their literature. At one rowdy meeting, their bag of literature was snatched away, breaking the handle. Hudson lost his hat and glasses and unfortunately his spectacles were not returned.

In one pagoda which was five storeys high the missionaries caught sight of hundreds of various sized idols.

When the two men set off for Tongzhou their Chinese companions warned them to stay away as the people were rough and rowdy and the soldiers very cruel.

But after much prayer they left, telling their friends to wait for a time and if they did not return, one junk was to leave for Shanghai to report their absence while the other waited in case they arrived later.

Several days later Hudson and John found themselves walking along the muddy roadway towards the city. People gathered to see the foreigners in their strange black clothes and shouted out to them, 'Black devils!'

Hudson's wheelbarrow man became afraid and refused to go any further.

As the missionaries approached the city gate a strongly built, drunk man grabbed John Burdon by his shoulders. As Hudson turned to see what was happening they were surrounded by a dozen of his friends who began roughly shoving them along.

They were told they were being taken to the chief magistrate and along the way suffered the abuse of the excited men who thought their captives were rebels from Shanghai or members of the Taiping forces.

Hudson found that his bag of books was becoming heavy, but he staggered along under its weight. Suddenly he was grabbed by the hair and almost knocked to the ground. Another man grabbed his collar and attempted to choke him, in the process badly bruising his arms and shoulders. It was during those trying minutes that he remembered a verse of a hymn that his mother had quoted in a recent letter:

> We speak of the realms of the blest,
>> That country so bright and fair,
> And oft are its glories confessed:
>> But what must it be to be there!

He began to think that they were soon to become martyrs. Thoughts of Scripture teaching filled his mind—to be absent from the body meant being in the presence of Christ in the land of righteousness where never again would he be harmed by Satan's malice. Both men considered it a privilege to suffer for Christ, and they encouraged one another as they were being knocked about.

John Burdon courageously began to distribute Christian literature until one soldier, in a furious rage, demanded that he be handcuffed.

Fortunately these could not be found, but it became impossible to continue the distribution of the literature. All the missionaries could do was quietly accompany their captors wherever they were being taken.

As they made their way along the road they heard the men discussing what should be done with them. Some suggested they be immediately killed, while others argued for a visit to the city official.

While being pushed and dragged along the road Hudson was able to take from his pocket a Chinese card bearing his name. When the men saw it they began to treat them more kindly. He demanded that his card be taken to the chief city official and that he and Mr Burdon be taken to his office.

Hudson continues the story:

> Oh the long weary streets we were dragged through! I thought they would never end; and seldom have I felt more thankful than when we stopped at a place where we were told a Mandarin resided. Quite exhausted, bathed in perspiration and with my tongue cleaving to the roof of my mouth, I leaned against the wall, and saw that Mr Burdon was in the same state. I requested them to bring us chairs, but they told us to wait, and when I begged them to give us some tea, received only the same answer. Round the doorway a large crowd gathered, and Mr Burdon, collecting his remaining strength, preached Jesus Christ to them. Our cards and books had been taken in to the Mandarin, but he proved to be one of low rank, and after keeping us waiting for some time referred us to his superior in office.
>
> Upon hearing this…we positively refused to move a single step and insisted on chairs being brought. After some demur this was done, and we were carried off. On the way we felt so glad of the rest the chairs afforded and so thankful for having been enabled to preach the gospel in spite of Satan's malice ….
>
> When we arrived at the Ya-men I wondered where we were being taken, for though we passed through some great gates that looked like those of the city wall, we were still evidently within the city. A second pair of gates suggested that it was a prison into which we were being carried. But when we came in sight of a large tablet with the inscription *Min-chi fu-mu* (the Father and Mother of the people) we felt more at ease, for this is the title assumed by civil magistrates.
>
> Our cards again were sent in, and after a short delay we were ushered into the presence of Ch'en Ta Lao-ie (The Great Venerable Grandfather Ch'en), who…knew the importance of treating

foreigners with civility. Coming before him some of the people fell on their knees and bowed down to the ground, and my conductor motioned me to do the same, but without success. This mandarin… came out to meet us with every possible token of respect. He took us to an inner apartment, a more private room, followed by a large number of writers, runners, and semi-officials. I explained the object of our visit and begged permission to give him copies of our books, for which he thanked me. As I handed him the New Testament with part of the Old (from Genesis to Ruth), and some tracts, I tried to say a little about them, and also to give him a brief summary of our teachings.…He listened very attentively, as of course did all the others. He then ordered refreshments to be brought, which were very welcome.…

After a long stay, we asked permission to see something of the city and to distribute the books we had with us before returning. To this he kindly consented. We then mentioned that we had been most disrespectfully treated as we came in…we requested him to give orders that we were not to be further molested. This also he acceded to, and, with every possible token of respect, accompanied us to the door of his ya-men, sending several "runners" to see that no trouble arose.…We distributed our books well and quickly…It was amusing to see the use the "runners" made of their tails. When the way was blocked by the crowd they turned them into whips and laid them about the people's shoulders to right and left!…

Early in the evening we got back to the boats in safety, sincerely thankful to our Heavenly Father for His gracious protection and aid.

This was Hudson's first real experience of danger from the people he wanted to evangelize.

The British and Foreign Bible Society was so impressed with his work that they supplied him with all the Scriptures he could use and contributed to his living costs.

Safely in Shanghai he began searching for a city house that Dr Parker could use as a dispensary.

Sixth Missionary Journey

Hudson decided that he should make another journey further afield, hoping to reach Nanking. All the time he was searching for new premises that could be used as a home base when venturing inland. This sixth journey commenced on 8 May and lasted for twenty four days.

Hiring a junk he made his way inland almost reaching Zhenjiang which was approximately two hundred miles from Shanghai.

During this journey he distributed two thousand seven hundred Scripture sections as well as other Christian literature.

At one place he met an eighty year old Mandarin, exchanged books and spoke on a variety of subjects, including the old man's conviction from observations that the earth moved about the sun. The old man, who was convinced that a moral life would result in happiness, listened intently to all he had to say.

At another place some drunks pelted him with mud, but generally the people and city officials welcomed him. On several occasions the citizens ran away in fright when he appeared.

He treated patients, preached the Word and became more accustomed to their way of life, making good use of chopsticks. His boatmen and others suggested that he ought to wear Chinese clothing and shave his head as was the Chinese custom.

All the time he walked closely with God, reading the Word and praying for Jehovah's blessings upon his labours in Christ's name. He also realised more than ever that medical work was the means of attracting people to him where he could preach the gospel.

Before returning home on 1 June, he remembered the unpleasant problem he had in his room—rats and mice! They were everywhere, even jumping on his bed while he tried to sleep. Seeing a cat with two kittens he purchased them and took them home.

Now he hoped his problem would be solved!

17

A Change of Direction

Hudson and the Parkers faced new difficulties when the LMS indicated it would soon need the house in which they were living. The CES, unwilling to commit any funds to building in a Treaty Port as its policy was to establish a work in the inland provinces rejected Hudson's proposal for consolidation of the work in Shanghai.

At this time he had been reported to the British authorities by a magistrate from Jingjiang for breaking the law restricting foreigners to the Treaty Ports and an area not exceeding thirty miles from those cities.

Despite this setback he preached five or six times a day, lived in cramped quarters with the two other families and was physically unwell. Having rented rooms near the South gate of the Chinese section of the city he opened a school there. They were also used as a chapel and Dr Parker visited the place several times a week giving medical assistance.

Then Dr Parker announced that he intended leaving Shanghai for Ningbo to establish a hospital, the support of which was guaranteed by the merchants and citizens.

This proposal upset Hudson, who, in the hot weather, was physically unwell and needed some new accommodation himself.

What was he to do?

He bowed before his God and pleaded for guidance from the One who held the affairs of all men in his hands.

Seventh Journey

On 8th June, accompanied by John Burdon and William Parker, he set out for Ningbo. Along the way they preached the gospel, distributed Christian literature and gave medical assistance wherever necessary.

In Zhapu, Hudson was separated from his companions and, much to his satisfaction, spent the night with a Chinese family, using chopsticks and sleeping on a straw bed.

Reaching Ningbo, they found a city of six or seven million people with a bustling foreign settlement and some well organised missionary establishments. Surrounding the city was a beautiful countryside.

One establishment with an excellent reputation was Miss Aldersey's school for girls. Two young English women teaching at the school were Burella and Maria Dyer, the daughters of the late missionaries, Rev. and Mrs Samuel Dyer.

Hudson inspected the city, even keeping an eye out for insects to add to his collection.

When a message was received that John Burdon's child was desperately ill the decision was made to return to Shanghai.

With Dr Parker making a final inspection of Ningbo, Hudson made a momentous decision—he would adopt Chinese clothing for everyday wear, shave his head, grow a pigtail and live as did the Chinese. In this way he knew he would blend in with the native population and not attract the rowdy element that always caused problems when missionaries arrived dressed in their strange European clothes.

In mid August Dr Parker was ready to move to Ningbo. By that time Hudson, realising that medical work was a means of attracting people, where they could hear the gospel preached, wrote to his mother: 'I wish that when I was in England, I had been able to procure a medical diploma *independent of the* [the CES], as then I could easily have got a position of £300 or more per annum, without preventing my doing missionary work....'

He was sick and confused about his future. In three months he had distributed nine thousand pieces of Christian literature, given medical assistance to well over a thousand patients and preached many times. He was also very concerned about the loneliness he'd face when Dr Parker and his family left for Ningbo.

Eighth Journey

On 23 August Dr Parker asked Hudson to accompany him part of the way to Ningbo. By so doing he would determine if his new appearance was acceptable to the locals.

Before leaving he was finally able to rent a house of five rooms—two upstairs, two downstairs and one for servants across the courtyard. Then after hiring a boat he found a Chinese barber.

His head was shaved except for a small tuft on the back of the skull, which after dyeing, had a plaited pigtail of black Chinese hair securely attached. A piece of black ribbon was tied to the pigtail and the hair-do was finished. With his new suit of Chinese clothes he truly looked like a Chinese scholar.

On 24 August, he and Dr Parker set sail for Ningbo accompanied by servants and a barber to care for his new hairstyle.

In the Hangzhou Bay area both men distributed literature, preached and Dr Parker gave medical help wherever possible.

Leaving Dr Parker to travel to Ningbo, Hudson moved on to Haiyan where he proved the value of his new appearance.

However, his new appearance didn't impress the citizens of the Shanghai European Settlement. He found himself the object of the scorn and laughter of the British merchants who believed he had degraded their nation in the eyes of the Chinese and brought disgrace upon the European community. Even members of the missionary community ridiculed his action.

Most Europeans saw him as an unordained man, without academic qualifications, receiving no church support and dressed like a Chinaman. But he knew he had taken a step that would produce results to the glory of God.

Despite the shortage of finances, he continued to receive money from William Berger, to be used as he saw fit.

About that time Mr Charles Bird of the CES alienated many people who had supported the work of the Society. As a result of failing mental health he had written many offensive letters to people. This was possibly the reason why Mr Berger posted money to Hudson direct.

Correspondence from Elizabeth Sissons encouraged him to believe he may have found a wife, but soon after, a letter from her father cast a shadow over his hopes. It seemed that he and his wife had no objections to their daughter's marriage if he lived in England, but Elizabeth's mother strongly objected to her daughter marrying a missionary and then moving to China.

Hudson still hoped that the matter would be resolved and they could marry.

Meanwhile in Ningbo, Dr Parker rented premises large enough for his family and live-in patients. Returning to Shanghai he gathered together his belongings and, with his family, were farewelled on 24 September, leaving Hudson alone.

More Difficulties

In his new living quarters in the Chinese area, he lived a very lonely, frugal existence. The weather was very hot, food quickly decayed and there was no sanitation with the result that a vile smell wafted through the suburbs.

Despite his difficulties his spiritual life was blooming. He exhibited an infectious love of God and devotion to Christ that had a marked effect upon the boys attending his school. He found patients attending his clinic in large numbers—people who wanted to hear more of his teaching. Many were showing a deep interest in the Christ he proclaimed, and it was about that time that his faithful servant Guihua was converted.

Ninth Journey

This journey was undertaken by Hudson and his devoted Christian Chinese servants to Chongming and Xinkaihe. He had previously visited Chongming where he had given a copy of the New Testament to the Chief Magistrate and obtained approval to return when the Old Testament was available.

On 19 October, after landing at Xinkaihe he began preaching and distributing literature to those able to read. Without any difficulty he rented rooms above a factory and paid six months rent. Here Hudson received many visitors and carried out eye surgery on patients who visited him. He was also able to preach to crowds numbering many hundreds. Because of his Chinese appearance he was welcomed as an equal.

Since the island was close to Shanghai, he returned whenever necessary to obtain fresh supplies. On one return journey he received a cheque for fifty pounds from the faithful William Berger.

While in Shanghai during November a writ was received from the Chongming Chief Magistrate accusing him of having broken the Treaty of Nanking regulations relating to areas where foreigners could live. It indicated that those involved in renting the living quarters to the 'foreign devil' would suffer the consequences of their action.

Later Hudson found out that behind the writ were some doctors who objected to the free medical treatment he gave to his Chinese patients.

During this time several Chinese were soundly converted, including a blacksmith and a grocer. Tsien and Deng, who had returned with him to advise him concerning the writ, continued to preach Christ fearlessly. He treated many patients finding great comfort in the words of Scripture: 'Call upon Me in the day of trouble. I will deliver you, and you shall glorify Me.'

When he failed to receive a formal order to appear before the Chief Magistrate to answer the charges, he visited Chongming City hoping to meet him, but as he was supervising examinations Hudson indicated he'd return later to discuss the affair.

He continued his medical work and when faced with a demand for a bribe to let the writ lapse, he refused. Despite the fact that the amount demanded dropped from thirteen dollars to three dollars he still refused to pay the bribe. The corrupt doctors, in league with some junior city officials, then extorted the money from the city druggists.

Soon news arrived that all those involved with his visit would be liable for a punishment of between three hundred and one thousand blows.

Back at Shanghai the Vice Consul sent a formal letter requesting Hudson to appear before him.

He was most concerned about what might happen—he could face fines as large as five hundred dollars, and so he immediately wrote to the CES asking whether they would meet any fines, especially as they wanted him to preach in inland areas.

He argued his case well before the authorities, stating that priests were living in the inland areas without any objections being raised— even flying French flags over their residences. He also pointed out that foreign manufacturers had a silk factory outside the Treaty Ports.

Hudson, being warned that he was not to live at Chongming Island, or face fines, finally gathered his servants and helpers together and all returned to Shanghai with the intention of appealing the decision to Sir John Bowring, who was soon expected in Shanghai. However, he failed to arrive and the matter was forgotten.

Knowing that he could not depend upon the CES for support, he decided to make his own plans for the future.

In the midst of all the turmoil he received an upsetting letter from Elizabeth Sissons stating she did not love him.

This was followed by news from England that some Christians were critical of him for not standing firm at Chongming, but Miss Stacey came to his defence saying that he had acted as the apostles had done—'If they persecute you in one city, flee to another.'

Hudson returned to his South Gate house and there not only lived with Chinese, but absorbed their culture, their ways and attitudes.

Towards the end of 1855, with his Chinese Christian friends, Deng and Si, he preached to congregations of up to three hundred people.

God had not deserted him!

18

William Burns

When William Burns, an experienced Presbyterian missionary, who had established a thriving congregation in Amoy, visited Shanghai, he met Hudson Taylor. Burns was greatly loved by the Amoy Chinese, many of whom he had rescued from the slaughter between the Triads who occupied the city and the Imperialist forces.

Having returned from Scotland he attempted to make his way to the Taiping forces at Nanking. When this project failed he visited Shanghai where he met a man after his own heart in Hudson Taylor.

During the time Hudson spent with Burns he realised the importance of the 'evangelist' as an office in the church. Burns in turn saw the value of dressing in Chinese clothes and decided to make the change sometime in the future.

Both men were utterly convinced that Christ's command to go into the whole world and preach the gospel surpassed every command of man—including the Treaty of Nanking regulations which confined foreigners to the Treaty Ports and the immediate surrounds.

Hudson knew it was unwise to revisit Chongming, as his presence would endanger the locals who had graciously received him into their community. As he and Burns had the common goal of preaching Christ to the Chinese no matter where they lived, they spent much time in prayer, seeking God's guidance.

Tenth Journey

On 17 December, 1855 they set out in two boats manned by Chinese and accompanied by Song, a teacher. Tsien and Guihua were to join them along the way.

The boats were more comfortable than anything Hudson had used on previous journeys: 'a comfortable boat, that…gives me a nice little room for myself…My little room has an oyster-shell window that gives light, but prevents persons peeping in; a little table at which I write and take meals, a locker…over which my bed is placed at night, and a seat round the remaining parts, so that two friends can sit with me…How differently the Master was lodged!' He even believed the accommodation was suitable for a wife—if he had one!

The men planned to visit as many towns and cities as possible, passing through Songjiang and visiting cities near the Great Lake—Tai Hu. Along the way Hudson was introduced to Burns' practice of avoiding the central part of a city as soon as he arrived, initially spending time preaching on the outskirts without attracting the attention of the rough elements. Both men preached wherever the opportunity presented itself—in temples, streets, tea shops—anywhere people gathered together.

Reaching Nanxun they heard that an immoral play was in progress in a tent village outside the city which was well known for vice and immorality.

William Burns decided to confront public sin where it was found, and fearlessly both men made their way to the place where Burns mounted the stage, interrupted the play and preached righteousness and the reality of hellfire for unrepentant sinners. Those organizing the play grabbed the missionaries and led them away.

The next day when they returned and again preached they were once again quietly moved from the camp. The men made a third attempt to preach the gospel to the immoral actors and their watching crowds, but again they were escorted from the area.

Burns spoke out against the widespread prostitution, but few seemed concerned. Some townspeople urged the missionaries to try again and bring the immorality to an end.

Hudson made his way to the tent city and wearing his Chinese clothes was able to move undetected past the brothels and gambling tents. Then standing on the stage he ordered the play to end and began preaching. When some men tried to get him off the stage he told them to sit down and listen to what he had to say. Before he was dragged away, he again preached the gospel.

Mr Burns, who had, unknown to Hudson, arrived in Chinese clothes began asking the men if they would like their wives and daughters to become involved in prostitution. Finally they were hustled to the canal where they spoke of Christ to the prostitutes who lived on the junks.

The next port of call was Wuzhen where they preached in the God of War's temple and distributed Christian literature to those who could read.

Some illiterate Chinese who wanted booklets attacked the boats while Hudson was having lunch. He wrote: 'a battering began, the roof was at once broken in. I went out…and found four or five men taking the large lumps of frozen earth…weighing…from seven to fourteen pounds each—and throwing them at the boat…a considerable part of the upper structure…was broken to pieces.'

Only Tsien's quick action saved the boats from further damage.

Next came a demand from some salt smugglers for ten dollars and a pound of opium, with the threat that the boats would be destroyed if the payment was not made. Hudson, who had a badly inflamed knee decided that he should return to Shanghai leaving William Burns to continue preaching the need of repentance and a saving faith in Christ. No payment was made to the standover men.

Burns returned to Shanghai on 26 January, 1856.

Eleventh Journey

Little is known about this preaching tour to Songjiang which commenced on 29 January and lasted for about two weeks, except that the cold weather froze Hudson's face cloth while he was shaving.

Twelfth Journey

Hudson was facing continual financial difficulties because the CES failed to fully support his work; in fact most of his credit was cut off except for his small salary. The allowance he received from the Bible Society to distribute the Scriptures, supplemented his meagre CES allowance.

With just one hundred dollars remaining from William Berger's last gift, he was obliged to dispense with the services of Tsien and Si. In order to meet the freight on six boxes of printing blocks sent to Dr Parker from Lobscheid, Hudson sold his stock of candles and soap to raise some ready cash.

His faith in God to supply his needs was strong. The Lord had proved his faithfulness in England and China and he knew that God would never let him down.

But what did the future hold for him?

At a prayer meeting held at the home of Dr Medhurst, Captain Bowers from Swatow was present. He begged Hudson and William Burns to visit the crime infested region and preach the gospel. Merchants had established themselves in the city but there was a desperate need for the moral influence of missionaries.

In a letter to his mother Hudson described Swatow: 'About two hundred boxes of opium are imported monthly…you will not be surprised to learn that the people are wretchedly poor, ignorant, and vicious.'

He also wrote of the cruel coolie trade where on the pretence of earning big money Chinese were enticed on board ships bound for foreign shores. Once on board, they were captives. If an attempt was made to escape they were whipped and placed in the locked ship's hold. Many died in the cramped quarters that sometimes held over one thousand prisoners, very few of whom ever returned to their homeland.

Hudson was more conscious than ever of the Lord's calling to move to Swatow and evangelize the citizens held captive to sin. With the offer of a free passage, both missionaries agreed to accompany Captain Bowers.

Hudson had no idea of what lay before him and before leaving Shanghai wrote: 'As to Swatow we go looking to the Lord for guidance and blessing.…As we are led, we shall return sooner or later or not at all.…May the Lord be with us, bless us abundantly, and glorify His own great name.…Oh, pray that we may be kept from sin and used of God in the conversion of sinners.'

The *Geelong* sailed on 6 March, 1856 and upon reaching the city, the men couldn't find accommodation in the Chinese suburbs, even though both spoke the language and wore native clothing. Captain Bowers cared for them until Mr Burns met a Cantonese merchant who was so impressed with his command of the language, that he used his influence with a relative, to obtain rental accommodation for the missionaries. This was a very small room above an incense shop, the only entrance being up a ladder and through a hole in the floor.

Of this room Hudson wrote: 'My bedroom is on the south. Mr Burns takes the north side, and the strip on the west we use as our study. The partitions are made of sheets and a few boards....We are promised a trap-door next week, and then we shall have more privacy.

'Our beds are...boards, and our table the lid of a box supported on two bags of books....So for the present...we have completely furnished the house—with two bamboo stools and a bamboo easy-chair.'

The two missionaries found themselves surrounded by poverty, crime and immorality.

Late one night, several weeks after moving into their new quarters, both men for several hours heard the 'heart-rending' screams from two women. The next morning when Hudson asked what had been the cause of the distress he was told that they were unwilling prostitutes being tortured and beaten until they submitted to their cruel owners.

Life was dangerous as both men faced the risk of being taken captive by the local criminals and ransomed for a healthy profit. However, they openly proclaimed their Lord and Saviour, and as Hudson, who was being tutored by a local farmer, became proficient in the local language, he joined William Burns preaching to crowds of interested citizens.

Letters from home were always welcome and the two he received involved his sister Amelia. One revealed that his close friend Benjamin Broomhall was interested in her as a future wife. The other was a letter from Amelia which caused him some disappointment, as she was very critical of his wearing oriental clothing.

To her he replied that he was sorry his change in clothing had upset her, but she needed to understand that now he could enter areas for lengthy periods without experiencing any difficulties. He then explained that English clothing was as barbarous to the Chinese as their clothing was to the British.

Again the CES failed to forward any money, and Hudson found himself dependent upon the continuing gifts from William Berger. He was so concerned by the lack of support that he considered resigning from the Society and told Mr Pearse that this was very likely.

With his better command of the local dialect he began visiting the dock area preaching the gospel. His visits to the countryside were much better received than in the city area, but he was finding the very hot weather tiring. On 21 May, his twenty-fourth birthday, he was sunburnt and worn out. With a rented house in Topu he thought his problems were solved, but when he met the landlord he was told it was no longer available as the nearby residents objected to the presence of foreigners.

As it was too late to return to Swatow he found accommodation with a barber. With a room above the shop he was able to explain the gospel to the hospitable family below. But falling ill with dysentery he returned to Swatow where he found some welcome mail awaiting him.

This time Amelia indicated that she wanted to come to China and assist him in his work. In another letter some friends urged him to return to England and complete his medical studies which would then give him some status and respect in the European missionary community.

Hudson was again vacillating about the value of medicine in his missionary work, believing he should devote his time totally to preaching the gospel: 'I have a very low opinion of the value of medicine, and I believe it to be oftener a hindrance than a help to a missionary, from the time it takes up.'

However, when the local mandarin came to him seeking medical help, which proved successful, he changed his mind. As the Mandarin advised him to make use of his medical skill he wrote: 'God blessed the medicines given, and grateful for relief, he [the Mandarin] advised our renting a house for a hospital and dispensary. Having his permission, we were able to secure the entire premises, one room of which we had previously occupied.'

While waiting for their new premises, the two men remained in their tiny attic where it was so hot they couldn't touch the roof tiles. Hudson, suffering from dysentery, was undecided what he should do.

Following a time of prayer the decision was made that he should return to Shanghai in order to recover from his continuing sickness, while Mr Burns laboured on at Swatow.

Hudson arrived in Shanghai on 14 July hoping to return to Swatow when he recovered, but to his disappointment he discovered that the LMS place where he had stored his medical equipment had been burned out, destroying everything, including thirty thousand copies of the New Testament.

Then came the news that at the outbreak of war in southern China, Mr Burns had been taken captive and sent to Canton as a prisoner. Later he returned to Swatow where his work was greatly blessed by God. He travelled far and wide preaching the gospel, even reaching Peking where he spent four fruitful years.

Hudson and William Burns never again met!

19

Ningbo again

Hudson discovered that his mail, including a letter of credit from the CES had been forwarded to Swatow leaving him almost destitute. The CES was experiencing continual financial problems, as giving was down and the bank in which their funds had been deposited, collapsed. Only Mr Berger's faithful giving saved him from destitution.

Then he heard of the arrival of the Jones family who had sailed from England with the promise that funds would be forwarded by the CES—if they were available. This godly family were already in Ningbo working with Dr Parker.

The CES caused further embarrassment when *The Gleaner* printed an article critical of the missionary societies in China. Hudson rebuked the CES, as he had received generous help from the LMS and the CMS when his own society had failed in their responsibility to support him as they had promised.

When the Jones' family reached Shanghai, almost destitute, it was the LMS that took them in and then conveniently arranged a missionary journey to Ningbo, meaning they were provided with free travel to the Parkers.

Hudson continued his usual work in Shanghai, distributing the Scriptures and tracts and preaching the gospel, but rejoicing that a change was taking place in the missionary community—Joseph Edkins was now wearing Chinese clothes!

Thirteenth Journey

On 22 July, gathering together his few possessions which he had left with Alexander Wylie, Hudson, with his one box under his arm containing books, his collection of insects, watches, camera, photographs and the Bible his mother had given him and with his sleeping mattress over his shoulder, set off for Ningbo.

At Songjiang he discovered that some of his property was missing, but he moved on, preaching Christ wherever he had the opportunity. The countryside was suffering severe drought and he used this to show that the idol gods were incapable of sending the drought-breaking rain.

Reaching Jiaxing he found boat travel impossible and set out walking to Haining.

So far he had handed out two hundred copies of the New Testament and almost three thousand pieces of Christian literature.

He hired several coolies to carry his belongings, but they were so slow, he moved on ahead. Later it was shown they were opium addicts.

At Chang'an, after waiting for the hired men to arrive with his property, he was obliged to stay overnight in a room having eleven 'beds'—planks resting on tressels with a shoe and umbrella as a pillow. He paid his account only to later discover that the landlord had cheated him with his change.

Reaching Haining he enjoyed a meal of rice gruel and having no place to sleep was obliged to spend the night on the stone steps of a temple. This proved to be a frightening experience. He carefully hid his money by using it as a pillow and was almost asleep (despite the cold weather) when he heard someone approaching. It was one of the many beggars who saw Hudson as a victim to rob. After watching the 'sleeping' missionary he began searching through Hudson's clothes only to be asked, 'What do you want?'

The man went away without answering.

Hudson quietly hid his money in his sleeve and used a stone jutting out of the wall as a pillow. No sooner had he dozed off than he heard the 'noiseless' footsteps of two men approaching.

Again he prayed to his Heavenly Father, seeking his providential protection.

Quietly and gently one of the men began to feel about under his head, hoping to find the cash, but when Hudson spoke, both men sat down, saying they were going to spend the night with him. As there was plenty space, he ordered them to sit on the opposite side so he could watch them carefully. However, they stayed close, waiting for him to drop off to sleep.

As he pulled himself up against the wall the men suggested 'You had better lie down and sleep; if you do not, you will be unable to walk home tomorrow. Do not be afraid; we shall not leave you, and will see that no one hurts you.'

'Listen to me,' he replied. 'I do not want your protection; I need it not; I am not a Chinese; I do not worship your senseless idols. I worship God; He is my Father; I trust in him. I know well what you are, and what your intentions are, and shall keep my eye on you, and shall not sleep.'

One man stood up and walked away, returning with a third friend. Hudson, feeling somewhat uneasy prayed to God for help.

Occasionally when the men checked to see if he was asleep, he said, 'Do not be mistaken; I am not sleeping.'

To keep himself awake and alert he sang some hymns and prayed aloud in English much to the annoyance of the Chinese, who still hoped that he would eventually fall asleep.

Shortly before the sun rose, the men walked away, giving him the opportunity to catch a little sleep.

After a breakfast of gruel and tea he again unsuccessfully searched for his property which had been stolen several days before at Songjiang.

He then set out to return to Shimenwan, but after eight miles of heat and blistered feet he was ready to collapse. Spending the last of his money he bought a meal of two eggs, some cakes and tea and fell asleep.

When the cool of the evening came he recommenced his journey, but finding himself being closely watched by an official he knew he had to return to Shanghai. He spent the night in an open boat, but found sleep impossible due to mosquitoes and the cool, moist, night air.

Having no money it seemed an impossibility to obtain a boat passage to Shanghai. However, a kind man hailed a mail boat and asked the captain to take Hudson, who would pay his fare when he reached Shanghai. If he did not, the man assured the sailor he would pay the fare himself.

'After a pleasant and speedy journey,' recorded Hudson, 'I reached Shanghai in safety on August 9, through the help of Him who has said,

"I will never leave you, nor forsake you…Lo, I am with you always, even unto the end of the world".'

Along the way, as the mail was delivered, Hudson took the opportunity to preach, praying that his witness would bear fruit, to the glory of God.

When he later found out that one of his servants had stolen his property, some friends suggested he bribe a city official to use his authority to force the thief to either return his belongings or pay compensation.

Hudson refused the suggestion knowing that the thief might well be cruelly treated and end up in prison, which was not in accordance with the teachings of Christ. In a letter home he said:

> So I have sent him a plain, faithful letter, to the effect that we know his guilt, and what its consequences might be to himself; that at first I had considered handing him over to the ya-men, but remembering Christ's command to return good for evil I had not done so, and did not wish to injure a hair of his head.…I told him… that I freely forgave him, and besought him more earnestly than ever to flee from the wrath to come.

He asked the man to return those pieces of his property that were of no use to him and sought the prayers of others that the man might be saved.

His missionary friends offered to make up his loss but with a gift of forty pounds from Mr Berger, and the proceeds from the sale of his last few pieces of furniture he had the funds to replace his medical equipment.

In England, when George Müller heard of his loss, he sent a gift of forty pounds to cover the cost of replacing everything. In fact George Müller became a faithful supporter of Hudson's work.

Fourteenth Journey

On 18 August Hudson left for Ningbo where he found Dr Parker's medical work progressing very well. Supported by the local community and friends in Great Britain he had seen nine thousand patients in twelve months. Missionaries from other societies supported him by visiting his premises and preaching Christ to the waiting patients. The relationship between the various mission groups was very cordial, convincing Dr Parker that Ningbo was an excellent place to both consolidate missionary endeavour and use as a base to move into the interior. To him it was the equal of Shanghai.

He had purchased a site for a hospital and suggested that a special effort should be made to teach the many illiterate Chinese to read.

Hudson was welcomed into the midst of the missionary community and when Dr Parker met him he was surprised at his Chinese appearance.

Soon Hudson was to meet Miss Aldersey and two unmarried young women teaching at her school—Maria and Burella Dyer.

Miss Aldersey was widely respected, but many thought her a tyrant. One wrote of her: 'The impression she made on the Chinese whether Christian or pagan was profound, the latter firmly believing that as England was ruled by a woman so Miss Aldersey had been delegated to be the head of our foreign community. The British Consul, they said, invariably obeyed her commands.'

Several minor earthquakes alarmed the citizens, who attributed the disturbances to her magic power. They alleged that they had seen her on the city-wall before the dawn of day, opening a bottle in which she kept some strong spirits which shook the earth.

> The only wonder is that they did not burn or stone her as a witch.... The year round she was accustomed to walk on the city-wall at five o'clock in the morning, and with such undeviating punctuality that in winter she was preceded by a man bearing a lantern. A bottle she carried in her hand did really contain "strong spirits", spirits of hartshorn, which she constantly used to relieve a headache and as an antidote for ill odours. In summer, unwilling to leave her school for the seaside she would climb to the ninth storey of a lofty pagoda and sit there through the long hours of the afternoon, sniffing the wind that came from the sea....Many indeed...are the households that call Miss Aldersey blessed, and I can truly say that in the long list of devoted women who have laboured in and for China, I know no nobler name than hers.

It was not too long before Hudson found himself the object of her scorn when he made known his affection for Maria, a sweet young woman of nineteen years.

Maria met and was attracted to Hudson when he accompanied the Parkers to their weekly meal with Miss Aldersey.

During his stay he became close friends of the Jones' family and often with John Jones ventured outside the city to distribute Christian literature and explain the gospel. The seven weeks he spent at Ningbo were very peaceful, yet his intention was to return to Swatow and recommence his labours with William Burns.

Fifteenth Journey

On 15 September twenty pounds arrived from William Berger and several weeks later another gift of forty pounds. Buying the medical supplies he needed, he gave Dr Parker a donation of fifty dollars towards the hospital building fund, and prepared to return to Shanghai. However his departure was delayed so that some sick people could be readied for the trip. John Jones and his little son occupied one boat and the Way family the second.

The journey to Shanghai was very difficult due to sickness, the heat and the plagues of locusts that were swarming everywhere. However, the city was reached on 4 October.

Sixteenth Journey

As Captain Bowers was in Shanghai ready to leave for Swatow he offered a free passage to Hudson who gratefully accepted and had his belongings transferred to the *Geelong*. He was looking forward to the trip as it meant a reunion with his dear companion in the faith, William Burns.

Thirty pounds from William Berger arrived in the mail, but again the CES failed in its responsibility. It appeared that nothing now would prevent Hudson's return to Swatow!

When unexpected news was received that William Burns and his workers had been arrested, Burns being sent under arrest to Canton, and his Christian Chinese companions being thrown into prison, it seemed to be an unwise move to return to Swatow.

What should he do?

He prayerfully considered the situation concluding that God had closed the door to Swatow; a fire had destroyed the equipment he needed in Swatow; Burns was in prison; Burns' helpers were suffering at the hands of their Chinese tormentors; the British authorities had issued a warning to everyone that they should abide by the Treaty laws; his goods had been stolen and he had cut his ties with Shanghai. The decision was made—he would gather his few belongings together and return to Ningbo!

At that time the relationship between England and China was very tense with the danger of war breaking out at any time. This meant it was not safe for foreigners to move outside the Treaty Ports.

This danger was reinforced by news of the horrible treatment meted out to a French priest who received one hundred lashes across the face, each blow being hard enough to knock out teeth.

Then he received one hundred strokes with a rattan cane across the back, followed by torture with an iron chain. After that he was suspended in a cage, 'so constructed that the sufferer's feet scarcely touch the ground, whilst his head is suspended above the cage by two boards, hollowed out a little, and fitted to the neck, so as to cause all the sufferings of strangulation, and yet leaving sufficient freedom of respiration to allow the patient to live for some time—even as long as five or six days. The sufferer...is placed in front of the prison and exposed to the public gaze.'

The priest survived this terrible treatment for two days, after which he was beheaded and mutilated with a cutlass and his remains thrown to the dogs.

Hudson made the decision to accompany John Jones and his son back to Ningbo and assist Dr Parker in his work.

Before leaving they met Peter, a Chinese national who had travelled overseas, even visiting England. He had met the Parkers on his travels and v as on his way to Ningbo to assist as a nurse.

Hudson intended travelling by boat to Songjiang where he was going to preach, and as Peter indicated that he wanted to learn of Christ, they settled down to what they hoped would be an uneventful journey.

The first morning, when the boat was not far from the shore Peter accidentally fell overboard, head first. By the time Hudson reached the deck he had disappeared.

Hudson immediately lowered the sail and began a search by jumping into the muddy water. Seeing men trawling for fish with a net and hooks, he pleaded with them to come and assist in the search.

The reply was simply, 'Veh bin!' (It is not convenient!) No, they wouldn't come to save a life as it meant a break from fishing. Hudson offered them money if they would help and after much time spent bargaining, for the sum of fourteen dollars they slowly made their way to the general area where Peter had disappeared.

A minute after dragging the area his body was found. Despite the fact that Peter had been submerged for a long time Hudson performed resuscitation, but without success.

He later told this story many times, using it to illustrate the attitude of the ungodly to human life. He wrote:

To myself this incident was profoundly sad and full of significance, suggesting a far more mournful reality. Were not those fishermen actually guilty of this poor Chinaman's death, in that they had the means of saving him at hand, if they would have but used them? Assuredly they were guilty. And yet, let us pause ere we pronounce judgment against them, lest a greater than Nathan answer, "You are the man." Is it so hardhearted, so wicked a thing to neglect to save the body? Of how much sorer punishment, then, is he worthy who leaves the soul to perish, and Cain-like says, "Am I my brother's keeper?" The Lord Jesus commands, commands me, commands you, [go] into all the world, and preach the gospel to every creature. Shall we say to Him, "No, it is not convenient"? Shall we tell Him that we are busy fishing and cannot go?...Before long "we must all appear before the judgment seat of Christ; that everyone may receive the things done in his body."

Let us remember, let us pray for, let us labour for the unevangelized Chinese.

Hudson returned to Shanghai and after much trouble left Peter's body with his mother and sister—and the money to meet the cost of his funeral.

On the second attempt to reach Ningbo the junk ran aground and broke up. Fortunately all lives were saved and the Chinese boatmen rescued Hudson's luggage. Walking overland they found another boat leaving for Ningbo which they safely reached on 20 October, 1856—which was the Christian Sabbath!

20

Political Unrest

The *Arrow* incident[2] on 8 October, 1856, gave the British government a reason to pressure China into opening her territory even more to both opium and general trade. Tensions grew worse when in Canton on 14 December, the Cantonese burned several foreign banks, destroyed foreign owned factories and then offered cash for the murder of foreigners.

Three days after Hudson and John Jones reached Ningbo, on 23 October, the bombardment of Canton commenced. Two weeks later the citizens of Ningbo heard the news.

On 14 January, 1857 an attempt was made by a Hong Kong baker to poison every foreigner with bread laced with arsenic. Four hundred fell ill and two died. Then on 18 January a plot was uncovered to kill every foreigner in Ningbo.

Arriving there, Hudson made his way to the Parkers' premises, while John Jones and his son Tom went to the Goughs of the CMS, where his wife Mary was staying. John, who was suffering from dysentery and renal colic was forced to spend time recuperating.

For a time Hudson lived on his boat, but as danger increased he moved to Dr Parker's Bridge Street property using the attic as his home.

During his stay he soon learned that he was held in low regard by the local missionary establishment. To them he was a nobody! He had no academic standing, was not ordained and to make matters worse, wore Chinese clothing and lived as did the Chinese. As he was rarely invited to conduct worship on the Lord's Day, he again began to wonder if he should return to England and gain qualifications that would give him some status within the missionary community.

When Mr Sissons indicated he would withdraw his objections to the marriage of his daughter to Hudson if he returned to live in England, he was tempted for a moment, but knew he could not turn his back on God's gracious call to service in China.

So he continued working, distributing the Scriptures and preaching the gospel wherever he had the opportunity. His relationship with John and Mary Jones grew closer—so much so that he looked upon them as a brother and sister, a couple in whom he could confide his closest secrets, joys and problems. With John he carried out evangelistic work amongst the Chinese, also visiting a group of Korean sailors who were in Ningbo.

Early in his stay he was included in a group who regularly had meals with Miss Aldersey, but she immediately took a dislike to this unusual Englishman. She considered his clothing to be due to his eccentricities, and when she heard that the party had completed their return journey to Ningbo on the 'Sabbath', she concluded that all she had heard about his theology was correct—an exclusive brethren and a Sabbath breaker. Miss Aldersey however, was unaware that some of her English friends held Hudson in the highest regard.

At those meals, Hudson met Maria and from the very start she was attracted to the unusual evangelist. She was good friends with Mary Jones and Mrs Gough, visiting them frequently.

Christmas, 1856 was a happy occasion for Hudson who spent the day with the Goughs and later wrote of this joyful time: 'We had a famous dinner—beef and plum pudding—and in the afternoon the Misses Dyer enlivened us playing some duets on Mr Gough's pianoforte, a very superior one, so with the party and my mail I had quite a treat. You see you have not all the good things at home....'

The day following, Maria and Mary Jones spent time visiting the locals and in the evening he had the pleasure of escorting Maria home.

Again he found the CES failed in its responsibility to provide the support he had been promised. The Jones family suffered in the same way, but the regular gifts received from the Bergers made it possible for him to survive by living a very frugal lifestyle.

When almost destitute, the mail brought another cheque for fifty pounds from William Berger. God had not let him down!

On 12 January, 1857, Hudson wrote a letter to his mother which summarized his feelings:

> Last month Mr Bird sent me twenty-five pounds instead of seventy, "hoping next mail to do more,"—but next mail nil. True, Mr Berger has sent me fifty pounds…and the Tottenham people have sent me five pounds, so that the Lord provides for me…but this is not the way to have the mind at rest, or a position to get married in….In the midst of this maze I sometimes think I must come home and try to get a degree and a wife….The Parkers think the best thing I can do is to go home and qualify. The Jones think of China and wonder I can think of leaving the field—and Mrs Jones thinks she knows what would make me settled, and recommends me to try and get married, promising me her influence in my favour with Miss Aldersey's assistant Miss M. Dyer…I am not in a position to marry and am not supplied with funds enough to keep me *alone* in European style….I cast all my care on the Lord and feel my burden lightened….The present state in China is…very critical. Soon we may be obliged to move for safety, in event of general war….

When Hudson and John Jones learned that the CES was borrowing money in an effort to meet payments to their missionaries, Hudson concluded that if funds were not available, then their work was not of God, because the Lord would provide all that was required to carry out his purposes. He knew the situation demanded a decision and, assisted by the prayers and wise counsel of John and Mary Jones, made the decision to work from Ningbo. The friendship with the likeminded John and Mary Jones and no doubt the attraction of Maria played a big part in the decision he reached.

Maria had recently declined a marriage proposal and was now looking favourably on Hudson. Her rejection of Joseph Edkins became public knowledge and Mrs Bausum, a close friend, gave her some wise advice on dealing with suitors. She told Maria not to embarrass a rejected suitor by laughing about his interest in her affections. In the discussion that followed she confided in Mrs Bausum of her affection for Hudson. Mrs Bausum responded by telling her she didn't think Hudson had any interest in her as a future wife.

With the discovery of the plan to kill the foreigners living in Ningbo, Miss Aldersey who was in the process of selling her school, sent all the girls home while she made preparations for escape if the situation grew worse. Of the situation Dr Parker wrote:

> The peril that threatened us was so great…that the merchants of the Settlement prepared for flight by keeping at single anchor the vessel on which their valuables had been stored. They and some others had their houses guarded by armed men; and after much prayer several missionaries, including Mr Jones and myself, were led to send our wives and children to Shanghai.

Shanghai seemed to be the only safe port in the event of war and Hudson was asked if he would escort the families to that safe destination.

On 24 January Miss Aldersey suggested that Maria and Burella go to Shanghai, but they refused declaring their readiness to remain with her and the others, including their motherly friend Mrs Bausum.

Miss Aldersey refused to move to the safe section of Ningbo, declaring that she had a coffin and coffin bearers at the ready. If the city erupted into war she would be carried to safety in her coffin!

Seventeenth Journey

On 25 January, 1857, Hudson, with his precious cargo of missionaries left for Shanghai. John and Mary Jones and their family, Mrs Parker and her children, Mrs Gough and her children boarded the *Japan* and without any difficulties arrived safely at Shanghai, where the LMS cared for everyone.

Soon afterwards Hudson heard that the CES had sent another three missionaries to China—at a time when they couldn't meet the costs associated with the ones already on the field.

When the danger in Ningbo eased, Dr Parker visited Shanghai to collect his family, and return to his hospital work in Ningbo.

In Shanghai, Hudson again spent his time distributing literature, preaching in the open air and teaching smaller groups.

As the fighting between the various warring factions created a class of people who had very little, he and John Jones became involved in the alleviation of their physical needs. Of the situation Mr Jones wrote:

> We took food with us and sought out others. Many of these poor creatures…have their dwelling literally among the tombs. Graves, here, are often simple arches, low, and from ten to twelve feet long. One end being broken through, they creep inside for shelter,

specially at night....We found them in all stages of nakedness, sickness and starvation.

Hudson also wrote of the tragedy being experienced by many Chinese:

> In our search we came upon the remains of a house bearing witness to the troublous times through which Shanghai had passed.... Affording some little shelter from the weather, it had been taken possession of by beggars, and in it we found a large number collected, some well and able to beg, others dying of starvation and disease. From this time we made regular visits to these poor creatures, and helped those who were unable to help themselves....We found, as is always the case, how difficult it is to care for body and soul at the same time. We did, nevertheless, as far as we were able, and I trust the seed sown was not without fruit in the salvation of souls.

At that time Hudson received word from William Burns that the way was open to join him. However, he had decided that Ningbo, where other CES missionaries were established, should be the centre for his future labours. The city seemed to be an ideal place to consolidate a work before moving inland.

He was very fond of Maria and wanted to know if she had any emotional interest in him. Thus he wrote her a letter, unburdening his heart, asking a reply and suggesting that if she was not interested in his 'proposal' she should burn the letter. He posted it on 23 March, just two days before Mary Jones became ill with smallpox. In order to care for her and the three small children Hudson placed himself in isolation for several days till she recovered.

When Maria read the letter she was overjoyed as was her sister Burella. Miss Aldersey however, was horrified that such a person— a nobody—should dare make such a proposal to Maria.

While Maria didn't want to discourage Hudson's attention, Miss Aldersey insisted that she write and immediately end his hopes. This she did, but worded the letter in such a way that it gave him some hope, even though he was told not to make any such future contact.

Then commenced a protracted dispute with Miss Aldersey who was determined to prevent Maria wasting her life on such a 'good for nothing hypocrite.' The dispute overflowed into the missionary community which took sides in the drawn out saga.

During this time Hudson and John Jones were carefully considering their position with the CES. The decision was that on 29 May, 1857 Hudson resigned his membership from the society. In part he wrote to Mr Pearse:

If I possess any legal right on the Society to draw, or sue for salary due, but not sent, I now relinquish that right. You feel you owe me a fixed sum every quarter, which your funds do not enable you to send, and...monies sent to me...I do not feel free to use....If the Lord blesses you, and leads you to send anything to me...I hope to receive it as from Him, and with thankfulness to Him and you.

He then went on to say that his travels inland could burden the Society with heavy fines and this he did not want. He continued: 'To avoid this, *I resign my connection with the Society entirely, from this time forth.*'

Several days later John Jones also forwarded his resignation to the CES. This opened the way for a missionary outreach from Hudson's premises in Bridge Street, Ningbo.

Eighteenth Journey

With the arrival in Shanghai of the three missionaries who were to be supported by the CES, and the LMS having the need of the accommodation being used by the refugees from Ningbo, it was decided to return to the city which was again experiencing settled times.

On 16 June, 1857 Hudson escorted the Jones family and others back to Ningbo where he commenced an independent missionary work.

21

A Romantic Interlude

Maria's Aunt and Uncle Tarn had agreed to their nieces accompanying Miss Aldersey to Ningbo but they remained the girls' legal guardians. Miss Aldersey, having reached sixty years of age was soon to retire and hand the school over to Mrs Bausum, who would then accept the oversight of the Dyer sisters.

Returning to Ningbo, Hudson avoided Miss Aldersey, knowing that she was totally opposed to any romantic relationship between himself and Maria.

When Mary Jones invited Maria to accompany her on a visit to some Chinese homes, Miss Aldersey said, 'No!'

Expressing her dislike of Hudson she ordered the Jones' household to do all they could to keep the young people apart.

The Goughs had a similar visit from Miss Aldersey.

During those months the relationship between the British and Chinese became very tense. The Cantonese in Ningbo became involved in a minor, but serious skirmish with the Portuguese which resulted in the death of many Chinese. Dr Parker gave medical assistance to the injured, but was warned by the British authorities that as Britain was a neutral power at that time he should not do anything to indicate he was taking sides. Dr Parker, however, freely assisted everyone in need. Consequently the locals gave large donations towards hospital improvements.

Hudson, wanting to spend time with Maria, decided to face Miss Aldersey and answer her objections to him. Quickly and precisely she outlined why Maria was not to have any dealings with him.

First, Maria was a minor and all contact with her should be through her guardian, Miss Aldersey. After some questions he elucidated that she was not Maria's guardian, but believed she was acting in accordance with the wishes of the Tarns in England who would never approve of such a relationship. He then suggested that before he asked for formal approval to meet Maria he should know her feelings on the subject, otherwise there was no point in asking for permission.

Miss Aldersey accused him of being a Sabbath breaker and a member of the Exclusive Brethren who had strange theological views. Hudson's reply was unacceptable to her.

However, she admitted that she had dictated Maria's response to his letter and had refused to give her permission to seek advice from her aunt and uncle in England. Then she objected to Hudson's faith which relied upon God to provide for his every need. In the end it was simply that she considered Maria too good for him.

After the interview Hudson knew he had to meet Maria and seek permission to write to her guardians in England. His efforts at first were frustrated, but Maria, distressed by the actions and words of Miss Aldersey wrote to her aunt and uncle revealing her feelings and speaking highly of Hudson. She also unburdened herself about Miss Aldersey's action in preventing her writing to them at an earlier date.

In mid July a Ladies' Prayer Meeting was held in the Jones' home and Maria attended with Mrs Bausum. Hudson was in the attic doing some writing when a sudden downpour of rain prevented the ladies leaving. The arrival of a missionary who wanted to speak with him meant that he came downstairs for the short interview.

Mr Jones told Maria that Hudson was present and asked if she would speak to him. This was just what Maria had wanted for some time—to speak with Hudson; and with Mrs Bausum present they met.

He apologized for the difficulties he had caused and asked permission to write to the Tarns seeking their approval for a closer relationship with her.

Maria was delighted and said that she had already written and then divulged that her letter to him had been dictated by Miss Aldersey, causing her great distress. After a short prayer Hudson left the two ladies with hope in his heart. He immediately wrote to the Tarns:

Mrs Hudson Taylor (née Maria Dyer)

I know that my love is reciprocated, that her first declining my
proposal was compulsory, and I have her full consent...to write.
Gladly therefore do I commit the matter to Him who has the
direction of all events in His hands, and pray that He may guide
you to a right decision—and hope you may be led either to sanction
our union, or to permit Miss M. D. to act for herself in the matter
as the Lord may lead her...'

During this period of romantic turmoil Hudson worked hard. Living at his Bridge Street home, he continued his hectic preaching timetable with John Jones and assisted the many who were in physical distress because of the civil war and disturbances with the foreign powers.

When Miss Aldersey heard that Maria had met Hudson she was furious with everyone concerned. Maria was called to give an explanation for meeting someone of whom she did not approve—someone who was a nobody. Then she sent a blunt letter to Hudson

> Sir, when you favoured me with a call you remarked...that you were not aware...that [Miss MD] was a minor...however you might be at a loss to know the right course of action through want of information as to the priorities which obtain at home, but now Sir you have placed yourself in a very different position with respect to my estimate of your character as a *man* and still more as a *Christian* for, when you *did* know from me that Miss M.D. was a minor you went to [the Ladies' House] determining if possible to take advantage of her youth to induce her to trample on the prohibition which had been laid on her...I now beg to say that if you persist in continuing your addresses, not awaiting the permission of Miss M. D.'s aunt I shall be constrained to take steps of a more formidable character than you are prepared to meet....I am Sir yours faithfully....'

Hudson showed the letter to his friends and Maria who complained bitterly to her aunt and uncle of Miss Aldersey's actions.

Mrs Bausum thought it wise to speak to Hudson and discover his theological position. After the discussion she went away very satisfied and Maria wrote to her aunt and uncle informing them of the result of Mrs Bausum's talk with Hudson.

Rumours circulated that if Hudson had a degree and was an ordained missionary Miss Aldersey would have a different opinion.

All the time he and John Jones worked on, never once neglecting their missionary endeavours. About this time Hudson met Nyi, a business man, who came to hear him preach. At the conclusion of the meeting Nyi rose to his feet and said, 'I have long sought the Truth, as did my father before me, but without finding it....In Confucianism, Buddhism, Taoism, I have found no rest; but I do find rest in what we have heard tonight. Henceforward I am a believer in Jesus.'

These words encouraged Hudson especially when Nyi accompanied him on some of his preaching trips in the city. On one such occasion

Nyi asked, 'How long have you had the Glad Tidings in England?' To this Hudson replied several hundred years.

'What,' exclaimed Nyi, 'several hundred years! Is it possible that you have known about Jesus so long, and only now have come to tell us? My father sought the truth for more than twenty years, and died without finding it. Oh, why did you not come sooner?'

When his good friend, Mr Quarterman caught smallpox it was Hudson who cared for him during his last days, ignoring the danger of infection.

And all the time Miss Aldersey kept up her tirade against him greatly upsetting Maria. Mrs Bausum decided that it was time to inform the Tarns of the truth about the situation and wrote, speaking highly of Hudson's godliness.

Hudson fell ill and during his high fever hallucinated that Maria was with him. In his dream, Maria touched his hand and forehead causing his headache to subside. He heard her say that he was hers and she was his.

He then heard that Miss Aldersey planned to have Maria moved to Shanghai. She moved Maria to Mrs Bausum's home not realising that Hudson was there to discuss the delicate situation with Mrs Bausum. He was invited inside but told to wait as Maria was in the house, but before she had the opportunity to get Maria out of the way she entered. In Mrs Bausum's presence, when he divulged Miss Aldersey's plans, Maria said she would not go.

When Mrs Bausum told Miss Aldersey of the meeting she was furious and encouraged some local, unattached men to show an interest in Maria.

This upset Hudson who believed that everyone should be made aware of their close friendship.

In mid November some friends who were soon to leave Ningbo agreed to arrange for the lovers to meet. With Hudson at their home they sent a note to Maria asking her to come over at once. They knew that she would come and if she met Hudson then all the better.

At first Maria was frightened fearing that Miss Aldersey would find out, but for six hours she and Hudson were able to sit and talk. Many years later Hudson said, 'We sat side by side on the sofa, her hand clasped in mine.' At the time he confided, 'She gave me a sweet kiss.'

At that meeting it was decided to make the announcement of a formal betrothal. Such would keep all of Miss Aldersey's suitors at arm's length and everyone would respect the relationship that existed between them.

It was Hudson who took the news to Miss Aldersey, who listened without much comment. She was however, furious!

Mr Russel, in whose home Miss Aldersey was living, told Hudson that he was not to visit his home again. Miss Aldersey then wrote to Maria demanding that she pack her bags and come and live with her.

In the midst of the animosity shown by Miss Aldersey and her supporters a letter from the Tarns arrived, and Maria read the words she longed to receive: we 'fully approve of your choice.' Hudson's letter contained the words, we 'entirely approve of the proposed union.'

They also wrote that they were very disappointed with the behaviour of Miss Aldersey. They had sought information concerning Hudson and were delighted with what they heard.

Upon reading the long awaited letter Maria wrote to Hudson:

> My own dear,
> I have received a letter from my Aunt, and she tells me that she and my Uncle certainly have not heard anything to induce them "to oppose my wishes".
> Do come quickly.
>
> Your own loving
> Maria.

Bridge Street was still being used as a home, chapel and food dispensary for those needing help. The times were hard and Hudson and the Jones family were reduced to poverty.

So destitute were they that another missionary bought a dictionary and some soap from them, insisting they repurchase their property when finance arrived.

They had no money to meet the burial cost of a man who had died at the hospital, nor had they any to provide food for the hungry poor. There was no oil for the lamps, and the mail was not expected for another week. As their need was very real, they prayed in faith, knowing that Jehovah would not forget them!

Monday was the day when the coffers would be totally empty. But the mail arrived a week earlier than expected and a letter from William Berger contained a credit note for $214 for John Jones. Hudson again rejoiced in the truth of the words written on the scrolls at Bridge Street: 'Ebenezer'—'Hitherto has the Lord helped us', and 'Jehovah Jireh'—'the Lord will provide.'

The destitute people did not go without, but John and Hudson decided they were going beyond God's purposes for them, otherwise money would be given for the work. Thus, for a time they cut back on their charitable activities.

Christmas 1857 was a very happy time for Maria and Hudson, and the rest of their friends. After Christmas, when everyone gathered for a pleasant afternoon, an incident occurred which showed that fun was part of the Ningbo missionary life:

> One evening the young people were seated round a table playing a game that required their hands to be hidden beneath it. To his surprise Mr Nevius received an unexpected squeeze. Guessing at once it was a case of mistaken identity, and enjoying the situation he returned the pressure with interest. In a moment Maria…discovered her mistake, but when she would have withdrawn her hand it was held fast by its captor's strong fingers. Not until flushed cheeks, and almost tearful eyes warned him that the joke had gone far enough did he release her. Those were days when to laugh was easy!

On 28 December, the British bombardment of Canton commenced resulting in the death of many citizens.

But this didn't prevent arrangements being made for the marriage which was set for the day when Maria turned twenty one.

At that time Hudson and John Jones were almost penniless. With just one eighth of a penny left they decided to sell an old iron stove as scrap metal. With the money they would be able to buy food for the table—and Maria was expected for tea.

But the men were unable to reach the foundry and returned home to have just a cup of cocoa. With a childlike faith they prayed, 'Give us *this day* our daily bread!'

Mary Jones had enough food in the house to give the children their evening meal, but nothing remained for the adults, including Maria who was expected to arrive very soon.

Suddenly without warning, there was a knock on the door. The mail had arrived and in one letter was a credit note for forty pounds from Mr Berger. Hudson wrote to him explaining their joy: 'Oh! Dear Brother, you do not know how tears of joy filled our eyes at the sight. We thanked God, borrowed a few cash and got something to eat, then went and got this bill cashed—and thus God fed us.'

Never again was he placed in such extreme poverty, but only a little money was left after meeting all their expenses. When he told Maria of their situation he gave her the opportunity of turning down the forthcoming marriage to such a poverty stricken missionary. To that suggestion she replied, 'I have been left an orphan and God has been my Father all these years. Do you think I shall be afraid of trusting Him now?'

On 20 January, 1858 Hudson, dressed in his Chinese best, and Maria dressed in a grey silk gown and wedding veil, took their vows.

Miss Aldersey didn't attend the wedding, but those present enjoyed themselves after the ceremony at the home of Mr and Mrs Way, good friends of them both.

Six weeks later Hudson wrote: 'Oh, to be married to the one you do love, and love most tenderly and devotedly...that is bliss beyond the power of words to express or imagination to conceive. There is no disappointment there. And every day as it shows more of the mind of your Beloved, when you have such a treasure as mine, makes you only more proud, more happy, more humbly thankful to the Giver of all good for this best of earthly gifts.'

Hudson and Maria were very happy!

22

Difficult Times

Much was to happen between 20 January, 1858 and 19 July, 1860 when Hudson, Maria and their little daughter, Grace Dyer Taylor, boarded the *Jubilee* to return to England.

After a honeymoon which was punctuated by work obligations, Hudson and Maria decided to make their home near East Lake, about nine miles from Ningbo. However, Maria contracted typhoid fever and required medical care. No sooner had they returned to the Parkers than Hudson fell ill.

When their health improved they returned to Bridge Street, making their home in the attic above the downstairs rooms which were used as a school and chapel.

Hudson started work, making the room a home for Maria. He wrote home asking his mother to send out some cutlery, a tablecloth, crockery and even some wine glasses. Later on, when Maria was ill he asked for a bed to replace the hard bamboo slats on which they slept as he was of the opinion that a new soft bed would benefit his dear wife. He also thanked his mother for the cookbook which he said resulted in an improvement in Maria's housekeeping skills.

It was a happy time when Maria discovered that she was pregnant, but joy turned to sadness when the baby was born prematurely and died.

When an harmonium arrived from England Maria was delighted. It proved a wonderful aid during worship.

Maria again fell pregnant and a daughter, whom they named Grace Dyer was born on 31 July, 1859. During the latter months of her second pregnancy the city was in turmoil. As there was a danger of an uprising against the foreign citizens, Hudson kept a boat in the canal beside his house just in case they had to make a hurried escape. As the danger increased he sent Maria to the Parkers' home.

During this time, open warfare broke out between Britain (and other European nations and the USA) and China, which resulted in the Treaty of Tientsin which was signed on 26 June, 1858. It was some time later, in October, 1860 that the Emperor, when faced by the British fleet was forced to ratify the Treaty.

This Treaty opened up China to increased trade, but as far as missions were concerned, the country was open to the preaching of the gospel. One Treaty clause assured freedom to all who wished to travel into China's interior, giving assurances that Christianity would be tolerated. This meant that 'persons teaching it [Christianity] or professing it should alike be entitled to the protection of the Chinese authorities.'

Tragically the traffic in opium received legal status.

The Taiping rebels caused much destruction with their internal disputes and warfare with the Imperial forces which resulted in the death of hundreds of thousands of citizens. Before Hudson and Maria left Ningbo it was feared that the rebels would reach the city, which they did for a short time in 1861.

Sickness plagued the missionary community and Hudson and Maria suffered with the rest.

Miss Aldersey commenced speaking with Maria and Hudson, but showed her distaste of Mrs Bausum's part in their romance by influencing the Presbyterians who ran the school to dismiss Mrs Bausum. Consequently she returned to England with her children.

Hudson contacted Miss Stacey of Tottenham asking if she would arrange for her ladies' group to help Mrs Bausum with an annual gift of one hundred and sixty pounds. Years later she returned as a missionary.

John and Mary Jones found their health deteriorating—Mary was suffering from TB and John from kidney stones. To make matters worse the promised CES support didn't eventuate and before long the CES collapsed!

The living conditions experienced by the missionaries who lived in the Chinese suburbs were appalling. When Hudson went to help the Goughs who had just lost a baby, he spent the night watching over the little body to protect it from the rats that thrived in the area.

The terrible 'coolie' trade continued where Chinese were tricked into travelling overseas in the hope of making their fortune before returning home.

Of this cruel trade Hudson wrote: it 'is rapidly assuming all the features of the African Slave Trade!!! The poor men are stolen and kidnapped, bought and sold just like cattle, packed in the hold, not indeed as slaves used to be, but in such numbers that a fearful amount die from disease...'

Now that they were married Maria helped him in his outreach and medical work. She accompanied him on visits to outlying villages, talking to the women who eagerly gathered to hear her speak. After that she taught children in the Bridge Street School for six or seven hours each day.

Later Hudson arranged for Miss Stacey and her friends to send out printing equipment which she used to publish large quantities of literature for distribution to the Chinese.

There were times when finances ran very low, but generally support from friends in England ensured that their work continued. Whenever Hudson had more than he needed, he helped other needy missionaries. On several occasions, when he had an excess of funds, he wrote to his mother asking for some books for the Jones' children and a microscope for their father. He also sent twenty pounds to his grandmother and thirty pounds to his parents when they suffered a financial loss.

William Berger faithfully supported his work, and on one occasion wrote asking if he could help by supporting a native evangelist or rent a property in the country.

The CES had failed to support Dr Parker, who survived on gifts from local and overseas friends. He charged private patients and used any excess money to support the six ward hospital. In one year he examined fourteen thousand patients.

Hudson devoted a lot of time and effort helping those addicted to opium and in many cases he had success, especially with those who turned to Christ.

There was the continual round of street preaching during the week and the Sunday services at Bridge Street. He also gave instruction to those preparing for baptism.

Hudson assisted Dr Parker in his new hospital, doing what he could to take some of the load off the overworked man. He enjoyed many hours visiting in-patients, explaining the way of life.

Again and again he faced the nagging question concerning his lack of formal qualifications. This had created problems when courting Maria and while everything had settled down, there was still the problem of his acceptance by his well qualified brethren.

Believing that in the future he might have the opportunity to complete his medical studies, he began to do some dissecting. The smell of the dead bodies was putrid and when the burning of incense didn't control the foul odour he wrote to his mother asking her to send out some little china 'cutty pipes such as I used to smoke.' He hoped the smell of the smoke mixed with the sweet smelling burning incense coils would overcome the nauseous smell of the dead bodies on his dissecting table.

He and Mr Jones developed a new policy towards missionary endeavour. The Treaty of Tientsin opened the inland to the missionaries, and while some immediately took advantage of the new regulations to move inland, they believed they should first consolidate the work at Bridge Street, building up a strong congregation to support missionary work. They also began training selected Chinese nationals for missionary work.

Hudson wanted more foreign and Chinese missionaries, who would settle in the inland provinces and preach the gospel. When they established a congregation they were to move on to another area and do the same. He was now developing a workable plan for the evangelization of China.

The men saw some fruit for their labours. An ex-Buddhist, Ni, often accompanied John Jones on his preaching tours. Tsiu was the third of the Chinese to be baptized, followed by a basket maker, Feng Neng-gui. Tragically many Chinese who supported the missionaries suffered persecution from their ungodly countrymen.

The end of 1859 saw the first death of one of the little flock at Bridge Street. Old Dzing, who had been converted in the last year of his life, spent his time speaking of his Lord to those to whom he peddled his wares.

After catching bronchitis he was admitted to Dr Parker's hospital where his Christian friends showed him great kindness. As his earthly life drew to an end and his breathing became more difficult, he said many times, 'If only the Lord would take me!'

Hudson replied, 'He will just as soon as you are ready. He loves you far better than we do, and will not let you suffer a moment longer than he sees needful. He wants you to trust Him, and to be willing to wait His time. Will you show your love for Him by being patient, even in this?'

Before old Dzing died, he said, 'Tomorrow is the Lord's day, but I shall not be able to join in worship.' Hudson reminded him that the Lord was always near His people.

'Yes it is so,' replied Dzing. 'He has promised never to leave me, and He never has; and soon He will take me to Himself.'

On Sunday his friends read to him passages of the Scripture, including Psalm 23. He was greatly encouraged when he heard them sing some hymns, including the words:

> Who are these in white array,
> Brighter than the noonday sun?

When he heard those words he whispered, 'I shall soon shine too, but all the praise will belong to Jesus.'

In his last moments one of the Christians by his side asked, 'What do you want, Elder Brother?'

He opened his old eyes and with a smile replied, 'Jehovah my Shepherd.' And with those words he fell asleep in Christ his Saviour.

On 25 August, 1859 Mrs Parker fell ill. In order for Dr Parker to devote his time to his wife, Hudson took over the supervision of the hospital and patients. When she failed to respond to the treatment and passed away to be with her Lord and Saviour, Dr Parker decided to return to England, leaving Hudson in charge of the hospital. This resulted in a sick John Jones being made responsible for the Bridge Street chapel. Hudson found that he had to help John which meant he was very much overworked. With funds in short supply he had to depend upon the Church congregation for financial and physical help and to uphold him in prayer.

The day came when the hospital cook approached Hudson with the news that the last bag of rice had been opened. Soon there would be no more food!

Trusting in the Lord to answer his prayer for help, he replied, 'Then, the Lord's time for helping must be close at hand.'

Before the pantry was emptied, a letter containing fifty pounds arrived from the ever faithful William Berger, who explained that his father had died, leaving him his estate. Being wealthy, he wished to use the money in the Lord's work and thus fifty pounds was enclosed for Hudson to use as he saw fit. The only requirement was that he be told how the money was used and if there was a need for more help.

In March, 1860 Hudson wrote to his mother about his health:

> ...I should inform you that for some time past it has been failing, and that I have felt more and more unequal to my work. It is a very difficult thing to be one's own physician...I think however...that my chest is affected with tubercular disease...attacks of ague caused by going about at night to see [seriously ill patients]...have more or less injured my spleen...I may be able to continue the work...Or it may be that I may be sent home for a season...Dearly I should love to see you...

On 24 April he added, 'I do not feel well enough to write much...I am just now quite laid aside from hepatitis and jaundice...I feel my health is so thoroughly breaking down that I may suffer much if spared to reach or pass through another summer.'

He didn't have time to rest as he and members of other missions saw many Chinese responding to the preaching of the gospel. Bridge Street had a congregation of twenty-one members and in February, 1860 he was instructing twelve new candidates for baptism. The revival that was spreading throughout many European countries and North America was being felt in China. Hudson was preaching several times each day and with his other duties he wrote: 'My work already exceeds my time and strength.'

Much of his work involved treating people injured by the rebels who were fighting their way towards Ningbo. One young man had been shot through the neck, but by careful treatment he saved his life and when he responded to the gospel, Hudson had further reason for rejoicing. Many of those he treated were in a terrible physical condition. One man was so injured that he had to amputate both of his legs. Within a fortnight his wounds were fully healed.

Overworked and sick Hudson faced the reality that he needed a break. But how could he leave when there was no one well enough to take his place? He wrote home to his parents and friends wondering if they knew any men and women, filled with the Holy Spirit who were willing to step out in faith and come to Ningbo where there was a work to do. This call for help indirectly led to James Meadows offering himself for missionary service.

With his health deteriorating, Hudson was advised by local physicians to return to England. It was even suggested that his health was so poor that he might never return to China.

When the decision was made for the family to return to England a godly Chinese Christian, Wang Lae-djün volunteered to accompany them in order to help him translate some hymns and books into Chinese.

On 19 July, 1860, the *Jubilee* left port on her way to England with the Taylor family on board—William Berger having underwritten the cost of the fare!

23

A Trip Home

If Hudson and Maria expected a pleasant journey across the high seas they soon discovered their mistake. Little Grace was teething and her crying upset the rough ship's captain who ordered Hudson to keep her quiet. Maria was so seasick that Lae-djün found himself taking care of Grace.

Sleep was difficult because of seasickness and the bedbugs that had made their home in the cabin. For entertainment Hudson caught and recorded his catch of about forty each day.

Later he and Maria became ill with dysentery. When Maria's condition worsened he knew that a special diet was essential, but the captain refused. Using a tin cup, he secretly cooked some arrowroot over a candle or a small spirit lamp. Occasionally he screwed up pieces of paper and setting them alight boiled his brew which worked wonders and by the time they reached the Cape of Good Hope Maria had recovered, and much to their joy was pregnant!

His relationship with the captain deteriorated even further when one Sunday he refused to translate for him when some Chinese traders drew alongside wanting to sell fresh supplies. He faithfully upheld the sanctity of the Lord's Day by refusing to become involved in Sunday trading. Consequently Captain Jones went out of his way to make the remainder of the trip as unpleasant as possible.

On board there were two other passengers—the captain's wife who was terrified of her husband, and an insane woman he kept tied up, usually to the mast. Many times he cruelly whipped her for no apparent reason.

The first mate, however, was a Christian and despite the captain's godlessness he allowed Hudson to conduct worship services for the crew.

Having decided that he would pray for five missionaries to replace him at Ningbo, he and Lae-djün spent much time before the throne of grace seeking the blessing of God upon missionary work in China.

Any spare time was spent with some of the crew studying the Scriptures, and translating hymns for the Ningbo Christians. Hudson also conceived a plan to produce a Romanized translation of the New Testament in the Ningbo dialect.

With improving health and England drawing close the spirits of all on board became brighter, especially Hudson who would meet family and friends again and introduce them all to his family and Chinese companion.

After just over four months at sea, on 20 November 1860 the *Jubilee* dropped anchor off Gravesend. Following last minute packing, the unconventional looking group disembarked to catch the train to London where they made their way to Amelia and Benjamin Broomhall's home.

Home at last

As they walked along the street of an upper class London suburb, the Broomhall neighbours must have wondered who were the strangers walking by.

Lae-djün led the way, dressed in his national clothing, pigtail flopping behind and carrying a little girl dressed in unfashionable clothing. Beside him walked Maria, also dressed in clothing well out of fashion and to any who watched they probably appeared to be husband and wife. Behind them walked Hudson, a smaller man, also dressed in Chinese clothing.

When they reached 63 Westbourne Grove the door was flung open and a wonderful reunion took place. Even Louisa was there. They were expected, as Dr Parker had brought the news of Hudson's health and the necessary preparations had been made to receive the weary travellers.

Out came new clothing and soon Maria and Grace were dressed in stylish clothes. A return trip to the customs' house was necessary to collect their possessions, and a letter was written to Barnsley saying they would be visiting before the end of the year.

A doctor's visit resulted in the suggestion that Hudson should be well enough to return to China within a year! This meant there was little time in which to accomplish much.

Despite the dissolving of the CES due to the shortage of funds, his friend George Pearse was ready to support his New Testament translation project. A meeting with the faithful William Berger resulted in a lifelong friendship and his welcome encouragement for the Ningbo New Testament.

Translation work

The agreement with the Religious Tract Society to publish a new Ningbo hymnal was followed by the Bible Society's approval of the New Testament translation. This meant a lot of effort as he also wanted it to contain the useful cross references.

In this work he was ably assisted by Lae-djün and Rev. Frederick Gough of the Church Missionary Society, who was home from Ningbo on furlough.

He and Mr Gough were close friends from their days in Ningbo when his wife, Mary, had supported Maria against the tirades of Miss Aldersey. On another occasion he had guarded the body of their dead child from rats.

The work took years and at times there was considerable friction between the two translators as Hudson wanted to hasten the job, but Mr Gough, a scholar by nature, was inclined to a slower, more careful approach. The Chinese characters had to be analysed for their sounds and then translated into the Romanized script, while there was a continual reference to the original Greek, ensuring an accurate translation.

Often the Bible Society considered terminating the work, but the influence of George Pearse guaranteed their continued support.

As Hudson intended recommencing his medical studies a house was rented at 1 Beaumont St, East End, which was near the London Hospital. It was here that Herbert was born on 3 April, 1861.

East End was a working class, outer London suburb through which the Thames River flowed. At that time the river was little more than a sewerage trench into which was thrown all the rubbish and filth from the surrounding houses.

Drunkenness was common and life was almost unbearable due to the stench from animal hides, manure, alcohol, human waste and the filth found in the streets and drains. In fact the hospital was situated in an area described as 'noisy, crowded...where even the children never seemed to go to bed.'

This was not an ideal place for the quietness needed for study and translation work.

There were many interruptions, and on one occasion they were called to give assistance to a Chinese who had been stabbed.

Mr Gough and Lae-djün returned home as they couldn't stand the sight of the man's stomach hanging out of his body. As Hudson repaired the wound he spoke of Christ. When the pain became unbearable he administered the new medical miracle—chloroform.

With a map of China on the wall, the translation continued, supported by the prayers of his friends, that God might bless their labours and raise up godly men and women to preach the gospel in that pagan nation.

Medical Studies

Hudson now appreciated the value of medicine in his missionary work because the many Chinese awaiting medical attention made up a congregation. Even though he had often scorned academic qualifications he now thanked God for the opportunity to recommence his studies at London Hospital which hadn't changed much since his previous student days.

There were some trained nurses who showed kindness and care to the sick and dying, but there was little understanding of the cause of disease, and epidemics continued to kill thousands. Chloroform, though available, was not widely used.

In July 1861 he was welcomed back by many who had been his teachers and after paying his fees commenced studies and practical work, to become a surgeon.

He was now involved in translation work, writing, visiting and studying for examinations. During those days he was often down to his last penny, not knowing from whence the food for the next meal would come, only trusting in God to provide.

On one occasion when food was in short supply, Mrs Jones' sister arrived with a parcel of supplies including 'a goose, a duck, and a fowl.'

Another time Hudson had put aside the money needed to pay the rent. The day before the landlord called to collect his money he discovered he was one pound short. He'd made a mistake in his counting and would soon face a landlord who was known for his anger. That night he took his need to the Lord, knowing that God would make the necessary provision. All day he waited for the landlord to knock and create a scene, but he didn't come.

The next morning a sovereign arrived in the mail which was all he needed to pay the rent.

In answer to prayer, he was granted credit for medical work done in China, and on 29 July 1862 he became a Fellow of the Royal College of Surgeons and now could add to his name, 'FRCS'.

He enrolled in the diploma course—'Licentiate of Midwifery'— knowing that the skills he learned would be very useful on the mission field where so many women died during and after childbirth. He passed the examinations for this qualification in October, 1862 and now became Dr J. Hudson Taylor, FRCS, LM(RCS) England.

With the pressure of examinations out of the way he devoted more time to translation work and promoting missionary interest in China.

He prayed fervently for the day when five new missionaries would join Mr Jones in Ningbo.

Mr William Berger

Now that Hudson was home his friendship with William Berger grew stronger each day. He became one of Hudson's closest friends, prayer supporter, financial patron and later treasurer of the China Inland Mission.

They had met briefly before Hudson sailed for China, but now their relationship became very close. He had faithfully supported Hudson's endeavours to take the gospel to that needy land.

Mr Berger was a very rich Christian, being the owner of a well managed starch factory. With his financial ability he gave Hudson much wise advice. At Saint Hill, he lived in a mansion, surrounded by lawns and gardens. So concerned was he about the spiritual well-being of his workers that he had a chapel built at his factory and another at his home. Many times Hudson conducted worship at both places.

Charles Judd wrote of Mr Berger: 'He was one of the finest men I ever met in my life...He was a man that God had clearly raised up for the work...At one time he gave up his business and retired but later took (it) up again simply that he might support missionary work...his wife, was as good as he was...a loving bright energetic little body, but she did everything so quietly that you seldom knew she had done it... She prayed incessantly. (And her husband) a godly prayerful man who really walked with God (and) loved his Bible...He had been the means of the conversion of a number of people in the neighbourhood.'

Mrs Berger invited the Taylor family to their home soon after their return to England and there cemented a lifelong friendship; Mrs Berger treating Maria as a daughter. The two men spent many hours discussing the needs of China and praying for guidance as they formulated plans for the future.

James Meadows

Hudson's prayer for missionaries was made known, with the result that the doors of heaven were stormed with requests for help for Mr Jones.

When Hudson's father spoke to a friend of the need, Mr Bell replied that he knew of just the person, James Meadows, who had been converted several years beforehand.

He approached James, asking him, 'James, I have a job for you to do. Will you do it?'

To this question James replied 'What job?' He answered, 'Go to China.'

James said, 'I will go,' but asked for time to pray about it. He fasted and went into his workshop and prayed, and was reassured of his decision.

Nearly half a century later he wrote of his decision '...I have never regretted from that day to this that I acted upon it.'

In October, 1861, twenty six year old, James Meadows, who was betrothed to Martha, joined the family group at 1 Beaumont Street, with a view to becoming a missionary in Ningbo.

Years later he wrote his impressions:

> The first thing that struck me about Mr Taylor, was his utter indifference about his uncomfortable and poverty-stricken surroundings. His cook, who was the family washerman as well, was a Chinaman [Wang Lae-djun]...everything about the rooms, beds and linen looked..."seedy". Scarcely a dozen hot coals in the

firegrate and it was bitterly cold too. The crockery was all odds and ends and the cutlery at sixes and sevens!

But none of these things moved our dear brother Mr. Taylor. Even his personal appearance struck me as being very untidy for a man in his position, the bottoms of his trousers were bespattered with mud....The next thing I was struck with was the gentle earnest piety of Mr Taylor and dear Mr Gough....I found that the good man was in poverty himself and had no means nor money to send me out to China! I had come all the way from Yorkshire to London and had left my weekly earnings which enabled me to live in greater comfort than that in which I found dear Mr and Mrs Taylor were living!...His strong, yet quiet faith in the promises of Scripture, his implicit confidence in God, this it was which compelled submission on my part to whatever he proposed for me.

He had a dear affectionate friend in the person of Mr. Wm Thos Berger—a wealthy man...

Hudson found James to be a man after his own heart and immediately realised that he was the first of the five to be called of God for missionary work in Ningbo.

James collected his possessions and returned to an overcrowded Beaumont Street, to commence his training. Soon after, a second house was rented to accommodate everyone.

As funds were not available to send him and Martha to China, Hudson wrote to his parents asking if they would start making some collections to meet the expenses involved.

This proved unnecessary as the sailing ship Challenger was ready to sail for China and Mr Berger was told that a cabin was available for any missionaries he knew. He at once told Hudson and with a gift of money from Mr Berger the costs were well covered.

James immediately returned to Barnsley, married Martha, and gathered their few possessions together in readiness to leave.

Quickly Hudson and Maria purchased what they knew the couple would need: 'For James they had bought a cap, a carpet-bag, an overcoat, a suit of black cloth and one of light material, a dozen collars, two dozen shirts, drawers, hose, umbrellas, etc. For Martha, stockings, gloves, nightcaps, shawl and scarf, stays, bonnet, etc. The cabin furnishing included bedding, sheeting, towelling, chair, washstand, looking glass and toilet set, lamps, candlestick and matches, hammer, nails and screws.'

Martha and James, a 'Scripture Reader', were farewelled by their friends and relatives in Barnsley and boarded the ship which sailed on 8 January, 1862, little knowing what lay before them! James left England acknowledging Hudson as his overseer and professing total dependence upon God.

About that time a weekly Saturday prayer meeting commenced at 1 Beaumont Street, for the missionaries and their work in China, especially that being undertaken in Ningbo. This prayer meeting spread world wide and continued for well over one hundred years.

Martha and James sailed into a war zone, where the Taiping rebels were about to invade Ningbo. However, they were repelled by the European forces and when terms for peace were offered, the rebels fired shots through the rigging of the Allied ships, announcing a bounty of a hundred dollars for every dead Westerner.

The Allied forces ordered a force of several hundred soldiers to attack thousands of armed Taiping warriors. On 10 May, 1862 the British Captain Dew launched a surprise attack to retake Ningbo. He reported to his Vice Admiral that the warships pounded the walls and area where the rebels were encamped—and this at point blank range, 'which was replied to with much spirit from guns and small arms…[By noon] having silenced the guns and knocked down the battlements, exposing the top of the wall…where I intended to scale, *I ceased firing and went to dinner.*'

James Meadows couldn't speak the dialect and was unable to talk with people. This upset him: 'I have just got up from my knees. I have been weeping at the feet of Jesus because I cannot learn the dialect quick enough. Tens of thousands of souls are perishing all around me, and I cannot tell them about the Saviour…'

He and Martha found it uncomfortable mixing with the well educated missionaries and his lack of education meant they were not readily accepted by the other missionaries.

Martha, who felt particularly out of place, wrote to Hudson's mother expressing her sadness: 'It is well for me that Mrs Jones is homely and condescends to persons of low estate, else I should be most miserable, not being able to enter into the conversation of the ladies at Ningbo.'

James found that his Methodist background and infant baptism, meant that he was not welcomed by Mr Lord (who was caring for the Bridge Street assembly) at the Lord's Table.

He set to work at Bridge Street with the small Christian community, doing all he could to help them with their physical and spiritual needs. Dr Parker (who had remarried) and a sick John Jones gave him all the help and guidance they could, but generally he did as he saw fit.

Life in Ningbo was very precarious. On 17 December 1862 the infant son of Dr and Mrs Parker died. Mr Jones' health was so bad that his family planned to return to England.

Then Dr Parker had a fatal accident. The honour in which he was held by the Chinese and European population was shown by the huge crowds that gathered for his funeral on 4 February 1863.

Two days later, the Jones family sailed for England, but news was received that John had died on 4 May.

In April 1863 James fell ill with chicken pox and again Martha, now in her eighth month of pregnancy moved in with Mrs Parker. Mr Lord visited James each day as he was confined to bed. During this time, James studied the Scriptures which prepared him for the difficult days ahead.

In June, a son was born and the Meadows rejoiced. However the work amongst the professing Christians was disappointing as many returned to their old ways and the congregations almost died.

When the rain began to fall, James took his family home to Bridge Street arriving there on 1 September. Without warning Martha fell ill and died three days later. Writing to Hudson, he said that during the night he heard Martha call his name:

> I was frightened that something was wrong and ran immediately for the doctor, with all my might. The doctor came with me immediately, but, oh, my dear Brother, my beloved wife was dead before we could reach her…she has entered into peace, she is at rest in her bed, and because, Lord, you have done it, I will be silent, you shall find no murmurings in my heart at your ways….

Because of the sudden costs involved with a funeral and a wet nurse, James was penniless—so much so that he could not afford the cost of sending a letter to Hudson. When he eventually did, he said that he was often dependent upon his old servant woman for food. Finally, he was forced to sell Martha's possessions to make ends meet.

Hudson immediately sent funds to him and his situation improved. With Mrs William Parker caring for the baby he gave more time to language studies and evangelistic work.

Dr John Parker, who replaced his brother, often accompanied him on preaching trips into the countryside, but James was tired, homesick and lonely. He longed for Hudson's return and wrote of his terrible circumstances:

In my walks through the city I meet with some horrid sights, some heart-rending scenes...the poor beggars and refugees...When I consider these poor creatures...homeless, destitute...contending daily with starvation...disease and...Death, I say to myself, "Why in the world is Mr Taylor staying there making books, while thousands are perishing to whom he might administer medicine both to their souls and bodies?"

Jean Notman

When Mrs Lord wrote indicating she needed help with her work amongst the Chinese women, the Taylors and others prayed with greater fervour. Mrs Lord conducted a school and much of her time was occupied with that work. Help would free her to spend more time with the Chinese women.

George Pearse suggested a Miss Jean Notman who wished to become involved in the faith work, and it was decided that if she was suitable she could leave immediately.

Jean indicated that she was willing and an outfit of clothing and equipment were put together at once.

The expenses were met by Mr Berger, Miss Stacey and others and on 19 December, 1864 she sailed for Ningbo, sharing a cabin with four women and an *amah*, all of whom were Christians.

The first sign of problems came when, dissatisfied with sharing a cabin, she transferred to a more comfortable one, and sent the account to Hudson.

In Ningbo she helped Mrs Lord, but resigned soon after and married a local.

Another Volunteer—Stephan Barchet

Stephan Barchet, a German who had come to England to enjoy the social life visited Hudson in 1864 following his conversion.

He had been given a copy of the small booklet *The Lord's Dealing with George Müller* which he left in his room without reading.

In London, he visited a friend, and together they enjoyed the sights and the social life. After several days away he returned to find his friend dead on the apartment floor. On his way home he asked himself the question: 'Where should I be now if I had died like that?'

When safely home in his room he prayed for mercy from God and searched the Scriptures for the answer to his problem of sin. He also read the story of George Müller which the Holy Spirit used to bring him to saving faith in Christ.

After a visit to Hudson, he became convinced of his call to the Chinese mission field, and commenced the study of the language and medicine.

In March, 1865, there came news of the availability of two free passages to China on the new ship *Corea*.

But who would go? The offer was made to Stephan Barchet and another young man, Richard Truelove, who had also been studying with a view to mission work in China. Both men were very excited and although it meant Stephan would not continue with his medical studies he agreed to leave at once. At Coborn Street residence which had been rented in order to accommodate everyone, both men rejoiced in their decision, dressing up in Chinese clothes.

Hudson and Mr Berger visited a West End congregation that was offering to support Stephan, who would soon be working with James in Ningbo. This was a farewell gathering and to their surprise they found themselves with a group of people who in their poverty were willing to undertake Stephan's total support. Hudson spoke to the gathered Christians and what they heard and saw had a marked effect upon Mr Berger. Filled with shame that he had so much and yet was not doing all he could to support the work of Christ's Church, he said that, by God's grace, in future he'd do much more, even one hundred times more than he had done in the past.

Richard Truelove proved to be a disappointment. After failing to board the ship with Stephan and being lost for a time, he eventually caught up with the ship before it left England.

All went well until *Corea* reached the Bay of Biscay, where they found a deserted ship containing a valuable cargo of coal. The captain decided to tow it back to England so his employers could claim their prize.

Richard Truelove, who had been very seasick, rejoiced when he again set foot on English soil. Stephan was then given the unpleasant job of telling Hudson that Richard would not be going to China.

This very much upset Hudson, not just because a free passage and outfitting expenses would be lost, but one less missionary would be on his way to Ningbo.

George Crombie had been living with the Taylor family, studying for the Ningbo mission and it was suggested that he should replace

Truelove. George had been engaged to Anne Skinner for four years and expected to be married before leaving.

When Maria put the proposition to him he asked for an hour to pray and make his decision.

During his time of prayer Anne took him aside and quietly said, 'Go! And show that you love the cause of God more than me.'

The ship's captain and owner agreed to the change of passenger and in the short time available, George had his clothing made. On 12 April, 1865 he and Stephan commenced their long journey to China.

Before the ship sailed Hudson, Stephan, George and others gathered for prayer, committing the two young men to the God of all grace. They also prayed that Anne would soon have a passage to China, a suitable escort appointed and funds given to provide her with all that she needed.

George Crombie was so certain that God would answer their prayer, that when he sent mail back to England from the Canary Islands he posted no letter to Anne as he believed she would already be sailing to China.

In fact she had left England just two weeks after George. People were well aware of the sacrifice both she and George had made and consequently money was readily given to meet the cost of her outfit and goods needed in China. She was provided with 'the usual iron bedstead, bedding, table and chairs and looking-glass for the cabin, a swimming belt, cutlery, crockery—and baby linen.'

On 24 July, 1865 George and Stephan were met by a rejoicing James Meadows. In September Anne disembarked, and her marriage took place in Ningbo on 1 October where there was much rejoicing amongst the sixty men and women who made up the growing Bridge Street congregation.

The fifth person to leave for China in answer to Hudson's prayers was John Stevenson and his wife Anne. He was a Scot who had spent considerable time with Hudson, learning the language and giving valuable assistance in many tasks, including the New Testament translation. He and his wife sailed for China on 3 October, 1865.

With five new missionaries working in Ningbo, Hudson could devote more time to complete the revision of the Ningbo New Testament, and develop his plans for China.

24

A New Direction

The newly rented house in Coborn Street, not far from 1 Beaumont Street proved successful in accommodating those whose interviews were successful. There they commenced the study of Chinese.

As Hudson's reputation grew he was invited to address many Christian groups where he stressed the spiritual need of the Chinese people. Consequently he met men and women who believed they were called to serve on that missionfield.

On 16 April, 1865 when he prayed at a worship service attended by Dowager Lady Radstock, she was so touched by his sincerity that she asked one of the leaders, 'Who was that little man who prayed so earnestly? I should like to be introduced to him.'

As a result he was invited to her home at Langley Park, Norfolk where he won the support of many wealthy, influential families.

On one visit to address some meetings that had been arranged by Lady Beauchamp, the sister of Lord Radstock and her husband Sir Thomas, he witnessed an example of their Christian liberality.

He never appealed for financial support, but the Christian couple, whose business had left them short of ready money, wanted to give. They prayed over the matter and concluded, 'Why not trust the Lord about the conservatories, and contribute the amount almost due for insurance?'

Langley Park had widespread greenhouses and being near the coast suffered from severe winter storms. However, they decided to give their insurance money to Hudson for his work in China. Many years later he heard the story of the gift. Several months after making the contribution a violent storm swept in from the coast severely damaging other properties in the area. But, by the grace of God the storms passed their extensive glass conservatories.

Often Hudson visited this loving family where he addressed meetings and played with the children who loved to hear his exciting stories of life in China and on the high seas.

Many years later, Rev. Sir Montagu Beauchamp, who gave thirty years service to the CIM, recalled with much pleasure the days when Hudson—'the pigtail and chopsticks' man—visited their home.

Hudson was also busy preparing articles for the 'Baptist Magazine', but the material was returned with the suggestion that they be published in book form as a way to generate interest in the Ningbo mission.

As he wrote, his vision for China expanded. He formulated plans for a bolder work, but he was tired, overworked and his faith was being put to the test.

At Coborn Street he observed the many applicants for missionary work living in peace and harmony, despite coming from a variety of church and social backgrounds. He asked himself, 'Why should this not be the same in China?'

He believed that Chinese congregations could, when strong enough, send out and support native colporteurs and preachers with missionaries.

He also prayed that soon he would return to China with additional missionaries to take up the work he had left. And all the time he heard the call of inland China to come and preach the glorious gospel of salvation.

Prayer and discussions with those close to him created a spiritual turmoil. Monetary gifts were arriving at 1 Beaumont Street, where accurate records were kept of income and expenditure.

In June, 1865 he first used the name 'China Mission' instead of 'Ningpo Mission' and later that month Mr Berger, when auditing some accounts wrote 'J. H. Taylor in account with China Inland Mission.'

The plans of both men were being crystallized—they were most concerned about inland China!

All the time Hudson's thoughts turned to those millions in China who faced a Christless eternity because he was not using his influence and skills to promote a new missionary organisation. His troubled mind and inability to step out in faith distressed him greatly and he found sleep difficult. He knew what was needed, but questioned whether he could accept the responsibility for sending raw recruits into inland provinces, depending totally upon God for the supply of all their needs. And yet Chinese were dying without Christ while he thought about a project.

His friends were so concerned about his health that Mr George Pearse invited him to stay with him at Brighton for a weekend. There he was to preach at the evening service, but following the morning worship he quietly strolled along the sandflats.

There he cried out to the One who heard and answered prayers—the God who had cared for him in so many difficult experiences. He realized that his life must be one of total surrender to the God he loved.

He thought: 'Well, if God gives us a band of men for inland China, and they go, and all die of starvation even, they will only be taken straight to heaven; and if one heathen soul is saved, would it not be well worth while?'

Of that 'Brighton experience' Hudson later wrote:

> On Sunday, June 25, 1865, unable to bear the sight of a congregation of a thousand or more Christian people rejoicing in their own security, while millions were perishing for lack of knowledge, I wandered out on the sands alone, in great spiritual agony; and there the Lord conquered my unbelief, and I surrendered myself to God for this service. I told Him that all the responsibility as to issues and consequences must rest with Him; that as His servant it was mine to obey and to follow Him—His, to direct, to care for, and to guide me and those who might labour with me. Need I say that peace at once flowed into my burdened heart? There and then I asked Him for twenty-four fellow workers, two for each of eleven inland provinces which were without a missionary, and two for Mongolia; and writing the petition on the margin of the Bible I had with me, I returned home...'

Elsewhere he wrote: 'How restfully I turned away from the shore when this was done. The conflict was all ended. Peace and gladness filled my soul. I felt almost like flying up that hill by the station to Mr Pearse's house. And how did I sleep that night! My dear wife thought that Brighton had done wonders for me; and so it had.'

In his Bible Hudson wrote the words: 'Prayed for twenty-four willing, skilful labourers, Brighton, June 25/65.'

On 27 June, he accompanied Mr Pearse to a bank where they opened an account in the name of 'China Inland Mission' (CIM). A deposit of ten pounds was made and from that time receipts were issued in that name.

China: Its Spiritual Need and Claims

Hudson now devoted much time to the finalization of his book. Because of his Brighton experience the manuscript now spoke not just of Ningbo, but the whole of China.

This meant that he and Maria spent much time in the sitting-room researching up to date information.

The week days were very busy organizing the structure of the new CIM. This meant meetings with those who would become involved in the Mission and the screening of volunteers for mission service. Those accepted as spiritually, medically and temperamentally qualified commenced a study of the land and its language.

A continual round of meetings were attended where he delivered speeches concerning China's needs. This meant that Sunday became the day on which much writing was done. He and Maria never neglected the Lord's Day worship, but when they had time they retired to the sitting-room where he dictated while Maria wrote.

Later in life he commented about those hours of writing: 'Every sentence was steeped in prayer. It grew up while we were writing— I walking up and down the room and Maria seated at the table.'

His words are as true today as in 1865 when he wrote of Christians: 'Instead of honouring him with the first-fruits of our time and substance, are we not content to offer him the fragments that remain after our own supposed need is met?'

Reminding his readers that Christ had commanded his people to evangelize the world he described China—its history and people, always stressing the huge population that inhabited that largely unknown land. Assuming that the nation's population was two hundred and fifty million:

> How immense is this number! what mind can grasp it.... If a railway train could go twelve hours without stopping to relieve the driver or to take in water, and were to travel the twelve hours at the uniform rate of thirty miles an hour it would make three hundred and sixty

miles a day. Seven years and a half of such travel, without a single day's intermission would not accomplish *one* million miles; and had a train commenced to travel at this rate on the first day of the Christian era and continued every day since…it would not yet have accomplished 250 million miles.…Were the subjects of the court of Peking marshalled in single file, allowing one yard between man and man, they would encircle the globe more than seven times at its equator. Were they to march past the spectator at the rate of thirty miles a day, they would move on and on, day after day, week after week, month after month; and over seventeen years and a quarter would elapse before the last individual passed by.

He followed this by saying that if all those Protestant Chinese confessing faith in Christ were to line up, they would pass by in less than one day.

Then came a brief outline of the work and success of the various Chinese missions.

Sprinkled throughout the writing were photos of places and people in China plus a retelling of many incidents he faced during those difficult early days.

He retold the story of Peter, asking:

My reader, would you not say that these men were verily guilty of this poor Chinaman's death, in that they had the means of saving him at hand, but would not use them? Surely they were! And yet, pause ere you give your judgment against them, lest a greater than Nathan say, "You are the man".…The Lord Jesus commands *you*, my brother, and *you* my sister. "Go," says He, "Go into *all* the world, and preach the Gospel to *every* creature." Will you say to Him, "No, it is not convenient"?…Ere long "we must all appear before the judgment seat of CHRIST, that everyone may receive the things done in the body." Remember, oh! remember, pray for, labour for, the unevangelized Chinese; or you will sin against your own soul.

He wrote of the roads, the rights given missionaries by the treaties signed and the ripeness of the people for the gospel after years of social upheaval caused by war and opium, and of the gospel and hymns readily available in the Chinese language.

This was followed by a call for labourers to serve with the China Inland Mission.

Stressing that all who laboured with the CIM did so trusting in God to supply their every need he wrote: 'Upon past EBENEZERS we built our JEHOVAH-JIREH. "They that know Thy name will put their trust in Thee.'"

This book called ordinary Christian people, uneducated by worldly standards who were converted in the revivals of the late 1850s, to use their gifts in the Lord's service. The CIM provided such an avenue for service.

When Mr Berger and his wife read the manuscript they were so impressed they agreed to meet the cost of printing three thousand copies, wanting them available for the Mildmay Conference which was to be held just ten days later.

China: Its Spiritual Need and Claims was a paperback book of over one hundred pages, and at lunch on 25 October the first copies were delivered. The following day at the Mildmay Conference Hudson saw eighty two copies of the book sold and many more ordered which meant that a second edition had to be printed in February, 1866 with more to follow.

When the conference concluded he received an invitation to dine with Dowager Lady Radstock who introduced him to more influential people. This was an age when many titled people openly displayed their Christian faith and he was often invited to luncheons with the cream of the upper class. In some circles it became fashionable to be associated with missionary endeavour in the Far East, especially China. Facing people dressed in their elegant evening dress, he spoke of China's desperate spiritual need.

Many of these people openly supported the work of the China Inland Mission for decades with gifts of money and personal service.

As word spread, money began to flow into the newly opened CIM account. Lord Radstock posted a letter to Hudson, containing a gift of one hundred pounds and the suggestion: 'Dear brother, enlarge your desires and ask for one hundred labourers and the Lord will give them to you.'

In the midst of all the rush and hurry, on 29 November, 1865 he was elected a Fellow of the Royal Geographical Society.

The China Inland Mission

Now Hudson and his close friends and advisors—especially Mr and Mrs Berger put some 'leaves on the newly sown CIM tree.'

All working for the CIM acknowledged Hudson as their leader, agreeing to follow his advice. The Mission was responsible for training and outfitting those accepted for service. This meant agreement to continue their studies whilst travelling to China.

All Mission members were to dress and live as the Chinese did, often in depressed areas. The specific aim of missionaries was to preach the gospel throughout the land. Having preached Christ and sown the seed they were to move on leaving the reaping of a harvest to the local church.

The mission would not appeal for money, but pray for the Holy Spirit to open pockets and purses that men and women might freely give support. This meant a total trust in Jehovah to provide for their every need. Nor would there be any borrowing of money. Hudson said, 'It is really just as easy for God to give beforehand; and He much prefers to do so. He is too wise to allow His purposes to be frustrated for lack of a little money…And what does going into debt really mean? It means that God has not supplied your need….If we can only wait right up to the time, God cannot lie, God cannot forget.'

Both male and female missionaries were welcome and no educational or social standards were set. All had to be regenerate men and women, so filled with the Holy Spirit that they could do nothing but work for the salvation of souls.

Men and women of any Protestant church, holding to the fundamentals of the Christian faith, were welcome to apply, with the assurance that as far as possible people of the same theological outlook would work together.

Hudson stressed that he would not live from money donated to the CIM, but that he and his family would cast themselves on the mercy of God to provide for their needs.

He also stressed that the CIM missionaries were to go forward into the unknown interior of China, trusting in Jehovah for protection, not treaties or British gunboats.

Mr Berger accepted responsibility for the Mission in Great Britain, while he cared for the work in China.

Hudson now realised that if his plans for the Mission were to be fulfilled he needed to select a group of missionaries and leave for China as soon as possible.

This meant publicity and prayer that God would raise up men and women for mission service. When he was asked how many he expected to accompany him he replied, 'If the Lord sends money for three or four, three or four will go; but if He provides for sixteen, we shall take it as His indication that sixteen are to sail at this time.'

He was relieved of his part in the final stages of the New Testament revision and after almost four and a half years of work, Mr Gough and Rev. George Moule finished the translation.

Publicity for a new mission

As the Perth Conference was one of the better known Christian meetings Hudson decided to attend in an effort to gain permission to speak. With about two thousand delegates from the major denominations present he knew that an address on behalf of the spiritual needs of China would publicise the CIM.

The programme had been arranged and when he asked if he might address the gathering he was told by the Convener: 'My dear sir, surely you mistake the character of the Conference! These meetings are for spiritual edification!'

Undeterred he handed several letters of introduction to those responsible for the organization and pleaded for an opportunity to tell them how two thousand Chinese would die during the time of one session. He also mentioned his close friend and worker, the well known and respected William Burns.

Consequently he was given twenty minutes to speak of China's spiritual need. That evening, 5 September, 1865 he was called upon to pray, which he did with great solemnity.

The next day, following a sermon by the great Free Church minister, Rev. Andrew Bonar, he was called upon to speak. He was almost unknown and as he stepped forward it seemed that he was struck dumb. Then in the midst of a lengthy period of silence he said, 'Let us pray'.

For almost five minutes he poured out his heart to the God he loved and faithfully served.

Then he launched into his address, graphically painting the scene of Peter drowning before an uncaring group of Chinese. He concluded with: 'We want lay men to come out to China, to teach Christ, and to live Christ before the people. Some four months of study will prepare anyone to be a labourer there.'

Those who listened went home to speak of a young missionary, who without any denominational backing had gone to China and was now calling others to follow in his footsteps.

General Sir Alexander Lindsay took him home to hear more. He arranged for other meetings which were announced to the Conference delegates before they left. At those gatherings Hudson spoke of China's situation and spiritual needs. He also told them of the much loved William Burns, and his valuable missionary work.

As news began to circulate about Hudson Taylor and the newly formed CIM, many men and women offered themselves for service in inland China. Soon he found himself exhausted from his many speaking engagements throughout Great Britain.

And this all happened while Hudson was busy organising the departure of John and Anne Stevenson, and George Stott who had come to faith in Christ while recovering from the amputation of a leg due to tuberculosis. He returned to teaching, but the call to service in China was so strong that he resigned saying, 'I do not see those with two legs going, so I must!' This meant extra difficulties arranging for his departure as he had to be supplied with the usual outfit plus spare wooden legs.

On 3 October they left for China.

1865 drew to a close with many prayers of thanksgiving to God for his goodness to the Taylor family and all those associated with the Mission.

The news from Ningbo was encouraging. The spread of the gospel resulted in increased numbers attending worship at Bridge Street, and a letter from George Stott encouraged everyone with the news that the CIM missionaries were moving out from Ningbo: 'On arriving at Ningbo, I had no plan of operation in view; but after consulting with Mr Lord and Brother Crombie, we have determined (DV) to proceed to Fenghua, a town about twenty miles from Ningbo, and if possible pitch our tent there…I intend to plant a school at once…We may have some difficulty in gaining a footing, as there never has been a foreigner living there.'

For the first time, 31 December was designated a day of prayer and fasting—a day of thanksgiving to God for his many blessings, and of petition for the blessing of God upon all who proclaimed Christ—especially to those working with CIM.

Volunteers for service

In England Hudson evaluated almost thirty prospective missionaries for work with the CIM. Some were rejected because of poor health or unsuitability for such a work and several were advised to commence a Christian work in Great Britain. One such person was Tom Barnardo.

The list of those who finally sailed for China was: J. H. Taylor, Maria and their four children, Lewis Nicol and his wife Elizabeth, George Duncan, Josiah Jackson, William Rudland, John Sell, James Williamson, Susan Barnes, Mary Bausum (13 years of age), Emily Blatchley, Mary Bell, Mary Bowyer, Louise Desgraz, Jane Faulding, Jane McLean, Elizabeth Rose (who was to marry James Meadows).

As the prospective missionaries made their way to Coborn Street, Hudson found it necessary to rent the vacant house next door.

It is not possible to comment on all of these people, but several deserve our attention. Elizabeth Rose was a close friend of James Meadows' late wife. He wrote to her proposing marriage. Hudson didn't know the young lady but when his mother spoke of her sweet Christian character he congratulated James on his wise choice.

While working at his forge William Rudland had read a report of Hudson's address to the Perth Conference. Believing God had called him to missionary work in China he asked his Christian employer if he could attend the Mildmay Conference and meet Hudson personally. His boss didn't want to lose a good worker and attended the conference in his place, promising to tell him what had taken place. This he failed to do, and when William talked about China and his wish to accompany Hudson to that part of the world he produced a Chinese book and asked, 'See, this is the language they talk over there! Do you think you could ever learn it?'

William's reply was, 'Has anybody else learned it?'

'A few' replied his employer.

'Then why not I?' William asked.

His friend Annie Macpherson then posted him a copy of *China: Its Spiritual Need and Claims* with the suggestion that he accompany her to the Saturday, Coborn Street, prayer meeting.

When he told his employer of this he said, 'Yes, you must take a day or two, but as sure as you cross this threshold you are on your way to China.'

William joined the CIM and proved himself to be a devoted servant of the Lord Jesus Christ, serving till his death in 1912.

Hudson's reputation and the needs of China spread. Those selected for service by him and Mr Berger, came from a variety of social, educational and church backgrounds, but they were united in the desire to promote the glory of Christ in China. Having common goals they proved they could peacefully live together. They were not required to sign any formal agreement, as both Hudson and Mr Berger agreed that a verbal agreement sealed with the shake of hands was sufficient amongst Christians.

Preparations for Departure

Towards the end of 1865 Maria once again fell seriously ill. Her pregnancy had to be induced with the result that little Jane Dyer Taylor lived only half an hour. However, pregnancy was not the cause of Maria's sickness. She was seriously ill with a common illness—pulmonary tuberculosis. She had been coughing up blood.

Hudson became so convinced that he would lose his wife that he wrote to his parents: 'It is very solemn to feel that all our married happiness may be so near to its close…She is resting happily in Jesus.… Ask grace for me to mean and say, "Thy will be done".'

But God was gracious and spared her life.

He made arrangements for his mother to care for the children and Maria was able to spend some time recuperating at the Bergers.

No date could be set for departure as a suitable ship could not be found. The overland route would be impossible due to costs and the large amount of cargo that accompanied the missionary group.

Hudson and Mr Berger decided to publish an *Occasional Paper* to outline the work of the CIM and publish audited accounts of income and expenditure.

With a need of almost two thousand pounds to cover the expected cost of both travel and outfits, it was decided to make mention of this need. The paper was to go to press on 6 February, the same day that a daily prayer meeting was commenced. This prayer time was from noon till 1 pm and was specifically a time of prayer for God to supply the material needs of the missionaries who would soon depart for China. Till that time only one hundred and seventy pounds had been received to meet these costs.

However, God stirred his people to give and in the first five weeks of 1866 one hundred and seventy pounds was given. By the end of the next five weeks almost two thousand pounds had arrived.

10 March proved to be a day when the mail contained big gifts to the Mission. Lord Radstock sent an envelope containing cheques to the value of two hundred and eleven pounds. In the same mail there was a gift of six hundred and fifty pounds from a Mr Richard Houghton. These amounts were vast sums in an age when a worker could expect

about fifty pounds wages a year. Amounts, large and small flowed in from a variety of sources.

The first *Occasional Paper* which was expected to be published in February was delayed by a fire, with the result that Hudson's mention of the need of finances was well out of date. To Lord Radstock he wrote: 'Before we could get the *Occasional Paper* into circulation stating that £1,500 to £2,000 would be needed...the Lord had sent the whole sum. None can now say the 'Paper' has done it. No! The Lord has done it—His alone is the glory.'

Before the first *Occasional Paper* was distributed Hudson included an insert indicating that the monetary needs of the Mission had been met.

The second *Occasional Paper* carried the story of God's gracious provision of the finances needed for the journey to China.

Many people began asking for CIM money boxes so they could save. As a result Mr Berger paid for all the boxes which were freely given to anyone who wanted one. Photographs of the various missionaries were distributed to encourage people to pray for that person.

By the end of April all that was needed was suitable transport— a ship large enough to accommodate everyone and with a Christian captain.

On 2 May Hudson travelled to Hertfordshire to address a meeting organized by Colonel Puget, Lady Radstock's brother. He had stressed that no offering was to be taken, but at the conclusion of his address, the Colonel stood and, realizing that the audience had been moved by Hudson's words to give generously, suggested an offering would be taken.

Hudson interrupted saying that he was not there to raise money for the CIM, but suggested they go home and if they felt moved by God to give, then their offerings could be sent to the CIM. He stressed that neither he nor the Mission asked for money, but trusted in God to open the wallets and cheque books of those who could afford to give.

That night at supper Colonel Puget commented, 'You made a great mistake, if I may say so. The people were really interested. We might have had a good collection.'

Hudson again explained the policy of the CIM, speaking of the God who supplied all needs.

The next morning the Colonel arrived late for breakfast and it was obvious that he had not slept very well that night. He handed Hudson several donations and then said: 'I felt last evening that you were wrong about the collection, but now I see things differently. Lying awake in the night, as I thought of that stream of souls in China, a thousand every hour going out into the dark, I could only cry, "Lord, what will you have me to do?" I think I have the answer.'

He handed Hudson a cheque for five hundred pounds with the comment, 'If there had been a collection I should have given a five-pound note. This cheque is the result of no small part of the night spent in prayer.'

On 4 May, Hudson received a letter announcing that accommodation was available for everyone on the *Lammermuir*. He packed his bags, left for the shipping agents and paid the five hundred pounds cheque as a deposit on the berths. Then he set off to Coborn Street with the news.

Now the pressure was really on everyone involved in the last minute preparations. People passing Coborn Street could clearly hear the happy group singing psalms and hymns of praise to God as they sewed clothing and did everything necessary to prepare for departure.

Each person gathered their clothing and personal gear while a weary Hudson continued promoting China's spiritual need. He also met with Mr Berger and others to ensure that the Mission ran smoothly even though members and supporters were separated by thousands of miles. God sustained him in this extremely busy period.

30 April saw the first of many farewell meetings held in Josiah Jackson's home in Scotland.

Some people expressed surprise and concern that Hudson was going to China with his family, including four children, when he would serve a good purpose staying in Great Britain to promote the work and remind people of the needs of the missionaries. To those people he responded with: 'We are taking our four little children, and I never need anyone to remind me that they need their breakfast... dinner...supper. And I cannot imagine that our heavenly Father is less able or less willing to remember His children's needs, when he sends them forth to the end of the earth about His business.'

Gifts of money, food and clothing arrived and when the time came for loading their cargo onto the boat, two hundred and sixty eight heavy cases were at dockside, as well as personal baggage.

As the day for departure drew near the missionaries accompanied by friends and relatives made their way to the dock. Hudson and Maria spent the last couple of nights alone in their empty house, sleeping on straw.

Hudson's mother arrived to see the party off, but his father couldn't come. He was too shy, but sent a message: 'I can't mix with strangers— I shall ever pray for you.' While he had no difficulty preaching Christ, enjoying the company of his grandchildren and working with friends, he could not easily mix with strangers. But his heart was with his son who was doing a work he wanted to do years before.

The last item to be loaded was the harmonium.

The 26 May dawned a lovely day. Hudson, now thirty four years old, with his family, fellow missionaries, relatives and friends met on the *Lammermuir* to hold their final prayer meeting.

As the boat was towed out from the docks they sang the hymn: 'Yes, we part, but not for ever.'

The wife of the first officer of the *Lammermuir*, a Mr Brunton who had an unpleasant personality, reported his comments, 'It was a pretty go, they were going to have a whole shipload of missionaries psalm-singing all day long, and he wished he was out of it.'

The last to say goodbye to the ship's company was Tom Barnardo, who in his own small boat farewelled the passing ship off the coast at Gravesend. There he handed over a supply of wine and groceries.

The *Lammermuir* made her way out of British waters to the open sea, commencing the long journey to China.

25

Rough Seas (1866)

The twenty-two *Lammermuir* passengers faced a long four to five months at sea which was to be a time of learning to live together. They looked upon the thirty-four members of the crew as a missionfield to be won to Christ.

Captain Bell was a Christian, who gave permission for services to be held. Several others of the crew were professing Christians, but the majority were hardworking, rough sailors. The first mate was a token member of the Roman Catholic Church, who terrorized the crew with his vile language and physical abuse.

The ship carried dogs, sheep, pigs, geese, ducks and chickens, which were of great interest to everyone, especially the children. No doubt some animals ended up on the dinner table.

All were given the freedom of the ship and allowed to mix with the sailors whose friendship they quickly won. They quickly learned the nautical terminology for parts of the sailing ship and at times helped repair broken equipment.

Life at sea was very pleasant for many weeks, and some days, in strong breezes, the ship covered almost two hundred and fifty miles. Study of Chinese continued, but there was ample time for sunbathing and exercise in the warm climate. On one occasion a very courageous Hudson climbed the ship's highest mast from which he counted ten ships making their way along the coast of Portugal.

Jennie Faulding wrote of those peaceful days:

> We almost live on deck...the sea is so lovely and the air so
> beautiful...the captain makes great pets of the children. The
> sunsets are so lovely and I never saw the moon so bright....There
> is no unpleasantness with anyone on board...and the young men
> don't trouble me in the least...Mr Taylor has a (tin) bath and an
> apparatus by means of which we can get the water in at our cabin
> windows so I enjoy a sea-bath sometimes...

Hudson kept everyone busy in an effort to prevent boredom that could
harm relationships.

Captain Bell's enjoyable, long meals, helped pass the time and gave
an opportunity for passengers and crew to get to know each other.

Hudson, surprised at the variety of delicious meals provided, asked
his mother to keep the news to herself, as he feared that those supporting
the Mission would think their giving was being squandered. However,
he could not resist outlining the menu:

> We began (to-day's dinner) with hare soup and chicken soup. Then
> preserved mutton, minced hare, chicken and ham, with potatoes, and
> turnips followed. Next plum pudding, (bottled) apple pie, (bottled)
> damson pie, (preserved) black-currant tart, (preserved) rhubarb tart.
> Then biscuits and cheese. Lastly dessert: nuts, almonds, Malaya raisins,
> figs. Time occupied at a table, one and three-quarter hours....

An unexpected huge wave caused some excitement when it struck the
port side of the ship, smashing portholes and flooding beds, bedding
and boxes.

Hudson gave medical lectures, and when a pig was slaughtered he
gave an illustrated talk, demonstrating the way in which the heart and
blood circulation worked. When a shark was caught he gave a lecture
on the structure of the eye.

His medical skills were useful with injured sailors who needed attention
and Emily Blatchley had her tooth extracted without anaesthesia.

Hudson devoted much time and skill helping Maria who was
pregnant and suffering from toxaemia, morning sickness and a threatened miscarriage following a fall.

Daily prayer meetings were held as well as the weekly one hour
prayer meeting for the success of the gospel in China.

Prayer and witness to the crew in words and life resulted in the
conversion of many, but some disharmony so grieved the Holy Spirit
that until peace was established blessings were withheld.

The Chinese language class caused problems! The slow learners were jealous of those who found the subject to their liking. When they in turn complained that the slow learners were holding them back, Hudson and Maria commenced extra lessons in an effort to pacify both groups.

This was followed by a dispute over clothing. Josiah Jackson complained that the Presbyterians had received better clothing, while others grumbled that they had not received as many new dresses as others.

The jealousy faded away after a prayer meeting was called to deal with the grievances. As brothers and sisters in Christ, repentance and expressions of sorrow brought the issue to a satisfactory conclusion.

God's blessings fell and there was much rejoicing when they saw a change in the cold, hard heart of Mr Brunton, the vile tempered Roman Catholic, ship's mate. This was an answer to prayer and Elizabeth Rose, who was to marry James Meadows, wrote of the circumstances:

> Every means was used to help him, and again and again requests came from those who were going to converse with him, that they might be prayed for. One night Mr. Sell came running down from the deck at twelve o'clock saying that Mr Brunton had just asked him to go to his cabin and pray with him…but he did not find peace that night, nor for many weeks following.
>
> By the first week in August, matters came to a climax….He was wretched…it seemed a life and death question….On the night of the 3rd, his watch ended at twelve o'clock. Mr. Taylor went just after and had a long conversation with him, those who were up retiring to the stern-cabin for prayer. When Mr. Taylor came down and the answer had not yet been given, he and another continued in prayer till three o'clock. The Bible Class next day was turned into a prayer-meeting, another special meeting was called in the forenoon; and a third would have been held later, but bad weather prevented it….Mr. Taylor again met Mr. Brunton at midnight, in his cabin; and while he was explaining to him the passage, "When I see the blood, I will pass over you," light broke! He saw the plan of salvation; peace and joy took possession of his heart; and he at once poured out his soul to God in praise and prayer—remembering us each one by name, all who were unsaved on board, and his own wife and children….It is impossible to describe the rejoicing of that day!

The good news quickly spread amongst the members of the crew, and they were heard to say to one another, 'If the mate is converted then there is some chance for us.' The mate's conversion was genuine as he took the time to fellowship with Mr Berger and Hudson whenever his ship called in at a nearby port.

Another hard-hearted sailor was almost scalped when he fell from a mast. Hudson was called to give him medical help and as a result of his close call with death he began reading his Bible.

As the ship made her way towards Java there were times of calm seas followed by strong winds causing rough seas. Great care had to be taken in this region, as the ship sailed through unchartered waters, where there were many hidden reefs.

On 23 August the *Lammermuir* dropped anchor near Anjer, a settlement of Chinese and Malays. Here the ship's larder was restocked and mail collected and posted.

Of that enjoyable day ashore Hudson wrote: '...we had tea at the hotel, being waited on by Chinese servants; and then, after resting in the garden and singing some hymns, we went back to the boat, tired out with our long, happy day.'

Many bought small mementos of their stay, while some of the crew bought monkeys and birds as pets.

During this stop-over, Hudson baptized Jane McLean, Elizabeth Rose and Mary Bowyer to prevent criticism from the paedo-baptists if the ceremony was held in China.

Mr Brunton was disappointed that Hudson wouldn't also baptize him. He gave the reason that other newly converted members of the crew would have felt slighted that they were not asked to be involved.

It was expected that with a couple of weeks of good sailing the *Lammermuir* would be dropping anchor in Shanghai.

But this was not to be!

It seemed that when entering the China Sea, Satan made a final attempt to destroy the missionaries who were determined to undermine his kingdom in China.

The ship was making good speed, but on Monday, 10 September, while the crew was busy painting and cleaning to make the ship a credit to all when they reached Shanghai, it was noticed that the barometer was falling.

In the sky above they saw the 'sailor's warning' of dangerous times ahead—the sign of a typhoon. With rising seas the crew quickly tied down everything, ready for the mountainous seas that would soon be pounding the ship.

Hudson called everyone together and there they approached the mercy seat seeking God's protection for all on board.

Like David, who was protected by Jehovah as he walked through the 'valley of the shadow of death', they called upon God who controlled the weather, to place his protective hands about them and bring them safely to Shanghai.

What followed were days of towering seas that washed across the decks of *Lammermuir*, tearing away and washing overboard many fixtures. Some of the crew were seasick and fearful that their end was drawing close. Of this first typhoon Jennie Faulding wrote that it was

> ...fearfully rough, with a wild sea, and the rain descending as if the clouds were coming down bodily; while the raging of the wind made it exceedingly difficult to pass orders. More than once the whole of the watch were nearly washed overboard by the heavy seas that swept our deck...we could only...commend ourselves, and more especially the crew, to God's keeping...dogs, sheep, geese and fowls all got drenched continually and narrowly escaped with their lives. It poured in torrents and the sea came over the poop and got into the saloon till there was hardly a dry place anywhere...It was impossible to sleep in bed...We thought it not impossible that the vessel might be lost, the largest boat was washed away...the sea was very grand but I have no desire to be in another typhoon... I didn't feel frightened but my head ached and it was thoroughly uncomfortable.

Several days later Hudson removed the cause of Jennie's aching face— a tooth was extracted, again without anaesthesia.

The *Lammermuir* had been blown well off course, and instead of passing between Formosa and the coast of China, she passed on the outer side of the island.

But the rough seas were not at an end. Following a day of fine weather the seas again began to rise and the ship was forced to plough its way through the churning surf, with all on deck fearful that she would end up on one of the many shoals in the area.

The *Lammermuir* was forced to tack its way towards Shanghai, which was only a couple of days away in normal sailing conditions. After several days of huge seas, during which one sailor was almost killed the weather began to clear.

On Sunday, 16 September the weather was fine so Hudson conducted worship, thanking God for their deliverance. It was his plan to conduct a communion service in the afternoon as Mr Brunton and another seaman were eager to sit at the Lord's Table with the missionaries. Just as Hudson was about to break the bread, George Duncan and Josiah Jackson stood up and walked out in protest as they believed that neither man was qualified to sit at the Lord's Table.

As their behaviour upset everyone present, Hudson immediately drew them aside to speak to them. After some discussion they realized they should not have set themselves up as judges in the matter and agreed that both sailors were indeed converted and had a right and duty to sit at the Lord's Table with the saints.

During those hours the seas again began to rise and the ship faced the fury of another violent storm. During the prayer meeting that night all present sang some of the great hymns—'Rock of Ages,' 'God our help in ages past,' but often their voices could not be heard above the noise of the howling wind and the waves crashing onto the ship. Hudson knew the situation was perilous as the seas were more violent than ever before. Jennie Faulding wrote:

> Our mainsail was torn to ribbons; the jib-boom and fore, main and mizzen-masts were carried away, and it seemed impossible we should weather it. I am glad to say we were all kept calm, ready for life or death. We were making water fast. The broken masts were hanging over our heads as if by a thread, swinging about fearfully and threatening every moment to fall—which if they had done, the deck or side of the vessel must have been staved in, and we should have gone down in a few minutes....I had the strongest conviction that our lives would not be lost.
>
> William Rudland took up the story: 'All through the storm Mr. Taylor was perfectly calm. When almost at its height the men refused to work any longer. The Captain had advised all to put on life-belts. "She can scarcely hold together two hours", was his verdict. At this juncture he was going to the forecastle, where the men were taking refuge, revolver in hand. Mr. Taylor went up to him. "Don't use force," he said "till everything else has been tried." He then went in quietly and talked to the men, telling them he believed God would bring us through, but everything depended upon the greatest care in navigating the ship, in other words, upon the men themselves. "We will all help," he added; "our lives are in jeopardy as much as yours." The men were completely reassured by his quiet demeanour and friendly reasoning, and the officers, midshipmen, and the rest

of us went to work in earnest at the wreckage, and before long got in the great iron spars that were ramming the side of the ship.

Sunday, 23 September was the first Lord's day on board that could not be kept as a day of rest. The possibility that the ship might founder meant that all able bodies were hard at work keeping the ship sailing.

On Monday the pumps stopped working, but several missionaries successfully carried out repairs. There was about four feet of water in the hold, but two days later this had fallen to about ten inches. With sails repaired and hoisted, the ship was again making good progress towards Shanghai.

Emily Blatchley wrote: '...we in our hearts thanked God for the great deliverance...Though some of the crew met with severe bruising and such like hurts, not one life was lost, and not one limb broken....'

On 30 September the *Lammermuir* dropped anchor. All had reached China safely, and in appreciation of the missionaries' help Captain Bell invited everyone to use the ship's facilities as accommodation for as long as was necessary.

26

A Stay in Shanghai

A foreign ship dropping anchor always created an interest amongst the European community in Shanghai. This ship was special as it needed repair having survived the full fury of several typhoons. Interest waned, however, when it was discovered that the ship contained a load of missionaries.

Hudson, convinced that God would provide suitable accommodation for the members of his Mission, thanked Captain Bell for his kind offer of the ship's cabins for sleeping quarters and went ashore to find suitable housing. He knew that as God had called them all to China, he would also provide living quarters for them. Much prayer had been made seeking God's providential care and he knew God answered the believing prayers of his people.

Mr William Gamble, a friend from his days in Ningbo, and a worker for the American Presbyterian Mission Press had recently purchased a warehouse—a 'go down'—and made it and his own home available to the missionary group. The kind offer was accepted on the condition that he accept payment for the rooms.

After the coolies moved their possessions to the new living quarters everyone set about unpacking, washing, drying and repacking clothes and other property.

While everyone was settling in, Hudson made a quick trip to Ningbo to present James Meadows with his wife to be, Elizabeth Rose. Mary

Bausum accompanied them to be reunited with her mother. Arriving at Bridge Street, the congregation warmly welcomed Hudson home.

His stay was only brief as he had to return to his friends in Shanghai and get them organized to leave for an inland city.

He was accompanied by Mr Tsiu, one of his early converts, who was doing a very fine work evangelizing his people in Ningbo and the surrounding towns. He had grown his fingernails to a length of one and a half inches—a sign that he was not a manual labourer, but a scholar.

Three other Chinese returned with Hudson to help with the day to day work, and teach the local language to the missionaries.

During his absence work was done to make the warehouse liveable. Rooms were divided using some makeshift material, but everything was rather rough. One of the party wrote:

> There is no lack of ventilation, the windows being unglazed, square openings, supplemented by plenty of crevices in the roof. The wind makes noises ghostly enough for any romance; and the rats keep up a perpetual scuffle among our boxes and the loose straw. On windy nights our linen walls are very restless indeed; but there is not much difficulty sleeping after a long day's work.

Jennie Faulding, usually the life of the party wrote humorously: 'Missionary work under the most favourable conditions.'

During their short stay in Shanghai they saw many amazing sights including the great variety of idols in the temples. They noticed the influence of Western lifestyles upon the local Chinese and the wide assortment of goods for sale in the shops. The homes of the well-to-do were surrounded by high walls to keep out unwelcome visitors.

The regular sound of the gong calling people to temple worship reminded the missionaries that they faced a great task in turning the people to Christ.

George Duncan was impressed with the Chinese courtesy: 'They are very quiet and polite with us; far more than many of our countrymen would be with them...I believe...that the only way of reaching the Chinese is to become Christian Chinese, and live like them...We must show them that we come to seek their good and not oppose their customs.'

Everyone was saddened at the sight of a Chinese funeral and the fear the mourners had of the evil spirits supposedly surrounding them. Fireworks were exploded to drive away the demons, while others burned imitation money which they believed would be of use to the departed one in their new world.

Walking was the easiest way to get about, but for payment they could be carried in a wheelbarrow or a sedan chair. The well to do Chinese rode their horses.

Several prominent British Government representatives had their own horse drawn carriages which really set them apart from the common people.

Jennie Faulding expressed the feelings of the group when she wrote: 'I'm glad we are not going to stay in Shanghai—the Chinese here are money-loving…and the English are so worldly and stylish, everyone knows everyone's business. I suppose we are pretty well talked about.'

The missionaries were the subject of whispers and gossip, particularly when they changed into Chinese clothes. This was not the done thing as far as the proud British were concerned!

For the ladies it meant a change of clothing, but the men had to have their forehead shaved and the queue[3] attached.

William Rudland told Mr Berger: 'When we were in Shanghai, every dog was barking at us; but no sooner had we put on the Chinese costume, than the dogs left off…I did not like the dress much at first, but I like it better now…and hope to be spared to wear it for many years to come.'

Lewis Nicol, who later caused so much heartache when he refused to wear the Chinese clothing, wrote: 'The Chinese costume…has been a trial to me; but when I think it is for God and not man, it eases my mind; and that I also vowed to my God when at home, if He sent me to China, by His grace I was to count nothing dear to me but the glory of God and the salvation of souls; and by his grace I hope to spend and be spent for Him.'

Maria knew that it was not just the wearing of clothing that was necessary, but a total change in lifestyle. If Chinese dress was not accompanied by the customs and courtesies they would stand out more than when they wore European clothing. For Maria it meant that she could no longer walk arm in arm with her husband, but would have to walk several paces behind him.

The local papers reporting the arrival of the new members of the CIM referred to the group as the 'pigtail mission'.

Everyone had high expectations that God would bless their endeavours to take the gospel to areas where the name of Christ was unheard.

Hudson saw the work at Ningbo as a good model for what he planned for the CIM. There, the gospel had been preached and a congregation established. After teaching the Chinese the truths of Scripture they in turn moved into new areas where Christ was preached.

Congregations had been established in Shaoxing and Fenghua and these later would be used as bases for further outreach.

Hudson planned to establish his headquarters at Hangzhou, the capital of the adjoining province which would be the first time that European women travelled away from the 'Treaty Ports'. This decision became the subject of much comment and criticism in the European community. He and Maria were convinced that the ladies would do a fine work amongst the Chinese women, a work not open to men.

Before they left on their long boat journey he had to arrange for passports and registration papers.

Hudson hired four good quality junks and the crews necessary to man each boat. The men and women occupied two different junks while the third was used as a kitchen, laundry and sleeping quarters for the Chinese servants. The fourth small junk was hired for John Sell whose continual coughing from bronchitis proved an annoyance to anyone trying to sleep.

On 20 October it was time to say farewell to Shanghai. Some missionary groups gathered for prayer seeking the blessing of God upon the gospel work that was to be carried out. It was with tears that they farewelled the crew of the *Lammermuir*. They had been through so much together, and many sailors owed their salvation to the passengers God had used to bless them.

Before leaving, Hudson baptized Mr Brunton, the ship's mate, and after cleaning the warehouse, he gave Mr Gamble the agreed rent—a hundred dollars.

Captain Bell, who had been presented with a Bible and travelling rug by the grateful Mission members, heard that they had no butter, so he sent them a gift of two pots of butter, a jar of treacle, some cheese and meat. Mr Gamble came to the wharf to say farewell, and as the junks moved away he left the rent money on a seat as a gift to the CIM.

The journey to Hangzhou was a learning experience for everyone on board. Each day Chinese language studies continued and time was set aside for prayers and other spiritual fellowship. The junks stopped at many towns and cities where everyone had an opportunity to mix with the locals and use their newly acquired language.

Along the way Hudson investigated the availability of rental accommodation which could be used if an effort was to be made to establish a Christian congregation. As they travelled they saw the horrific damage done in the civil war. The once great city of Songjiang was in ruins, with three quarters of the population dead from the effects of war. Disease and starvation added to the high death rate.

During the journey each missionary took a Chinese name by which they would be known to the local population. The bright, joyful Jennie Faulding was named Fu Guniang which meant 'Miss Happiness'.

During the journey Hudson's son Bertie fell overboard, but was rescued by the quick action of one on board. This was the cause for much thanksgiving to God.

With practice, everyone became skilled in the use of chopsticks, even when eating rice, the staple diet.

Bickering between some of the party created much heartache, and living in cramped quarters added to the problems. The weather was turning cold and with winter approaching some of the boatmen wanted to return to their homes and prepare for the cold weather. When dysentery broke out, the cramped living conditions caused a drop in morale.

There was much excitement when they again met William Gamble who was accompanied by an English speaking Malay, Mr Wu. He had been travelling to Japan when the typhoon struck—the same typhoon the *Lammermuir* travellers had endured. Faced with death, and knowing the gospel, he had thrown himself on the mercy of Christ for salvation. Arriving in Shanghai he wanted to speak to a missionary and Mr Gamble took him to catch up with Hudson. This meeting took place at Songjiang where Hudson baptized him and preached from the deck of a junk to the crowds gathered on shore.

That meeting was to produce wonderful results in the future.

Several times Hudson and his companions went shooting. He had a shotgun and was able to shoot some birds which proved to be a welcome change of diet.

On 21 November the great city of Hangzhou could be seen. Encircling the city proper was twelve miles of walls and scattered about the countryside were azaleas, magnolias and camellias.

As the water in the canal became shallow the junks came to a stop several miles from the city. Now the party had the same problem as they did when they arrived in Shanghai—where could they find accommodation? Much prayer had been made that God who wonderfully provided accommodation there would do the same in Hangzhou.

The following day, while Hudson and Mr Tsiu searched for a suitable house to rent, Maria called everyone together for prayer, that God would again meet their need.

The two men visited Mr Green of the American Presbyterian Mission and there discovered what they needed. As Mr Green's missionary friend, Mr Kreyer, had rented a property and was in Ningbo collecting his wife, his home was available for them to use during his absence.

The missionaries divided into small groups and with their meagre possessions inconspicuously made their way to the house in which they would stay. To prevent attracting the attention of the locals, all the heavy luggage had been left in Shanghai. This was also necessary until they had somewhere permanent in which to store everything.

Having settled into their new home Hudson and Mr Tsiu began house hunting. Before long they came to No 1 New Lane which was a run down mansion, having about thirty rooms. The building had an upper storey which would provide excellent sleeping quarters.

In discussions with the landlord they discovered that the rent being asked was twenty dollars a month with a two hundred dollar key money payment. However, there were five or six families living in the house who could not be evicted until a month had passed.

Hudson knew that the house was just what he wanted, but he also knew the landlord was taking him down by asking more for the property than it was worth. He concluded negotiations saying the rental being asked was too high and he would look elsewhere for a suitable house. There were no negotiations the next day as it was the Lord's Day and the owner of No 1 New Lane took this to mean that Hudson had found another house. Again there was much prayer for the Lord to bring the negotiations to a satisfactory conclusion.

The following day the landlord appeared and after lengthy discussions a contract was signed—fourteen dollars a month with eighty four dollars key money.

By the time the Kreyers returned to their home the missionaries had moved.

With their new residence, the CIM was well settled in China. Hangzhou, the capital of Zhejiang province was about a hundred and fifty miles from Ningbo and sixty miles from Shaoxing where the Stevensons were labouring. In Fenghua the gospel was also being preached. The work of the CIM was now well under way!

The next day, the unexpected arrival of James Meadows and George Crombie from Ningbo encouraged everyone. Hudson and his two friends then took the opportunity to preach Christ in pagan Hangzhou.

27

Hangzhou—A new start

A new start in a new city in a new province lifted everyone's morale. All were thrilled to know that now the good news was being preached by CIM members in a new part of China. With James Meadows and George Crombie, Hudson visited Xiaoshan where he saw a great opportunity to begin a new work. As Hudson saw this city as God's answer to prayer for a new preaching centre, he rented a suitable house quite cheaply.

He then notified Mr Berger of their whereabouts, the postal address and the banking facilities which were available in order to receive money from England and to maintain communications with the CIM office and supporters in Great Britain.

Number 1 New Lane was a hive of activity with all the work that was necessary to turn the house into a home. Some Chinese carpenters commenced work on the house while the missionaries scrubbed the walls, floors and ceilings and wallpapered wherever possible. Several destroyed walls and ceilings were replaced with wooden frames covered with paper.

The windows were often just holes in the wall through which the cold wind blew. As glass was not available the spaces were covered with white paper which allowed the light to penetrate, but kept out the cold breeze. And it was getting cold as winter was on the way! Heating was primitive compared to what everyone had in England. Brass pots, filled with burning charcoal provided some warmth.

On one of the dining room walls someone wrote two Biblical texts in large letters: *'I must work the works of Him that sent me,'* and *'Even Christ pleased not Himself.'*

Everyone wore their Chinese clothes and lived as did the Chinese. Chopsticks and Chinese food graced the table and gradually European ways were put aside.

Language studies were easier because of the opportunities to mix and speak with the locals. Because of the adoption of Chinese ways the locals looked upon them as friends and showed a willingness to hear what they had to say. Jennie Faulding wrote of the efforts to evangelize the people, especially the families still living at No 1 New Lane:

> It seems something like beginning missionary work. The woman A-lo-sao seems very pleased. I found I was intelligible to her (though unless they talk slowly I cannot understand them very well)....I am so glad for them to have been here...I could not have visited them out of doors...but I go and read and talk to these women every day...[A-lo-sao]...has given up burning incense and says that since we came she has begun to pray to God...As I read they often take up their [tobacco] pipes and have a few whiffs almost choking me with the smoke.

Those who attended Sunday services did so because 'they feel much more at home with us, seeing that we eat rice and dress like themselves.'

In early December, 1866 an encouraging letter arrived from the great missionary William Muirhead who was overjoyed that Hudson had young women with him who were ready to go inland and preach the gospel. He wanted some firsthand information about the CIM and warned him that he was sure to meet opposition.

Hudson was pleased to reply, outlining the structure and aims of the interdenominational CIM. All members were agreed upon the fundamental truths revealed in the Scriptures, but where there were differences concerning church government and baptism each member taught as he understood the Scriptures.

He outlined his plan of total reliance upon God to provide everything needed by all CIM missionaries. He gave the name of the Mission banking company suggesting that any giving could be placed in the Mission account.

As the CIM was ready to move into new areas, Stephan Barchet and Lewis Nicol visited Xiaoshan (about ten miles from Hangzhou) and made final arrangements with the landlord, noting a clause in the rental contract that the missionaries living in his premises would wear Chinese clothing. Hudson saw the possibility of the Nicol family settling in the city.

About that time a gift of one hundred and twenty-six dollars was received from the crew of the *Lammermuir* with an accompanying letter of encouragement written by Mr Brunton.

Another letter arrived from Mr Wu with a gift of money which was the amount needed to rent the house in Xiaoshan.

Before Christmas, 1866, Sunday services attracting congregations of more than fifty were being conducted. The chapel was set up so that the women and men could be seated separately as Chinese custom demanded. Jennie Faulding wrote of those unusual services:

> You would be amused at many things we see; a man nursing an immense dog all through the service; a woman mending a large man's shoes; and another, close by me giving a lesson in the approved style of dressing children's hair, using her thin fingers as a comb. She evidently thought she could do two things at a time, for she certainly listened to what was being said.

Soon the preaching and witness started to bear fruit. Many came to hear the gospel preached on the Lord's Day while others came along to listen to the daily readings of the Scripture. Some attended services because of the kindness shown by the missionaries, while others wanted to hear what was being said in stammering speech about a Christ who died to save sinners.

Reports soon were heard of people disposing of their idols and refusing to burn incense. In the months that followed crowds of almost two hundred attended the services, feasting on the truths they heard. Some were asking for baptism as the sign that they had been converted to the Christian faith.

Jennie Faulding commenced her own work amongst the women which quickly bore fruit. One woman invited her to her home where she found a congregation of about thirty waiting to hear her speak. Following the time of teaching, Jennie was given some tea and cakes and asked to come again. Writing to her parents she spoke of this meeting:

> …the woman next to me said, with an air of satisfaction. "Your clothes are like mine." I am very glad to wear it, though most missionaries

are unwilling to give it a trial; it is certainly an advantage. If I had on English clothes, the women would at first be afraid of me and if I succeeded in winning their confidence, my dress would be the one subject of their thoughts…'

One woman, after hearing Luke's account of the crucifixion said, 'We ought to believe in Jesus.' Jennie's comment on her words were, 'She is a nice old woman…and I believe she would do anything for me. She has a great deal of taunting to endure from her relations for "eating foreign rice" as they call it.'

Hudson did all he could to visit the other members of the CIM, but early in 1867 he went to Ningbo to defend his role in having the Bible Society produce a new version of the New Testament. Many Ningbo missionaries believed he had acted improperly in the matter. They were also under the impression that he was ignorant of Greek and should not have been involved in such an important project.

Hudson's defence was that he could read Biblical Greek and had been assisted by the well-known and respected Rev. Frederick Gough of the Church Missionary Society, a competent Greek scholar who had at one time tutored George Moule at Cambridge University. Instead of condemnation the assembled missionaries heartily thanked Hudson for the work he had undertaken.

In February, 1867 Hudson opened his surgery in Hangzhou. The nearest doctors were at Shanghai and Ningbo which meant that soon his waiting room was overcrowded by people requiring medical attention.

Later Jennie Faulding wrote of the scene at Hudson's surgery:

> Mr Taylor has over two hundred patients daily. People bring their wares and stay near our door, in the hope of getting more custom from the numbers that gather here than they could elsewhere. Sedan chairs with their bearers are generally waiting, to carry those who cannot walk. The evangelist spends most of his time talking to the patients, and Mr. Taylor gives a short address. We have some most hopeful enquirers.

In England, Mr and Mrs Berger had made all the necessary arrangements for John McCarthy, his family and Jane McLean's twin sister Margaret to be outfitted and leave for China.

On 23 February, 1867 they arrived. So busy was Hudson when they walked in, that all he could do was give a wave and shout out a welcome before continuing his address while standing on a table.

Before long John McCarthy was hard at work in the surgery assisting wherever he could.

In England, Mr Berger found life with the CIM very demanding of his time and energy. His home was used to interview prospective missionaries and he found it necessary to use a cottage on his estate to accommodate those who came to be interviewed.

He was responsible for organizing the CIM prayer meetings, the publication of the *Occasional Papers*, keeping accounts, issuing receipts and auditing statements as well as the many other matters that had to be done. He was also responsible for the publicity which ensured financial support for the Mission.

So heavy was his secretarial load that he had to employ a secretary to assist. Yet with all the many duties not once did he miss sending mail to Hudson.

When suitable men or women were accepted by the Mission it was largely Mr and Mrs Berger who organized the necessary outfits, booked passages, furnished the cabins and organized public farewells. Under God they proved very successful in their labours for the Lord Jesus.

Mr and Mrs Berger were the CIM in Great Britain!

In the midst of all the joys and heartbreak in Hangzhou, Christmas, 1886 proved a happy time. Everyone discarded their Chinese clothing and for a short time became British in a foreign land. Out came their British clothing as well as plates and European cutlery. Christmas was enjoyed in the traditional manner. Jennie wrote of the occasion:

> It was quite delightful to be once more in our barbarian dress. Mr. Taylor thought it rather condescending for a Celestial [himself] to consent to sit down at table with such barbarians as we had made ourselves...The pressure of work and of different matters he has to attend to all at the same time, seem sometimes too much for him....Emily and I thought we might as well be English altogether while we were about it, so I did my hair in my old way...and she put on my black silk dress and I the mauve one and we turned out collars and brooches and made ourselves presentable to English eyes once more.

For Christmas dinner Hudson and Maria had arranged a meal of pheasants, venison, fruit pies and good old plum pudding.

However, all was not well in the camp. Dissatisfaction between some members was beginning to raise its head and before long Hudson feared that it would engulf the mission and destroy its effectiveness, giving Satan a victory.

28

Trouble in the Camp

The person responsible for causing disunity was Lewis Nicol, an arrogant man who before the end of 1866 was complaining about wearing Chinese clothes. He disapproved of Hudson's leadership and the plans for the CIM. Then there followed complaints concerning the amount of money given to Mission members. He was furious when he discovered his wife had not received the same amount of money as did the other ladies when they reached China.

George and Adelaide Moule, who had disagreed with Hudson, listened to the complaints of Mr and Mrs Nicol. Then, inviting other members of the CIM to their home they questioned their guests about sleeping arrangements at No 1 New Lane.

Mr Moule and his missionary companions, travelled in hired sedan chairs and dressed in the clothes of the Church of England upper class ministers, believing themselves to be of a superior race to the locals.

Suspecting that Hudson's relationship with the young unmarried women whom he was supposedly chaperoning, was improper, he took him to task.

Hudson immediately held a meeting of his missionaries and after some serious discussion thought the problems had been sorted out. In reality much worse was soon to follow!

When Nicol wrote to England complaining of Hudson and the policy of the CIM, Mr Berger did not believe what he read and forwarded copies of the correspondence to Hudson.

Maria wanted to write to Mr Berger explaining the true situation, but Hudson believed the least said the better.

Early in January, 1867 Lewis Nicol made his way to Xiaoshan to establish himself in the house Hudson had rented with the assistance of James Williamson.

On 25 January he arrived back in Hangzhou with the request that Mr Tsiu return with him and begin work in the newly set up chapel. When he met Mr Nicol, Hudson saw at once that he had broken the agreement he had with the landlord. Nicol was dressed in his British clothes!

The group returned to Xiaoshan and following the chapel opening, Mr Nicol and Mr Tsiu began preaching the Christian faith in the streets. One night, a crowd of Chinese, led by the city magistrate, made their way to the Nicol residence demanding an interview. In response to Mr Tsiu's call, he came downstairs where the crowd of Chinese who had entered the chapel, pushed him around.

He was then ordered to sit before the magistrate who refused to look at his passport.

Mr Nicol suggested they have a cup of tea, but the drunken magistrate refused to drink with a foreigner. James Williamson produced his passport but again the magistrate brushed it aside.

When Mrs Nicol appeared, the magistrate after passing some rude remarks, made his way through the house. He then turned his attention to Mr Tsiu, a Chinese citizen and ordered that he be beaten. Nicol described what happened then:

> Two took hold of him, one by the (bianzi)[4] and another by the feet, and held him down. The two men then began their brutal work of beating him on the thighs whilst lying on his face on the ground, and they gave him six hundred lashes on his bare skin...This done, he then received a hundred lashes on the sides of his (face), fifty on each, with a thing like the sole of a shoe, made of leather.

The magistrate then ordered Nicol and his companions to leave the city.

The following day carrying as much of their belongings as possible, the distressed group arrived in Hangzhou, demanding that Hudson, as head of the CIM, take immediate action against the offending magistrate. Hudson replied by asking who was offended, Mr Tsiu or the CIM?

Mr Nicol's report of the events was not totally truthful, but his companions corrected him in their statements. Hudson then wrote to the British Consul formally complaining of the magistrate's assault of Mr Tsiu.

When this news became well known in Great Britain, the action of the magistrate was the cause of an international incident.

Mr Nicol was greatly offended by the actions of the Xiaoshan Mayor, but Mr Tsui wrote that when he 'was ill-treated by the Mayor of (Xiaoshan), and punished with beating, he thought this truly is not real disgrace: though deeply painful, there is joy in it,' because he considered it a privilege to be counted worthy to suffer for Christ.

When Hudson reminded Mr Nicol of his promise to wear Chinese clothes he was rudely told: 'No, I won't. I will not be bound neck and heel to any man.'

Nicol, dressed in his British clothes, offended those living at No 1 New Lane. Many of the locals who regularly visited the compound refused to come as they were frightened of the newcomer. John Sell sided with him and also began wearing his European clothing. Some of the ladies agreed with their actions.

During this troubled period Mr Nicol continued to write letters of complaint to Mr Berger—letters that were full of untruths. When he received an apology from those who assaulted Mr Tsui, Nicol and his associates returned to Xiaoshan.

At No 1 New Lane Hudson's medical work attracted crowds. He prescribed medicines, opened abscesses and did surgery on the eyes of many patients. There was always great rejoicing when people, almost blind from cataracts, were able to see again.

While awaiting treatment, the patients listened to Mr Tsiu as he explained the Scriptures. Hudson's companions took the opportunity to mix with the waiting people and speak to them of Christ. George Duncan found this difficult, and longed for the day when he could speak the language proficiently.

There was much rejoicing when on 3 February, 1867 Maria gave birth to a daughter.

About this time Wang Lae-djün finished his contract with another missionary group in Ningbo and was invited to Hangzhou to pastor the small, but growing congregation.

The arrival of the McCarthy family and Margaret McLean greatly encouraged everyone, and Hudson found John McCarthy a great help with medical work, particularly as he was seeing as many as one hundred and sixty patients each day.

With some ill-feeling still existing between Mission members, Hudson called a meeting to hopefully solve the disturbing problems.

When he asked for the understanding each had of the agreement to wear Chinese clothing Mr Nicol replied, 'Until we had got the language we should wear English dress for our own protection.' John Sell sided with Nicol in the discussions.

James Williamson understood the agreement as did Hudson: 'I understood according to the views you have expressed,' about the wearing of Chinese clothes and financial arrangements.

Nicol then began spreading a rumour that Hudson had been seen kissing the unmarried ladies. George Moule passed the rumours as facts to friends in London questioning Hudson's morality.

Maria responded by stating that such stories were very much untrue and greatly offended the single women.

In England, Mr Berger hearing the gossip about Hudson wrote: 'I am at a loss to comprehend it as I have a copy of a paper signed by all the sisters.' In their letter the ladies had denied the accusations made against Hudson.

Many in China and England treated the vicious rumours with the contempt they deserved.

New tales

Following the Taiping rebellion and other activities in which European forces had played a part, many Chinese hated foreigners. Rumours began to spread of the supposed gruesome activities of some members of the foreign settlement. In Ningbo in 1866 stories circulated of Chinese being kidnapped by some who worked for foreign ships. These people were supposedly kidnapped at night by having a sack thrown over their head and taken to a ship to be transported to foreign shores to do forced labour.

In Hangzhou stories abounded of locals being drowned in wells, and Hudson heard the story that he poisoned patients at his surgery. Another tale was that he had killed a girl by cutting out her kidneys.

Elsewhere stories circulated about some Europeans who had supposedly killed seven children and salted down their bodies.

As a result the numbers attending Hudson's surgery dropped. Stones were thrown at the compound and there were disturbances by angry Chinese on the roadway outside.

In the midst of all these rumours he remembered that he had brought from England a box of human bones which he intended to use, teaching the Chinese about the human anatomy. If these were found everyone would believe the rumours to be fact. Consequently he had several of his friends quietly remove the box of bones to Ningbo.

Following the throwing of stones at No 1 New Lane, Hudson and members of other missions knew it was time to visit the city officials and restore the peace.

In his Chinese attire of 'a long blue silk robe, confined by a girdle round the waist, and over this, a short jacket of dark brown satin; black satin boots, and a cap with a very broad brim, red tassel, and a gilt button (the mark of literary distinction)', and accompanied by Mr Green and Mr Valentine in their European clothes they set off to visit the prefect. Mr Tsiu had given Hudson plenty of practice in the way of bowing before such an important city official.

The city prefect was not interested in speaking to the missionaries, so he sent word that he was too busy to see them which was viewed by the locals as permission to renew their attacks upon the foreign missionaries. Mr Green, however, said in a voice loud enough to be heard, that they would put the matter into the hands of the British consul.

Immediately the prefect came in and welcomed his visitors, who bowed correctly and when told to sit, sat in the seats for people of lower classes. At once he invited them to take an honourable seat.

They talked and left feeling assured that the citizens would now make them welcome. When matters returned to normal Hudson found his surgery filled with patients and Mr Tsiu and others freely preached the gospel throughout the city.

When the British consul heard of the wise action of the missionaries, he wrote praising them.

The next day the prefect's secretary arrived in his private capacity to look over the premises. After a tour of inspection he left the compound very impressed by what he had seen.

Hudson knew that because of his visit they would be accepted by everyone. Pleased with the success of their labours, but tired and in need of a break he left the city with James Williamson for a couple of days' rest in the countryside.

At Bridge Street, James Meadows witnessed some progress, while in Fenghua the Crombies and Fan Qiseng and his wife worked on. They also had reason for rejoicing because in December, 1866 their first baptism took place.

At Ninggongqiao, Stephan Barchet and one-legged George Stott were working with a small group of faithful Christians. In Shaoxing, John Stevenson saw little progess for his labours. These godly missionaries largely worked independently, wearing their British clothes, as they had not been involved in the promises made by all who had travelled to China on the *Lammermuir*.

Meanwhile, Mr Nicol returned to Xiaoshan, having received from the offending city official gifts of fruit, twenty-two handkerchiefs, cigars, crockery and tokens of repentance. Still refusing to obey the promises he made before leaving England, Hudson tolerated him working and living as he pleased for almost two more years, before terminating his services with CIM. During his time in Xiaoshan he had few friends.

Everyone at No 1 New Lane needed a break so Hudson took his shotgun and spent some time shooting on a nearby lake. John McCarthy spent the day in the surrounding hills and returned to announce that he had discovered just the holiday retreat they all needed. This dilapidated temple in which lived several priests was an ideal place for rest, and with the agreement of the priests Hudson returned with some of the residents of No 1 New Lane to enjoy a stay in the pleasant countryside.

After loading a boat with supplies, he set out for 'Pengshan' with his family and half a dozen others. Here they could enjoy life without all the courtesies and rituals of China. On one of the house doors they were overjoyed to find a tract which had been put there by a woman who heard the gospel while waiting for medical treatment.

Jennie Faulding and Emily Blatchley stayed at Hangzhou and Jennie wrote of the others: '(They have) gone gypsying to what (we) call a fairy spot...in the midst of the hills and flowers, where they can roam about at will....'

Hudson rejoiced when some Chinese were won into Christ's kingdom. Aliang, the cursing laundryman of No 1 New Lane had been brought to saving faith following the faithful witness of Louise Desgraz. She often spoke to him about his sinful cursing, while George Duncan read him the Scriptures as he worked. Aliang often corrected his speech and this raised a question—why should these missionaries come all the way to China, leaving a life of comfort to teach them of the saving work of the Lord Jesus. Before long he confessed his faith in Christ. At once he contacted his brother Liangyong, who, after hearing the gospel explained, also confessed his love of Christ. Both then faithfully served the CIM as evangelists.

Writing home, Jennie Faulding kept her family in England informed of events in China. She wrote of the work being carried out and of the need of more missionaries. Often she outlined their toil amongst the Chinese women and then explained the difficulties she daily faced— the insect bites that made her body itch and the bedroom rats that ate her candles, flowers, books and stockings.

Maria established a school for women where she taught sewing and read the Scriptures as they worked. When she was absent another of the ladies stepped into her place, reading the Scriptures and teaching the class of Christ and the salvation to be found in Him.

The men visited the tea houses where they sipped tea while gossiping the gospel. William Rudland found the Chinese language very difficult to learn and concluded that he was a failure. To help him, Hudson gave him a job with Dengmiao the bookbinder. William became proficient at printing and through his constant conversations with Dengmiao his language skills improved remarkably.

In May 1867 four men and two women were baptized and soon more followed.

With Wang Lae-djün as the new pastor of the congregation numbers attending worship increased and a block of land was purchased on which to build a new chapel. He had intended leaving his wife, a godless, cranky woman behind in Ningbo, but she came along. The united prayer of all who knew Wang resulted in his wife's conversion. She then faithfully assisted him in his new work.

With success in Hangzhou, Hudson began to look for a new city in which to begin a work, but before this eventuated sickness struck the camp.

Stephan Barchet had smallpox, but was on the way to recovery. However the disease was very contagious and the next to become ill was John Sell. He had come to Hangzhou to escort his wife-to-be, Jane McLean and her bridesmaid back to Ningbo for the wedding. When it was thought he was recovering, he suffered a burst blood vessel and died within two hours. Then Josiah Jackson fell ill with the same disease, but recovered.

Experiencing more disorder from Nicol, Hudson thought it best to call together all Mission members who had dealings with him to sort out their difficulties.

Nicol, discovering that his landlord wanted his house for a relative, asked Hudson to come down to Xiaoshan as he wanted to talk over the problems that existed.

Hudson decided that a time of prayer and fasting would be held, to seek guidance from God on what should be done. In the middle of the prayer meeting in walked Nicol.

On 10 May, with the Hangzhou members of the CIM, discussions commenced. The outcome was that Mr Nicol was proved to be untrustworthy in what he had been saying. A statement was prepared and signed by all present, including Mr Nicol, outlining the principles and practice of the Mission and clearly stating that if they were to succeed in the work, they had to act as a family, bound together in love.[5]

This historic document which was signed by all the missionaries, clearly acknowledged Hudson as the leader of the CIM.

The sudden, unexpected death of John Sell who had sided with the dissenters, filled the hearts of both Mr Nicol and Mr Jackson with fear.

Jackson wrote to Nicol explaining that he wanted nothing more to do with his complaints and lies: 'I have fully made up my mind not to have anything more to do with these unhappy affairs, moreover I believe them to be most wicked and opposed to the teaching of Scripture. I therefore give you clearly to understand that I decline to answer any further communication from you or anyone else....'

To this Nicol responded: 'I want to drop these things. I wish they had never been. Therefore I would say with you, bury them for ever from our sight, and let us live in unity as brethren...May God stay His hand now....'

Then came news that Mrs Nicol was ill. She was pregnant and became Hudson's patient during her pregnancy. In Xiaoshan, he found a new home for Mr Nicol and leased it for ten years in the expectation that he had truly reformed his ways and was a good and faithful member of the CIM. This was not to be!

In England the rumours and letters from the disgruntled Nicol and others were causing problems. Finally Mr Berger arranged a meeting with several officers of the CMS where he defended Hudson so well that the chairman brought the meeting to a conclusion before its time. As the months passed and more information came to light, Hudson's name was cleared and Mr Berger's support for the CIM and Hudson was vindicated. Even George Moule who had contributed greatly to the problems found himself isolated by those who learned the full story.

> Following a visit and discussion with his friend William Gamble, Hudson reached the decision in June, 1867 that the time was ripe to commence a new work. Mr Gamble had said, 'I hope you will not delay any longer to find fields of labour for each of the gentlemen of your party. This is now the most important matter connected with your Mission. Medicine and printing and everything else is of minor importance. I was pleased with Jackson's spirit. I see he is very anxious to find his field...

Hudson had already reached the decision that Josiah Jackson should move out on his own. His rebellious attitude had been forgiven and great things were expected of him.

Accompanied by Mr Tsiu, John McCarthy, George Duncan and two other Chinese, Hudson set out along the Qiantang River to investigate the possibilities of establishing a new centre in the Yanzhou prefecture.

29

A Hard Year Concludes

As the weather was too hot for walking, it was decided to travel by boat using the public transport which went daily between Hangzhou and Fuyang. This meant a night journey, but Hudson saw it as a good learning experience for his companions.

They were allocated an area in front of the foremast on the large eighty ton junk. Soon they were surrounded by Chinese travellers eating meals, talking, laughing and smoking. They were surprised to be with Europeans wearing Chinese clothing and speaking the native language. An even bigger surprise was when they saw them eat their evening meal with chopsticks.

The night started well with a cool breeze and no mosquitoes, but after prayers, sleeping on the solid wooden decking was difficult because only four had room at any time to lie down.

Fuyang was reached in the morning, not by sail, but by men pulling the junk along. The breeze had dropped during the night!

Before disembarking Hudson conducted worship, reading the Scriptures, singing a hymn and preaching.

During the day they all walked about selling books and preaching in the once great city which had suffered death and destruction during the Taiping rebellion.

The second stage of the journey was on a smaller junk where sleeping was head to toe. But this time they were under cover, and how they praised God for his providential care when torrential rain fell and they were dry.

George Duncan found himself beside a prisoner in chains. He was a murderer's accomplice who had been banished from the province and was under escort to the border.

Some passengers were important city officials, while others enjoyed their opium smoking. Here they met a Mr Yu who claimed to be a doctor, moving about, practising his skills. He was an intelligent man and Hudson invited him to teach Mandarin in Hangzhou. Mr Yu accepted the offer and spent some years at No 1 New Lane teaching Mandarin Chinese.

When the men pulling the junk stopped for a smoke, usually of opium, Hudson took the opportunity to preach the gospel.

Nearing Yanzhou, John McCarthy wrote a description of the missionary group:

> First came Mr Duncan, his shaven crown protected by a white straw hat of considerable dimensions, in one hand a palm-leaf fan, and in the other a live cock, which we secured for dinner. Next came Mr. Taylor with other purchases under his arms, and the same head-gear, followed by myself with one thousand cash—the change of a dollar—slung around my neck. Our gowns had once been white, but alas! a week's wear in travelling had changed their colour considerably....

Dressing as the Chinese did won the confidence of the locals who gathered to listen to their words. And all the time Hudson searched for accommodation which could be used when attempting to establish a congregation.

As he had rented some rooms in Yanzhou, it was decided that John McCarthy and Aseng should remain behind for a month or so to learn the local dialect and preach the gospel. One intelligent local was hired to give language lessons.

Hudson set out for Lanxi which he believed would be an ideal spot to start a work that would become a base from which to move into other provinces.

The first difficulty was finding somewhere to stay. Sitting together in a 'restaurant', speaking in the Ningbo dialect they were approached by a man who began speaking to them in the same dialect. He was far from home, homesick and thought he'd discovered people he could call friends. As they talked it became obvious that he thought highly of the missionaries and said he could find the accommodation they needed. He excused himself for a short time and before they had finished their meal returned with the news that they could all sleep in a loft. When they reached the spot they found a shocking mess:

> Dust lay in royal profusion on every hand, broken bedsteads, old oars of boats, baskets of rags and rubbish, bamboo matting, boat-covers, firewood, charcoal, etc, etc, etc, lay in the most indiscriminate profusion…sweeping and dusting followed…but at last we got the room into occupiable condition, had our bedding and mosquito curtains arranged, and began to feel in something like order.

This was to be home for a short time while the gospel was preached and tracts, printed in Lanxi, were being distributed amongst the people.

When Hudson and Dengmiao left to return home, Duncan, Zhumou and Mr Tsiu were left alone to continue the precious gospel work. Hudson visited the CIM missionaries in the area—even the Nicols who were in their new house in Xiaoshan.

For George Duncan this was his first experience of being separated from European company, but he knew that this was why he left England for China. While he didn't see any immediate fruit for the short time he and his friends spent in Lanxi, some years later he met a man who wanted membership in a CIM church. He confessed his faith in Christ, declaring that after he'd heard the gospel preached in Lanxi in 1867 by a foreigner and his Ningbo companion he'd destroyed his idols and commenced to worship the God spoken of by the missionaries—the God who had given His Son to die for sinners.

In Hangzhou the work was progressing and No 2 New Lane was rented to provide sufficient space for all the work being done. More room was needed for worship, a school was being set up and there was news that three more men were about to leave England for China.

In late July Hudson visited as many CIM centres as he could, encouraging the workers and thanking God for their perseverance in stressful times. During July and later, the problems between Mr Nicol and Hudson had taken a back seat.

Meanwhile in England the Bergers found life very busy. They were responsible for looking after the Mission finances; answering the continual supply of correspondence from China and throughout

Great Britain; organizing the distribution of *China: Its Spiritual Need and Claims*; interviewing applicants, organizing everything necessary if they were accepted and have the *Occasional Paper* printed and distributed. This magazine usually consisted of forty or more pages and required a lot of work editing the material received from China. Mr Berger and the supporters of CIM stood firm against the criticism by those who had been fed with lies by Mr Nicol and others.

The financial position of the Mission was excellent, but the criticisms of Hudson and the principles of the CIM proved an irritant to the Bergers.

Maria wrote to them clearly explaining the situation in China and so boosting the confidence of those who promoted the Mission.

During the year Hudson had continued to outline his understanding of the Biblical injunction to be all things to all men in order that some might be saved (1 Corinthians 9:19-23):

> I have never heard of anyone who after having *bona fide* attempted to become a Chinese to the Chinese that he might gain the Chinese, either regretted the step he had taken or decided to abandon the course...We wish to see Christian (Chinese)...We wish to see churches and Christian Chinese presided over by pastors and officers of their own countrymen, worshipping the true God in the land of their fathers, in the costume of their fathers, in their own tongue wherein they were born, and in edifices of a thoroughly Chinese style of architecture....Let us adopt their costume, acquire their language, study to imitate their habits and approximate to their diet as far as health and constitution will allow. Let us live in their houses, making no unnecessary alterations in external appearance....Knives and forks, plates and dishes, cups and saucers, must give place to chopsticks, native spoons and basins (and food).

Hudson's absences proved a heartache to Maria and the children. The letters flowing between the two, gave all the news, and expressed words of love and affection for each other.

During his absences Maria made the decisions, but was always careful not to offend the Chinese in any way. Objections were raised by a servant when William Rudland started treating their sick cow. He had been a farm hand, but was told that a Chinese cow should receive Chinese treatment and medicines.

Calmly Maria rebuked the servant: 'Very well,' she replied, 'when [you] are unwell [you] must not come to Mr Taylor for medicine.' That short rebuke resolved the matter and the cow recovered.

A magistrate, whose daughter Hudson had successfully treated wanted to show his thanks with a gift of goodies—a couple of hundred eggs and many baskets of peaches. Everyone knew Chinese etiquette, so a portion was accepted gratefully and the remainder politely returned. In this there was no insult to the magistrate.

In mid 1867 Jennie Faulding wrote home about life in Hangzhou: 'If I could have fifty lives, I would live them all for poor China…We look before long to have stations far and wide in the interior….' Then she expressed her longing to see her language teacher converted. The letter finished with a PS: 'Excuse grease spots; a rat was scrambling about and in taking up my lamp to send him off some oil dropt out.'

Many Chinese were being converted and by mid year the congregation was fourteen men and four women members, with fifteen applicants for baptism and membership. By October the membership stood at thirty nine (which was why No 2 New Lane was rented).

Now that the Chinese authorities in Zhejiang province had formally recognised Christianity as an approved religion, the climate was right to move safely throughout the cities preaching the Word.

In Ningbo, James Meadows and Josiah Jackson were ready to make their way to the distant city of Taizhou. Jackson, no longer supporting Nicol's rebellious activities, was ready to play his part in extending the work of the CIM.

Hudson wrote to Josiah, encouraging him in the project, even suggesting that he was the one responsible for this forward thinking move.

Money was sent to rent premises for six months plus sufficient to meet living costs. Hudson gave him advice about the careful use of his money and committed the new work to God's care.

On 5 July, 1867 James Meadows, Josiah Jackson and Feng Nenggui, the converted basket-maker arrived at Taizhou, a beautiful city surrounded by hills through which a river flowed. Josiah wore Chinese clothes as he had promised.

He soon saw the advantage of this when the locals gave him the freedom of the city, while James Meadows, dressed in his foreign clothes was the object of abuse. They called him, 'White devil!' and 'Red-haired man!' and generally made his life miserable.

With temporary accommodation in the rooms of a temple Abbot, the carriers were paid off and the missionaries went down town to purchase food. The locals ignored Josiah Jackson and Feng Nenggui but James Meadows found himself the target of stones thrown by the local trouble makers. That night they ate well and thanked God for their safe arrival.

The next day following a visit to the city prefect, Feng returned with the news that they were welcome in the city of Taizhou.

That night they returned to their tiny upstairs room containing three beds and one window in the wall about four metres from the street. Here they thought they could rest safely. But such was not to be!

During the night thieves broke in and stole almost everything they possessed. Josiah Jackson lost equipment valued at about one hundred dollars as well as his shotgun and pistol which he had kept beside him during the night. However, the robbers had somehow missed out on the silver dollars they had with them.

The missionaries complained bitterly to the prefect, who promised to do all he could to catch the criminals.

When James Meadows returned to Ningbo, Mr Jackson and evangelist Feng rented a four roomed house in a busy part of the city. Most of the stolen goods were recovered and the evangelists were well received by the local citizens who considered them as one of themselves because they dressed as they did and ate Chinese food with chopsticks.

When funds ran low and his preaching attracted very few Chinese, Mr Jackson, believing that it was not God's will to be in Taizhou wrote to Hudson for advice and financial help. He needed money to repay a loan so set out for Ningbo to get help from James Meadows.

Hudson, having received a letter from Mr Jackson, wrote a letter of encouragement, urging him to return to his city and get on with the work to which he had been called.

He urged him to consider the great advantages that lay before him. He had no reason to feel defeated, but should continue in the strength of God—learn more of the local dialect and preach the gospel. He also reminded him that God would provide and there was no need to borrow from any man nor trust in the power of a gun or man. Then he indicated that money had been allocated for his use even before he knew of his need, and that James Meadows would add another twenty dollars to cover the losses incurred in the burglary.

Josiah willingly returned to Taizhou a chastened, but wiser man, and was working hard when George Scott arrived towards the end of the year.

Gracie's death

The first summer in Hangzhou was a difficult time. In William Rudland's room his thermometer reached one hundred and two degrees. Covered with prickly heat rash it was decided he should visit George Duncan at Lanxi where it was cooler. When he returned to Hangzhou it was with a 'friend'—a new cow to provide milk for the children!

Sickness was rife at No 1 New Lane—Hudson had conjunctivitis; six year old Herbert had been bitten on the face by a dog and everyone feared hydrophobia; four year old Freddie (Howard) had several convulsions; Maria was very ill, and eight year old Gracie complained of feeling sick and not enjoying her food.

Hudson believed it was time to find some cooler territory for a time. Some Mission members left to visit other CIM centres while the majority packed their bags and set off for the pleasant, cooler region of Pengshan, leaving Lae-djün and James Williamson to care for the New Lane property.

They reached their holiday hideaway on 5 August and made their way to the rooms which they had used on other occasions. Maria was so unwell that she had to be carried to her bed. Several days later when Gracie began complaining of piercing headaches Hudson believed that the cooler weather would overcome her sickness.

As he escorted his children around the temple grounds they came upon a man who was carefully carving an idol.

'Oh, papa, that man does not know Jesus!' Gracie exclaimed. 'He would never make an idol if he knew Jesus. Do tell him about JESUS!'

Hudson described what followed: 'I had not so much faith as to the result of the message as my dear child had; but I stopped and told the man the story of GOD'S great love in the gift of his Son. Then we went on our way; and the man went on making the idol.

'After we had gone a little distance we sat down under the trees, and I said to my dear child, seeing that her heart was burdened, "What shall we sing, Gracie dear?" She said, "Let us have 'Rock of Ages, cleft for me'."

'We sang the hymn, and then I said to her, "Will you pray first?" She did so; and I never heard such a prayer as she offered. She had seen the man making an idol...and she prayed to God on his behalf...I was so moved; my heart was bowed before God; words fail to describe it.'

In the midst of Gracie's sickness Hudson received a cry for help from a sick missionary. While he was absent for some hours Gracie became very much worse, lapsing into unconsciousness.

Despite their prayers, Hudson realised that Gracie would soon be in the arms of her Saviour. He took Maria aside to a secluded spot and there told her what he believed would soon happen. Together the broken-hearted parents gave their little daughter back to the God they loved, asking that He might do what was best in the circumstances.

The family and friends gathered at Gracie's bedside and together sang songs of praise to God and prayed. Hudson knew that when he committed his life to missionary work in China, he also committed the life of his family.

To his friend William Berger he wrote during those trying days:

> I seem to be writing almost from the inner chamber of the King of kings. Surely this is holy ground! I am striving to pen a few lines from beside the couch on which my darling little Gracie lies dying....It was no vain or unintelligent act when, knowing this land, its people and climate, I laid my precious wife and children, with myself, on the altar of consecration for this service. And he whom... we have been seeking to serve...has not left us now. "Ebenezer" and "Jehovah-Jireh" are still precious words."

On 19 August, at ten minutes to nine in the night Gracie took her final breath and was totally at peace.

Later he again wrote to Mr Berger: 'Beloved brother, the Lord has taken our sweet little Gracie to blossom in the purer atmosphere of his own presence. Our hearts bleed; but

> "Above the rest this note shall swell:
> Our JESUS hath done all things well."

Heartbroken, Hudson and Maria arranged for their immediate return to Hangzhou. Owing to the Chinese superstition about death, Gracie's body had to be taken home secretly. Dressed in her fine clothing her body was hidden in a bath which James Williamson hoisted on his broad shoulders and carried to the boats. The oarsmen had no idea what was taking place. Reaching Hangzhou Mr Williamson again carried her body in the bath, reaching New Lane well and truly before anyone was out of bed.

Hudson and Lae-djün went out and bought a new coffin for Gracie's body—a coffin with sides, and bottom six inches thick. All night Lae-djün worked hard preparing the coffin. On Sunday morning, the lid was closed over the body of little Gracie, dressed in her Chinese clothing and holding a single flower in her hands. Some of their Chinese friends said of her death: 'The Gardener came and plucked a rose.'

Wang Lae-djün, who had known Gracie all her life and loved her dearly, spent three weeks polishing and lacquering the coffin, then decorating it with gold leaf until it shone with a great brilliance. Finally the coffin was laid to rest in an above ground tomb in Gracie's rock garden.

It was at that time that six men and one woman stepped ashore in Shanghai. Manpower was available to move away from Hangzhou.

A New Centre—Nanjing!

The time had come for the establishment of a new centre at Nanjing. With Hudson filling the role of CIM administrator the work of church planting fell to those who knew the language well enough to move out on their own. George Duncan had reached that point of maturity.

On 29 August, with two faithful Chinese companions, Li Tianfu and Ling Zhumou, George left the security of Hangzhou and began the boat journey to Nanjing.

Along the way they preached the Word and distributed tracts to interested Chinese. George was thrilled when he found that the people who gathered around could understand his message. At Wuzhen, where Hudson and William Burns had been forced to leave by the salt smugglers, people gathered to hear of Christ's saving work. George was disappointed that he was unable to speak the local dialect.

Reaching Suzhou where they spent ten days, the boatsmen were paid off and a room rented. Then the missionaries checked out the city's banking facilities and accommodation, all of which would be necessary if ever a congregation was to be established. Here, more than ever, George Duncan saw the desperate spiritual plight of the citizens.

On 18 September, the missionaries reached Nanjing. The large city was surrounded by thirty five miles of walls, much of which had been destroyed during the days when the Taiping rebels were a strong political and military force. The city was recovering and was again a centre of commerce, the arts and education.

In order to ensure their safety George and his two companions visited the city prefect to announce their arrival. Politely he invited them to lunch and not knowing that custom demanded a polite refusal with thanks, George accepted the invitation. Immediately runners were sent out to warn those with rooms to rent that the foreigner was not to be given accommodation. Rooms were readily available for George's Chinese companions, but he was obliged to spend the night on the junk. This was a costly exercise and George knew it couldn't continue for long.

In the city was a Drum Tower where the drum was sounded to announce the night watches or in the event of a fire. The priest who controlled the tower had not heard the prefect's warning and opened a loft to George.

Later Hudson described it as 'a miserable little side compartment formed by pieces of matting…where the noise of the drum at various hours of the night, and the multitude of rats which shared his little tent, in no way added to his comfort.' This was George's home for over three weeks.

When it was realized that George and his companions presented no danger, a local carpenter rented him an upstairs room which he shared with his Chinese companions. By listening to the family below George quickly picked up the local dialect.

Later he obtained permission to use half the room below the sleeping quarters as a chapel.

At the end of the room George placed a table and chair which he used as a pulpit and the congregation sat along the wall on benches.

He soon experienced financial difficulties when one bank failed and the other moved out of town. When Hudson tried to transfer money to him the Hangzhou bank returned the funds as they had nowhere to send them.

George, knowing that he could trust God to provide for his every need, took his increasingly desperate situation to the Lord in prayer. In Hangzhou, Hudson and his missionary friends also prayed that God would somehow provide for their friend.

God knew George Duncan's need and had already put into operation a train of events to prove that he ruled the universe to his own glory and for the benefits of the saints. Unexpectedly William Rudland had arrived at Hangzhou and hearing of George's needs volunteered to take some money to his friend.

The first part of the three hundred and twenty mile journey which commenced on 29 October proved easy going. The wind blew briskly in the right direction and soon he was days ahead of what he expected.

Reaching Danyang he decided to travel overland and save several more days. He hired a wheelbarrow, packed it with his belongings and set off for Nanjing.[6]

But the going was hard. The weather was hot, his feet blistered and his body wracked with aches and pains. However, he pushed on, knowing that his friend George Duncan was in need.

Reaching the outskirts of Nanjing, William met and hired a donkey, cared for by two boys. He was an amusing sight as he made his way through the city walls seated on the animal.

Meanwhile George had almost reached the end of his tether. He had been very economical in the use of his finances, but the day had arrived when nothing was left. One morning, after breakfast his servant announced that there was nothing left to eat for dinner and asked what should be done.

'Done?' replied Mr Duncan, 'we must trust in the LORD and do good, so shall we dwell in the land, and verily we shall be fed.'

As he picked up his tracts and books and was about to leave for his day's work his servant offered him a 'gift' of five dollars. George asked whether it was given with the expectation of being returned when some money arrived, but when assured that it truly was a gift he accepted the money with thanks.

The cash lasted several more days, but when it was all spent the servant again asked, 'What is to be done?' He also added that all of his wages were gone and he was now as poor as his master.

Again George urged the man to trust in God and left for another day of gospel witnessing. It was during that day that William Rudland arrived riding a donkey and with money in his pocket.

As evening fell, the servant, seeing his weary master slowly walking home ran to greet him with the words, 'It's all right, sir, it's all right; the dinner is ready. Mr Rudland has come and brought some money.'

George put his hand on the man's shoulder and said, 'Didn't I tell you this morning that it was all right? It is always right to trust in the Lord and do good; so shall we dwell in the land, and verily we shall be fed.'

Nanjing was now secure and would prove a springboard for further missionary activities up the mighty Yangzi.

A riot in Huzhou

Huzhou, a city well known for its wickedness, had been visited by Hudson and George Duncan early in 1867. They were anxiously waiting an opportunity to visit the city a second time. Hudson wanted to get on with the work of church planting, but knew that whoever tried to settle in Huzhou would face many difficulties. He wrote of the inhabitants: 'This city...is inhabited by a people peculiarly turbulent and irritable. Their situation in a district infested by such lawless hordes as the notable Great Lake robbers, may in part account for this. Their own magistrates seem to have but little power over them, and are...afraid of the people whom they nominally rule.'

When James Williamson visited the city he found that accommodation was available and believed that Christian missionaries would be welcomed.

On 18 September Hudson, with James Williamson and their Chinese companions set out for the distant city. Upon arrival they presented themselves to the local officials who made them feel welcome and assisted them in finding suitable accommodation. Liu Jinchen had paid a deposit on the house and they were assured they could take possession in the near future. As everything seemed settled Hudson returned to Hangzhou.

James Williamson and Liu Jinchen lived on a boat and spent the days preaching the gospel and distributing tracts to the many citizens who eagerly gathered to hear the good news.

Some problems arose concerning moving into the house but they were unable to discover the cause. Suddenly James became very ill and before Hudson could come and give medical treatment he also fell ill. As it happened James Williamson had malaria and was sent home, to be replaced by John McCarthy.

Soon there were signs of difficulties. Some local citizens began to parade with placards denouncing the missionaries and foreigners in general. The visit of another missionary, Carl Kreyer, dressed in European clothing did nothing to help the situation.

On 13 November, John McCarthy and his two missionary companions, Yi Zewo and Liu Jinchen found themselves confronted by an angry Chinese mob. As they walked through a narrow lane one drunken man began to abuse them and Christianity. As soon as John McCarthy had passed they grabbed Mr Yi and began to knock him about. John quickly made his way to their boat to get passports and a copy of the treaty which allowed them freedom of travel throughout China. Liu sent for the constable while John McCarthy and Yi confronted the shouting mob.

The ringleader grabbed Yi and began slapping him about the face. When an official arrived he commanded Yi to accompany him. But as he walked along, the crowd attacked him with whatever weapon they could find. When John tried to follow, the gathered crowd prevented him.

Hoping to get some security, Yi called out, demanding that the city prefect provide both protection and justice. But the infuriated crowd pushed John McCarthy out of the way and set upon Yi, knocking him to the ground. The assault continued until he could barely move. Then the mob turned away thinking they had killed him.

John McCarthy, a big man, picked up his friend and carried him back to the junk where he ordered the boatman to return at once to Hangzhou where Hudson would give medical treatment. John sent a brief note with Yi explaining what had happened and declaring he would remain on duty till he heard otherwise.

When Yi reached Hudson he had no idea where John McCarthy and his Chinese companion were to be found. For all he knew they could be dead.

Hudson dragged himself from his sickbed and after attending to Yi, dressed himself in his finest Chinese clothes, and accompanied by Carl Kreyer, set out in sedan chairs to visit the city rulers. They carried a letter of formal complaint to the local governor—a letter which could not be ignored since the mob at Huzhou had violated the treaty made with Britain, which ensured safety for foreigners travelling in China.

Having made their official complaint Hudson returned to his sickbed and Carl set out for Huzhou where he could make some official protest about the events. He took with him a new Chinese companion for John McCarthy.

Soon after Carl Kreyer had departed Liu Jinchen arrived, battered and needing medical treatment. He had been assaulted by the angry mob who had tied a huge weight to his body and were about to throw him in the river, when he had been rescued by some sympathetic Chinese, who quickly put him on a boat which was returning to Hangzhou.

The result of the complaints was that several city officials were made scapegoats for the affair. In fact some innocent officials were punished. The one responsible was a Sing Tsin-si, one of the literati who was high in office and largely untouchable.

Hudson decided to withdraw John McCarthy and to return with Maria and the family—as well as Emily Blatchley and Louise Desgraz and get to the truth of the matter.

They left the security of Hangzhou in a houseboat, while Hudson travelled in a boat capable of more speed. Amongst their belongings he carried his shotgun!

Again there was a problem concerning the house on which a deposit had been paid. The landlord would only allow occupation if there was an official proclamation made in favour of the missionaries, thus guaranteeing his safety.

However, other problems surfaced. It was December, the time when many merchants made their way to Huzhou, a city well known for drunken brawls at that time of the year. It was so dangerous that even mandarins had been dragged from their sedan chairs by drunken mobs and brutally beaten.

Huzhou was not yet a place of safety, so Hudson and his entourage returned home.

Yet all was not in vain as during the riot a barber had supported the missionaries. He had been converted when James Williamson had visited the city. Some time after the riot he visited New Lane searching for more instruction about the Christ he loved.

Early in 1868 John McCarthy went back to Huzhou in order to see if their protests had borne fruit. He was received respectfully, even being permitted to enter the city gates after they had been closed, but he sensed that the city was still a dangerous spot for foreigners.

It was not till 1874 that a second attempt was made to enter the city. This resulted in a second riot.

Social change unwelcome in many quarters

The people behind the Huzhou riot were the influential members of the educated class—the literati. These men were the Confucian, Buddhist and Taoist scholars who through their education had gained positions of importance in government office. They loved the old ways and didn't want any change to a society which was set in its ways. They wanted nothing to do with the steam engine, international trade and the telegraph. Western society was seen as responsible for the vile opium trade and the terrible heartache it was doing to the Chinese way of life.

Christianity also was seen as a danger to the old ways because it threatened the stability of the family. Christians advocated human rights and justice to all groups in society, which undermined the authority of the literati.

Consequently these influential men organized riots against Westerners, despite the Treaty obligations which gave foreigners the right to travel without danger to their lives.

A move in another direction

One-legged George Stott had spent time helping James Meadows in Ningbo and George Crombie at Fenghua. George was a capable missionary, ready to move out to establish a new congregation. After discussions with Hudson the decision was made for him to leave for Wenzhou.

Thus in Ningbo, with James Meadows and two evangelists, Mr Zhu Xingjun and the basket maker Feng Nenggui, he gathered together the necessary equipment and booked their passage on a boat. But when James Meadows became very sick he remained behind.

Mr Zhu, a well educated businessman, who had turned his back on a bright future in the business world to serve Christ, had plenty of contacts in Wenzhou.

Nenggui had been a sickly boy and this continued into his adult life. He was a basket maker who suffered greatly because of his conversion to Christianity, but was a great servant of Christ in the Bridge Street congregation.

These three missionaries were joined by Josiah Jackson at Taizhou and made their way to Wenzhou, arriving there in November. Next came the difficulty of finding suitable accommodation, especially as George Stott still wore his Western clothes. In fact it was mid January, 1868 before they were able to rent a house. Josiah Jackson then returned to his own work.

A busy life

Life was very busy in Hangzhou. It was the centre for activity and there was a continual coming and going. Hudson found his hands full with medical work and visiting his CIM workers whenever he was able. He travelled about using the quickest means of transport which meant travelling night and day.

Correspondence occupied much of his time.

In the midst of all the hustle and bustle there was an answer to prayer when it became obvious that little Freddie (Howard) was converted. He confessed that Jesus had given him a new heart.

The conclusion to a busy year

Towards the end of the year new arrivals were expected from Great Britain—Henry Cordon and his wife, and Henry Reid. William Rudland went to Shanghai to meet the new arrivals and ensure their minds were not poisoned by Lewis Nicol who was back to his trouble-making ways.

As William Rudland was to be married to Mary, Hudson and his family, including the bride to be, also set out for Shanghai to meet the new arrivals and be present for the wedding. After the marriage he intended escorting the newcomers back to Hangzhou.

When the newcomers arrived earlier than expected, William set off for Hangzhou, expecting to arrive there before the wedding party left. But their ships passed and both groups were unaware they had missed each other. Reaching Hangzhou and discovering that the bridal party had left William began the return journey.

Finally they met and on 23 December, 1867 were married.

It was a happy occasion when the missionaries opened gifts from the Bergers and others which had been sent with the newcomers. A tin bath was there for Jennie—a gift from her parents; a mouldy Christmas cake and many other gifts—many spoilt by the long ocean trip—for the others.

Christmas was a very happy occasion for all at New Lane. December 31 saw a big crowd gathered for the annual prayer meeting of praise and thanksgiving. The work of the Mission had survived, and now there was hope for more expansion in the new year.

30

A Taste of Rough Times

1868 saw the start of difficult and even violent times for the CIM and other foreign missions as they attempted to move inland. This was a period when Western powers were flexing their muscles and Great Britain was exercising 'gunboat' diplomacy.

When Europeans began plundering China's treasures all foreigners were considered guilty. Many demanded that all missionaries should be removed from the land.

All was well in Hangzhou where Jennie Faulding conducted a well-run school and a programme of home visitation for the Chinese women. Under the direction of godly Lae-djün the congregation was in good health and growing.

Hudson's life was largely involved with administration. There was continual correspondence with the Bergers and much time spent revising *China: Its Spiritual Need and Claims*. He dictated while Maria wrote his words!

Medical work occupied considerable time, especially as the number of married missionaries increased and he was called upon to deliver babies and care for families in times of sickness.

He also visited the various CIM centres, encouraging and advising as plans were made for future expansion and overseeing the distribution of finances to the various Mission members.

With the accommodation in the New Lane homes overcrowded with newcomers, he realised the time had arrived to open up new centres as the Mission policy dictated.

All were aware of the need of total honesty and wise planning when dealing with citizens in a new area.

On one occasion a servant of another mission had rented premises saying that a shop would be opened. When the landlord found out his premises were to be used as a mission he demanded the missionaries move elsewhere. When this was refused the landlord had the door walled shut and the roof removed.

In Jinhua James Williamson was forced to leave because of anti foreign tensions. The local mandarin had ordered the landlord of the CIM house to be given four hundred lashes because he had rented his house to a 'foreign devil'.

When James visited the landlord in prison he found him 'in a den with a number of criminals…like so many wild beasts in a large cage'. The man's legs were 'fearfully bruised and swollen' from his beatings. In order to save others from a similar assault he decided it was wise to leave the city.

In February, 1868 two new couples arrived in Shanghai, Mr and Mrs C. Judd and Mr and Mrs J. Cardwell, who suffered greatly from 'culture shock'.

Mrs Judd, who wrote of her experiences, was soon dressed in Chinese clothing and aboard a boat ready to leave for Hangzhou. When dinner was ready she and her husband found themselves with chopsticks and a basin each of soup with some strange pieces of food floating in it.

'Will you take puppy-dumplings, Mr. Judd?' Maria asked with a smile.

Immediately Mr Judd thought he was eating dog flesh—after all he'd heard about the Chinese eating dog flesh! But when he looked closely he was relieved to discover his meal was pieces of pork in dough.

That night the newly married Mrs Judd was horrified to discover cockroaches crawling out of crevices between the boards in the boat. She disliked the creatures intensely and the thought that they might spend the night crawling all over her made her cry out to Maria: 'Oh, Mrs. Taylor, I really cannot go to bed with all these cockroaches about!'

Then Mrs Cardwell turned up the light as she intended sitting up all night—she had no intention of sleeping with cockroaches crawling all over her!

Maria calmly spoke to her: 'Dear child, if God spares you to work in China, you will have many nights like this, and you will not be able to afford to lose your sleep. Can you not lie down quietly, and trust Him to keep you?'

With those words Maria calmly went to sleep. Mrs Judd likewise lay down and keeping one eye on the marauding cockroaches fell asleep and had a good night's rest.

In Hangzhou they found that life was very plain. Tables were simply bare boards resting on trestles and beds were simply coconut fibre ropes on which was thrown a thin mattress. The food was all Chinese, eaten with chopsticks.

In February the old problem of the complaining Nicol and the McLean sisters again created much tension.

Hudson knew it was time for expansion, but in April in Taiwan some missions were invaded and destroyed by angry mobs who forced the missionaries to flee.

In one riot a catechist was caught by some of the local violent men, murdered and then had his heart torn out and eaten by those responsible for his death.

When the reports of the violence reached the mainland, the literati began to spread false rumours about the activities of the missions in an effort to rid the nation of foreign influence. Charges made centuries before were revived: the 'barbarians were kidnapping children and using their eyes, livers, hearts and other organs to make medicines.'

Directed at the Roman Catholics was the complaint: 'When a (Chinese) member of their religion is on his death-bed...while the breath is still in his body they scoop out his eyes and cut out his heart, which they use in their country in the manufacture of false silver.'

Hudson concluded that the CIM should open a branch in Suzhou which could be used as a base for moving inland. Before making a move he knew he had to obtain a public proclamation from the city administrator to the effect that the missionaries were to be treated with all the respect and courtesy demanded by the treaties with Western governments.

However, such proclamations were few and far between due to the fact that Westerners were unwelcome in those places where the educated, literati exercised influence.

Nicol again began to spread lies about Hudson and the CIM. He complained that Hudson had changed his mind when they reached

China, forcing them to wear Chinese clothes when large quantities of material and English clothing were stored away.

He said that Hudson would rather see this store of clothing eaten by insects and rot away in preference to handing them to the ones for whom they were intended. Again, these charges were nothing but lies!

The time had come for Hudson to move on and it was Zhenjiang on the Yangzi River that attracted his attention. In mid May he and his party left for the city and spent months looking for accommodation. After finding a house and being assured that he could take possession within two weeks, he notified the Rudlands to come, bringing the printing equipment and the Chinese employees who worked the printing presses.

However, Hudson was unaware that a local magistrate was extremely anti-foreigner and ready to cause trouble for any who arrived in his district.

When the landlord suffered some pressure from the official, he refused to allow the Mission to take possession of the house, making Hudson the laughing stock of the local population.

There was nothing to do but move to the nearby city of Yangzhou about fifteen mile distance along the Grand Canal. The city was known for its evil ways.

Again there was no house ready for occupation so while Hudson searched for something suitable, his family and others lived on their boat. However, the influence of the literati frustrated the search. The rain began to fall and on the houseboats it seemed that every joint in the roof allowed the rain to leak through. Huddled under umbrellas Maria and the children (and the others) found life very difficult. In desperation Hudson decided to rent rooms in a local inn, and on 8 June everyone was settled in dry, pleasant surroundings.

He again tried to find a suitable house in Zhenjiang, but on 8 July posters appeared claiming that young women and children were being given drugged food, kidnapped and killed. Then their eyes, sexual organs and livers had been made into drugs. These accusations, together with the hot summer weather, resulted in many Chinese being ready to take violent action against the 'foreign devils'.

From Suzhou came news that a Chinese Mission preacher had openly taught that the highly respected Confucius was in hell because of his sins. The Chinese did not appreciate this accusation and the work suffered a severe setback.

In Hangzhou a crowd of antagonistic locals had gathered outside the New Lane compound, but Charles Judd had been able to control the situation.

In Yangzhou, Hudson finally rented a house in July and everyone moved in. Soon after, the printing presses and workers arrived.

Then there appeared handbills and posters accusing the missionaries of terrible activities. One stated that they 'scooped out the eyes of the dying, opened foundling hospitals to eat the children, [and] cut open pregnant women (for the purpose of making medicine).' These pamphlets stirred the local citizens into action against all foreigners.

Hudson then asked the local city Prefect to issue a proclamation denying the truth of the rumours, in the hope that the locals would be more tolerant.

When one of the employees of the Roman Catholic orphanage was caught attempting to dispose of the body of an infant who had died from malnutrition it was assumed that he was about to use the body parts for medicine. As a result the chief mandarin ordered the exhumation of all the bodies of people who had died recently. Despite the lack of evidence of any mutilation no proclamation was issued clearing the Catholic orphanage.

When, on 16 August, it was rumoured that twenty-four children were missing a crowd gathered at New Lane, ready for violent action. The mob broke through the compound gates, but backed off when Hudson invited them to come and look over the house in a couple of weeks when the carpenters had done their work. In the meantime he appealed to the city officials for protection—a protection which was guaranteed by law. When it was not forthcoming the mobs prepared for action.

One of the literati class by the name of Koh stirred up the crowd by announcing that it was time to drive out the missionaries. When nothing eventuated, Koh set to work to create more problems.

On 22 August the American Chargé d' affaires visited Yangzhou, dressed in his foreign clothes. His visit, plus new rumours that twenty-four children were missing stirred the crowds to action.

The compound gates were broken open and with much difficulty Hudson drove the howling mob out of the immediate area, allowing carpenters in to repair the damage.

George Duncan arrived to find a great crowd accusing the missionaries of eating twenty-four children. As night fell the armed crowd, becoming more courageous, began throwing bricks.

247

Hudson again sent to the Prefect seeking help, but no help arrived. Then the crowd—estimated at twenty thousand—began to pull down the compound wall and with a shower of bricks broke the windows and shutters.

Hudson decided that he and George Duncan should personally face the Prefect and demand protection as guaranteed by the international treaty. They hadn't gone far before they were recognised and the cry went up that the 'foreign devils' were escaping.

Thinking they were trying to escape through the East Gate of the city wall the crowd took a short cut to cut them off. When the crowds realized what was happening they chased both men, throwing a shower of stones in their direction. Exhausted and hurt they finally reached the Prefect's home.

The gate-keepers were closing the gates when they heard the call for help in Chinese: 'Save life! Save life!'

Such a cry was to be answered by the mandarin no matter when it was heard, but it was almost three quarters of an hour before the Prefect appeared. All the time they could hear the distant crowd rioting, but had no idea what was happening to their loved ones.

Several hours later the Prefect returned to assure Hudson that the military forces had everything under control and that those responsible would be punished.

The Prefect then sent for chairs and Hudson and George Duncan were escorted back to what remained of the house. During the trip back they were told that all the foreigners had been killed.

Hudson's story continued: 'When we reached the house, the scene was such as to baffle description. Here a pile of half burned reeds showed where an attempt had been made to set the premises on fire; there debris of a broken down wall were to be seen; and strewn about everywhere were the remains of boxes and furniture, scattered papers and letters, broken workboxes, writing-desks, surgical and other instrument cases, smouldering remains of valuable books, etc; but no trace of inhabitants could we find within!'

Henry Reid and William Rudland were left to face the fury of the mob who were out for blood. While they attempted to guard the entrances to the house the women and children had made their way to the upper rooms. Because of the bricks and other missiles it was unsafe to remain in the rooms at the back of the house, so in Maria's room they huddled together, crying out to God, for His care and protection in the difficult situation. They also prayed for Hudson and George Duncan, who they trusted would safely reach the Prefect's house and return with help.

William Rudland appeared, covered in mud, with the news that the mob had broken through the back of the house and were searching every room. It was possible to close the trap-door leading into the upper rooms, but that would have cut off Henry Reid's escape route.

Then came Henry's voice warning everyone to escape the best way possible as the crowd had set fire to the building.

Quickly grabbing some blankets from the bed they began the dangerous task of lowering people over the tiles and down to the road. Mrs Rudland, Ensing, the printer's young wife, and Herbert were safely lowered to Mr Reid who hurried them away to safety.

When a semi-naked man burst into the room where Maria and the others were hiding she faced him demanding to know if he were ashamed of attacking women and children. The man replied that he was from the Prefect and for a sum of money would protect them all. Really he wanted to know where any money might be found.

When, to gain some time, Maria demanded his Prefect's card he became frustrated and began to search everyone for valuables. Emily Blatchley had a few dollars in a bag attached to her dress which he ripped away. The man then asked for more money threatening to cut off her head if more was not produced. Turning to Louise Desgraz he searched her, stealing her hair ornament. Then he began rifling through drawers and any boxes he could find.

While searching for anything of value one man noticed Maria's wedding ring, which he roughly tore off her finger.

During the disturbance the nurse, Annie Bohannan, grabbed the baby and hiding behind a man carrying away a large box was able to escape downstairs. Running through the fire she hid herself and the baby in the outside well-house.

Meanwhile William Rudland began lowering out of the room the youngsters, Howard, Samuel and the little Chinese girl who had been adopted by Louise Desgraz.

Below, Henry Reid called out for those still upstairs to escape as the fire was spreading. Louise Desgraz was safely lowered to the roadway, but because some men threw burning material below the escape route, Maria, Emily Blatchley and William Rudland were trapped.

Someone grabbed Mr Rudland by the hair and as he was dragged over the tiles, his clothing was searched for anything of value. William had a watch which he pulled from his pocket and threw away hoping his attacker would leave him and search for it in the semi-darkness. However, when the thief became furious and tried to push him off the roof, Maria and Emily grabbed him and pulled him to safety.

The thief then grabbed a brick and was about to smash it on William's head, when the two ladies grabbed his arm, saving him from almost certain death. The thief, now alone facing William, called to his friends for help, 'Come up! Come up!'

It was time to escape, but where could they go? Then they heard Mr Reid shouting, that he had removed the burning material from below the window and that he would do all he could to break their fall when they jumped.

Maria jumped from about fifteen feet and landed safely. Emily Blatchley was next, but as she did Mr Reid was hit in the eye by a brick which stunned him causing almost instant blindness. Emily landed heavily and for a short time lay on the courtyard before she made it to her feet.

William Rudland jumped next and then led everyone, including Mr Reid, who could not see, to a place of safety.

Moving away from the burning house they made their way over the debris to a closed door where they hid while Mr Rudland collected those hiding in the well-house and led them to the safety of a neighbour's home.

There in the darkness, they thanked God for their deliverance and prayed that God would care for Hudson and George Duncan.

It was an upset group that hid away from the rioting Chinese. Mr Reid was groaning in agony, the children wanted to go to sleep, Maria had almost fainted from loss of blood and Emily was in pain, particularly from a severe cut in the arm. Soon after, with their Chinese servants, they found their way to safety and waited for help.

Following the arrival of soldiers the rioters were dispersed and guards set watch over the house and surrounding area. However, it was some time before Hudson and George arrived on the scene.

Together all praised God for their safe delivery from the satanic forces. Property damage amounted to about five hundred pounds, but all were alive and ready to continue serving God.

They returned to their house as neighbours had extinguished the fire fearing that their own houses might also go up in flames.

The children were bedded down and soon everyone fell asleep, safe in the knowledge that soldiers were on guard. However, when their time of duty ended, they left the area without being replaced. At once the crowds began to reassemble and loot what was left, thinking the house was vacant. But when the missionaries appeared they began to disperse.

Standing on a broken chair, Hudson addressed the rioters telling them that they had come with the gospel which would bless their hearts. He warned all who listened that they would face the wrath of God for what they had done.

Then stepping down from the chair and walking through the crowd he went to the Prefect's house to lodge a formal complaint. While waiting for the Prefect the rioters again caused more damage at the house, but this time the Prefect sent soldiers to disperse the crowd. He interviewed Hudson inviting him to write a formal letter of complaint.

Returning to the wrecked house, Hudson wrote his letter of protest, which, when read was destroyed, as the complaints were of such a serious nature that the city Prefect would be in trouble.

When a more acceptable letter was written the suggestion was made that Hudson and his party should move to nearby Zhenjiang where they'd be safe.

When the British Consul, General W. Medhurst heard of the riot he decided a display of force was the appropriate response.

In England when an exaggerated report was published the editorials suggested that it was because the Chinese had no fear of British retaliation. Hudson and the CIM won the sympathy of both the British and local press.

Fearing that the rioters might cause disturbances at the foreign settlement in Zhenjiang the British gunboat *Rinaldo* arrived on 4 September. A French frigate was nearby in case it was needed.

Medhurst decided to visit Yangzhou to demand an explanation from the city officials and for show he travelled on the *Rinaldo*, accompanied by seventy marines in dress uniform.

When the local Prefect heard of his arrival he went to a gate of secondary importance with the intention of welcoming the British and escorting them to his home through the back streets.

Medhurst on the other hand, disembarked with his marines and marched through the dominant city gate, along the main streets, and, with his guards on duty, made himself at home in the Prefect's residence. A very humble city official willingly held discussions with the Consul.

Accommodation was made available in the Zhenjiang foreign settlement and everyone settled down in rather cramped quarters.

Hudson recommenced his administrative duties especially with correspondence to William Berger, explaining what had occurred. This was followed by letters to the other Mission centres.

In Hangzhou Nicol was again causing trouble, and Hudson faced the necessity of making a firm decision concerning his future with the Mission. He concluded that all trouble makers should be asked to resign before the work of consolidation began and new areas opened up to the gospel. Three provinces appealed to him—Henan, Anhui and Jiangxi.

He now realised that he was no longer needed in any existing CIM work as all appeared to be working satisfactorily. The gospel was bearing fruit and he greatly rejoiced when he heard that two men had walked forty miles to Taizhou to hear the gospel preached. Some time before they had received the gospel of Luke and the book of Acts. They indicated that at home another twenty men were waiting to learn about Christ.

Receiving a letter of agreement from Mr Berger concerning the dismissal of Lewis Nicol from the Mission, Hudson set about composing the letter. John McCarthy, who was in total agreement was asked to hand-deliver the letter to Mr Nicol in Xiaoshan.

Not only did he resign, but the McLean sisters and Susan Barnes followed his action.

Hudson and James Williamson, realizing that a step into the unknown was necessary, made preparations for a journey along the Grand Canal. Their plan was to visit the city of Qingjiangpu, some one hundred miles distant and see if it was a suitable place from which to move into the interior. Their journey commenced on 26 October, 1868 and lasted about ten days. Both men were convinced that it was a vital centre for future missionary endeavour.

At the same time Consul Medhurst set off for Nanjing, this time with a flotilla of war ships including the flagship HMS *Rodney*. The purpose was to display British gunboat power and hopefully ensure the safety of all British citizens living in China. One local paper made the comment concerning this move: 'We hope for the sake of the Chinese themselves, that they will yield to what is asked, and not await the seventy-eight guns of the *Rodney*!'

31

Difficult Days

The Yangzhou riot resulted in much sympathy for the CIM and Hudson in particular, but soon attention was diverted to the perceived wounded pride of Great Britain. One newspaper correspondent wrote: 'The case has now grown beyond a mere question of reparation for injuries sustained. Our political prestige has been injured and must be recovered.'

The consular representatives decided that a show of force was necessary to make the Chinese understand that British citizens had every right to travel throughout China without the fear of injury. Consul Medhurst, accompanied by several hundred marines and travelling on gunboats arrived at Yangzhou on 17 November, 1868.

As Mr Medhurst and Hudson were escorted to a large meeting house two heralds walked along shouting out to the watching citizens, 'People—take care not to hurt the foreigners; or to call them "foreign devils"; but to give them the titles of great men.' The city official however deliberately escorted Consul Medhurst through the back streets which was seen as an insult to British pride.

Consequently the next day the marines paraded through the main streets, concluding with a firing of field guns as a warning to the Chinese that they were to honour the treaty obligations or suffer the consequences.

It was agreed that the Mission house be repaired, all involved in the assault be punished and reparations for damage to property and personal injuries be paid. A proclamation was issued by the Chinese: 'Be it known to all that British subjects have liberty to go into the interior without let or hindrance as clearly stated in the Treaty ratified by the Emperor....Hereafter should anyone insult, hinder or annoy (British subjects) they shall be immediately seized and severely punished. No mercy shall be shown them. Tremble at this!'

23 November saw Hudson, his family and friends back in their repaired home which was reason for great joy and praise to God for His continuing mercies.

Six days later Maria gave birth to a son who was named Charles Edward.

Hudson learned some valuable lessons from the recent events at Yangzhou. In future, itinerant visits would be made to any city before the Mission established a permanent centre. To avoid unsettling the citizens the missionaries would walk to their headquarters in small groups carrying little luggage.

When the Judds arrived at Yangzhou they were warned that life was dangerous, despite all the efforts to establish peace following the riot. Several times they faced angry mobs and on one occasion some soldiers saved Mrs Judd from an angry mob.

Hudson noticed that Mr Judd was not well and in need of exercise so he asked George Duncan, who had some knowledge of horses, to purchase a good riding horse for him. When it arrived, Hudson asked Mr Judd to look after it for him, so he bought a saddle and began to exercise the animal—little realising that it was simply Hudson's scheme to give him some exercise.

Later, when Mr Judd was asked, 'Did Mr Taylor never ride it?' there came the reply, 'No, never! He was far too busy. But he was careful to pay its expenses. It was simply his way of providing horse exercise for one who could not otherwise have taken it. And it did me a world of good...And Mrs Taylor was just the same, loving, unselfish, thoughtful of others.'

Mr Judd was asked, 'Was she really kept free from care amid the practical concerns of everyday life?'

To this he replied, 'Wonderfully so! I never saw her worried.'

Again Mr Judd was questioned, 'Not with Chinese servants, or with the children?'

His response was, 'Not with servants, children, or anything else! I can never recall any part of her conduct, in the few years I was privileged to know her, without seeing her face shining with the brightness that comes from the Holy Spirit's anointing.'

Relations between the Chinese and Europeans were tense as Mr Judd discovered one day when riding the pony. He was attacked by a crowd of several thousand Chinese who stoned him as he was crossing a plank over a creek. Fortunately he escaped the angry mob.

When the news of the riot reached England the papers expressed support for the British missionaries, but soon attitudes changed.

When it was suggested that Hudson had been responsible for calling upon Mr Medhurst to send out the gunboats the question was asked: 'Could such an incident involving a small, largely unknown missionary group involve Great Britain in war with China?'

Then appeared the usual criticisms of Hudson and his Mission— Why had he taken single women into such a dangerous situation? Why were the ladies dressing in Chinese clothing similar to that worn by Chinese prostitutes?

This was followed by accusations of immorality—Hudson had kissed the ladies goodnight at the end of each day and when everyone was sleeping there was only a half inch wall between the rooms occupied by the single women and the men.

This bad publicity resulted in a drop in giving to the Mission and in a letter to Hudson (written during 1869) Mr Berger said, 'Once or twice in the past year the amount in my hands has been as low as twenty pounds; yet to the praise of God's grace I can say it has never been necessary to send money to China without my being able to do so, and even the full amount that I desired.'

During those difficult days George Müller faithfully forwarded money as did the many faithful Christians who refused to believe the lies that appeared in the papers.

On 9 March, 1869 the Yangzhou affair was the subject of debate in the British House of Lords. The Duke of Somerset asked, 'What right have we to send missionaries to the interior of China?' He stated that missionaries had no right to expect a gun boat to be at their disposal when they faced trouble and demanded that all missionaries working in inland China be recalled.

Another member of the House suggested that missionaries should follow the businessmen, arguing that when the Chinese saw value in trade, they would more readily accept the gospel.

However, the godly Bishop Magee, in his first House of Lords speech spoke out in favour of those who propagated the gospel. He criticised the British sale of opium to the Chinese and demanded equal rights for all British citizens in China, whether they sold 'Bibles or cotton.'

Gradually the truth became known that Hudson had not sent for a gun boat to protect the interests of the CIM. He refused to defend himself but in May, 1869 a friend, Miles Knowlton issued a report stating that people were ignorant of the facts and explained that Hudson and other missionaries had sought and received permission to enter inland China. He retold the story of the vicious placards and handbills that aroused the Chinese to action, concluding that the reason behind the riot was very simple—it was not that the Chinese hated the Christian gospel, but there was a 'hatred to all foreigners, as such.'

Towards the end of 1868 James Meadows and James Williamson set off by boat, up the Yangzi River, for the city of Anqing which was fifty miles distant from Nanjing, where George and Catherine Duncan had settled with Mary Bower and Elizabeth Meadows and the two children. The two men arrived at their destination on 8 January, 1869 and for a time were unable to find a house to rent.

With their boats moored in a creek amongst the many boats already there, they spent their time, with their Chinese assistants, preaching the gospel, gossiping the gospel in tea houses, but all without much success. The people just weren't interested and no one was willing to rent them a house.

After some time an inn-keeper near the West gate took them in, giving them rooms in the city. But they needed a home and no one was willing to risk renting a house to the 'foreign devils'.

In desperation James Meadows one day exclaimed, 'I wish I could find some scoundrel who feared nobody, but wanted money, and would be willing to let us a house!'

Very soon afterwards an eighty year old citizen called at the inn and told James that he had heard of his need and that he had a house for rent. His building needed some repairs and he asked for a year's rent in advance. The deal was made and soon the repair work commenced.

As time passed the missionaries found out that indeed he was a well known old scoundrel, who couldn't care less about the gospel of the risen Christ. When he was warned that he must repent of his sins and turn to Christ his usual reply was, 'Oh, I'm all right; I have got my coffin.'

With the return of Mrs Meadows and the children, witnessing commenced in earnest. To avoid public disturbances the men walked the streets selling gospel portions and speaking privately to any who would listen. Everything seemed peaceful and quiet.

Meanwhile Hudson and Maria found life very busy in their new Yangzhou home. He was responsible for all members of the Mission, which meant a continual round of visitations to encourage and guide all workers. Often he had to arrange his itinerary in order to be present at the birth of babies. He was always on call to give medical treatment when needed.

Being responsible for accounting, the distribution of the mission finances and the daily grind of letters to read and write, meant that he spent little time with Maria and the children.

At last it was decided to take a holiday. He, Maria, the children, and Emily Blatchley set out for the island of Putuo which was well known for its pleasant sandy beaches, the many temples and the masses of flowers, particularly the rhododendrons that were to be found everywhere. So lovely was the island that many Shanghai and Ningbo people made it their vacation resort.

The rest proved to be physically, mentally and spiritually refreshing. From 20 May until 5 June, 1869, Hudson put Mission duties aside, enjoying happy times with Maria and his children.

When he returned to 'civilization' he discovered that he was again being attacked by the local press for causing unrest on the holiday island. The falsehoods made good reading and one paper, *The Shanghai Recorder* even went so far as to say: 'Giving Mr Taylor full credit for his clerico-surgical character, we imagine that he has forsaken his vocation. In various parts of Great Britain there are to be found institutions (in many of which) the possession of a surgeon who could also officiate as chaplain would be an inestimable advantage. Among the institutions of this kind which present themselves to our memory one stands out with exceptional clearness—The Hospital for Incurable Idiots. We wish Mr Taylor could obtain admission in some capacity to this excellent asylum. Were he an inmate, much trouble that now occurs would be prevented....'

Before Hudson could reply, a ship had left for England, carrying copies of the untruthful newspaper reports. He felt very downhearted by what had been unfairly said of him during what was just a pleasant holiday.

Trouble followed in Anqing where James Meadows and James Williamson were settling in. Anti-foreign placards declaring that

Christianity should be crushed before its evil influence spread throughout China began to appear. Rumours were spreading that as many as two hundred and forty children had been eaten or disposed of by the missionaries.

In September the local magistrate warned the missionaries that as the annual literary and military examinations were soon to take place the best course of action would be to keep out of sight, even leaving the city for a time. It was well known that many of the candidates were unruly at examination times when much alcohol was consumed. Anything could happen!

On 2 November a large placard was displayed in the examination hall urging the students to attack the 'religious brigands' and destroy their house. James Williamson and James Meadows approached the city official to demand protection, but when he refused to interview them the students took this as an invitation to riot. Both men were assaulted and cried out for help from the official, 'Save life!'

While they were protected the students milled around shouting that the 'foreign devils' should be put to death. The request to see the official immediately was ignored because he was eating his rice. Giving orders for them to wait in a small side room he assured them that he would send some officials to prevent any damage being done at their residence.

The rioting students however turned their attention to the house where Mrs Meadows and the children were awaiting the men's return.

Quickly they battered down the door and invaded the house. Mrs Meadows described what happened:

> Each one for himself tore open drawers, boxes, and cupboards, carrying off everything in them...now an armful of crockery, now one of clothes, another of books, now and then stopping to break out the windows....I got downstairs somehow, receiving some severe blows....I did not know where to go, but went first to the teachers' room hoping there to be protected....There was a gentleman in the room whom I had not seen before, and he was helping us, taking all he could from the thieves and stowing them in his room. He made way for me to get into the room and kept the mob out as long as he could, getting his face bruised for his pains.

The rioters tried to drag little Louise from her arms, but in the struggle the little child was saved.

The magistrate arrived, and led by a faithful Christian servant, Mrs Meadows was escorted through the milling crowd to be reunited with her husband. When darkness fell the city officials put the missionary party on two little boats with some food, money and bedding and left them to fend for themselves.

It was a very miserable night. The wind was blowing which made for poor travelling conditions. After five days and nights they reached the city of Jiujiang where they were welcomed by the members of the foreign settlement and given free passage on a steamer which was leaving for Zhenjiang where they were met by the Rudlands. Soon Maria and Hudson joined them to hear them describe how they had lost their earthly possessions in the service of the Lord.

Again British officials came to the aid of those who suffered in the riot and received a promise from the Chinese that the damaged house would be repaired and compensation paid.

On 23 February, 1870 James Meadows and James Williamson returned to Anqing where they were welcomed by people and city officials alike. The city official who had not assisted the men when they needed help welcomed them into his home and then escorted them both to the door of his mansion. This was a great act of courtesy and indicated to the citizens of the city that the missionaries were to be made welcome.

When James Meadows returned to the repaired house, he went to a spot in the earthen floor and after digging a small hole recovered one hundred and three silver dollars which he had hidden before the riot.

Before long his wife Elizabeth returned to assist her husband in his work. James Williamson also had plans—he wanted to get a boat and begin a missionary journey, preaching and living on his junk.

The spirits of both men had not been dampened by the Anqing disturbance!

Another man who was to make his mark with the Mission was Mr J. Cardwell who arrived in China about seventeen months after the *Lammermuir* group had settled in. He had for a long time set his heart upon serving Christ in the province of Jiangxi.

While in England he met with a friend, who encouraged him to leave for China: 'One day, while talking with me about it, happening to have a map of China in his room, he said, "Dear brother, look at that map; you see the province of Jiangxi; you see the Poyang lake, and rivers in all directions, by which one might reach nearly every city. Shall we pray that, if it be the LORD'S will, you may be sent there, to labour on that lake?"'

He continued, 'We did pray over the matter, and at the end of seven years I went to China, not to the Poyang Lake, however, but to the city of Taizhou in Zhejiang, a long distance from the province for which we had been praying.'

While in Taizhou both he and his wife found it difficult to adjust to the new life and he was plagued with sickness. Hudson was very concerned about Cardwell's health and then found out that instead of calling him to oversee her pregnancy and the birth, Cardwell had sent her to a hospital in Ningbo, despite the fact he didn't have the money to meet the expense involved. He simply charged it to the Mission!

Some of Mr Cardwell's friends suggested he should return to England, but Hudson decided he should be given the opportunity of visiting the Lake Poyang area. Instead of using cheap transport he booked a passage for his family on a steamer—again the cost of which he could not meet. In his dealings with the shipping company he so upset the merchants that they refused in future to give discounts to any missionaries travelling on their ships.

Reaching Jiujiang in December, 1869, Mr Cardwell's health began to improve and with the change of scenery and better health he threw himself into the work he had so long wanted to do, with the result that soon he was known for his courageous trips into areas untouched by missionaries.

His church at Jiujiang grew in numbers and proved to be a faithful centre of CIM labours.

32

Death of a Dear One

The year 1869 witnessed a world-wide spiritual movement that had profound effects upon Christians including Hudson Taylor and most of the members of the CIM. As a result of the 'Holiness' movement which was born in England, Christians were told of a spiritual life on a higher plane. This Holy Spirit, revitalized life produced a life of devotion to the Lord Jesus, far beyond what was already being experienced.

It was claimed that this second blessing was usually the outcome of a crisis experience which caused the Christian to rest more firmly upon Christ for power to live the victorious Christian life.

At that time Hudson, with other members of the Mission, was experiencing hard times. The work was difficult, conversions were few, giving to the work had fallen and there was the continual threat of riots.

He was overworked with his many duties, frustrated with a lack of co-operation from some of the Mission members which resulted in frequent emotional outbursts. So concerned was he about sin in his life that on one occasion he said, 'Oftentimes I am tempted to think that one so full of sin cannot be a child of God at all...I hated myself; I hated my sin; and yet I gained no strength against it.'

Determined to have the victory over sin he spent more time meditating upon the Word of God and at prayer. When he made resolutions and fasted, he failed. He knew the answer to his spiritual problems were to be found in Christ: 'Every day, almost every hour, the consciousness of failure and sin oppressed me...I began the day with prayer, determined not to take my eye from Him for a moment; but pressure of duties, sometimes very trying, constant interruptions, sometimes so wearing, often caused me to forget Him. Then one's nerves get so fretted in this climate that temptations to irritability, hard thoughts, and sometimes unkind words are harder to withstand.'

Most of his friends felt the same concerning their sins and relationship with Christ, with the result that they examined their heart, praying that God might bless them with greater spiritual strength.

Many were reading a small booklet that Hudson had sent to every member of the CIM—*How to Live on Christ* by Harriet Beecher Stowe. This book had a deep influence upon those who prayerfully meditated upon its teaching.

John McCarthy, who had experienced a great blessing from the Lord wrote to Hudson of his experience:

> I do wish I could talk to you now about the way of holiness. At the same time you were speaking to me about it, it was the subject of all others occupying my thoughts...to find some way by which I might continuously enjoy that communion, that fellowship at times so real, but more often so visionary, so far off!...Do you know, dear brother, I now think that this striving, effort, longing, hoping for better days to come, is not the true way to happiness, holiness or usefulness...I have been struck with a passage from a book of yours left here, entitled *Christ is all*. It says: "The Lord Jesus received is holiness begun; the Lord Jesus cherished is holiness advancing; the Lord Jesus *counted upon as never absent* would be holiness complete.
>
> "This (grace of faith) is the chain which binds the soul to Christ, and makes the Saviour and the sinner one..."
>
> "A channel is now formed by which Christ's fullness plenteously flows down. The barren branch becomes a portion of the fruitful stem....One life reigns throughout the whole."
>
> "Believer you mourn your shortcomings....Help is laid up for you in Christ. Seek clearer interest in Him. They who most deeply feel that they have died in Christ, and paid in Him sin's penalties, ascend to the highest heights of godly life. He is most holy who has most of Christ within, and joys most fully in the finished work. It is defective faith which clogs the feet, and causes many to fall."

In Zhenjiang on 4 September Hudson opened the letter and read its contents with spiritual excitement. As he prayerfully put it down the truth dawned upon his heart: 'As I read,' he later wrote, 'I saw it all. I looked to Jesus; and when I saw, oh how joy flowed!'

He stood up, a new man with a story to tell. Gathering together everyone in the house, he explained what God had done to him as he read the letter from John McCarthy. His words were used of God to touch the hearts of the others in the room. Now they knew the truth of Christ's words: 'whoever drinks of the water that I shall give him will never thirst. But the water that I shall give him will become in him a fountain of water springing up into everlasting life' (John 4:14). Hudson now saw each Mission centre as a spiritual centre from which flowed the 'fountains of living water.'

When he returned to Yangzhou his spiritual change was easily seen by everyone. Mr Judd spoke of meeting him at that time:

> When I went to welcome him he was so full of joy, that he scarcely knew how to speak to me. He did not even say, "How do you do?" but walking up and down the room with his hands behind him, exclaimed: "Oh, Mr Judd, God has made me a new man!…The Lord Jesus tells me I *am* a branch. I am *part of Him*, and have just to believe it and act upon it. If I go to the bank in Shanghai, having an account, and ask for fifty dollars, the clerk cannot refuse it to my outstretched hand and say it belongs to Mr Taylor. What belongs to Mr Taylor my hand may take. It is a member of my body. And I am a member of Christ, and may take all I need of His fulness. I have seen it long enough in the Bible, and I *believe* it now as a living reality."

Mr Judd and others couldn't help noticing the change in Hudson's life:

> He was a joyous man now, a bright, happy Christian. He had been a toiling, burdened one before, with latterly not much rest of soul. It was resting in Jesus now, and letting Him do the work—which makes all the difference!…a new power seemed to flow from him, and in the practical things of life a new peace possessed him. Troubles did not worry him as before. He cast everything on God in a new way, and gave more time to prayer. Instead of working late at night, he began to go to bed earlier, rising at five in the morning to give two hours before the work of the day began to Bible study and prayer. Thus his own soul was fed, and from him flowed the living water to others.

In a letter to his sister Amelia he explained the change in his life:

> But how to get faith strengthened? Not by striving after faith, but by resting on the Faithful One....I looked to Jesus and saw (and when I saw, oh, how joy flowed!) that He had said, "I will never leave you." "Ah, there is rest!" I thought. "I have striven in vain to rest in Him. I'll strive no more. For has *He* not promised to abide with me—never to leave me, never to fail me?" And, dearie, *He never will!* I saw not only that Jesus would never leave me, but that I was a member of His body, of His flesh and of His bones. The vine now I see, is not the root merely, but all—root, stem, branches, twigs, leaves, flowers, fruit: and Jesus is not only that, He is soil and sunshine, air and showers, and ten thousand times more than we have ever dreamed, wished for, or needed. Oh, the joy of seeing this truth!

Hudson's newly experienced spiritual strength helped him face the difficult days that lay ahead.

The riot at Anqing and the rumours of the death of his missionary comrades was faced with a quiet confidence that the affairs of the world were controlled by God.

Money was in short supply and while it was not possible to have the foods that were common in England, Christmas was a happy time for everyone.

On New Year's Eve a letter was received from Mr George Müller which greatly encouraged everyone. He wrote how the Lord had stirred him to even greater prayer for the work of the Mission and enclosed was a heap of cheques made out to individual Mission members.

In the same mail Mr. Berger asked Hudson to send Mr. Müller the names of every member of the Mission so that no one would be overlooked when in the future money was sent out.

The love and continuing support of people such as the Müllers and Bergers proved to everyone that God was indeed caring for them and would, through his people, provide for their every need.

However, times had changed and it became obvious to Hudson and Maria that their children should be sent to England as continual sickness and moving from place to place was no life for them. Five year old Samuel had an ulcerated stomach which made eating and drinking very painful. He was so sick and in need of continual medical attention that they took him with them on their journeys.

When the decision was made it was Emily Blatchley, suffering from tuberculosis, who was asked if she would accompany Samuel, Herbert,

Howard and Maria to England. She was always ready to help and willingly undertook the task.

The decision was also made to keep little Charles with Hudson and Maria as he was just one year old.

Maria made clothes suitable for the English climate while Hudson prepared three months schoolwork for the school age children, including Greek lessons for nine year old Herbert.

Then it was off to Shanghai to book a passage on a French ship that was to sail for Marseilles in mid March, and back to Yangzhou, hoping to arrive there for Emily's twenty fifth birthday celebration on 24 January, 1870. He arrived home to find five year old Samuel very sick. The little boy died several days later on 4 February and his body was laid to rest in Zhenjiang.

There was much sadness with the imminent departure of the children with Emily. She had been a wonderful support to both Hudson and Maria for many years and would be greatly missed.

Maria, wanting to make sure Emily would be well cared for, wrote to Hudson's mother: 'Receive her as a daughter for our sake to begin with, but soon you will continue to do so for her own sake....And... call her Emily and not Miss Blatchley...she has been to us a daughter and a sister, both in one.'

In the same mail Hudson wrote to his mother: 'Dear Miss Blatchley's love and self-sacrifice we can never repay. Next to ourselves, the children love her and she them.'

Towards the middle of February the small party set out for Shanghai. The trip was not the easiest as there were places where the water was so shallow that the boat was stuck in the mud for days on end.

Arriving at Suzhou they were met by Jennie Faulding and Mrs Wang Lae-djün. Jennie and Emily had been friends for what must have seemed like ages. They had travelled to China on the *Lammermuir* and parting was difficult.

In Suzhou they met a young Chinese convert, Ren who was greatly influenced by what he saw of the spiritual life of the CIM group. Later he became a teacher in Jennie's school, marrying Wang Lae-djün's daughter.

But farewells had to end and the travellers moved on to Shanghai where they were met by the Cordons. Mrs Cordon, who was expecting a baby kept close to Hudson at all times, as she was unsure of the expected date of the baby's birth.

On 22 March, Hudson and Maria, with Emily and the children, boarded the ship which was to depart at half past five the following morning. Little did they know that they would never see their mother again.

Several weeks later a sorrowful Hudson expressed his feelings to Mr Berger:

> I have seen them awake, for the last time in China. Two of our little ones we have no anxiety about; they rest in Jesus' bosom. And now dear Brother, though the tears will not be stayed, I do thank God for permitting one so unworthy to take any part in this great work, and do not regret having engaged and being engaged in it. It is *His* work, not mine nor yours: and yet it is ours—not because we are engaged in it, but because we are His, and one with Him whose work it is.

With the children and Emily safely on their way to England, Hudson and Maria returned to Suzhou, Mrs Cordon following in their footsteps expecting to be delivered of her baby at any moment. When they reached Suzhou they received news that Mrs Judd was seriously ill at Zhenjiang.

Hudson, accompanied by the expectant Mrs Cordon continued on by boat to be with her. Maria, who was pregnant, made the decision to travel the thirty miles home over rough roads on a springless wheelbarrow. Late in the evening Mr Judd heard the noise of a wheelbarrow approaching the mission house and looking out of the window was surprised to see Maria making her way to the door.

As soon as she entered the room she took over from an exhausted Mr Judd who wrote:

> Suffering though she was at the time and worn with hard travelling, she insisted on my going to bed and that she would undertake the nursing. Nothing would induce her to rest.
>
> '"No," she said, "you have quite enough to bear, without sitting up any more at night. Go to bed, for I shall stay with your wife whether you do or not."
>
> 'Never can I forget the firmness and love with which it was said, her face shining meanwhile with the tenderness of Him in Whom it was her joy and strength to abide.'

Several days later Mary Bower arrived and assisted Maria caring for Mrs Judd.

When Hudson arrived he believed she would die. He also found the place so overcrowded with the Judds, the Meadows' family and Mr Duncan that he spent his nights on the boat, sleeping and carrying out the ever present administrative duties.

When the Meadows returned to Anqing, they left behind little Sammy. As Elizabeth Judd was improving he ordered her and her husband to Putuo Island for a break. Mary Bower accompanied them to give whatever help she could.

For a time Hudson was fully occupied with correspondence and medical work. Regular reports had to be sent to William Berger and letters of advice and encouragement written to the Mission members. As he had become the medical advisor for the European citizens in many centres he found his trips regulated by sickness and the delivery of babies.

Despite being assisted by many good men and women who knew what was expected of them and worked to the glory of God, there were others who were a continual headache.

Charles Fishe, newly arrived from England, proved to be a man of considerable ability and as Hudson had lost Emily Blatchley Charles was asked if he would become Hudson's personal secretary. When he agreed many burdens were lifted from Hudson's shoulders.

With Mrs Cordon still at Zhenjiang awaiting the birth of her child, Hudson, thinking he could make a quick visit to Yangzhou, left Maria in charge. During his absence she ably delivered Mrs Cordon of her infant.

News travelled slowly and it was with anxious hearts that both parents awaited news of the safe arrival of their children in England.

They were met at Marseilles and after spending several days in Paris left for Dover where they were welcomed by the Bergers on 24 April, 1870. Everyone had changed so much that they didn't recognize the travellers until they noticed Herbert's Chinese shoes. Emily Blatchley also had changed due to the difficult times in China and the tuberculosis that was taking its toll upon her health.

Mrs Berger immediately wrote to Maria telling her of the safe arrival of the children and Emily. Her letter finished with words that Maria never read: 'The Lord throw around you His everlasting arms!'

After a very happy time at Saint Hill with the Berger family, Emily with her precious children, moved to Amelia and Benjamin's home. With good food and loving care the children's health improved greatly.

Emily, who was quite ill, helped Mr Berger prepare reports about the Mission for publication in the *Occasional Paper*. Amongst her writings she commented about Maria and Hudson's love of their children. After Maria's death she wrote to Hudson: 'It often comforts me about the children to remember how much she prayed for them.

I have seen her at night, when she thought all were sleeping, with head bowed, kneeling for a long, long time on the bare floor. And when I picture her so, I always feel that she was praying most especially for you and the dear children.'

In China, the tension which was growing between the locals and foreigners was to boil over in mid June, when many would lose their lives in the riots.

However, tension didn't prevent the work of the CIM and other missionary groups who were ever reaching out into new areas with the precious gospel of a risen Christ.

George Stott who was working alone in the distant city of Wenzhou longed to have a wife to share his life, but there were no European women living in the region. Having met Grace Ciggie in London before he left for China he wrote proposing marriage. Grace, who hardly knew George, longed to work in China, but had spent her time helping the underprivileged Glasgow women. When the proposal arrived she accepted and on 4 December, 1869 sailed for Shanghai hoping that the trip would take no more than one hundred days. She wanted to be in Shanghai on 12 March, 1870, the twenty-fifth anniversary of her birthday. This in fact happened and she was met there by George, who escorted her to Ningbo where the marriage took place after the one month residency requirement.

George wanted to immediately return home with his new wife, but had to wait until a convoy of junks sailed with a gunboat protection from the pirates who roamed the seas. As a result Gracie spent two weeks waiting and travelling before she finally reached her 'home' which was a small upstairs bedroom beside a living room, situated above a noisy school room.

She soon found herself the centre of attention amongst the Chinese who, having never had a white foreign woman in their midst, visited her in droves.

This friendly relationship changed after the Tianjin riot and massacre which took place in late June. Feelings ran high throughout the land and for three months Gracie stayed inside her 'home'. When placards appeared charging the Stotts of killing babies and salting down their bodies Gracie found her rooms forceably opened to the Chinese public who wandered through each room keeping an eye out for the 'missing children.'

Whenever George ventured out to buy food he faced abuse and the occasional shower of stones. So dangerous was the situation in most

CIM stations that many men sent their wives and children to safer regions. Gracie, however, would not leave her husband and faced the wrath of the Chinese with the man she had married.

Life was difficult and dangerous for the members of the fourteen CIM outposts and those Chinese who had befriended them.

Twenty-first June, a riot in Tianjin struck fear into the hearts of every foreigner. Prior to the riot rumours had been spread of the supposed criminal activities of foreigners. On 14 June the acting Consul General at Zhenjiang advised Hudson: 'I have to warn you to be exceedingly cautious...not leaving your house after nightfall and (when this is found impracticable) carrying a lantern with your name in Chinese upon it....I need hardly remind you that when the passions of the people are roused the authorities have not always the power even where they have the will to protect you from outrage.' Hudson in turn forwarded copies of the letter to all Mission stations urging care to avoid creating tension with the locals.

In Tianjin anti-foreigner rumours were reaching fever pitch with the nuns at the Roman Catholic orphanage being accused of removing the eyes and hearts of infants for use in the production of drugs. It was true that some unwanted babies had been purchased by the nuns in order to be baptized and cared for but when one Chinese cook declared she had seen the babies killed, tempers flared. In early June an epidemic resulted in the death of many infants in the orphanage which was considered proof of the accusations, despite the fact that when the bodies were exhumed no evidence of criminal activities was found.

On 21 June the Chinese mobs attacked the French consulate, looting, murdering and burning everything they found before turning their attention to the Roman Catholic orphanage which was about a mile from the consulate.

The mob dragged out the ten nuns and after hacking them to death burnt their bodies. Then followed attacks and killing of other foreigners.

The threat of war hung over the region for some time, but French involvement in war in Europe made reprisals impossible. For a time foreigners were left to defend themselves, and while not given any assurances of protection from the Western forces in the area, the presence of British warships helped establish a degree of peace.

Hudson and his CIM workers knew that British weapons were not to be their protection in those dangerous times, but the all powerful

God they loved and served. They all rested in the words of Scripture, 'The name of the LORD is a strong tower; the righteous flee unto it and are safe.' In the correspondence that circulated at that time the words, 'God reigns' were to be found scattered throughout the messages.

July was a very hot month and on 5 July Maria who was expecting her baby, became very ill. Despite extreme pain and sickness she didn't wake anyone for help, but when Hudson entered her room the next morning he was shocked to see her so unwell.

By 7 July she appeared to be recovering so he thought it safe to leave her for a short time while he farewelled Mr Williamson who was leaving for Anqing with little Sammy Meadows, and bought a small bottle of brandy for Maria.

However, when he returned home he was greeted by a baby's cry. Maria was very ill and he had to make surgical repairs to prevent a continuing severe haemorrhage.

Later he wrote to his parents of the joy of the new baby: 'How I stroked the soft, silky hair, and nestled the little one in my bosom! And how she loved him, when with a father's joy and pride I brought him to her for her first kiss, and together we gave him to the Lord.'

The little boy was named Noel, simply because Maria liked the name which meant 'peace'. For a time, little Noel did well, but when Maria suffered an attack of cholera and was unable to feed him, he fell ill. With thrush and diarrhoea his prospects for recovery were not good. A Chinese wet nurse was found, but on 20 July little Noel died.

During these difficult days Maria's health deteriorated, but she was able to select several hymns to be sung when Noel was laid to rest. On 22 July Hudson conducted the funeral where Noel's body was buried beside that of Samuel. Following the service he spoke prophetic words to the grave-digger: 'I trust I may not have to trouble you again.'

Sad of heart, he wrote to his parents, expressing the comfort which Maria found in Christ: 'Though excessively prostrate in body, the deep peace of soul, the realization of the Lord's presence, and the joy in His holy will with which she was filled, and in which I was permitted to share, I can find no words to describe.'

Hudson made arrangements to have Maria moved to the home of a friend who lived in a cooler part of the city, but when he arrived home he found Maria much worse. Being very hot, she asked, 'Could I have my bath there as often as I like?'

When an exhausted Hudson fell asleep, she watched over him until he awoke at about 9:30 pm. She then told him that Mrs Rudland had a cup of tea waiting for him.

This was just what he needed, but as he was drinking some tea, Hudson heard his name called and rushing to Maria, found her standing, unable to speak or return to her bed. He picked her up in his arms and gently placed her in her bed. He realized that Maria was dying, so asked the Rudlands to gather the members of household together for prayer.

The next day when Maria complained of being hot, especially about her head he painstakingly thinned her hair with a pair of scissors, carefully putting the locks aside. When he was finished Maria felt what he had done and smiling commented, 'That's what you call thinning out, is it?' Hudson wrote of the events that moment: 'And she threw her loving arms—so thin—around me, and kissed me in her own loving way for it.'

It was 23 July when suddenly he was called to Maria's side:

> By this time it was dawn and the sunlight revealed what the candle had hidden—the deathlike hue of her countenance. Even my love could no longer deny, not her danger, but that she was actually dying. As soon as I was sufficiently composed, I said:
>
> "My darling, do you know that you are dying?"
>
> "Dying?" she replied. "Do you think so? What makes you think so?"
>
> I said, "I can see it, darling. Your strength is giving way."
>
> "Can it be so? I feel no pain, only weariness."
>
> "Yes, you are going Home. You will soon be with Jesus."
>
> My precious wife thought of my being left alone at a time of so much trial, with no companion like herself, with whom…to bring everything to the Throne of Grace.
>
> "I am sorry," she said, and paused as if half correcting herself for the feeling.
>
> "You are not sorry to go to be with Jesus?"
>
> "Oh, no! It is not that. You know, darling, that for ten years past there has not been a cloud between me and my Saviour. I cannot be sorry to go to Him; but it does grieve me to leave you alone at such a time. Yet…He will be with you and meet all your need."

Later, writing to Maria's cousin he said:

> The Chinese servants and teachers who all respected and loved her, came into her room. She had a message for each, and an earnest

exhortation for those who were unsaved to come to Jesus and meet her in heaven. She gave me her dying kisses for her little ones in England, and messages for them. Then language failed her and her last act of consciousness was to put one arm around my neck and one on my head, to look up to heaven with a look of unutterable love and trust. Her lips moved but no sound was uttered...Then she fell asleep...Her sleep became lighter and lighter, and it was not easy to say when it ceased and her ransomed spirit entered into the joy of her Lord.

Mrs Duncan also wrote of those last minutes of Maria's life:

I never witnessed such a scene. As dear Mrs. Taylor was breathing her last, Mr. Taylor knelt down—his heart so full—and committed her to the Lord; thanking Him for having given her, and for the twelve and a half years of happiness they had had together; thanking Him, too, for taking her to His own blessed presence, and solemnly dedicating himself anew to His service.

It was 23 July!

The weather was very hot so Hudson at once bought a Chinese coffin into which he gently placed Maria's body saying, 'The Lord gave and the Lord has taken away; blessed be the name of the Lord.' Then he went to a room to have a time with his Lord.

He conducted Maria's funeral. Eight Chinese carried the coffin preceded by Charles Fishe and Thomas Harvey who were dressed in white, the colour of mourning in China. Hudson and all their friends from the Mission and the foreign settlement followed. Sad though the occasion was, he rejoiced in the knowledge that his Maria was now with Christ experiencing a joy beyond the understanding of anyone present.

The next day Hudson fell ill with dysentery and fever which lasted for several months. But sickness didn't prevent him from conducting the funeral service of a sailor who died.

He wrote to the Bergers on 1 August expressing the deep feelings of his heart:

When I think of my loss, my heart, nigh to breaking, bursts forth in thankful praise to Him who has spared her from much sorrow and has made her so unspeakably happy. My tears are more tears of joy than of sorrow....I feel like a person recovering from a long prostrating illness—yet I am not really weak, I was able to take the service at the Consulate and three Chinese services yesterday.

Then he wrote to his children, enclosing locks of their mother's hair for each of them. So precious was that hair that he divided it into two parcels and posted them on different ships, just in case one didn't reach its destination. He prayerfully told the children of their mother's last messages for them.

Alone he returned to his work.

At Tianjin eighteen rioters were beheaded for their part in the atrocities—not as common criminals but dressed in silk because these men were considered heroes. The Chinese officials who had encouraged the rioters were left largely untouched. To have them executed would have insulted the Emperor and that could never be!

Now Hudson was alone and ill with three graves at Zhenjiang and one at Hangzhou. His three other children were in England and little Charles was being cared for by Mrs Gough at Ningbo. There was a real danger of more anti-foreign riots and he felt responsible for the safety of each member of the Mission. He missed Emily Blatchley's help, but found Charles Fishe to be a competent assistant. However Hudson was sick and tired and in a letter to Jennie Faulding he simply said, 'I am almost worn out.'

As the Crombies were very sick, Hudson with the help of other Mission members sacrificially gave to pay their return fares to England. Mrs Crombie had lost three children and was again pregnant.

Hudson travelled to Shanghai to bid them farewell, trusting that the expected baby would be born without problems in England. On the night before the ship sailed Anne had a miscarriage and being too ill to be moved he decided to accompany them as far as Hong Kong in case his medical skill was needed. This brief absence was a pleasant break from the workload he faced.

Returning to Ningbo he saw little Charles as his only link with Maria. The little boy was unwell with croup, but Hudson had to move on to Hangzhou where he would be with a group of close friends. The stopover did him the world of good.

Then came the distressing news from England—Emily Blatchley was very unwell. Her doctor gave her no hope of recovery from the advancing tuberculosis. The Bergers were also unwell.

For many many years they had borne the burden of Mission administration in England, supporting Hudson and the Mission when under attack by Nicol and others.

In letters to Hudson William Berger wrote, 'I bear burdens too heavy for me...I get weaker year by year...I am very weakly in body but the Lord knows my need.'

Hudson was ever on call to the sick members of the CIM. Godly, hard-working George Duncan in Zhenjiang was seriously ill, coughing up blood. He died two years later. Hudson intended that the Meadows family should return home before the heat of the 1871 summer.

Looking back over 1870 he wrote:

> Thus wave after wave of trial rolled over us; but at the end of the year not a few of us were constrained to confess that we had learned more of the loving kindness of the LORD through these experiences than in any previous year in our lives.
>
> Perhaps, also, more was really accomplished during this time in teaching the native Christians not to lean upon the arm of foreign protection and support, but upon God alone, on whom, as they could not but see, the missionaries themselves had solely to depend in the hour of trial and danger.

Hudson knew the reality of God's sustaining grace and John McCarthy wrote: 'Dear Mr. Taylor seems kept in perfect peace amidst all the sorrow and difficulty.'

The year had been difficult, but progress had been made as A. J. Broomhall wrote:

> During the less tense periods Stevenson had extended the Shaoxing church to Xinchang beyond Sheng Xian where he had begun work in 1869; Wang Lae-djün had opened a country chapel at his own expense; the Hangzhou evangelists had returned to Lanxi on the Qiantang River, and to other cities; McCarthy had made an evangelistic journey north-east from Hangzhou, Harvey northwards into Anhui and Nanjing, and Rudland and Edward Fishe in two directions from Taizhou. The freehold of the Nanjing house had been successfully purchased, and the land outside Zhenjiang on which to build. The invisible signs of progress were not long in making themselves apparent when churches came into being in those cities in which beleaguered young men and women had thought they were achieving nothing.[7]

33

A New Year—1871

An exhausted Hudson knew he had to make a change in his lifestyle or he'd have a complete physical breakdown. Going to bed before 10 pm and not rising before about 6:30 am was a step in the right direction. He also made Charles Fishe responsible for preparing *The Monthly Gleaner*.

His oversight of the Zhenjiang congregation meant conducting as many as six daily services with the result that his health deteriorated to such an extent that in the April, 1871 copy of *The Monthly Gleaner* Charles Fishe commented, 'Mr Taylor has been very unwell for the last three months, almost wholly unable to engage in any work.' With a constant pain in his side and chest he realized that he needed a good rest and his thoughts turned to England. Emily and his four children had been living with Amelia and her family, but owing to the collapse of her husband's business, help was urgently needed to care for Hudson's family.

The Bergers were both so sick that they sold a portion of their estate and spent most of their time in a coastal home. They were overworked and their continued support of the Mission had sapped them of their energy. Giving to the work of the CIM had declined and they were convinced that a speaking tour by Hudson would revive interest in the Mission's work.

Over several years they had purchased, packed and forwarded thirty-two large containers of supplies. They were distressed when they learned of Maria's death and of the sickness and danger faced by other members of the Mission. The news of the Tianjin massacre discouraged them as they became more fully aware of the danger faced by missionaries.

Because Mr Berger was seriously questioning the doctrines of eternal hell and election he believed he should no longer remain the British representative of the Mission.

Hudson knew that he was needed in England and some of his friends suggested he should return and marry Emily Blatchley.

As much as he loved Emily he knew they could never marry as she was so desperately sick that she could never fulfil the role of wife of a missionary in China. In a letter home he said: 'I am, however, rather looking forward to reunion with my own Maria, than to any earthly union.'

He was encouraged by many good things happening in China—John McCarthy's training school for new missionaries was doing well, and Ren was amongst the students who were taught the Scriptures and given opportunities to preach the gospel. Occasionally they visited tea shops to sharpen their language skills and speak of the Lord Jesus. Others accompanied Pastor Wang on preaching tours.

On one occasion Hudson walked hundreds of miles visiting the Mission members at Ningbo, Fenghua, Taizhou and Wenzhou.

In Hangzhou Jennie Faulding and Mrs Wang were happily visiting women in their homes which produced good results. Jennie's school was functioning well and two of her students knew the New Testament (except for two gospels) by heart.

Wang Lae-djün had, at his own expense, established four outposts serviced by seven evangelists and colporteurs. He had travelled along the Qiantang River as far as Qu Xian.

In Zhenjiang Henry Reid was supervising the school for women and children and John Cardwell had evangelized the area of the Poyang Lake, travelling along the Fu He River to Fuzhou. At Fuzhou he was greeted by a shower of stones, thrown by some of the locals who hated foreigners.

'Is this the way to treat a visiting stranger?' he asked. The more tolerant in the crowd then ordered the stone throwers to stop their dangerous activity.

On another occasion when a person called out, 'Foreign devil' he took the man's hand and placing it beside his he asked, 'They are the same! Then why do you call me a "foreign devil"?'

Mrs Hudson Taylor (née J. E. Faulding)

He argued that if they had similar bodies and he was a 'foreign devil' then the person before him must be a 'native devil'. As a result many locals no longer called him a 'foreign devil'.

In Anqing, opposition to the Mission increased and in Yangzhou, Hudson faced great difficulty when he attempted to purchase some property.

277

Following the Yangzhou riot he had been guaranteed his right to the property rented by the Mission. This house was owned by a General Li, who hated Europeans. He had retired from the Chinese army, but still had at his disposal several gunboats and soldiers if ever they were needed. Hudson's negotiations with Li's uncle were proceeding well, until the new city officials urged General Li to bring them to a conclusion.

Li wrote to his uncle demanding that he get rid of the foreigners one way or another before 4 May, warning 'that if they were not out of the premises by that time, [the uncle]...should go to the premises, close the first gate and commit suicide within, upon which, "I will at once come and avenge your death." He warned the uncle not to attempt to escape, "for if you do, I will seize on your wife and children and kill them."'

When the terrified uncle pleaded with Mr Judd to leave he reminded the terrified man that as the deposit had been paid and the contract was ready to be signed the CIM would not be leaving the property!

Everyone knew of the warnings and there was an expectation that riots would soon take place. For the sake of safety, Hudson and Mr Judd decided to close the school and send Louise to Zhenjiang. Mr Judd decided to return to the house and defend what was rightfully Mission premises. As 4 July drew near, the local trouble makers prepared for the invasion of General Li's property and the killing of Mr Judd, the foreigner.

The Governor of Jiangsu Province, knowing that such violent behaviour would invite the wrath of the British, warned the Yangzhou city officials that they would be held personally responsible for any harm done to Mr Judd.

The decision was then made that a city official's friend would purchase General Li's property, paying whatever price he asked. He in turn would lease the property to the CIM for an initial period of five years, thus preventing any loss of face to the Chinese or British. Later the CIM would be permitted to purchase the property outright.

About that time (3 June, 1871) the cable link between Shanghai and San Francisco was completed which meant that messages could be quickly relayed between Shanghai and London via San Francisco.

The time arrived for Hudson to return to England. He was most unwell, but was still caring for several pregnant women. Arrangements had been made for Jennie Faulding to accompany the Meadows family following the birth of their new baby. When Mrs Meadows gave birth prematurely they could all return to England immediately.

Hudson collected his son Charles from Ningbo and when the Consul's wife and Mrs Judd gave birth there was no need for him to remain in China.

He left the Mission, consisting of twenty five missionaries, eighteen children and forty five Chinese workers, in ten cities, in the capable hands of Charles Fishe.

The CIM party, including Lanfeng, caught a steam ship for Hong Kong, but were very disappointed with the disgraceful third class accommodation. As an act of kindness, the ships' officers upgraded their accommodation to second grade which was greatly appreciated as most were in poor health. At Hong Kong they were transferred to the Ava which was bound for Marseilles, via Saigon.

This gave Jennie and Hudson a lot of time together, and as the days passed they fell in love. When she confessed her love for him he sent a message from the Red Sea to Mr and Mrs Faulding expressing his affection for their daughter and asking permission to marry. At that time he was thirty nine years old and Jennie twenty eight.

His love for her was real and all consuming, but she entered the relationship knowing that she could never replace the unique place that Maria held in his affections. In a letter to Elizabeth Judd following his wedding, he wrote:

> The last wish [Maria] expressed to me was that if she were removed, I would marry again....Seeing the love I have for her is not likely to undergo any change or diminution, I do not want one or two years, or five, to forget her. You do not know how I love her, nor how seldom for one hour she is absent from my waking thoughts.... And my dear (Jennie) would not wish it otherwise. She has her own place in my heart, which Jesus has given her, a place all the larger because her love is not jealous.

After the *Ava* berthed at Marseilles the little group made their way to Paris, then Southhampton and finally on 25 September, 1871 they arrived in London. There everyone went their own way; Jennie returned to her parents' home and Hudson set out for Barnsley and a happy reunion. He returned to London to visit the Bergers on 10 October.

As he needed accommodation in London he rented six rooms at 64 Mildmay Road on the outskirts of London.

In the house there was Hudson, his mother, Emily Blatchley, Lanfeng and the four children—Herbert, ten years; Howard, eight years; Maria, four years and little Charles who was just two.

He and Jennie wanted to marry, but faced opposition from Jennie's mother who demanded that as they were both unwell they should wait one year. Every time he met Jennie he knew that she was upset—there were telltale marks of tears which had been running down her face.

On 10 November, he wrote a very blunt letter to Mr and Mrs Faulding saying that their objections to an immediate marriage were unfounded and as a doctor he knew their health would improve after marriage. He reminded them that they were of age and well able to make wise decisions. The result was that they were married on 28 November.

Following the wedding they returned to their London home and continued working. Hudson's mother was then able to return to Barnsley and Emily Blatchley had a short holiday.

During marriage preparations Hudson corresponded with the British Foreign Minister who was attempting to curtail the activities of the CIM in Yangzhou because of possible violence.

He also was faced with the Bergers relinquishing their formal association with the CIM because of Mr Berger's theological differences. Both were sick of the tension caused by the political and newspaper criticisms of the activities of the Mission and were spending most of their time in their coastal home. More than ever Emily and Hudson found the administrative work of the Mission resting upon them.

It was in March, 1872, after spending five days with the Bergers, that the work of the Mission was formally handed over to Hudson who knew that he could not handle it alone.

Meanwhile, news from China wasn't good. Charles Fishe, who started off so well as the administrator, had fallen very ill and was incapable of carrying out the essential duties required of him. He was forced to let things go, which meant that correspondence went unanswered and funds were not distributed even when the need was very urgent. John McCarthy had suffered a robbery, yet the much needed finances had not been forwarded to him. In Hangzhou the boarding school was without funds and Wang Lae-djün was obliged to pawn some of his clothing in order to obtain some necessary money.

Robert White was wearing European clothing which was a waste of money as the Chinese charged foreigners a higher price for goods and services than local citizens. On one occasion when some Chinese carriers charged the higher price White very smartly assaulted them. On another occasion he dragged three local citizens to the city mandarin and there sat with him in judgment of the three. After the guilty decision was handed down the men were sentenced to a whipping. Hudson knew that such incidents could well result in the British authorities stepping in and ordering the troublesome missionaries out of the area.

With other missionaries and their families sick he saw the need for his return to China. However, this was impossible until replacements were found for Mr and Mrs Berger.

The news from China was not all bad. John McCarthy was faithfully at work establishing a truly indigenous church. In the *Monthly Gleaner* of November, 1871 he had published an article putting forward his proposals for such a work. He wanted to see the Chinese Christians taking the gospel into areas as yet unreached. These Chinese could work to earn their keep and thus be a real 'tent ministry', pushing forward the aims of the CIM.

George Duncan and Thomas Harvey who built the first Protestant church at Nanking carried out a journey from Wuhu to Ningguo, then to Yanzhou and finally to Hangzhou. When Thomas Harvey became ill, George continued on with a Chinese Christian to the Lake Chao area and then to Lüzhou which was about two hundred kilometres from Anqing. There, even under threat of expulsion he preached the gospel and sold hundreds of Christian books.

Hudson advised him to obtain property in Anqing, as it would be a good spot from which to venture further into inland China.

Tsiang Aliang, the head printer urged William Rudland to find his brother Tsiang, who lived near Fenghua and bring him back saying, 'My little brother at home is feeding cows and is nearly as stupid as they are. I wish you could use him here in some way.' This William did and Tsiang Liangyong was later converted and appointed the pastor of Hangzhou church.

John Stevenson was most unwell for nine months, but as soon as he improved he made his way to Sheng Xian where he preached the gospel to spiritually hungry Chinese. He was a true man of prayer and constantly kept his arduous work before the Lord, pleading for the conversion of souls. It was there that he met a very learned Confucianist named Ning. This scholarly gentleman, a student of the Chinese classics, also studied Western science. The interesting story of his conversion to Christ is recounted by Mr and Mrs Howard Taylor:

> A leading Confucianist, proud of his learning and position, this Mr Ning would have been the last to have anything to do with the foreigner who came from time to time to preach strange doctrines in his city. But he was interested in Western science,

and happened to have some translation of a work upon the subject which he did not fully understand. Taking advantage, therefore, of one of Mr Stevenson's visits he strolled along to the mission-house and entered into conversation with the evangelist. Soon he was introduced to the young missionary, who talked with him of the matters about which he wished to inquire. Then turning to the New Testament lying on the table, Mr. Stevenson quite naturally went on: "Have you also in your library the books of the Christian religion?"

"I have," replied the scholar, "but, to be quite candid, I do not find them as interesting as your works on science."

This led to a conversation in which it appeared that Mr Ning was sceptical as to the existence of God or the soul, and considered prayer manifestly stupid.

"If there were a supreme Being," he urged, "He would be too far distant to take any notice of our little affairs."

Patiently the missionary sought to bring him to a better point of view, but without success; and at length, seeing that argument was useless, he availed himself of a simple illustration.

"Water and fire are opposing elements, we say, and can never combine. Water extinguished fire, and fire evaporates water. Very well, so much for our argument! But while we are talking, my servant has put on the kettle, and see, here is water raised to the boiling point, ready to make you a cup of tea."

"You say there is no God, and that even if there were He would never condescend to listen to our prayers: but believe me, if you go home tonight and take up that New Testament, and before opening it humbly and earnestly ask the God of Heaven to give you His Holy Spirit that you may understand it aright, that book will be a new book to you and will soon mean more than any other book in the world. Put it to the proof; and whether you pray for yourself or not, I will pray for you."

More impressed than he cared to show, the scholar went home ....
That night when alone, Mr. Ning took up the book in question with a feeling of amusement. How could any intelligent person imagine that a few words addressed to some unknown Being, who might or might not exist, would turn a dull book into an interesting one, or make any change in one's outlook upon life? Yet, incredulous as he was, he somehow wanted to put it to the test.

"O God, if there be a God," he found himself saying, "save my soul, if I have a soul. Give me your Holy Spirit, and help me to understand this book."

As evening wore on, Mrs. Ning looked into the room, to find her husband engrossed in study. At length she ventured to remonstrate, reminding him of the lateness of the hour.

"Do not wait for me," was his reply; "I have important matters in hand." And he went on reading.

The book had become a new book indeed, and hour after hour as he turned the pages a new spirit was taking possession of him. But for days he dared not confess the change to those nearest to him.... He knew that as a Christian he would be despised if not cast out by their relatives....Yet his heart burned within him. The wonderful Saviour of whom he read was becoming real to him as he could never have believed it possible....

"When the children are in bed," he said to his wife at length, "there is something I should like to tell you."

...he had no idea what to say or how to begin. But it committed him to some sort of confession of his faith in Christ, though he trembled to think how she would receive it.

Silently they sat on either side of the table when evening came, and he could not open the subject.

"Is there not something you wanted to say to me?" she inquired.

Then it all came out, he knew not how! and she listened with growing wonder. The true and living God—not any of the idols in the temples; a way by which sins might be forgiven; a Saviour Who could fill the heart with joy and peace: to his surprise she seemed to be following eagerly.

"Have you really found Him?" she broke in before long. "Oh, I have so wanted to know! For there must be a living God. Who else could have heard my cry for help, long, long ago?"

It was when the Taiping rebels had come to the city in which her parents lived, burning and pillaging everything. Their home had been ravaged, like the rest. Many people were killed; many committed suicide; and she, helpless and terror-stricken, had crept into a wardrobe to hide. She heard the soldiers ransacking the house, and coming nearer and nearer.

"Oh, Heavenly Grandfather," she cried in her heart, "save me!"

None but the true and living God could have answered that prayer. The idols in the temples were helpless to protect themselves, even, from the terrible marauders. But though they had been in the very room, they had passed over the hiding-place where she was crouching, scarcely daring to breathe. And, ever since, she had longed to know about Him—the wonderful God Who had saved her.

With what joy and thankfulness her husband assured her not only that there was such a Being—supremely great and good—but that He had spoken, had made Himself known to men! Did ever the story of redeeming love seem more precious, or heart rejoice to tell it forth more than that of the once proud Confucianist as he began to preach Christ in his home and city? So fervent was his spirit that it disconcerted those who thought to laugh him out of his new-fangled notions.

"You must control that disciple of yours," said the local Mandarin to the Chancellor of the University. "He is disgracing us by actually preaching the foreign doctrine on the streets. When I remonstrated with him he even began to preach to me! and said he was so full of the 'Good News,' as he calls it, that he could not keep it in."

"I will soon bring him to reason," was the confident reply. "Leave him to me!"

But the Chancellor fared no better than the Mayor, and...beat a hasty retreat. Loving his Bible, and helped by visits to Shaoxing, Mr Ning soon became a preacher of much power. Among the first converts he had the joy of winning was a man who had been the terror of the neighbourhood. Nothing was too bad or too heartless for Lao Kuen! What power had turned the lion into a lamb the villagers could not tell, but the old father whom he had formerly treated with cruelty and neglect could testify to the reality of the change, and, like his son, was soon a believer in Jesus.

In ever-widening circles the blessing spread, till it reached the keeper of a gambling-den and house of ill-fame in a neighbouring town. His conversion was even more notable than the others, for it banished the gambling-tables, emptied his house of bad characters, and turned his best and largest room into a chapel. It was his own idea to have it cleaned and whitewashed before offering it, free of cost, as a place of worship.

These and others formed the group of converts of whose baptism Mr. Stevenson had written. Ten altogether had followed Mr. Ning in confessing Christ, and there were not a few interested enquirers.

Later when Hudson had the opportunity of meeting Mr Ning and his fellow Christians he wrote: 'I could have wept for joy to hear what grace had done for one and another of those present...I have never seen anything like it in China.'

In England Hudson was obliged to oversee the working of the Mission from March until September 1872. During those months he attempted to establish an organisation to replace Mr and Mrs Berger.

First, as finances were low, he began speaking tours in an effort to stir up interest in the Mission. He was also involved in the production of a new edition of *China's Spiritual Need and Claims* which he believed would be used of God to bring about an increased support for the CIM.

Then came the 1872 Mildmay Conference which covered the days 26–28 June.

Following the singing of a hymn he rose to his feet to address the hundreds of Christians who were there for a time of edification. He immediately drew the attention of the people to the fact that missionary effort was carried out by Christians who obeyed the command of their Saviour to go out into the world and preach a risen Christ, the only Saviour of men and women. He reminded them all that such activity was only possible in the power of the Holy Spirit. He then spoke of the work being carried out in China, and the fact that many Chinese were being brought to a saving faith in the Lord Jesus.

One evening during the conference, he stood up and challenged those present: 'Now,' he said, 'have you the faith to join with me in laying hold of God for eighteen new men, to go two by two to the unoccupied provinces?'

Those present, including Henrietta and Lucy Soltau, Jennie, Emily and several men made a solemn covenant that they would each pray daily that Jehovah would answer their prayer.

Hudson then led in prayer.

Everyone knew that he was carrying an organisational burden that was too heavy for one man to bear.

In July, when visiting Mr and Mrs Richard Hill who were faithful supporters of the Mission, it was suggested by Mr Hill that a Council be formed to handle all Mission matters in England, thus relieving him of that burden and making it possible for him to return to China.

In August, after much prayer, a series of meetings were held where Hudson discussed the formation of such a Council with Richard Hill and Henry Soltau as Honorary Secretaries. During the weeks that followed a list was drawn up of people who could serve on the council.

On 4 September a meeting was held to farewell a party leaving for China. This group consisted of the Crombies and Lanfeng, who were accompanying Fanny Wilson and a Miss Potter.

Hudson and Richard Hill visited those people who had been nominated to serve on the CIM Council with the result that an important meeting was held on Friday, 4 October, 1872 to 'inaugurate a Council for the management of the Home affairs of the China Inland Mission.' This group was to act for Hudson during his absences from England. They were to implement the principles of the CIM which were clearly understood.

The 1873 Council consisted of John Challice (Hon Treasurer); William Hall; Richard Hill (Hon Secretary); Theodore Howard; George Soltau (training CIM candidates); Henry Soltau (Hon Secretary), and Joseph Weatherley, with a group of godly men making up the 'Referees'.

George Soltau was responsible for the selection and training of prospective workers with the Mission. This would be done at his school—the Lamb and Flag Ragged School and City Mission.

Hudson then commenced a speaking tour to promote the newly formed Council and recreate an interest in the work of the CIM.

During the tour he organised the packing of all that was needed for his return to China.

Sad farewells with family and friends followed and Emily, who was very ill was again left to care for the four Taylor children. She also helped the members of the newly formed Council carry out their duties.

On 9 October, 1872 Hudson and Jennie and a new recruit for the Mission, Emmeline Turner boarded the train. A large crowd was at the station to see them off, so large that Hudson's father was unable to get through the barrier and missed saying farewell to his son.

The party arrived at Marseilles and made themselves at home in the third class cabins on the steamer *Tigre*. This meant that Jennie and Emmeline shared a nine berth cabin, while Hudson and some other men shared accommodation next door.

On board the ship he and Jennie spent much of their time with correspondence as well as preparing the thirty-first edition of the *Occasional Paper*.

When the steamer reached Singapore they took on board another passenger—Miss Potter, who had become very ill during the voyage across the Indian Ocean and had been left at Singapore to recover. As there was room on board the *Tigre* she was able to continue her voyage. In China her continuing illness resulted in her returning to England where she died in July, 1874.

On 28 November, the first anniversary of Hudson's marriage to Jennie, the ship reached Shanghai. He was returning to a greatly depleted CIM which at that time consisted of nine men, five wives, Louise Desgraz and the newly arrived Crombies and Fanny Wilson.

34

Back in China

Hudson disembarked to be welcomed by a rather embarrassed Charles Fishe, dressed in his finest European clothing. He knew he was in the wrong, but tried to explain away his appearance by saying he would be out of place in Shanghai if he didn't wear his British best.

Hudson soon learned that Charles, on the verge of a total breakdown was ready to return to England. When he realized that Charles had failed to carry out his responsibilities, particularly the distribution of funds to the needy stations, Hudson at once shared the small amount he had amongst them.

Sickness was rife and some Mission families had lost children to the ever present diseases.

Hudson saw the immediate need to visit every Mission centre to encourage both leaders and congregational members and gain first hand knowledge of their needs.

Finances were urgently needed to meet daily running expenses, but before he set out the mail brought a most welcome gift. Faithful George Müller had again sent money for the various missionaries and in the envelope were cheques amounting to four hundred and ninety-five pounds.

Later in Zhenjiang, as a memorial to Maria, land was purchased for the construction of a boys' school.

At that time China was undergoing political changes. The boy emperor, Tong Zhi, reached the age where he could rule as an independent monarch. No longer was his mother, the Dowager Ci Xi the power behind the throne. The new emperor was a worldly young man who lived for horse riding, archery and immorality.

In October, 1872 he married and in this ceremony he snubbed the foreign dignities by refusing them permission to attend, or even look at his future wife as she made her way to the wedding.

When he finally met the foreign consuls, he humiliated them all by holding the activities in a hall normally reserved for the representatives of tributary states.

In 1873 the Chinese forces conquered the invading Muslim armies, but in the process emptied the state coffers.

About this time Hudson was giving serious thought to having his missionaries enter the western areas of China through Burma thus saving time and avoiding the opposition of the Chinese. He knew that delay meant that great numbers passed into eternity having never heard of the name of the Lord Jesus Christ. Many people prayed for guidance as plans were being formulated for the future direction of the Mission.

He wrote to Emily Blatchley on 1 January, 1873: 'I want you to pray daily that God will direct us as to which provinces we should attempt, and how....Ask for me more simple trust in Him, and boldness to attempt great things....Try to get friends to promise and seriously endeavour to pray daily about the opening up of new provinces to the Gospel. Christ must speedily be proclaimed in them: how and by whom we must ask Him.'

Finally he concluded that the work being done in the coastal provinces should be consolidated using Chinese evangelists who were more acceptable to the locals. Simultaneously, trained Christian men and women would venture into the interior provinces. But finances were needed! Money was available for work in new provinces, but the real shortage was of capital to extend the work along the coast.

In England Grattan Guinness and James Meadows were making tours speaking of the work and needs of the CIM. Gifts were being received and a Mrs Grace promised the Mission fifty pounds annually.

Grattan Guinness had opened a training school in the East London area for prospective missionaries. For practical experience they worked with Tom Barnardo in the slum areas of London. Arthur William Douthwaite, who would prove himself a faithful servant of

Christ in the CIM was directed to spend some time with the Grattan Guinness Training School before he left for China.

In December, 1872 Frederick Groombridge and John Donovan sailed for China with the best of references, but both men proved to be unsuitable, raising the need for better screening of prospective missionaries.

Hudson's tour of Mission stations revealed many downhearted Christians. Even the Ningbo, Bridge Street congregation suffered from the lack of oversight and encouragement. Of the work in Zhenjiang Hudson wrote to Emily, 'The work here is and has been utterly neglected.'

In England the treasurer of the newly formed Council, who had finances available, failed to forward the desperately needed money. As Jennie had been left a bequest by an Australian uncle, she was able to devote the interest and a portion of the capital to work in China.

Emily's health deteriorated as she coped with the four Taylor children who often needed a restraining hand, so Hudson could already see the time coming when he would have to return to England.

In a letter to Emily he wrote:

> Kiss the dear children for me. How I wish I could save you the trouble! [He was hoping to get Herbert and Howard into the City of London School.] A little rough discipline might...make them strike their roots deeper, give you more hold of their affections, make them men not girls....Expensive schools beget expensive habits, cheap ones often lead to vulgar habits, so it is very difficult to know...what to do.

Hudson and Jennie were at Nanjing when she went into a long, drawn out labour. Dr Macartney was called for advice and while helping, Jennie went into convulsions and gave birth to a still born infant.

The next day as she seemed well again he returned to his own surgery, but she again went into labour and gave birth to a second still-born baby.

This was a distressing time for both parents. However, the work of the CIM meant there was no time for rest, and Hudson wanted to introduce his plans for the inland provinces.

It was also time for John McCarthy to move to Anqing, leaving his family behind.

There he was frustrated by some Chinese who wanted all foreigners removed from the area. When the owner of his rented property demanded that he leave he failed to comply. Consequently the owner built a pigsty beside the entrance to the Mission property and all who wanted to enter had to wade through a filthy mud pool. As a result John moved into another house and continued his work.

J. Cardwell's work further inland was bearing fruit. He was based at Jiujiang and spent much time travelling by boat to the many centres of population around Poyang Lake selling thousands of copies of the Old and New Testaments and many tracts. To help the work expand more quickly he commenced training classes for prospective missionaries.

Opposition to the gospel was continually being stirred up by the literati, but Cardwell was not hurt.

Again Hudson, unsure whether the Mission should extend northwards along the Grand Canal to Henan Province, or westward beyond the city of Jiujiang to the cities where the Han River met the Yangzi River, turned to God for guidance.

He longed to see the very competent Charles Judd back in China to undertake a move into the inland. He begged him to return, even suggesting that he leave his wife behind. About that time he wrote to Henry Soltau suggesting he join the Mission in China.

Hudson and Jennie set out from Zhenjiang on 18 July to visit the Mission stations along the Yangzi River as far as Jiujiang. This trip ended when they returned to Zhenjiang on 5 August. The next day Hudson left for Yangzhou and Qingjiangpu. Life as an administrator meant prayer and continual travel to encourage and determine the help that was needed in each centre.

In England, Charles Judd announced that he was ready to return to China. Early in September, 1873 with his family, and accompanied by Frederick Baller, Henry Taylor and Mary Bower they sailed for China via America.

Mrs Grace gave the Judds £140 for the new work they expected to undertake, but at the last moment she increased the gift to £300.

Arthur Douthwaite delayed his departure for several months to be able to accompany James Meadows when he returned.

In China Hudson faced many disappointments. The Rudlands had become rather conceited with their work, others were sick, Groombridge was complaining like Nicol had done years before and John McCarthy's wife wanted to pack up and go home.

A message arrived from England that Emily Blatchley was so ill that the Taylor children had moved to be with Hudson's parents in Barnsley. Then came the news that some Chinese students were planning to destroy the Mission property at Hangzhou.

When help was requested for Wang Lae-jün's wife who was seriously ill, Jennie agreed to stay with her while Hudson went to Shaoxing to be with Anne Stevenson whose baby was due in a couple of weeks.

Word arrived during that troublesome period that Charles Judd and his party would soon reach Shanghai. Hudson, determined to meet them, set out at once for Shanghai via Ningbo burdened with the knowledge that he was needed in England to be with Emily before she died.

He had to make a hurried journey along rough roads and over narrow mountain passes, often travelling by mountain chair. He wanted to be in Shanghai to greet the newcomers before they could be influenced by what they saw and heard from the malcontents. He was experiencing difficult times because Groombridge and Donovan who had given their word to abide by Mission regulations were influencing others to change their ways.

On the track between Taizhou and Ningbo he met a postal courier on his way to Taizhou, carrying mail for him. There on the roadside he scribbled a short note to his mother expressing his concern for Emily, and saying he would have loved to see her before she passed into glory, but it was not possible as he was needed in China more than in England. Meeting the Judds and their companions was of primary importance.

Hudson, who tried to meet newcomers in Shanghai, saw the need of a permanent office in that city. The one manning the centre could meet incoming missionaries and be responsible for the ordering and receipt of goods which were to be distributed amongst the Mission stations.

It was in December 1873 that Lanfeng and his wife were appointed the official agents of the Mission, being responsible for all shipping, purchases and postal matters. In addition a printing press was set up and much valuable work was done in this area.

Arriving in Shanghai to meet the newcomers, Hudson rented a room, with four beds, two chairs and a table, at a Chinese inn.

On 5 November he welcomed the Judd family and for the first time met the new arrivals, determined that they would be quickly introduced into the ways of the Chinese.

Fred Baller recorded the meeting:

> We looked but could only see a Chinaman on a wheelbarrow. The barrow stopped and the figure advanced toward us. It was a good thing that there was someone to do the introducing, for we should never have recognised Mr. Taylor. The weather was cold, and he had

on a wadded gown and jacket. Over his head he wore a wind-hood with side pieces which fitted close to the face, leaving nothing but a medallion-shaped opening for nose, eyes and mouth. In his hand he grasped a huge Chinese umbrella, which he carried in true native style, handle foremost. In his wadded clothes he looked almost as broad as he was long, and to our foreign eyes was the oddest figure we had ever seen. He said he had made arrangements for the ladies and Mr. Judd to stay with friends in the French Settlement, and turning to Henry Taylor and myself added: "After we have been to the vessel, perhaps you will accompany me to my hotel."

The newcomers agreed and followed him through the slum areas. Again Frederick Baller wrote:

Lines of junks lie along the river here and trade and bustle are the order of the day. Here, too, are heaps of malodorous refuse, fish, vegetables, muck from the streets, filth of all sorts, while stenches, massive and unrelieved, assail the fastidious foreigner....Mr. Taylor threaded his way among the crowds till he stopped at the door of a native post office. Passing through the front part of the office, he led the way to a small door secured by a Chinese lock. This he opened and invited us to follow him up the stairs. It was pitch dark and very narrow, but we stumbled up till we came to a door which he entered. We followed him, and found ourselves in the "hotel". It consisted of a room about twelve feet square, innocent of any adornment, and containing a square table, a small skin-covered box, and a native food basket....A window opened out on to the street, but it had paper of a grimy hue instead of glass.

Mr. Taylor very courteously asked us to be seated, and after making enquiries as to our voyage, produced a Bible. He read the seventieth chapter of the Gospel of John, and asked what we thought was the meaning of the words, "That the love wherewith Thou hast loved me may be in them, and I in them.".…Reading over, we knelt down and had prayer together.

Hudson invited the weary travellers to a Chinese restaurant and before eating asked if they wanted to wash their hands:

We replied in the affirmative, but as there was no trace of either a washstand, soap, towel or basin, we wondered how the ablutions were to be performed. Mr. Taylor went to the door and called out something in Chinese, whereupon a man appeared who was, we understood, his servant. He went to the basket in the corner and fished out of its depths a wooden basin and what looked like a pocket-handkerchief. Leaving the latter on the table he descended to the street, and going to a hot-water shop bought enough hot water to fill the basin. On his return he placed it on the table, and, taking the rag...he dipped it in the water, and wringing it out handed it to Mr. Taylor....By the time he had gone over the area that needed cleansing, the cloth was nearly cold. This meant another dip...and a renewed application to face and hands, this time more in the way of polishing than cleansing....Here was plain living and high thinking...here was economy and cleanliness combined. Sponge, soap, towel—all were included in the magic cloth! We followed suit, and found the operation very refreshing, partly from its novelty and partly from its effects....We began to realise that we were in a land where money could be made to go a long way.

"Now," said Mr. Taylor, "let us go and have breakfast."...

After enquiry in one or two cook-shops as to whether they had a certain kind of vegetable, Mr. Taylor finally led us into one and invited us to be seated. Four narrow forms were placed around the table. The cooking was being carried on in the front part of the shop, while customers sat at a number of square tables in the back. Our table had once been new, and probably had once been clean, but it must have been many years before we were born. However, what it lacked in purity it made up in polish....A pair of chopsticks was brought and placed before each of us after having been carefully wiped on the shady cloth which dangled over the shoulder of our attendant...we had acquired some skill in the use of [chopsticks] while crossing the Pacific. We had often fraternized with the Chinese passengers, imitating them in the use of chopsticks till we could take up a bean without dropping it....

At last the supreme moment arrived, and the waiter brought in four basins of piled up rice and placed them before us. This was followed by several basins of hot vegetables and a large basin of chunks of fat pork, the pièce de résistance of the meal.

Mr. Taylor's servant...fearing that in our inexperience we should not make a good meal, chose out the fattest and largest lumps and laid them in triumph, with a winsome smile, intended to hearten us to the task, on the top of our basin. It had some interest for us the first few times; but steadily going through four or five pieces in succession...we had to appeal to Mr. Taylor to ask him to desist...

Such was our first meeting with Mr. Taylor in China, such our reception, such our first toilet and meal. Things have greatly altered since then, but I would gladly forgo all the improvements, if I could have the experiences of that morning over again...we took to Chinese dress, Chinese food, Chinese ways as a duck to water. Personally, I can never be thankful enough for that experience. I have been in many dirtier inns since then, in many parts of China, and have had far rougher accommodation than that of Mr. Taylor's "hotel", but the remembrance of his example has made things easy and silenced murmuring.

With this introduction to China, Hudson was sure he had two very good spiritual warriors. They in turn respected the man who would lead them to preach to the Chinese the wonder of salvation in the Lord Jesus Christ.

The newcomers were then escorted to Nanjing where Hudson spent a couple of weeks with them, introducing them to the Chinese culture and street preaching. Leaving both men with Mr and Mrs Judd, he returned to Shanghai visiting the many Mission stations and patients who needed his care. His plan was to reach Taizhou, where he expected to meet Jennie again. Eventually, at the mission house in Fenghua, they were alone for the first time since their marriage.

He sent new material to England for the next *Occasional Paper*, outlining the work of the Mission and indicating where finances had been used.

He also wrote to the English Council indicating the type of person that was needed on the mission field and pleading that they be given some practical experience in frugal living. They needed to know in advance the conditions they would face in China. He also indicated that third class travel was not luxurious:

> If two or three kinds of meat, two or three of vegetables, soup, bread and potatoes ad lib and one pint of wine per meal are not enough; or if the privation of a few weeks' loss of privacy, and separation in the case of husbands and wives, who must sleep in separate rooms, is too appalling, this is such positive luxury and comfort compared with what will be found here, that such persons would do well to stay at home. The only persons wanted here are those who will *rejoice* to work—*really* to labour—not to dream their lives away; to *deny* themselves; to *suffer* in order to *save*. Of such men and women there is room for any number and *God* will support *any* number— they are *His* jewels and *He* values and cares for them.

Support for work in untouched provinces was forthcoming. Mrs Grace, in December, 1873, added another £800 to the £300 she had already given, stipulating that it be used for work in new provinces. Then on 10 January, 1874 Hudson received word that James Meadows was returning to China, accompanied by Arthur Douthwaite.

He saw this as an answer to prayer, and with such an influx of good men and women, the leap into the interior would become a reality.

More time was spent in prayer, seeking the guidance of God on plans that were being formulated.

In his Bible on 27 January, 1874 he wrote on a blank page:

> Tai-chow, January 27, 1874: Ask God for fifty or a hundred additional native evangelists, and as many foreign superintendents as may be needed to open up the four Fus [prefectures] and forty eight Hsiens [counties] still unoccupied in Che-kiang (Zhejiang); also for the men to break into the nine unoccupied provinces. Asked in the Name of Jesus. I thank Thee, Lord Jesus, for the promise whereon Thou hast given me to rest. Give me all needed strength of body, wisdom of mind, grace of soul to do this Thy so great work. Amen.

The work was progressing well, and on 31 March Hudson indicated in a letter to those supporting the CIM that the Mission had over forty stations involving the work of one hundred native and foreign workers. Finances for general use were in short supply and in a letter to Jennie he outlined the situation very plainly: 'The balance in hand yesterday was sixty-seven cents! The LORD reigns: herein is our joy and confidence.'

When Frederick Baller heard this news he wrote, 'Twenty-five cents *plus* all the promises of God.'

On 14 April in Zhenjiang, Hudson met with the Judds and as many of the Mission workers as they could manage, to discuss and pray for the future activities of the Mission. Prayer was also offered to God that their supporters might open their wallets and give to the work being undertaken. There the decision was made to go west! Wuhan and beyond now attracted the attention of everyone. Hudson at once notified Richard Hill in England to forward seven hundred pounds of Mrs Grace's money as it could be used in this new venture.

A short time later Mr Cardwell appeared with his dying child for which nothing could be done. Hudson comforted the Cardwells and several months later a very sick Mrs Cardwell and her two remaining children were on a steamer bound for England.

He was also aware that he was needed in Great Britain, as a replacement had to be found for the dying Emily. Louise Desgraz volunteered for this work.

Before leaving for England he decided to again visit the southern areas of the Mission, where time and again he saw the spiritual poverty of the inhabitants. Many were seeking spiritual peace, but had nowhere to go to find the truth. In Taiping he met one such man, old Dzing: 'An old man found me out, I know not how, and followed me to our boat. I asked him in, and enquired his name.

"My name is Dzing," he replied. "But the question which distresses me, and to which I can find no answer, is—What am I to do with my sins? Our scholars tell us that there is no future state, but I find it hard to believe them."

"Do not believe any such thing," I replied, "for there is an endless future before every one of us. One must either burn for ever in hell-fire, or rejoice for ever in heavenly bliss."

"Then what *can* I do; what am I to do with my sins? Some say live on vegetable food alone (a popular method of fasting, supposed to be highly meritorious in China, as sparing animal life, and tending to keep under the body). Should I live on a vegetarian or a mixed diet?"

Hudson faced a situation where the man had never heard of the name of Jesus Christ. He would have to go back to basics and explain the way of salvation.

"There is no merit in the one or sin in the other," Hudson replied. "Both affect the stomach, not the heart."

"Ah, so it has always seemed to me! It seems to leave the question of sin untouched…I think and think and think again: but I cannot tell what is to be done with my sins. I am seventy-two years of age. I cannot expect to finish another decade. To-day knows not to-morrow's lot, as the saying is; and if true of all, how much more so of me. Can *you* tell me what is to be done about my sins?"

"I can indeed," was Hudson's reply. "It is to answer this very question I have come so many thousand miles. Listen—and I will explain just what you want and need to know." Gladly then Hudson spoke of a living, loving God—his Father in heaven; pointing to various proofs of His fatherly love and care.

"Yes," he interrupted, "and what are we to do to recompense such favour, such goodness? I do not see how it is to be recompensed. Our scholars say that if we worship Heaven and Earth and the idols at the end of the year, it is enough. But that does not satisfy me."

"And you do not know half there is to give thanks for," Hudson replied as he went on to speak of sin and its consequences, of God's pity, and the incarnation and death of Christ as a substitute—the innocent for the guilty, that He might bring us to God.

"Ah!" he exclaimed, "and what can we do to recompense *such* grace?"

"Nothing," I replied, "absolutely nothing but *receive* it freely, as God's free gift—just as we do the sunlight, wind and rain."

Hudson continued his story: 'The poor old man told me of all the idols he worshipped, and was quite overwhelmed to think that in doing so he was sinning against the true and living God....When my companions returned he listened again to the wonderful story of the Cross, and left us soothed and comforted—yet evidently bewildered—to think over all he had heard, more than glad to know that we had rented a house and hoped soon to have Christian colporteurs resident in the city.'

Hudson's visitation of the Mission centres continued and on 2 June he reached Jiujiang. This was to be a short stay as the steamer was to move on to Wuhan but while boarding the boat Hudson fell on the ladder, spraining his ankle and injuring his back.

Struggling to his feet he continued on his journey, reaching Wuhan the following day. When the Wesleyan pastor, Josiah Cox, heard of his arrival and of his injury, he insisted he move from the Chinese inn and stay with him in more comfortable surroundings.

Hudson believed his injuries were not severe and wrote to Jennie telling her that he was improving and able to stand up, putting weight on his feet.

During this time in Wuhan, Charles Judd obtained premises for use by missionaries when the move westward commenced. In Nanjing, Frederick Baller and Henry Taylor remained, waiting the arrival of Mr Judd and his family. Then came word that Mary Bower was very ill with smallpox.

When Hudson reached Zhenjiang he was met by a sullen John Donovan whose marriage proposal to Mary had been rejected. When Frederick Baller heard that she had smallpox, he left at once for her side, and there asked her to marry him. Mary accepted with delight-after all, they had become close friends on the trip to China. They were to become a very capable missionary couple.

Pained though he was, Hudson was fired with enthusiasm for the move westward. He had seen some of the millions of Chinese who were ready to learn of Christ. He had seen people converted and again prayed that God would display his saving power in bringing many souls to saving faith in Christ:

> My soul yearns, oh how intently for the evangelization of these 180 millions of the nine unoccupied provinces. Oh that I had a hundred lives to give or spend for their good....Better to have pecuniary and other outward trials and perplexities, and blessing in the work itself, souls being saved, and the name of the Lord Jesus being magnified, than any measure of external prosperity without it.

It was about this time that James Meadows with Arthur Douthwaite arrived in Shanghai where they were welcomed by Edward Fishe at the newly established Mission business centre.

Arthur's introduction to China was one of excitement, as several days later, on 3 May, 1874, he was involved in his first riot. The French had decided to move a cemetery in order to construct a new road—a proposal that was not well received by the Chinese. Many foreign owned homes were burned to the ground and seven locals killed when forces moved in to quell the disturbance. Arthur Douthwaite wrote home of the incident, outlining how Jane McLean's house and property were totally destroyed, and she was dragged along by her hair. Help arrived, but they too were assaulted. When the rioters understood that they were not French they moved on to other targets.

Many years later Arthur wrote, 'My first year was filled with a succession of riots in one of which I lost most of my possessions and narrowly escaped losing my life also.'

James Meadows moved to Shaoxing where he replaced John Stevenson. He would remain there as the congregational pastor for the next forty years.

Hudson had decided that he must return to England and when finances arrived, plus £500 of Jennie's legacy, he knew God had paved the way for him to depart, secure in the knowledge that sufficient finances were available to cover the Mission expenses.

On 30 August Hudson, Jennie, the Rudland family and the four McCarthy children boarded a French steamer, and began the journey home in 3rd class cabins.

Reaching Marseilles they received letters, one which contained the news that Emily had died on 25 July.

As Mary Rudland was much worse and unable to continue the journey when the group reached Paris, Jennie decided to stay with her for a day, giving her the chance to recover somewhat before catching up with Hudson and his party.

On 14 October, Hudson, William Rudland and seven children reached London. Hudson, however was now walking with the aid of crutches.

He was home, but was confronted with a chaotic situation!

35

Home at Last

They found Herbert was living with his grandmother, recovering from scarlet fever and Louise quarantined with Maria and Charles. Eight days after their return Mary Rudland died.

When Hudson's back condition became worse he was confined to bed. In early November he wrote to his mother: 'My spine has suffered from vibration of railways, cabs and omnibuses, etc, since reaching land; now I am forbidden travelling at all and need to spend much time on my back.'

And things only became worse!

However, there was work to be done. A group was being prepared to leave for China. Catherine Duncan was returning with two women— Lily Doig who was to marry Arthur Douthwaite, and Nellie Faulding who would marry Charles Fishe.

Soon after arriving home news was received of riots taking place in Huzhou where Arthur Douthwaite and James Meadows were settling in. A local society had been formed for the sole purpose of driving foreigners out of the city. The rioting proved that the literati had influence and foreigners were unwelcome! When Arthur Douthwaite was assaulted and had his belongings stolen from him he was learning the hard way that missionary work could be difficult and dangerous.

At that time Hudson followed with interest the efforts of the British to forge a trade route into China through Burma. An expedition led by Colonel Browne set off from Bhamo on 6 February, 1875 having received approval from Peking for this venture. However, the locals, who knew nothing of politics, saw the expedition as a large group of well armed foreigners encroaching on their territory. The result was that on 21 February, 1875 Augustus Margary, a British interpreter and six Chinese were speared to death in an ambush. This became an international incident of great importance.

It seemed obvious that Chinese officialdom was behind the ambush and the British Consul, Thomas Wade took the matter up with China's rulers in Peking.

At a Council meeting on 25 January, 1875, which met around his sick bed, Hudson informed the members of his plans concerning Burma and called for prayer for its success. John Stevenson had volunteered to go to Bhamo, which had a large Chinese population, and prepare for the venture while his wife and children remained in Great Britain.

In July that year a new edition of *China's Millions and Our Work Among Them* appeared giving up to date information of Mission work being carried out and of plans for entering China through Burma. Some readers considered Hudson was mad, but others saw the hand of God in such an ambitious plan.

In the publication there were encouraging articles describing the success of the gospel amongst the Chinese. One such story was of a man who was converted when he heard the gospel spoken by John Stevenson and saw the missionaries on their knees seeking God's blessing upon their labours, and giving praise for his grace and mercy. This particular man later became an evangelist.

In his articles, Hudson stressed the need of perseverance: 'We believe that the time has come for *doing* more fully what He has commanded us; and by His grace we intend to do it. *Not to try*, for we see no Scriptural authority for trying….In our experience, "to try" has usually meant "to fail". (The Lord's) command is not "Do your best," but "DO IT"…Do *the* thing commanded.'

The cover page had written in Chinese the word 'Ebenezer—Hitherto hath the Lord helped us' and 'Jehovah Jireh—the Lord will provide'.

John Stevenson sailed from Glasgow on 6 April, but before he left there was the round of farewells followed by a welcome surprise— Henry Soltau volunteered to accompany him to Burma. Both men arrived in Rangoon on 17 May only to be soon joined by a third man, Joseph Adams, who had received training at Grattan Guinness' School for missionaries.

This courageous move stirred the imagination of many in Great Britain, drawing attention once again to the work of the CIM.

Shockwaves from Margary's murder were felt in many parts of China. Charles Judd with several faithful Chinese Christians had moved into the Hunan province where he rented a house in Yueyang and commenced the evangelisation of the Dongtang Lakes region, but some of the locals, encouraged by the news of Margary's murder, attacked his little group. Protected by some friendly citizens, they were taken from the city by some men in an armed boat, sent by a local magistrate.

Josiah Jackson created further tension when he was rude to a Chinese magistrate. The matter was referred to the British Foreign Minister in London who in part gave Hudson and the members of the CIM a very clear warning: 'I have accordingly to instruct you,' he wrote to the British authorities in China, 'to inform the Taylor Mission that unless (Mr Jackson) and other members of the Mission exercise greater judgment in the future, Her Majesty's Government will find themselves reluctantly compelled to withdraw their passports.'

When Hudson heard of this memorandum he immediately notified each member of the Mission that just one offence could mean the cancellation of everyone's passport. Hence he advised: 'First, the absolute necessity of desisting from making any representation, private, semi-official, or official, of any difficulties in the work to HM Consul or consular offices.

'Second, if possible to avoid personal (dealings) with Mandarins. Communications with mandarins, if essential, must be in writing and worded very courteously, without demands or claims but as a favour. If refused, leave the matter entirely alone.'

Many aspects of Mission work would be difficult, but as Hudson often said of God's work: 'There are commonly three stages in the work for God. First impossible, then difficult, then done!'

Meanwhile, after arriving in London Jennie was found to be expecting a baby and Hudson's condition had worsened. He was so ill, and believing that he would die, drew up a new will, leaving his estate to Jennie.

Later came the news that the faithful evangelist, Mr Tsiu had died.

Hudson now was paralysed in his lower limbs, confined to bed and dependent upon others for all his needs. But he had time to formulate plans and take them to the Lord in prayer. Hanging at the foot of his bed was a map of China and again he pleaded with God for the eighteen missionaries needed to open up the nine untouched provinces. He had three of his eighteen—Fred Baller, Henry Taylor and Arthur Douthwaite—and knew that God would provide the others.

Mrs Grace had given eight hundred pounds for work in new provinces with a further five hundred pounds coming through Grattan Guinness.

Hudson was totally opposed to seeking financial gifts, but knew if he could put before the people of Great Britain the need for prayer, that God would bless the plans of the CIM. His appeal was published in some Christian magazines early in 1875:

> **APPEAL FOR PRAYER**
> On Behalf of more than 150 million Chinese
> There are nine provinces of China, each as large as a European kingdom, averaging a population of seventeen or eighteen millions, but destitute of the pure gospel. About a hundred Roman Catholic priests from Europe live in them, but not one Protestant missionary.
>
> Much prayer has been offered on behalf of these nine provinces by some friends of the China Inland Mission; and during the past year nearly four thousand pounds has been contributed on condition that it be used in these provinces alone ....Our present pressing need is of missionaries to lead the way. Will each of your Christian readers at once raise his heart to God, and wait one minute in earnest prayer that God will raise up this year eighteen suitable men, to devote themselves to this work? Warm-hearted young men, who have a good knowledge of business, clerks or assistants in shops...are well fitted for this work. They should possess strong faith, devoted piety, and burning zeal; be men who will gladly live, labour, suffer, and if need be, die for Christ's sake.

On 7 January, Jennie who was sharing a room with a prospective CIM missionary, Annie Knight, suddenly and unexpectedly realized she was about to give birth. She thought she had plenty of time and not telling anyone of her labour pains attended family worship at Hudson's bedside. Returning to her room she sent out a call for Louise to come quickly, but before she could arrive little Ernest was born. Both were well and not long afterwards Jennie was helping Hudson in every way possible.

With the growing numbers of applicants for work with the CIM, Hudson replied with a letter outlining the type of person who was needed: 'If you want hard work, and little appreciation of it; value

God's approbation more than you fear man's disapprobation; are prepared, if need be, to seal your testimony with your blood and perhaps oftentimes to take joyfully the spoiling of your goods...you may count on a harvest of souls here, and a crown of glory that does not fade away, and the Master's "Well done". You would find in connection with the China Inland Mission that it is no question of "making the best of both worlds"—the men who will be happy with us are those who have this world under their feet....If after prayerfully considering the matter, you still feel drawn to engage in such work, I shall be only too glad to hear from you again.'

Soon Hudson had sixty applicants of whom about fifteen seemed suitable. One was young George King, just eighteen years old who acted for a short time as Hudson's secretary before sailing for China on 15 May, 1875. The ship was wrecked off the coast near Singapore, but he lived to tell the tale and continued his journey to Shanghai.

Henrietta Soltau then assisted Hudson with secretarial work, but longed to be amongst the missionaries in far away China. Hudson however said that her health was so poor that her offer had to be declined. For many years she proved a great asset to the work of the mission in England, becoming responsible for training the women who were accepted for Mission service.

When Hudson's health began to show improvements he was again very busy.

Giving to mission work was declining, and between 4 and 24 May only sixty-eight pounds arrived when over three hundred pounds was needed to meet expenses. Calling all the members of the household together for prayer, he said, 'Let us ask the Lord to remind some of His wealthy stewards of the needs of the work'.

That very evening the postman delivered a cheque for £235.11.9.

Yes, they could depend upon God to provide all that was required by the Mission.

In June Hudson, using two walking sticks, attended the Brighton Convention where the subject was 'Scriptural Holiness'. Returning home he had a third class ticket and while waiting at the station he began speaking to a Russian noble who had attended the convention. Although he had a first class ticket, Count Bobrinsky travelled with him and after some discussion said he would make a small donation to the work of the CIM. When he handed Hudson a banknote he realised it was for fifty pounds. When Hudson asked if he really meant to give so much, and offered to return the money, Count Bobrinsky replied: 'I cannot take it back. It was five pounds I intended to give, but God must have intended you to have fifty; I cannot take it back.'

When Hudson returned to Pryland Road, he walked in during a prayer meeting in which requests were being made to God to provide sufficient money to meet a particular need in China. Another forty-nine pounds, eleven shillings was needed and the Christians knew that God would provide in his own way if asked in faith. He was able to put the fifty pound note he had received from Count Bobrinsky on the table, again proving that God knew their need and had made provision even before they asked.

Prayer was the lifeline of the CIM. Hudson and his workers testified to the miraculous ways in which God had providentially organized events so that when prayer was made the answer was on its way.

About this time George Nicoll, who had spent some time working and being trained with Grattan Guinness and Tom Barnardo, was accepted by the Mission and sailed for China in July, 1875.

The very difficult years seemed to be a thing of the past. Giving to the Mission was increasing and many were offering their lives to serve Christ in China. The 'Holiness Movement' had created an atmosphere where many Christians sought avenues of service for the Lord. The death of David Livingstone also helped create an interest in missionary endeavour.

The year 1875 was an important one because the CIM had been operating for a decade. Hudson prepared a report which he presented at the Mildmay Conference Hall, where he was able to point to a map of China and show his audience the twenty-eight CIM stations to be found in five provinces of China. He spoke of some six hundred who had received Christian baptism and the fact that some seventy of those were preaching Christ to their own people.

Of the sixty-eight missionaries who had sailed to China during the decade, fifty-two were still associated with the Mission. During that time God had not failed to provide the necessary finances to make their work possible. No appeal had been made for financial support, but some fifty two thousand pounds had been received.

In this work Hudson and his supporters gave all the glory to God testifying that God had answered the many prayers of those associated with the mission.

He was determined to see the two prongs of the work progress—consolidation in the provinces where the Mission had a foothold, and the entrance into the nine unoccupied provinces.

In China great historical events were taking place—events that would have a marked effect upon the working of the CIM. The young emperor, Tong Zhi died of smallpox on 13 January, 1875 leaving the Dowager Empresses Ci An and Ci Xi controlling China. Following his death there followed a series of mysterious deaths of the people who had a right to sit upon China's throne.

Empress Ci Xi wanted her nephew, four year old Zaitian, to become Emperor, but he had no legal or moral right to such a position. The powerful Ci Xi then pressured the officers of state to accept his nomination.

She ordered troops serving under Li Hongzhang to take up guard at the Forbidden City and then escort Zaitian to be proclaimed Emperor with the name Guang Xü. Everything was done in the still of night; the marching soldiers holding a chopstick between their teeth to remind them that there was to be no noise—not even speaking.

Now Ci Xi effectively ruled China, especially after the mysterious death of Empress Ci An. With a hatred of foreigners and Christianity, missions would soon feel her wrath.

36

The Curse of Opium

Hudson saw a change taking place in the work of the CIM. It seemed that the difficult days were coming to an end. God had answered prayers and now he found himself surrounded by many good men and women ready to preach the gospel in China. And money was readily available for work in the as yet untouched provinces.

In Rangoon, John Stevenson and Henry Soltau were well received by the large Chinese population. They had travelled to Mandalay where they held discussions with King Mindon of the independent kingdom of Upper Burma. He was pleased to meet them, even inviting them to establish a Mission station in Bhamo. He also gave them a letter to the local Governor, ordering him to grant a plot of land and assist them in obtaining material and workmen to build Mission premises.

On 3 October, 1875 they arrived in Bhamo, but the Governor didn't receive them very well and they were obliged to live in a shed by a roadway until a new governor was appointed. He gave them land near a city gate which was a popular Chinese thoroughfare.

Here they also met the wild Kachin tribesmen, armed with knives and spears, but they soon won them over with kindness and Henry Soltau's efforts with western medicine.

John Stevenson wrote home: 'The Chinese come by crowds and they have taken the Scriptures into China.' Both men expected no opposition if they crossed the border into Chinese territory.

Benjamin and Amelia Broomhall were invited to join Hudson at Pyrland Road and become involved in the management of CIM activities in England. They would be responsible for publications such as *China's Millions* and act as a host to the applicants for Mission membership.

G. Moore, who visited Pyrland Road where he lectured the missionaries in theology, wrote of his meeting the "great" Hudson Taylor:

> (His study) was largely occupied with packing cases and some rough bookshelves set along one of the walls. Near the window was a writing table littered with letters and papers. In front of the fireplace (unused) was a low, narrow, iron-bed neatly covered with a rug....I hardly think there was a scrap of carpet on the floor, and certainly not a single piece of furniture that suggested the slightest regard for comfort or appearance. Mr Taylor...lay down on his iron bedstead and eagerly plunged into conversation which was, for me, one of life's golden hours. Every idea I had hitherto cherished of a "great man" was completely shattered—the high and imposing airs, and all the trappings were conspicuously absent; but Christ's ideal of greatness was there....I strongly suspect that, by his unconscious influence, Mr Hudson Taylor did more than any other man of his day to compel Christian people to revise their ideas of "greatness".

By the end of 1875 Hudson was well on the road to recovery and announced that he had fourteen of the eighteen missionaries ready to open up the nine inland provinces.

M. Henry Taylor had in 1875 and 1876 ventured into the province of Henan with a Christian Chinese named Zhang where they preached salvation in Christ and sold copies of the Scriptures to all who showed an interest. At Runan he was welcomed by an inn keeper, but soon the local magistrate demanded that they leave the inn. The inn keeper replied that he had read the gospel and believed what he had read. There they found four believers who were standing firm in the face of persecution. The two major journeys lasted fifty-four days, with the final one, which ended in Wuchan on 15 January, 1876, lasting eighty-four days. The church was already born and growing in the province of Henan.

In England, men and women accepted for Mission service were leaving for China and with the departure of Francis James, Edward Pearse and George Parker in February, 1876 Hudson could say that God had given him the eighteen for whom he had prayed.

Women also made their way to China under the CIM banner. Elizabeth Wilson, a niece of Miss Stacey, was followed by another five in 1876.

Hudson was eager to return to China where his many skills were needed. He also knew that the members of the Mission looked to him for encouragement.

On 13 May he received the news that his dear friend, Miss Stacey, had died. This was not totally unexpected as she had been suffering ill health for some time, but he was greatly upset and for several weeks found it difficult to continue with his normal activities.

Before leaving he wanted some permanent headquarters for the Mission and successfully appealed for assistance in purchasing the properties being rented in Pyrland Road. With property and an administrative organization in place, he knew he could return to China.

A statement of principles was drawn up outlining what was expected of all who joined the Mission and before anyone left for China they were to sign the document, indicating their agreement with all clauses.

While the newcomers to China were venturing into new provinces the relationship between China and Great Britain was such that war was a real possibility. However, lengthy discussions between Sir Thomas Wade and Li Hongzhang produced the Chefoo Convention which was the formula for peace.

This Convention was ratified by the Chinese on 17 September, 1876 and Great Britain ten years later on 6 May, 1886 after clauses giving Great Britain the right to continue the sale of opium to the Chinese were added. The treaty gave foreigners complete freedom to travel anywhere in China if they had a passport. This edict was to be proclaimed in all Chinese cities ensuring a degree of safety for foreigners.

A new expedition into China from Burma was to be allowed and an indemnity paid by the Chinese for British losses in the first expedition. A letter of regret was to be sent to London and personally delivered by a mission of Chinese officials.

Now the inland provinces were truly open to the gospel—and the CIM was ready to advance.

Hudson left England for China on 8 September, 1876, rejoicing that his prayers had been answered. Legally the members of the Mission could raise the Christian flag wherever they wished. Meanwhile, Jennie remained behind to care for the energetic Taylor children. Herbert and Howard, both young teenagers were forever 'sparring with each other' and needed a strong hand of guidance. Jennie was also available to give advice to the newly established Mission Council.

Hudson's journey to China was an enforced rest as the box in which he had carefully packed all the papers he needed to work on was left behind and followed on another ship.

As soon as he arrived he accompanied John McCarthy to Zhenjiang, but fell ill with his old complaint 'enteritis' which put him to bed for a month. Here he wrote letters, arranged marriages between Chinese Christians and helped make plans for moves into the inland provinces.

Sickness, combined with a heavy workload, made life very difficult. Many times each day he was found upon his knees praying for strength and grace to continue working. Writing to Jennie in November, 1876 he said, 'It is difficult to realise that I cannot run about as I once did.' On another occasion he said that he was well and truly overworked, having much more to do than he could effectively carry out.

Although the 'Chefoo Convention' guaranteed freedom of travel by foreigners to all parts of the nation he was fearful that Peking might at any time repudiate the agreement. As the 'open door' might be closed at any time, he wanted Mission members settled in the inland provinces as soon as possible.

He also wanted to organize missionary conferences which occupied much of his time. His contagious zeal infected those in the outlying Mission compounds, creating the desire to visit the untouched provinces.

Soon after his return a move was made into the distant provinces of Shaanxi and Gansu.

On 8 November, 1876 George King, Charles Budd, George Easton, George Parker and their faithful Chinese evangelists set out from Wuhan to Xi'an. Hudson urged George Easton to take notice of the inns used by the officials who travelled the roads and by boat, as they would be suitable accommodation for Mission travellers.

The journey to Xi'an was by mule over rough territory. There the men divided into pairs to visit villages and cities along the way, selling Christian material and preaching the good news of salvation in Christ. In the larger centres they were pleased to find imperial edicts displayed giving permission for them to be there.

Before leaving Xi'an much prayer was made seeking God's blessing and protective care. George King wrote as they prepared to leave for Shaanxi province:

> We have resolved, in GOD'S strength to make our journey a season of special waiting upon the LORD for spiritual refreshment and blessing, for more likeness to Himself, more practical holiness and brotherly love…we are feeling very insufficient for the solemn and yet glorious work to which we are called; our cry is, "Lord, make Thy strength perfect in weakness."

Their last Sunday together was enjoyable as one of the group wrote:

> Spent some time to-day on a quiet mountain side, reading Mr. Spurgeon's sermon on "Predestined to be conformed to the image of His Son". What a blessed hope! I hope that we may indeed be conformed to Him in holiness and zeal while here below. May we, too, be about our Father's business, and eventually see much blessings amongst these cities. I feel that we are like the messengers sent out into the highways and hedges. Pray that we may bring in many to the feast!

George Easton, George Parker, Zhen and Zhang left for Gansu province which they entered on 28 January, 1877, being the first Protestant missionaries to set foot in this distant province.

Everywhere they travelled the gospel was preached and books sold to the crowds who gathered to see and listen to the foreigners in their midst. In one town a Mohammedan bought a tract which contained the story of the Prodigal Son. However, he soon returned as he was not happy with the illustrations: 'I am a follower of the Prophet. I do not want a picture with pigs in it!' With that he returned the book to George Easton.

After a time the party moved on to the city of Lanzhou on the Yellow River. Short of money and with only a few books left they turned around and began the return journey, arriving at Zhenjiang on 9 April, 1877 where they reported to Hudson all that had happened.

George King, Charles Budd, and the Chinese Christian missionaries Yao and Zhang visited as many places as possible in the province of Shaanxi. On one occasion, when they discovered that the local literati had put up placards urging the Chinese to oppose any foreigners who came into that area, they wisely withdrew. On 4 April, 1877 they returned to Zhenjiang to tell Hudson of their five month evangelistic journey.

When Henry Taylor and a Chinese Christian named Chu reached Queshan the house they had rented was occupied by a Chinese family. They soon discovered that the local literati didn't want them back and planned a riot to drive them out. While this didn't take place on the expected day, about six weeks later the landlord approached Henry seeking protection from an angry crowd. Henry immediately went to the local magistrate for protection, but while absent, his servant was badly beaten and it was thought best to leave. On 12 May, 1877 they arrived back at Wuhan, 'utterly sad'.

Nevertheless, the provinces were being penetrated by brave missionaries—British and Chinese—who glorified Christ as they went.

Another missionary expedition was that undertaken by J. Turner, who had been in China for just ten months, and Francis James, who had been there for only seven months. On 18 October, 1876 they left Zhenjiang for Nanjing, from which they departed on 23 October, 1876 with Yao and a Chinese evangelist. They carried three thousand gospels and one thousand three hundred booklets and tracts—and the precious gospel of Christ to preach wherever they went.

Their journey was one of one thousand seven hundred miles into the province of Shanxi, travelling by foot, boat, cart, donkey and whatever else proved necessary. When they reached the Yellow River they crossed over on a 'large flat-bottomed ferry-boat, a barge carrying two carts, forty mules and horses, some cattle and sixty men, some with loads, rowed (probably) by a dozen standing oarsmen.'

During their travelling the evangelists were amazed to see so much suffering from the effects of drought.

On 8 January, 1877 the journey ended in Wuhan, where after a day reporting to Hudson they commenced another expedition.

One of the greatest missionary journeys was that undertaken by John McCarthy, who crossed China from east to west, preaching the gospel as he went. In England when he told some close friends of his plan the reply was what he expected: 'Walk across China? What madness! Impossible; it never could be done!'

When the Chefoo Convention of September 1876 was ratified by the Chinese authorities, John realised he could freely move throughout all the provinces providing he had a passport suitably inscribed. Plans were being made, but John and Hudson kept the matter quiet in case the authorities refused permission for such a venture. Even when writing to Jennie, Hudson was vague about the proposed journey. He asked for prayer 'for him…as he may be in urgent need of it, and to continue every day till you hear further. If there be danger…McCarthy will be in it….No less than six or seven of the unoccupied provinces are being simultaneously attempted, and there can be no such extensive evangelism unattended with danger.'

John McCarthy wrote at the conclusion of his epic journey:

> My object in travelling in Western China was purely and simply a missionary one...while at the same time glad to obtain geographical and general information. The more frequently foreigners can travel among the people without exciting hostility, the sooner will the time come when, without let or hindrance, a more thorough and scientific knowledge of the country will be obtained...During the whole course of the journey I was not once called upon to produce my passport, nor had I once to appeal to any official for help or protection...Everywhere I received only civility and kindness. The journey...is but one of many which, within the last three years, have been taken by the members of the China Inland Mission...journeys which together represent more than 30,000 miles of travelling.... The spirit of the Chefoo Convention has been loyally carried out by the Chinese officials.

John McCarthy was accompanied by his faithful Chinese evangelist Yang Cunling and a teacher who was able to give advice concerning protocol when meeting Chinese officials and dealing with administrative regulations.

On 2 February, 1877 the party set off to walk to Bhamo in Burma, a journey of some three thousand miles when all diversions are taken into account.

The young man who accompanied John said, 'If Mr McCarthy, a stranger from a foreign land, does not fear; if he feels it laid upon his heart to carry the Gospel to western China, at the risk of his life, certainly I...a native of the country, and also a believer in the one true GOD, must have equal faith.'

In freezing weather he reached Yichang on 25 February where James Cameron and George Nicoll had established a beachhead. They were well received by the Chinese, but became involved in a riot when the local literati incited the mobs to violence. Even the local official who arrived to give help was assaulted. Damage was done to the mission house and when Hudson heard he referred to it as 'A little Yangzhou riot'.

On 20 March, John McCarthy and Yang Cunling moved on, preaching Christ along the way. At Chongqing they found five new Roman Catholic priests settling in. John was disgusted when he saw

Rome extending her influence while Protestants took it easy. Of the evangelization by Rome he wrote in his diary: 'Persecutions do not prevent them from coming here, but rather seem to send them in greater numbers.'

McCarthy kept a diary of what he did and saw, describing the towns, cities, people and the geography of the countryside. He found that the people were very friendly and often invited him to stay in their homes. At one spot near Guang'an—'The City of Broad Peace' they found a young man they had met previously. For two weeks they moved from house to house, village to village, taking the opportunity to rest from the tiring work of preaching in the larger towns and cities.

McCarthy wrote of his experiences in this area:

> It was an excellent opening. The people seemed really glad to hear, asked frequent questions, and listened long and attentively. Curiosity was rife as to life in foreign lands—steamboats, trains, telegraphic communication, etc.
>
> "Does it ever rain in your honourable country?" they would gravely enquire; "and does rain come down as it does in China?"
>
> "Have you any mountains and valleys, so far away?"
>
> "Does the sun shine on you as on us? And is it the same sun?"
>
> Kind and patient answers to these trivial questions removed misapprehension, and gained confidence, winning an entrance for the Master's message to darkened minds and hearts.

Families refused to accept payment for their overnight stays but were happy to receive some gospel literature.

Early in their journey, John and Yang found themselves the centre of attention to the curious Chinese, as foreigners were a rarity. He was often followed to the place where he was to stay overnight, and while eating his meal was watched by an inquisitive crowd. At times he felt like an animal surrounded by humans. As a result he and Yang usually stayed at the first inn, regardless of the standard of accommodation. By the time the news circulated that a foreigner was in town they had almost finished their meal. Refreshed and well fed they would then speak of Christ to the people.

They passed through areas where the opium poppy was grown and the majority of the people were addicts. John again saw the curse of what the English opium merchants had done and were still doing, all for the sake of making money from an immoral trade.

He described a meeting with an opium addicted mandarin:

He was only fifty-eight years of age, but was withered and decrepit from the lavish use of opium. Several times during the day I had noticed his sedan-chair left empty in the street, while he was somewhere indoors gratifying his depraved appetite. As we conversed together on the evils of opium-smoking, amongst other things, he was most emphatic in his condemnation of the practice, and in his expressions of astonishment that Englishmen should have any complicity in such a trade. I told him, of course, that if all Englishmen, and Chinamen too, for that matter, really believed in CHRIST JESUS, they would neither grow, nor sell, nor use the drug for any except medicinal purposes. He smiled very faintly [and] said, "Now every other man smokes"! Soon afterwards he withdrew to transact some "important matters," which my most pressing requests could not induce him to defer. A few minutes later this distinguished personage "the father and mother of the people" might have been seen lying, like any of his coolies, enjoying the opium pipe, regardless of Viceroy, Emperor, and all the world beside.

In many places opium was smoked by everyone in the home, even the young boys and girls.

In July John and Yang crossed into Yunnan province, a province that had never seen a Protestant missionary. When tracts were distributed and Christ preached they faced no opposition of consequence.

Travelling along the roadways they met many Chinese travellers, to whom they gossiped the gospel. Only two rebuked them for what they were doing. The two unfriendly travellers were men from the coast and when Yang offered them a book one replied angrily: 'Why do you go about the country like this selling the foreign devil's literature? Do you think we have no books of our own? Have you never seen the writings of Confucius?'

'Well, if you don't care for the book, there is no need to have it!' replied the young man and the trouble blew over.

For the remainder of the day the man would have nothing to do with the missionaries, but on the next day, when Hudson offered to share a cup of tea with him, he accepted and soon they became friends.

Burma was far away and the missionaries still had to pass through the country of the wild Kachin people who were well armed with knives and spears. However, with a faith that God would protect them, John and Yang continued on their way without any trouble. The end of the expedition was now in sight.

Geraldine Guinness wrote:

On a warm summer evening at the end of August [26th] he at last reached Bhamo and made his way up to the mission-station. Messrs. Soltau and Adams in that lonely station, so far from intercourse with the outside world, could hardly believe it possible that a foreigner had arrived.

"Who can it be?" they asked, bewildered, "and where has he come from?"

The answer to these questions—that it was none other than John McCarthy, and that he had come all the way from Shanghai, three thousand miles overland right across China—scarcely made the wonder seem less. And it was some time before, in their joy and surprise, they could believe it true. Little by little the story was told as the weary travellers rested from their long journey, and together they praised GOD, whose hand had indeed been with them for good.

John McCarthy was the first foreigner to cross China from east to west.

When he announced that he was ready to set off walking back the way he had come, the British officers in Bhamo refused permission as the journey was considered too unsafe.

He spent six months with the CIM, helping whenever possible, and hoping that the British authorities would have a change of heart and allow him to return the way he had come. This was not to be and after six months in Bhamo he returned to England.

Later he returned to China, but during his time in England he spoke out against the opium trade which had so degraded the people. He appealed for people to support the work of Chinese missions, who in bringing the people to Christ also liberated them from the tyranny of sin.

He had seen the degradation of women in China, especially in the province of Yunnan and knew that the gospel of Christ was their only hope. He knew that women missionaries were the only ones who could gain access to the women of China and his appeal for women missionaries touched the hearts of many who offered themselves for service overseas.

37

Conferences and Home

In January, 1877 Hudson wrote to William Berger:

> It will afford you no small joy to know that our prayers are so far
> answered that work had begun in six of the nine provinces....Can
> we be mistaken in trusting Him to do what He so easily can—to
> supply the men and means needed for carrying on His own work,
> and extending it? My glad heart says, "No," little as I know Him;
> and what is more, His word says, "He that spared not His own Son,
> but delivered Him up for us all, how shall He not, with Him also,
> freely give us all things?"

Hudson faced continued criticism by other missionary societies
because of his itinerant missionary policy, of living like the locals
and having women in areas where it was believed no western
woman should live. To win approval for the Mission policies
he took every opportunity to make himself known to other
missionaries.

While preparing for a conference, proposed by the Presbyterian
Synod of China to be held in Shanghai between 10 and 24 May, 1877,
he was concerned that the work of the CIM might be ridiculed by
the long established mission groups. Although the Mission was
independent he wanted others to understand and appreciate that it
was part of the body of Christ.

One evening, being unable to return to his quarters in Wuchang he sought overnight accommodation with E. Bryant of the LMS who lived in Hankou on the opposite side of the Yangzi River. This man held him in contempt and had threatened to 'expose' him in the local newspapers. Hudson took the opportunity to visit the man and impose on his Christian hospitality by asking for a bed for the night.

When the door was opened he explained his situation and of course Mr Bryant was obliged to offer a bed—what else could a Christian do? Before going to bed the two men discussed many subjects, making sure nothing controversial was brought up. After Hudson left the following morning Mr Bryant told others that he had had 'no idea Mr Taylor was so good a man.'

When Hudson later had the opportunity to reply to a critical article which appeared in the press, he was very generous in what he wrote of other mission groups. He spoke of the CIM journeys as 'working towards...more localized efforts than are now possible, (while) *besides this work*, we have fifty-two stations in five other provinces...being carried on by *resident* missionaries....We aim at being an auxiliary agency (to the great missionary societies); and but for the work of our honoured predecessors and...fellow-labourers from Europe and America, the work we are doing would have been an impossibility.'

The conference had attracted missionaries working as far away as a thousand miles from Shanghai and some shipping companies were offering special rates to any delegate who travelled on their ships. It was known that about one hundred and forty missionaries from eighteen mission organisations would gather to hear papers delivered, reports given and participate in prayer and worship of the God they loved and so diligently served. The conference was to be in English.

With such an important gathering Hudson decided to hold a local conference for CIM workers and any members of other missionary societies who wished to attend. The Sunday was spent in fasting and prayer and on the Monday a small group sat down together to hear the Scriptures opened. Present were six missionaries from the LMS, six Wesleyans, one from the American Episcopal Church and fourteen CIM members.

This was followed by talks on missionary activity and ways to integrate with the Chinese people. Griffin John, who had travelled far and wide spoke on the words of Scripture: '...but tarry in the city of Jerusalem until you are endued with power from on high.' In part he said, 'We have done very wrong in not waiting upon the Holy Spirit for power and guidance. We have been working like atheists, and I believe we have by this sinned awfully against the Holy Ghost.' Before the conference concluded, and thanks were extended to Hudson, the missionaries sat down together to commemorate the Lord's death. On the Sunday after the conference had concluded, three hundred Chinese Christians gathered with twenty missionaries for worship.

Hudson rejoiced that now those present would no longer consider the work of the CIM as 'aimless wandering.'

At the General Missionary Conference forty-five papers were delivered on a variety of subjects, Hudson speaking on, 'Itineration Far and Near as an Evangelizing Agency'.

The one Chinese present, Dr V. P. Su Vong praised the medical missionaries, but stressed that such men should not neglect the preaching of the gospel.

There followed some discussion of the relationship that should exist between the different Chinese churches.

One theological issue that many feared would split the delegates was that known as 'The Term Question'. Much had been written and said concerning the name to be used for God when preaching to the Chinese. When the subject was raised it was passed over as unity was of more importance than such a devisive issue.

One statement that had an effect on many throughout the world was: 'We want China emancipated from the thralldom of sin *in this generation*. It is possible...The Church of God can do it, if she be only faithful to her great commission.' In one form or another the words '*in this generation*' were repeated many times.

Reginald Radcliffe, at the 1877 Perth Conference declared, 'Let us pray God to gift 2,500 women at a stroke, and 2,500 men at a stroke and...to scatter them to the ends of the earth....I implore you to obey the Lord Jesus: "Go therefore and teach all nations."' Many in attendance saw such a time was then!

When the conference concluded, Hudson wrote to Jennie saying that the relationship between the CIM and other societies was now good. They understood more than ever, the man, Hudson Taylor, and the plans of the Mission.

He, however, was not well. He had toothache and had been sleeping in a downstairs room to give someone else a more comfortable room upstairs. When he was warned that overwork and lack of bodily care would shorten his life, he replied: 'Does it not say in God's Word that we ought to lay down our lives for the brethren?'

With the conference over, he faced a tour of the Zhejiang province mission centres. But before leaving he announced a convention for both Chinese and foreign missionaries—to be held at Ningbo- and the language to be spoken was Chinese!

A tour of mission centres commenced, but first a problem in Zhenjiang needed his counsel. One church leader had become an alcoholic and on one occasion was too drunk to stand during a communion service. In some centres, missionaries and people were downhearted and needing encouragement. Wang Laedjün sought him out for advice and then there was the continual job of preparing the next edition of 'China's Millions'. A lot of work went into the preparation of illustrations, articles on life in China and the work of the Mission. Before publication there was the slow, tiresome job of proof reading.

Despite his best efforts the magazine created problems with some readers. Lord Radstock wanted more information about Mission plans for the future, in order to encourage and give direction for prayer and complained that too much space was devoted to what the Mission had accomplished.

Hudson knew that he could never satisfy everybody!

On 8 June he set off to visit the many CIM stations in the south, accompanied by Elizabeth Wilson who was to stay at Wenzhou while he moved about. She, with her grey hair, became known as the 'Elder Sister' and was highly respected by the Chinese.

The church at Hangzhou was self supporting and reaching out into the surrounding district. On 7 July they reached Sheng Xian, which he believed to be 'the most successful of all our stations'. The people rejoiced to meet him again but soon he found out that some of the faithful Christians he had known had died. It was over three years since he had been in some of those regions and now heard many stories of God's saving grace.

The saintly, educated Nying, had done a faithful work and seen many won into the kingdom of the Lord. One of his sons in the faith, had seen a cotton-weaver saved in an unusual way. He was just a poor orphan young man, the slave of the family who had adopted him.

When he heard some laughter coming from the house next door he went to a hole in the wall where a knot had fallen out of the wooden plank and looked to see what was the cause of all the merriment.

The neighbour's son had returned from the city where he had heard the well-known gambler, Tao-hsing, who had 'eaten the foreign religion' and whose life had become so changed. He was repeating the story of the Prodigal Son.

The man listening heard the story with wonder and asked himself if there was a God, a heavenly Father who could love so much.

'Oh, go on, go on! Let us hear more of those good words!' he called out when the story ended.

When the response was laughter he later found his neighbour to once again hear the wonderful story of a God who loved and forgave.

At once he understood the message but when he told the story to the people for whom he worked, he was told to leave. This meant he had no occupation, nowhere to live and would lose the bride for whom he was working. It meant that he was cast out into the cold night, penniless and without a future, all because of this new religion. But he could not turn his back upon the Christ he now loved.

There in the street, with the freezing sleet falling upon his bare head he turned to God for refuge.

'A week or two later,' Mr. Taylor wrote, 'the family found they could not manage without him. After trying in vain to induce him to turn from the Lord, they took him back; and when we were there, there was hope of the conversion of several members of that household. Truly the Gospel is still "the power of God unto salvation"; we have no need to be ashamed of it, or fear for its success!'

Hudson wanted to move on, but money for general use was in short supply and on 1 August, he realised he had only two cents left.

During the journey which lasted five months he had kept up with all the correspondence that followed him, and devoted time to prayer, three times each day, never failing to mention each member of the Mission by name.

Soon it was time to return to Ningbo for the conference over which he presided. As he was soon to return to England, he left his travelling boxes in Shanghai ready to be transferred to the ship on which he would travel.

The conference, which lasted for eleven days with all papers presented by Chinese in their own language proved to be a real success, especially as representatives from other missionary societies were present. It showed that the churches could work together in the promotion of the gospel.

During this time evidence was mounting of the terrible famine in some of the northern provinces. Relief was needed and whilst the CIM was helping, much more needed to be done, giving another reason for Hudson to return to England.

On 17 October he sent a one word cable to Jennie—'Coming'. However the death of Edward Fishe delayed his departure for several weeks.

On 9 November and still wearing his Chinese clothing, he boarded a ship bound for home. He cabled Jennie to stay at home and not meet him in Paris. He had been away for fifteen months and wanted to meet his beloved Jennie in their English home.

It was just before Christmas 1877, on 20 December that he reached London and was again reunited with Jennie and the children.

38

Home Again

Homecoming was a joyful time for the Taylor family as it was Christmas time and, for a few days, work could be put aside. However, soon it was back to the preparation of *China's Millions* which was published each month. Articles had to be written, reports obtained from Mission members in China, illustrations had to be selected and the finished product proof read for errors. Life was busy!

One serious issue that was raised again and again was the terrible curse of opium upon the Chinese and Burmese, with the profits going to the British. J. Cardwell wrote of the effects of opium:

> It is eating out the very vitals of the nation. It is the source of poverty, wretchedness, disease and misery...It closes the eye to all pity, and the heart to all shame and sympathy. See that poor wretch with emaciated frame; he has parted with his land, his house, his furniture, his children's and his own clothing and bedding, and either sold his wife or hired her out for prostitution, and *all for opium*, to satisfy an insatiable appetite...until it has consumed his life.

However, the immediate issue was the terrible effects of drought in some of the northern provinces. Floods that had washed away the valuable top soil, followed by droughts, resulted in the deaths of tens of thousands—a number which mounted as the famine continued.

Members of the CIM who were travelling in those provinces gave graphic reports of the conditions. Many missions risked the lives of members as they worked to alleviate the distress of the starving people. The Chinese government was organizing help for the needy, but this was often a failure due to corrupt officials stealing the relief before it could be distributed. Often women and girls were exchanged for food.

Tianjin became a refugee centre for hundreds of thousands, but typhoid fever broke out causing the deaths of hundreds each day. A fire in a camp for refugee women incinerated nearly three thousand people. The animals hauling the much needed grain were often killed by hungry people leaving much of the grain to be eaten by rats.

Starving people walked towards the well watered sections of the Yangzi Valley through thousands of corpses scattered along the way.

In southern Shaanxi in late 1877, where a reported four million people were starving, it was disclosed that the trees had been stripped of their bark and eaten as food.

In Shaanxi the price of bread had increased seventeen times and rumours were circulating of people eating the flesh of those who had died.

Stories appeared in local press of the killing of locals for their flesh to eat. It was unsafe to be found alone in those areas!

When the rains came the farmers were often too weak to plant the crops.

During that terrible time seventy-five million people were suffering from starvation and over nine million died.

In all, aid from England amounted to a paltry fifty thousand pounds. Of this amount, eight thousand pounds worth of aid was distributed through the CIM and ten thousand pounds through other missionary societies—just a drop in the bucket when so many faced starvation.

Hudson however, knew that of more value to the suffering women in China would be a woman who understood the situation; a woman who could help women and children in particular; a woman who could redeem those women and children being sold and give them hope; a woman with organizing gifts and a faith in God to do great things in His name—and that woman was Jennie Taylor.

He suggested that Jennie should leave with a party of volunteers to oversee the orphanages and supervise the relief work.

At that time Jennie was just thirty-three years of age and the mother of two little children. Such a move would mean a great sacrifice, but she was willing to serve the Lord by returning at once to China.

When Amelia Broomhall heard of Jennie's plans she willingly offered her help to bring the plan to reality saying, 'If Jennie is called to China, I am called to care for her children.' This would mean another seven children added to her family of ten; this on top of all her work caring for prospective Mission workers.

Of course there were those who said that such a move was wrong. When one good friend, Mrs Robert Howard, privately told her that she should remain at home, Jennie took the matter to the Lord in prayer again, only this time she sought tangible proof that her proposed move was in accord with His will. She would put the Lord to the test as Gideon had done two thousand years before:

I felt like Gideon, that my strength in China would be, "Have not I commanded thee?" and I wanted some fleeces to confirm my faith, and as a token for those who would have me remain at home. I asked God to give me, in the first place, money to purchase certain requisites for outfit, as we had none to spare; and further, to give me liberally, as much as fifty pounds, so that there might be money in hand when I went away.

That very afternoon…a friend called to see Mrs Taylor, and before leaving said, "Will you accept a little gift for your own use, to get anything you may need for the journey?"

And the sum put into her hand was £10—just the allowance made by the Mission at that time towards the cost of an outfit.

No one knew, not even Mr Taylor, about the fleeces; and with a wondering heart she waited. Several days passed without bringing any further answer to her prayer.…

She continued, in a letter to Mr. Taylor's mother:

Yesterday (Sunday), I felt He would provide at the right time…and that in going I should learn more of Him and find His strength made perfect in my utter weakness.'

Glancing over the letters to see if there was one that might contain a gift for themselves, she came to the conclusion that there was not, and opened first a letter from Barnsley, thankful that Mr. Taylor's parents approved the step they were taking. And lo, from his father was enclosed a cheque for fifty pounds! Overwhelmed with joy and thankfulness, she ran to Mr. Taylor's study, but he was not alone.

'When I returned [for she was called away], he was reading your letter, and considering how the Lord would have the money applied.…

"'Oh," I said, "that fifty pounds is mine! I have a claim on it that you do not know of." And I told him all the circumstances.'

God had answered Jennie's prayer in a way that made her rejoice greatly. Ten days later, on 2 May, 1878 she and a group of three women and four young men boarded a ship for China. As she was leaving she was given a gift of one thousand pounds to assist in the relief work.

William Sharp, a new member of the CIM London Council who saw the party off recorded his impression of the separation of Jennie from Hudson: 'I felt just as if I were parting with my own wife, and the thought was altogether more than I could bear...and yet I suppose that if God called us to part, He would enable us to do so with the same calmness that you enjoyed yesterday.'

When Jennie and her enthusiastic party of missionaries arrived in China on 13 June, the women moved to Yangzhou to commence language studies, while the men went to Anqing. Immediately Jennie became involved in relief work which was well received by the local authorities, including many of the literati. When one missionary involved in relief work died, a senior Chinese official stated, 'that there must be something in a faith which induced the foreign gentlemen to come to China and gratuitously risk their lives, and even forfeit them' for the citizens of China.

One member of the CIM when he saw the death, misery and sickness about him said, 'It is probable that others of us will be called away. We must hold ourselves prepared, though of course we shall use every precaution against the fever. If I die...I wish to be buried here.' The love of God could be seen in the devoted, loving lives of the foreign missionaries.

After a bout of cholera, Jennie moved into some of the worst areas affected by the famine and established an orphanage in Taiyuan. She also opened an industrial school for destitute women.

When the rain fell giving the drought areas the prospect of a good season, disease broke out causing even more deaths than the famine.

Despite the relief support by citizens in England, Hudson made a cutting comment: 'Is it not humbling to think that the entire amount raised for the famine relief during 1878...is actually exceeded by the amount we through our Indian Government receive in three days from the sale of opium in China.'

The valuable relief work done by members of the CIM was praised, with Jennie receiving special mention by Alexander Wylie of the LMS: 'Among the earliest volunteers were members of the China Inland Mission...There is one...fact of such a noble character that I think it ought to be held up to view, I mean the conduct of the heroic lady, Mrs Taylor.'

Jennie was not alone in carrying out relief work on behalf of the CIM. In 1879 George Easton came into contact with the suffering refugees from the famine in Shaanxi. Many of the starving people were naked because they had sold everything they owned to buy food. Clothing was a necessity and George Easton, after distributing some meagre food supplies set off to Hanzhong where he obtained two thousand five hundred pieces of clothing. Packing it on mules he returned to Tianshui, arriving there on 3 February, 1880 and soon had distributed all the available garments.

George King, having heard of the clothing needs, sent five mules loaded with one thousand four hundred sets of clothes suitable for children which were greatly appreciated by the people.

In 1880, as a consequence of seeing China's great physical and spiritual need, Harold Schofield, physician and surgeon, joined the CIM and opened a new work in Taiyuan.

In England, and missing Jennie, Hudson was faced with problems in the Council. Funds were low and he spent time studying the accounts in order to be fully conversant with the situation. He realised that it was necessary for the churches throughout the nation to be made fully aware of the situation in China, and to call them to prayer. It seemed to him that many churches and Christians had slipped into a lazy, selfish way of living and needed to be awakened out of their stupor.

He also became aware that several members of the Council were not satisfied with an advisory role and wanted to play a part in administration. This he knew was unwise as those in England didn't have a true understanding of affairs in China.

So he set about visiting each Council member, explaining the true situation and appealing for prayer and help. This was followed by a round of talks at churches, schools, Sunday Schools and conferences; and as John Stevenson said of him: he carried an 'eighteen province revolver in his pocket.'

Congregations listened intently to his reports of the movement into the nine unevangelized provinces, financed by gifts earmarked for that work. He then announced that he was praying for another twenty or thirty men or women to implement the plan. He knew that if God was asked for manpower, he would raise up the men and women needed to carry out His purposes.

At a meeting of supporters, he said:

With current income not equal by so large a sum to the expense of the work, the question might well be asked, "Is the project of sending out twenty or thirty additional labourers at all a prudent one, even if men and women who appear suitable are found?"

Well we have looked the thing in the face, dear friends, and this is the conclusion we have come to: with the current income of the Mission we have nothing to do, but with God we have everything to do…we are asking GOD to send twenty or thirty.…He is just as able to supply them as he has proved faithful and loving in supplying those who have gone hitherto.

Up to the present, God has carried us safely through. As for the future—if by His grace He will only keep us, individually, *faithful to Him*, that ensures everything.

Again he testified to his faith in God—the God who answered the prayers of those who acted in accordance with His will.

Those who went to China as a response to God's call, faced the attack of Satan and his demons. The missionaries worked in areas where Christian morality didn't exist and Satan used the situation to undermine their faith. Thus, he asked for prayer that they might be kept faithful.

When he and his prayer partners prayed for extra manpower, answers soon began appearing. In 1878 fourteen men and fourteen women offered themselves for work in China and in March, 1879, four men departed, followed by another two in November.

At this time some substantial gifts were received by the Mission, including a gift from William Berger which brought his giving for the year to two thousand pounds.

When, due to overwork, Hudson's health deteriorated, the Beauchamps invited him, and the children, to accompany them to France and Switzerland.

This proved to be a very refreshing time, but the usual correspondence followed him wherever he was, which meant he spent much time answering as many as twenty five letters each day.

He missed Jennie's companionship, and from Sils Maria he wrote to her on 27 August, 1878, saying that their separation was for the sake of the Lord they served: 'Every day I look at the little Bible marker you gave me, with the words "For Jesus' sake," and I am thankful for the reminder. It is not for your pleasure or mine that we are separated, nor for money-making, nor for our children's sake. It is not even for China, or the missionaries, or the Mission; no—*for Jesus' sake*. HE is worthy!'

At that time he travelled to Paris to meet his dear friend William Berger and then it was back home and the continual round of meetings.

Hudson knew that some changes had to be made to the Mission organization in England before he could return to China.

Early in 1879, Benjamin Broomhall was officially appointed General Secretary in England, which meant that he was the overseer of its activities. Theodore Howard was appointed Director of the Council, while the Council was reminded that their function was to 'advise'.

Hudson planned to return to China after his meeting obligations were finished. He attended as many prayer meetings as he could to encourage these faithful people in their important work.

Life still had its stressful incidents. Towards the end of 1878, while attending a prayer meeting, a nurse rushed in with Mary Baller's baby in her arms. The little girl was suffering from 'croup' and had stopped breathing and appeared to be dead. Dr Hudson quickly grabbed the child and commenced mouth to mouth resuscitation. Soon the child began to breathe unassisted and years later became a CIM missionary in the province of Hunan.

Hudson was a man of prayer, but it was prayer associated with action. When the nurse brought the little girl to him for help a woman who believed in faith healing asked him to pray for the child's recovery. His reply to the woman was, 'Yes, pray while I work.' Later, one of his sons said of his father, 'He prayed about things as if everything depended upon the praying...but he worked also, as if everything depended upon his working.'

To enable Hudson's return to China, John McCarthy was given the responsibility for publishing *China's Millions* even though Hudson remained the editor.

Soon it was time for bags and boxes to be packed and loaded on board, but one box was mislaid—Hudson's medicine chest.

Before leaving England he spent time with William Berger, George Müller and C. H. Spurgeon. Spurgeon, who held Hudson in the highest respect, considered him to be a spiritual giant.

It is interesting to read Spurgeon's description of Hudson as it appeared in the *Sword and Trowel* (May, 1879):

> Mr Taylor...is not in outward appearance an individual who would be selected among others as the leader of a gigantic enterprise; in fact, he is lame in gait, and little in stature; but...his spirit is quiet and meek, yet strong and intense; there is not an atom of self-assertion about him, but a firm confidence in God....His faith is

that of a child-man...too certain of His presence and help to turn
aside...He provokes no hostility, but...arouses hearty sympathy,
though he is evidently independent of it, and would go on with
his great work even if no one countenanced him in it....The word
China, China, China is now ringing in our ears in that, special,
peculiar, musical, forcible, unique way Mr Taylor utters it...He did
not deny the fact (that he was already growing a queue).'

Hudson had to fulfil a speaking engagement in Holland before
boarding the ship at Marseilles, where he would join his missionary
group.

On the ship he progressively became unwell and really missed his
mislaid medicine chest.

By the time he reached Hong Kong his health had improved and
there he received a parcel of letters. Some outlined problems awaiting
his attention when he arrived in China, but the one that thrilled his
heart was from Jennie.

When word was received that Hudson and reinforcements were
soon to arrive, Jennie had transferred the orphanage and industrial
school to Anna Crickmay and set off for Shanghai, arriving there on 5
March to await his arrival.

On 22 April, 1879, Hudson was met by Mission members and his
Jennie. Noticing the lack of space at the Mission offices, he decided
that in the future new, spacious premises would be provided to cope
with all who needed accommodation.

In thankfulness to God for their safe arrival the first day on shore
was devoted to prayer and fasting.

Jennie soon saw that Hudson was run down and in need of a total
rest. When Dr Johnson of the LMS agreed, particularly when Hudson
became ill with dysentery, Jennie insisted that he have a complete rest.

With the heat of summer fast approaching he knew that his usefulness would be greatly undermined if he did not have immediate rest.
Soon he was on his way to enjoy the pleasant area of Yantai!

39

Rest for the Weary

Yantai (Chefoo) was a popular holiday spot for foreign traders, consuls and missionaries, who had established homes at Settlement Point.

Jennie, accompanied by Edward Tomalin and Joe Coulthard, was worried that Hudson, who was very ill and confined to bed, might not survive the journey.

He was unable to eat solid foods and lived on milk. What was supposed to be a two day trip by ship, turned out to take four days due to the heavy fog that settled over the ocean.

The milk that Jennie prepared for him curdled and the ship's supply ran out. Realizing that he was seriously ill, Jennie took the situation to the Lord in prayer. Describing the time to Louise Desgraz she wrote:

> In my distress I cried to God to help me. I asked Him to enable Mr Taylor to take the food we had, or to show me what I could get for him, or to make him better without anything...I pleaded too that the fog might clear away, and that God who loved His own child would undertake for him, as the responsibility was too great for me to bear....In the night he had a cupful of arrowroot, and next day was decidedly better....About 9:30 the fog cleared right away, and we had a splendid, moonlight night....It was between 9 and 9:30 that I had been praying about it before going to rest.

When the ship reached Chefoo, he was taken ashore on a Chinese boat. As inns were much too expensive, they accepted the invitation of Mr Ballard, a customs' officer, to stay at his home. Thus they became paying guests from 8 May till 9 December (1879). The fresh air, good company and nourishing food soon had him praising God for answered prayer.

As he recovered he saw the need of such a pleasant spot for Mission members who were suffering from physical exhaustion due to work, the hot summers or sickness. His vision extended to a school for Mission children, a hospital and a dispensary.

He rented premises only to hear of the Judds selling their furniture and preparing to return to England because of Elizabeth Judd's ill health. He sent word that they should spend some time enjoying the pleasant surroundings at Chefoo.

Soon the Judds moved into an unfurnished house. This was the 'Bungalow'—three small rooms and a warehouse. Charles Judd described the situation:

> There was no furniture to be had in Chefoo in those days, save one kind of a chair made of willow. It was altogether a new place; besides which, we had no money for anything except necessaries. Seeing a number of Chinese houses at no great distance however, I went over, and found a shopman selling off his shelves very reasonably. These I bought, and adapted to our requirements. Some of them did for beds, like berths on a ship, and didn't our boys enjoy them! I can truly say we lacked nothing—though it was a case of picnicking on the floor at first, which we did very willingly.

Thus commenced the first year of what became the CIM resort. Charles Judd was made responsible for the success of the venture, allowing Hudson to concentrate on other Mission affairs.

When Hudson had recovered sufficiently, he set out to visit some of the trouble spots needing his personal attention. The trip to Shanghai proved dangerous as the ship was struck by a typhoon. Again, he bowed before the throne of grace pleading for the safety of the ship and all on board. As he prayed he felt assured that all would be well. That day he wrote: 'I took off my swimming belt, turned the bedding over and found the underside moderately dry, and taking off my wettest things lay down in the others.'

Jennie was very conscious of the danger he faced when caught up in such horrendous weather, but when some of her friends expressed surprise that she wasn't unduly concerned, she answered, 'I did rejoice…that you were in such *safe* keeping…but when our Father had you in the hollow of His hand, why should I fear!'

After dealing with some problems, he sent the Moores, who were at Zhenjiang, to Chefoo for rest and recreation. At Yangzhou it was obvious that a new orphanage was required which meant drawing up plans and organizing supplies and labourers. Hudson was not the sort of person to stand back and watch others do all the work, so he rolled up his sleeves and in the extremely hot weather helped the builders. As a result he was overworked, lost weight and when he fell ill with dysentery he was compelled to return to Shanghai, and then to Chefoo.

More than ever he saw the value of a Mission rest centre at Chefoo and with Charles Judd spent time looking longingly at some land they considered to be ideal for their project. Both men knew that if they showed interest in the purchase of the property the price would automatically be raised.

One day as they were walking over a paddock the owner appeared and asked if they wanted to buy the field.

Unsure of what to say both men hesitated, but the farmer repeated his question: 'Do you want land?'

When they replied that they were interested in buying some property, to their surprise he asked, 'Then will you buy mine?' The sale price was not excessive and Mr Judd wrote: 'Then and there the bargain was struck. I never knew a piece of business settled so easily. The money was paid and we got the field, with a gully and fresh water running down beside it. Then neighbouring farmers were willing to sell theirs as well; and we bought all we wanted at a remarkably fair price.'

Next came the construction of some buildings. Again Mr Judd recalled:

> Neither Mr. Taylor nor I had any experience in house building. We employed men to quarry stone out of the gully, and made most of our bricks from the surface soil, which did well for that purpose. Then it occurred to us to make use of a ship called the *Christian* which had been wrecked in the bay. It had been built chiefly of oak and Norwegian pine, which served our purpose splendidly. We bought a large part of the wreck, using the deck for rafters and the oak for heavy beams. A Shanghai newspaper remarked…that the *Christian* had ceased going to sea, and had joined the CIM.
>
> From another wreck, the *Ada*, we were able to buy teak, which made the floors. The cabin-fittings from that wreck came in most

usefully. They were a splendid sideboard. We brought doors, locks, cupboards, everything we liked to take, at two dollars a hundredweight. We squared the doors as well as we could, got keys for many of the locks, and they answered all right. The worst of the teak was the holes that the bolts had left. We filled them up, but the filling was very apt to come out, leaving openings in very inconvenient places. I do not say that the house was well built, but it was wonderfully good considering our lack of experience. There were five rooms upstairs and about as many down, with outhouse and lean-to rooms besides...the Europeans in the Settlement were amazed at the rapidity with which it was put up. They could hardly believe their eyes when they saw it finished.

This change of work was very beneficial to Hudson, and the newcomers to the Mission found working with the Chinese a fine way of learning the new language. It also presented a wonderful opportunity to teach the gospel.

The finished building was the first section of the CIM Chefoo school. As the years passed other school buildings were added, plus a hospital and homes for the staff. The first pupils were two of the Judd children.

The school enrolled CIM children and others from the Consul and his staff and local merchants. By September, 1881, more than fifty boys and girls were attending, with some boarders. This school gained an excellent reputation in the Far East, because many of its ex-students made a great contribution to the society in which they lived.

Before long, student fees met the cost of running the school.

It was towards the end of 1879 that Hudson decided to transfer his office to Yantai. The pleasant climate meant he could spend more time attending to administrative duties without the continual sickness caused by the inland heat.

The mission was growing and numbered more than seventy Europeans and over one hundred Chinese, spread over sixty-four locations. He saw the advantage of Chinese nationals taking Christ to their own people, having written:

> No greater blessing can be desired for China than that there may be raised up...a large number of men qualified to do the work of evangelists and pastors...The sooner a few converts can be gathered in each of the interior provinces, the sooner may we hope to have men in training for Christian work in widely distant parts of the empire.

CIM missionaries were ever on the move. Many dependable men, with Hudson's blessing, made their own decisions concerning the work they would do. Some consolidated their work while others carried on itinerant ministries, taking the gospel to all parts of China and beyond.

His life was extremely busy visiting, encouraging, rebuking, organizing regional conferences, preaching and using his medical skills wherever they were needed.

During the years 1876–1883 the Mission expanded rapidly throughout the nation and instead of being looked upon as an insignificant, independent group ruled over by an authoritarian Hudson Taylor, other missionary societies and individuals considered the CIM in a new light. They saw the great successes being made by courageous men and women who preached the good news throughout China.

Hudson, accompanied by his faithful secretary Joe Coulthard, commenced a series of journeys hoping to visit each Mission station.

Their first journey, over the roughest of territory, with overnight stays in appalling conditions, covered three hundred miles in twenty-four days (9 December till 2 January, 1880) involving visits to Shandong, Jiangsu, Qingjiangpu and Yangzhou. On occasions at some very poor inns they were obliged to spend the night with their mules, who continually disturbed their sleep when they ate the straw being used as pillows.

A visit was made to Wuhan to farewell several groups of ladies as they left to work in the interior.

During one journey, he heard of sickness in the Pearse family and knowing his medical skill was needed, hastily made his way to Anqing.

Arriving he found Mrs Pearse recovering from a bout of dysentery, the eldest child suffering from whooping cough and the extremely ill baby died in his arms. He was not ashamed to weep with those who weep. He suggested that they spend time recuperating at Yantai, but the family remained at Anqing till Jennie arrived to escort them to the holiday resort. Hudson had the baby's little body placed in a small coffin and carried it with his own luggage, to be buried near Maria.

More widespread travelling followed and when he sailed for England on 10 February, 1883 it was estimated that he had covered fifteen thousand miles.

During those exciting years of gospel expansion, one man who travelled more than most was James Cameron, nicknamed 'the

Livingstone of China'. He was one of the eighteen who had sailed from England on 4 August, 1875. Soon after his arrival he was preaching the gospel in Anqing and later became the first member of the Mission to enter Sichuan province. His itinerant ministry lead him to Bhamo in Burma where he spent a short time with Henry Soltau and John McCarthy.

In January, 1878 he set off from Bhamo to Beiha and from there commenced a series of journeys in which he travelled through all but Hunan province. His plan was to continue his itinerant ministry everywhere he could. As he moved about he met CIM men and women in their stations, and all the way preached the gospel and sold Scripture portions and tracts.

Frequently he rejoiced when he met groups of Chinese Christians who were faithfully serving and worshipping the eternal God.

At the small village of Singkeng he met some of the Lord's people: 'I had a hearty welcome from an old farmer and his family. The news soon spread…so the Christians gathered…We sat down to a sumptuous supper and…I had the best room given to me. For a long time after I could not sleep for joy…on our way to the next city, many had a very intelligent knowledge of the gospel.'

During this journey he reached the border area of Tibet and was able to view the land that stretched into the far distance. Of that experience he wrote: 'We could see the houses of the Tibetans, but at a considerable distance. A good view was obtained of the border, as we had to walk just outside it for a long way. Near at hand were low-lying hills, and in the distance lofty, snow-clad peaks. As I gazed upon it I wondered when the messengers of JESUS would have free access there. *It will be open some day.*'

James Cameron became extremely disappointed with the lack of zeal found in the Protestant churches of Europe after he met Roman Catholic priests working in outlying parts of China.

His extensive journey in the southern and central provinces ended when he met Hudson at Yantai in mid 1879.

After a short stay he was ready to leave again for the north and north-western regions of China. He set out, accompanied by T. Pigott and supported by the Bible Society who met some expenses and provided a huge number of New Testaments and smaller Bible sections. Arrangements were made for more printed material to be sent to pre-arranged cities and in eight months, twenty thousand gospels, smaller Bible sections and thousands of tracts were sold.

Generally they were well received and only on a few occasions they faced any hostility. The literati generally objected to the preaching, but they made the time to speak with them, even offering them Scripture portions to take home and return if they didn't want them. Some purchased the books for their own library. There is no doubt that the tall Scot had a loving personality, which won him many friends amongst the Chinese.

His gentle nature was seen when his pack-mule fell down a mountain side and was killed. That mule had been with him when he visited Manchuria and they were good friends. The carcase was sold and when at the inn, the meal contained mule meat, he couldn't bear to be party to eating his own animal.

He travelled over mountainous areas, in freezing climates, along the roughest of roads, had property stolen and faced opposition, but was able to rejoice that God had cared for him, and eventually he went home again to Scotland to tell his story to the crowds who gathered to hear of the work of the CIM.

When in August, 1882 James Cameron sailed from China, he no doubt regretted that he had not visited the province of Hunan, the island of Taiwan, as well as Tibet and Chinese Turkestan (Xinjiang).

40

Women Members of the CIM

As Jennie Taylor had proved that women could work in safety in the inland provinces Hudson, while recuperating in Yantai, discussed with her his plans to invite ladies to give their life to the service of Christ in inland China with the CIM.

One of his last duties before leaving England in 1879 was to write an editorial for *China's Millions*, stressing the value of women in taking the gospel to the Chinese women. He wrote that frequently the religious and moral teaching of children was left to mothers. This applied especially to the boys and meant that mothers could exercise an influence for good with their sons. What was needed was a tenfold increase in the number of European women to take the gospel to the women of China, because custom prevented men entering the home to speak with them. In the days to come they would play a vital role in this work.

Hudson knew that these children and women could best be reached by their own sex and that Christ was the answer to their down-trodden plight.

Geraldine Guinness clearly described the terrible conditions faced by most Chinese girls and ladies in the middle of the nineteenth century. She wrote that one fifth of all the women in the world were to be found in China; one baby girl of every five in the world is suckled at a Chinese breast and in many cases unloved; and one fifth of all the young ladies in the world who goes to an unhappy marriage is found in China:

> *A woman's life in China*—what lies behind those words? A little lassie well-born in the 'Flowery Land' will probably be called 'Pure Filial Piety', 'Fair Flower', 'Delicate Perfume', 'Secure Silver', or some such title, if she is thought worth naming at all. Many are considered too insignificant for any appellation beyond that of 'big sister', 'second sister', 'third sister' and so forth, or simply 'one', 'two' or 'three'. Before her feet are bound she romps merrily enough with her brothers, running about as freely as our little ones at home. At ten or twelve, custom confines her to the house, but while under her parents' roof she is often kindly treated, and may be taught to read or write, though, as a rule, a knowledge of household matters, needlework, and delicate embroidery is considered enough learning for her and her young companions, who are 'only girls'....Bright and attractive, they set off their olive complexions, dark eyes, and glossy black hair to advantage by brilliant garments, flowers, and trinkets in abundance. Spent in 'the women's courtyard' their lives, though very different from their sisters in distant Christendom, are not wholly dark or dreary. Gleams of sunshine brighten almost every lot; and while health is good and fortune fair there may be a measure of happiness even under such unnatural conditions. Chinese mothers are fond of dressing up their children in showy colours, and seem to take pride and pleasure in them while they are young....
>
> The rest is a sad story.
>
> Betrothed in babyhood, she is transferred in her teens to the authority of her mother-in-law, and married to a man of whom she knows nothing, and who has never seen or spoken to her before the wedding day. So much is this change dreaded that sometimes the girls of a family, or clan, will bind themselves together by the most solemn vows, to take opium or some other poison, within a certain time of their marriage, and so put an end to their lives, rather than endure the misery that the future might entail. And when it is remembered that every man in China who can pay the price of a wife is married, no matter how unattractive, deformed, or vicious he may be, this desperate decision does not seem so strange.
>
> Should the bridegroom happen to be the eldest son, the girl's position is considered enviable. Her younger sisters-in-law have to bear the brunt of the hard work and worry of every day, while she takes her place as second in importance in the household. Should she become the mother of boys, she has attained the highest happiness open to her in life; but sad indeed is her condition if it be

otherwise. To have no sons in China is considered a sufficient cause for divorce, and in any case a second wife will be taken.

Enclosed within high walls, the only access to a Chinese mission is by the great, heavily barred gate that faces the south. Within are rooms for the retainers, kitchens and offices upon the first courtyard; guest halls and apartments for the men...while away at the back, opening out of these, are dwellings set apart for the women. Dark rooms, sometimes handsomely furnished, but always dirty and forlorn, opened from the court by curtained doors and papered windows that admit but little light and air. The ladies are often graceful and courteous, with an intelligent look, due to the lofty forehead, formed by pulling out the hair round the brow from the time of marriage. Perfumed, painted, and robed in silk, their rich, dark tresses elaborately dressed, and glittering with jewelled pins and ornaments, they are gay enough outwardly, at times, even in the unattractive surroundings of their often dreary homes. Rarely, very rarely, may they go out; and when they do, it must be in covered chairs, closely screened from view.

The mother-in-law is the absolute head of such a household. One or more rooms are given to each young wife, but the meals are usually held in common, and all the house-keeping is in the elder woman's hands. Husbands—good, bad or indifferent—are practically of far less importance than this domestic despot. Indeed, in some parts of China the young women are not supposed to speak to their husbands at all during the first three years of married life....

Feuds and jealousies, passion and strife, embitter every day; while ceaseless gossip and malicious slander banish all mutual respect and confidence....Dreary and monotonous at the best, too often such lives are further shadowed by sorrows the result of cruel selfishness and sin. Frequently the men are gamblers, opium-smokers, and worse; and the fate of the women and children—entirely in their hands—may be of the saddest. It is not an uncommon thing for wealthy families to be brought to poverty and shame through the vices of husbands and fathers; and men are at liberty even to sell their wives and daughters to obtain money for opium, or to pay their gambling debts.

Picture it! Ponder it! Pray over it! And think—do they not need us?

Not only these, however. Girls and women of the poorer classes, with harder work, fewer comforts, and less protection from cruelty, oppression, and wrong, need, even more, the help and blessing we can bring.

Little daughters-in-law living like slaves in the homes of their future husbands, whose parents, too poor to care for them, have been obliged to let them go as children to the families that have bought them for their sons—oh, how they need the protection of a friend! Thousands of these poor children continually endure indescribable sufferings from the unrestrained violence of those who have legal right to do with them what they will. It is the commonest thing for such little sufferers to take poison, or jump down a well, to end their misery.

One case may serve as an example for very many. The child, a bonny little lass of eight, had been brought to her mother-in-law some three years before I knew her. The neighbours said that then she was plump and as merry as a child could be. I saw her wan and wasted—silent, trembling, stupid with terror—and covered all over with scars of burns, cuts, and bruises, left by many a fit of passion vented upon her defenceless head. One bitterly cold autumn morning, drawn to the window by heart-rending cries, I saw her father-in-law, a tall, powerful man, who had dragged her out of the cottage without a scrap of clothing upon her poor shivering little frame, beating her violently with a branch from a thorn bush he had cut on purpose. Of course we interfered at once. But long ere this, that suffering little life has probably been sacrificed, as so many are in China, to persistent cruelty.

The awful fact that year by year in that dark land scores of thousands of women, oppressed beyond endurance, end their unhappy lives by suicide, speaks volumes in itself. Many such cases every missionary has witnessed; but the large majority are never heard of, never known, except to the heart of GOD....

By God's grace and in His strength we can deliver many at a time. And even where our presence and sympathy can bring no outward help, there is always the message of eternal freedom and blessedness for the soul.[8]

With Hudson in Wuhan, the time had arrived to implement this new aspect of Mission policy. Much prayer had been made to God that success would be the result of sending women into the inland provinces of Shaanxi, Gansu, Sichuan and Guizhou and finally Yunnan.

He asked George King and his new wife Emily, who had only arrived in China in November, 1878, if they would move to Tianshui in Gansu province to assist Mr Easton. The reply was a resounding, 'Yes' and with a load of eighteen boxes of books and personal luggage they set out on 18 September, 1879 for their new work.

Emily was the first foreign woman to enter the far west!

The next group to move inland was George Clarke and his wife Fanny, and George Nicoll and his wife Mary Ann, who were married in a double wedding at Shanghai on 15 September, 1879. The plan was for both couples to travel to Chongqing where the Nicolls would work. The Clarkes were to then move on to Guiyang and work with James Broumton. After much prayer and guidance the missionary party left Wuhan by boat on 3 November, 1879, to arrive at Chongging on 13 January, 1880.

This proved to be a dangerous and frightening journey as their boat was holed on one occasion. Before the boat sank the women scrambled ashore while the men made every effort to save whatever they could. Amongst the luggage were eleven boxes of books from the Bible Society. Most of the luggage was saturated, but there was time to dry out everything while the men raised the boat from the river bed. Nights were particularly difficult as many were spent trying to sleep under umbrellas as the wind and rain swirled about them.

A second accident with the boat meant the final section of the journey was covered by foot.

When Chongqing appeared, for the sake of security, the ladies entered the city in covered sedan chairs. At the 'Jesus hall' they were warmly welcomed. Mary Nicoll looked at her new surroundings—the place where her once bachelor husband had lived—'the pitiful little traces of bachelor ways and doings—the ragged table-cloth, the forlorn arrangement of the rooms, and the dust of a week swept up and left behind the door according to Chinese custom.'

A week later the Clarkes set out for Guiyang where James Broumton worked, leaving Mary, the only foreign woman in Chongqing. Soon she was the object of interest, especially amongst the Chinese women. She wrote of the situation: 'For nearly two months past I have daily seen some hundreds of women. Our house has been like a fair. Men also have come in large numbers to hear the gospel. They are spoken to in the front part of the house; the women I see in the guest-hall at the back, and in the court-yard before it, for the room is very soon filled. As soon as one crowd goes out another is waiting to come in.'

Mary was soon being visited by members of the upper classes and found their homes open for visitation. She worked on, helping her husband George preach the gospel and doing all she could with the women. There were times during the hot season she collapsed while speaking to visiting Chinese ladies. She recovered to find herself being fanned by the concerned women.

So busy was her life that there were days when she had to get out of bed at three in the morning in order to write letters and carry out

Mission duties. On many occasions she was called out during the night to help with attempted suicides.

For two years she didn't see another western woman. Some of the Chinese women sympathized with her, knowing she was overworked helping the local women spiritually and physically.

One senior lady showed her much compassion by sending her chair to the compound early in the morning asking Mary to come and rest. When she arrived she would send everyone away and in the heat quietly fan her to sleep. While she slept the kind lady prepared a delicious meal which they ate when she awoke. Mary would then be escorted home in the afternoon, refreshed and ready to face the next round of duties. On occasions the same woman would send her a delicious hot breakfast, just in case her cook hadn't prepared a meal.

Mary enjoyed teaching the gospel to the many women who attended her 'at homes', which proved to be very popular.

She was the only foreign woman in a province of over twenty million people. As one writer said, 'What an honour for her! What a shame to the Church of CHRIST!'

George and Fanny Clarke continued their journey overland to Guiyang where they met James Broumton on 5 February, 1880. The journey was over rough territory and 'the men often let her (mountain chair) fall…She was such a good traveller though.'

Fanny was the first foreign woman to live in the province of Guizhou.

Hudson also planned to send unmarried ladies into the inland provinces and the first to depart from Wuhan were Jane Kidd, who was described by Hudson as being as playful 'as a kitten', and Ellen McCarthy, whose husband William had died in June, 1879.

Hudson spent much time with the ladies and others in prayer and study of the Scriptures, preparing them for the work that lay before them. He also instructed them in practical matters such as Chinese etiquette and how to conduct business.

These two were to join the Clarkes at Guiyang. They were to be accompanied on their journey by Frederick Baller, the Chinese evangelist Yao, a Bible Society colporteur by the name of Lo, a Chinese woman, and for a portion of the journey by an independent missionary, Frank Trench.

The group left on 19 February, 1880 to first cross the province of Hunan.

The ladies were the centre of attention when they stopped in the towns and villages, but it was decided that they would keep out of sight in the cities.

Jane Kidd wrote of her experiences through Hunan:

> I like these Hunan women so much! They have been very kind, most willing to receive us and listen to our message. Amongst them our fair hair and unbound feet seem to pass almost unnoticed. The whiteness of our complexion strikes them most, and when they put their hands beside ours they laugh very heartily at the difference.
>
> Our native Christian woman was the greatest help. Never having seen foreigners before, the women along our route were naturally a little afraid of us at first. But she explained so nicely all about us and our presence in their midst, and soon they would draw near, take us by the hand and invite us to their houses. Once indoors, we were often surrounded by quite a crowd.
>
> One incident amused me much. We had anchored at a village for the night, and some women asked us to go ashore. Mrs McCarthy had face-ache, so I went alone. A woman of about half my size, with a baby in her arms, took hold of one of my hands, and a young girl of fifteen took the other, and thus they led me along the village street, telling me not to be afraid of the crowds, for they would take care of me! At our destination a large number of women came to see me, some of whom seemed to grasp the facts of the Gospel very clearly. The same little woman with the baby led me back to the boat. The LORD bless her, dear kind soul!

Along the way the gospel was preached and Bible portions sold to all who were interested. The only disturbing incident was once when some young ruffians grabbed the books from those who had made a purchase.

On 22 April, 1880 Guiyang was reached, much to everyone's joy. To Jane Kidd went the honour of being the first single woman to enter the region of far west China.

The next party to leave for the north west consisted of Miss Fausset, Elizabeth Wilson, the cook Zhou, and a leper Huang Kezhong who had been converted as a result of Charles Judd's preaching. This group was to work with the Kings at Hanzhong in Shaanxi province. George King had made the decision to remain at Hanzhong until his wife Mary had given birth to their baby. Before departure on 1 March, 1880, Hudson spent time with them in prayer, seeking the protective care of God. The journey was one of about one thousand miles, which was covered in just three months.

He ensured they had a suitable house boat with ample supplies. When the day arrived for departure a delay meant he was obliged to spend the night on the boat, sharing a cabin with Huang, the leper.

In the morning Miss Fausset complained about the foul odour that came from Huang's bedding. The stench was so strong it permeated the whole boat.

No sooner had the complaint been made than Miss Fausset realised that Hudson had spent the night in the same cabin without any complaint. He then went and purchased new bedding for the young man. When it was noted that the vegetable oil used for cooking made food unpalatable Hudson did what was necessary. Miss Fausset wrote that he went ashore and, 'When he returned he was carrying a basket on his arm (having no servant with him) in which were sweet potatoes, eggs and lard. One never could have thought a little lard capable of doing so much good, or making so enduring an impression.'

The journey was largely uneventful, except for the theft of some property one night. However, the thieves failed to find their money or passports. Again the ladies were objects of interest to the Chinese and on one occasion when everyone had settled down in the boat, the locals cut the mooring ropes. In the excitement, everyone came out, even the ladies, and so the Chinese had achieved their objective.

On 21 May, 1880 they reached Hanzhong to meet an exhausted George King. As well as his preaching, he daily was called upon to assist opium addicts. Opium was so widely available that in one street there were over two hundred outlets.

The gospel was preached by the women to the Chinese ladies who flocked to see the newcomers, and hear what they had to say. The result was that by the end of 1880 a small congregation of twenty baptized members met for worship. Zhou, the cook and Huang, the leper were ordained as congregational deacons.

Again, a sad feature of the situation was that the godly leper, Huang, was obliged to live outside the city limits.

George Easton, who had been involved in the distribution of clothing to refugees from Shaanxi was to marry Caroline Gardner. The marriage took place in Chefoo in August, 1881 and then with a newly arrived missionary, Hannah Jones they made their way to Hanzhong to take up further evangelization work.

In the midst of all the activity George Parker proposed to a Chinese girl, Shao Mianzi—'Minnie'. She had been a schoolgirl at Yangzhou and there their love had blossomed. Opposition to the marriage came from many quarters, including missionaries, George Parker's mother and particularly Shao's father. When Hudson, who was in England at the time, learned of the proposed marriage he advised caution, as to marry a Chinese girl meant marriage to the whole family which would create many problems.

Shao's father was eventually placated by paying him the costs involved in rearing his daughter. When that matter was settled the CIM had the legal right to arrange a marriage, with one condition— that Shao remain in China.

In June, 1879 Charles Judd informed Hudson of the situation and eight months later the marriage took place at Yantai. Mrs George Parker became the first Asian member of the Mission.

With Elizabeth Wilson they set off for their home at Tianshui where the newly married couple were welcomed into the community. When little Johnnie was born in February, 1881 their popularity increased even more.

During their journey to Tianshui, they stayed with Emily King when her baby was born. They heard the sad news of her death from typhoid four months later in Hanzhong, in the province of Shaanxi— the first Western woman to lay down her life for Christ and the Chinese women of the region.

Just a month before she passed into the presence of the God she loved and served she made the comment:

> Our little baby is four months old to-day. He is a great attraction and wonder to the Chinese, who cannot understand his being so white. Mr King gets grand opportunities of preaching. Lately he baptized two more men and a woman. Eighteen women have been baptized in all, and how many men I cannot exactly tell.
>
> The LORD is with us. He will never forsake those who put their trust in Him....The LORD is risen indeed.

A month later she was dead and six months after that the baby also died. Life in China for women and children was extremely difficult and at times heartbreaking.

In 1882 George Parker, accompanied by his wife and Hannah Jones, set off for the Qinghai border where they could evangelize the Tibetan women and Chinese who lived there.

George, who did some itinerant ministry by himself, visited Huozhou, where many Mohammedans lived. He was warmly welcomed in all the places he visited and later wrote: 'I could have sold a large number of Arabic and Persian Scriptures...but few can read Chinese.'

They returned to their home in Tianshui on September, 1882 having sold 'twenty-five complete Bibles, 183 New Testaments, 685 "quarter testaments" (a Gospel, Acts and some epistles) and 5,732 single Gospels...'

In the years that followed women played an important part in the Mission activities. Mrs Fanny Clarke was one such woman who valiantly served the Lord in the CIM.

She and her husband, George, moved into Yunnan, the most western province, crossing the border on 30 May, 1881. On 7 June they reached the capital city, Kunming, and on 24 June arrived at Dali. Theirs was the greatest distance from any European than any others working in the CIM. Mail took almost seven months to reach them and they found themselves facing problems from the beginning.

The house that legally was theirs was occupied by two Chinese families who refused to move. Sharing the place with the squatters they barely had sufficient room to carry out any activities. Even the small yard was the residence of pigs and fowls—and the children of the families living in the house. It took six months before the house became theirs alone.

Help was difficult to obtain but eventually a woman was hired. She and her child had escaped from her opium addicted husband who had sold two of their children.

Praising God for the house when it became available, Fanny commented, 'Mud floors are not very warm in winter, and it will be nice to have a real bedroom again.'

Fanny wrote of the city which was a den of iniquity:

> This is a terrible place. Sodom and Gomorrah could not have been more wicked. Just as I write the husband of my woman has come— a wrecked opium smoker—and taken her little girl away. Last year he sold her two other children; this one is only three years old. We can do nothing to prevent it. GOD help them! He wishes to sell his wife as well.
>
> One of our neighbours went further, and was going to kill his wife and child. My husband and three women held him. I never before witnessed such terrible scenes. Oh, what a land! Nothing but sorrow and sin!

When newcomers, George Andrews and Arthur Eason arrived, they exchanged localities for a time which meant that the Clarkes moved to Kunming for a period.

Here the landlord wanted them out. They couldn't obtain help from the local women who kept their distance for some time. It was not until Fanny started handing out text cards to the children that their parents showed any interest.

George Clarke continually preached and handed out tracts which he printed using wooden blocks. However, their time in Kunming came to an end and they returned to Dali, where Mrs Clarke gave birth to a son on 20 August, 1883.

Following the birth, Fanny's health did not improve as expected. Her husband became very worried as the nearest European doctor lived a six weeks' journey away and he had twice dreamt that he would be parted from his wife.

M. Geraldine Guinness takes up the story as Fanny Clarke's condition worsened:

> At last she became decidedly worse; complications came on, she could take no food, and suffered exceedingly from sickness, pain, and terrible thirst. Always gentle and patient, she tried every means her husband could think of to obtain relief, but in vain. The LORD had need of her. The home summons had come, and she knew it.
>
> On Friday, October 5th, thinking that she should never see another sunrise, she wished to take the Lord's Supper for the last time with her husband. The little baby, six weeks old, was by her side, its innocent eyes, warm breath, and tiny, clinging fingers sending a thrill of yearning through and through the mother's heart. On the eve of that last, long parting, and yet in perfect peace, those two together broke bread in their grief and isolation, remembering the Man of Sorrows. They reconsecrated their little son to GOD, christened with his father's tears, and committed themselves entirely to His hands, for life or death. Both were wonderfully at rest, and even joyful.
>
> 'Oh, read to me about the New Jerusalem!...I shall soon be by the river of the water of life and thirst no more,' she said.
>
> Tenderly her husband told her something of what she had been to him through all those years of loneliness; how he had always admired her devotion, and been uplifted by her Christlike spirit, in the midst of hardships and trials. 'No, do not flatter me,' she whispered. 'I am the least of all Christians. I feel I have done less than any woman in the Mission.'
>
> A group of Chinese women stole in to her bedside next day, and in the solemn hush of that chamber of death, she told them with joy and triumph of her perfect rest in CHRIST, and begged them, too, to put their trust in the Saviour. Others gathered round, some

Roman Catholics amongst them, moved by the earnest testimony she bore as to her faith in the finished work of CHRIST.

Then came the last, long night. Her husband watched beside her, as he had done, alone, for forty eight days past. The Lord's Day morning dawned, its shining radiance gilding the snow-peaks and lighting the blue lake-water—a silent prophecy and symbol of the uncreated light of the city that has "no need of the sun." She lay in great pain, longing to go home.

'Take care of my little son,' she charged the Chinese nurse. Thoughts of the dear child gone before seemed to be much with her.

'I shall have one little boy in heaven,'" she said to her husband, 'and you, one on earth.'

Twilight fell, and deepened into a perfect autumn evening, as the Lord's Day closed. Slowly the sun went down behind the mountains, flooding all the lovely scene with light. And in the gloaming, peacefully, she passed away to GOD.

'The LORD gave her to me,' wrote the heart-broken husband, 'and the LORD has taken His own....This is the deepest water He has ever caused me to cross. Blessed be His Name for the joy of knowing JESUS in every circumstance of life....Now I am alone. An empty chair stands beside me at my solitary meals. There is no dear face or voice to cheer me, save that of my motherless boy. Thank GOD for this solace! "The LORD is good—and does good".'

On Monday scores of women from the city came to look their last on the quiet face that they should see no more. Great was their surprise at its calmness, as of a sleeper in perfect rest. Amid heathendom's darkness, cruelty, and terror of the unseen, a peaceful death-bed is almost inconceivable. Silently the women stood, wondering much at that still presence, and at the story of those who had heard her dying words of joy and triumph. Never could they forget it, never lose the memory of that hour that brought them face to face with death robbed of victory, and the grave of its sting.

Far from the home-land a letter had been travelling for months to reach the hands and heart that now were still. It brought some little Swiss flowers from her loved mountains, and the day they came, her husband with his own hands laid her to rest. Outside the south gate of the city she sleeps in her lonely grave, with China all around her and the flowers on her breast.

A saint had gone home!

Medical help was one of the great needs of the women serving with the CIM. In January, 1880 Dr W. Pruen arrived in China, followed by Harold Schofield, an excellent surgeon.

In August, 1882 Dr E. Edwards, and Dr William Wilson, a nephew of Elizabeth Wilson arrived to give valuable service to the Mission. These men were an answer to Hudson's prayers for doctors to assist him in the huge amount of medical work that faced him among both the foreigners and the Chinese.

41

Time to Go Home

Between Hudson's return to China on 22 April, 1879 and the day of his departure for England on 6 February, 1883 the itinerant ministry of the many faithful, courageous, members of the CIM had penetrated every province, spreading the love of God.

John McCarthy had crossed China from east to west, preaching the gospel and selling Christian literature and gospels to the many spiritually hungry Chinese. In November, 1880, John Stevenson and Henry Soltau left Bhamo in Burma to become the first Europeans to walk across the land from west to east. Six months later they arrived in Shanghai, having preached and sold Christian literature all along their route.

The last great province to be penetrated by the gospel was Hunan, and this was the result of Adam Dorward's labours, who arrived in China in 1878. Again and again, with the assistance of faithful Chinese Christians, including Yang Cunling, he ventured into parts of the province where the name of Christ had never been heard. With a godly courage he faced the shouts of 'Beat the foreign devil!'

In places, even where he was made welcome, he had to sleep on a bed of straw. On many occasions he slept on table tops. For eight years he criss-crossed the province, walking thousands of miles, preaching the saving work of the Lord Jesus Christ. On one journey in 1883 he covered one thousand three hundred miles, selling seven thousand books and one thousand five hundred gospels.

Medical work was also underway and one man who deserves special mention was Dr Harold Schofield who arrived in Shanghai on 30 June, 1880. He was a brilliant Oxford graduate who was converted at the age of nine and held strongly to the great truth: 'What the Lord blesses everywhere is not great knowledge, but great devotedness of hearts to Himself.'

He had wide experience helping soldiers injured in war, but his heart loved the Chinese, much to the dismay of many of his friends: 'When I was preparing to come...some of my best friends tried to dissuade me on the plea that there was so much to be done at home. How I wish that they, and all who use this argument, could but live here for a while, and see and feel the need for themselves! They would then be disposed to ask, not whether I had a special call to go to China, but whether they have any special call to remain in England.' He saw his calling 'not those that need you, but those that need you most.'

At the age of twenty-nine, he and his wife were with Robert Landale in Taiyuan, in Shanxi province where he began his medical-missionary work several months later.

Well known for his street preaching he soon won the hearts of the people.

His medical work occupied much time and during his first year (1881) he treated about fifty in-patients and one thousand five hundred out-patients. Those numbers doubled during 1882. Chloroform was one of his innovations when doing surgical work.

He was a very spiritual man who was often heard pleading with God to raise up more doctors to come to China. His wife told Hudson that they had spent much time before the throne of grace pleading 'that God would open the hearts of the students at our Universities and Colleges to the needs of the Mission Fields of the world....He longed and prayed so earnestly for the best men in all respects to be sent to China.'

He kept meticulous records of his medical work, much of which would have appeared miraculous to the Chinese. 'One poor man,' he wrote, 'fifty-five years of age, with double cataract, practically blind, groped and begged his way to the hospital, a distance of fifty miles, taking about a fortnight to accomplish the journey. He recovered good vision in both eyes, and was greatly delighted at being able to walk home in two or three days....

'A woman aged forty-seven, who was dismissed from her situation because of blindness, attempted suicide, by jumping into a river, and down a well. A friend brought her to us and both eyes were successfully operated on. She is now able to sew and do housework, and will probably remain with us to attend the female in-patients.'

He spent many hours helping opium addicts, openly saying that the drug was a curse to society, morally, socially and physically.

In 1883 after treating a man for diphtheria he caught typhoid fever. His condition deteriorated quickly and of those last earthly hours his wife wrote:

> On the morning before he passed away his face was so radiant with a brightness not of earth, and since then I have often thought those lines were a true description of him,
>
> > "Jesus Himself, how clearly I can trace
> > His living likeness on that dying face."
>
> A short time after that he looked up, smiled, and said, "Heaven at last", and seemed as if he had recognized someone.

Before his early death on 1 August, 1883 he said to his wife: 'Tell Mr Taylor and the Council...that these three years in China have been by far the happiest of my life.'

Some twenty years later the CIM had fourteen doctors working in seven hospitals and dispensaries.

While God was blessing the labours of the CIM and the other mission societies, Hudson faced problems that almost brought his work to an end.

His policy was to send missionaries throughout China preaching the gospel. This itinerant ministry was considered by many to be the incorrect way to go, hence they supported the more settled ministry of the other missions. Hudson believed that the work of the CIM was to sow the seed and then move on, leaving others to build up the saints and oversee the newly established churches. As late as 1881 some were still saying of the CIM missionaries: 'Are they not unproductive and aimless wanderings?' However, attitudes were changing.

Alexander Wylie, in 1880, wrote of the CIM: 'They are opening up the country, and this is what we want. Other missionaries are doing a good work, but they are not doing *this* work.'

In the same year a Government report from the British consul in Wuhan, wrote of the CIM activities:

Always on the move, the missionaries of this society have travelled throughout the country, taking hardship and privation as the natural incidents of their profession, and, never attempting to force themselves anywhere, they have managed to make friends everywhere…Not only do the bachelor members of the Mission visit places supposed to be inaccessible to foreigners, but those who are married take their wives with them and settle down with the goodwill of the people of the districts far remote from official influence, and get on as comfortably and securely as their brethren of the older Missions under the shadow of a Consular flag and within range of a gun-boat's guns;…this Mission has…shown the true way of spreading Christianity in China.

Timothy Richard in the Shanxi province, created difficulties by renouncing the exclusive claims of Christianity and began to teach that spiritual truth could be found in all religions. He saw education and the teaching of morality as being the salvation of the Chinese people and believed that the world could be saved in one generation 'from wicked ones who tyrannize over the poor.'

He was of the opinion that if what was common to all 'faiths' could be made known to the literati, Christianity would become acceptable throughout China. He spent much time and energy preaching his new gospel and distributing tracts teaching a general morality. This, plus education, would help the people cope with natural disasters and so benefit society at large. In his tracts the name of Jesus was not mentioned.

Everyone was urged to have 'faith'; but faith in Jesus Christ, the Son of God as the only way of salvation was unacceptable, and sadly some of the members of the CIM were led astray and were forced to resign. This teaching greatly upset Hudson and his workers who remained faithful to the exclusive claims of Christ as the only way of salvation.

W. Martin proposed a more acceptable attitude towards ancestral worship arguing that Christianity could accommodate this practice—after all Christians held their ancestors in honour and kept photographs of their dead, loved ones.

However, ancestral worship was pagan as the living believed the dead were to be honoured and helped in many ways, and failure to do so resulted in sickness, and disasters. The Chinese saw their ancestors living an eternal purgatory, the pains of which could be alleviated by the living, who even printed money and burned it so their 'living dead' could use it. When the Chinese bowed before the tombs of their ancestors, many questioned whether this was any different to the Roman Catholics who bowed down before their idols.

The CIM could not tolerate any integration of ancestral worship with Christianity, despite the efforts of Mr Martin to do so. But conversion invited opposition as they were seen by their families as having failed in their duties to their ancestors. For many, following Christ meant ostracism from the family unit.

The views of Martin and Richard won followers and distressed Hudson, who had to discipline those who were led astray. In a letter to Lord Radstock he wrote: 'The faith of one brother has broken down, under the unhelpful influence largely of other missionaries, and we shall have to recall him.'

Hudson, who longed to be on the road preaching the gospel, found his life was burdened down with administrative duties in Chefoo. He travelled many thousands of miles visiting Mission centres, but was increasingly held back by bouts of sickness, especially his constant companion—dysentery. Often it was Hudson who required the encouragement of his brethren.

Another problem was caused by the failure of those in England to carefully examine those accepted for the Mission. Over a short period, two men were found to be epileptics, two were mentally ill and one refused to learn the language. This meant money was being wasted sending the misfits home.

Funds in China were in short supply, often because the treasurer in England failed to forward available monies. On many occasions the monthly income was insufficient to cover expenses, but still Hudson looked to God to make provision. Sometimes the giving in China was sufficient to make up the deficit. Many workers who looked to the CIM to provide their needs, failed in one fundamental Mission principle raised again by Elizabeth Wilson in November, 1880—'Our confidence must be in God, who has never failed those in the Mission who trusted in Him.'

Then there were some who having seen the apparent ease of others serving in different missions, began taking time off for their own activities. On one occasion Hudson wrote to Benjamin Broomhall : 'It is reported that CIM missionaries have nothing to do and do nothing.'

Others created a bad impression to the local population by living in luxury. Some had personality problems, continually being rude to everyone.

The disciplinary action that followed caused Hudson heartache, especially when he was unwell and needing quiet rest.

It was normal policy to have an open house for everyone who preached the gospel, but sometimes empty Mission premises were used by missionaries from other societies dressed in foreign clothing and armed with guns. The local Chinese often associated them with the CIM which caused trouble for the CIM missionaries when they returned.

Then came news of the death of close friends in various parts of China—men and women who were the backbone of the Mission.

In April, 1881 Empress-regent Ci Xi was able to act alone as her co-Empress-regent Ci An died in suspicious circumstances. The international situation in the Far East was very unsettled and this disturbed Hudson who bore the responsibility for sending men and women into the inland provinces.

Jennie was longing to return home to see her family, but for some time she felt unable to do so, because of Hudson's poor health. But home events made a return journey necessary.

In July, 1881 Hudson's mother died, followed by Jennie's mother in August of the same year. Thus on 13 October, 1881 Jennie sailed from Yantai, leaving behind a lonely, overworked and unwell husband. Before Jennie reached England Hudson's father also passed away.

Alone in China, and hearing of his father's death, Hudson wrote home:

> My dear and honoured father has been taken Home, painlessly and without a moment's warning. None was needed: to him, to die was gain. I realized very thankfully that the long, dreary winter we had dreaded for him, alone—without my dear mother, for fifty years his companion—would not distress him now; but I could not help a feeling of desolation at the thought of no more Father's or Mother's welcome; no old home to go to, should I return to England again. But it dawned on me that not only are they both at rest, in the presence of the Lord Jesus, but they are reunited, freed from infirmity and imperfection for ever....

Hudson's heart was burdened with the great difficulties confronting him. He knew that workers and finance were needed and humanly the need could not be met. In a note to Theodore Howard he said, 'Unless one could really cast the burden on the Lord, and feel that the responsibility of providing for His servants is His, one would be much concerned at the present aspect of things.' To a missionary friend he wrote in the same manner: 'When shall we get through our difficulties? Funds seem dropping lower and lower. We need much prayer. But God cannot fail us: let us trust and not be afraid.' Those living at Chefoo observed that Hudson spent many hours in prayer. When Mr and Mrs Nicoll made mention of his prayer times he replied, 'What would you do if you had a large family and nothing to give them to eat? This is almost my situation at present.'

In November, 1881 he made his way up the Yangzi River to Wuchang for a time of informal conference with some local Mission members and others who were passing through. On the wall in one of the rooms hung a Biblical text which encouraged everyone present: 'Although the fig-tree shall not blossom, neither shall fruit be in the vines; the labour of the olive shall fail, and the field shall yield no meat; the flock shall be cut off from the fold, and there shall be no herd in the stalls; yet will I rejoice in the LORD; I will joy in the GOD of my salvation.'

There the small group of missionaries met for prayer concerning the state of funds, the need of more manpower and the general principles that were used to guide the Mission work. Those present knew the difficulty they faced: 'GOD is rich and great...He has opened to us doors of access on all hands in this once-sealed land. The needs are overwhelming; the opportunities wonderful! *How is it that the labourers are so few?*'

Facing so many difficulties, reason would indicate—'hold the fort', but inland China was ready to hear of Christ. Hudson knew that effective prayer had been made that those provinces be opened up to the gospel. God had graciously answered this prayer, but he knew that concentrated, believing prayer had not been made for the extra workers.

At that time the CIM consisted of ninety-six missionaries, which included wives, and about one hundred Chinese workers. Fifty-six extra personnel could be used immediately! Hudson believed that if God provided the extra manpower He would also provide the necessary support.

Praying about the matter, a text of Scripture came to his mind 'the Lord appointed seventy also, and sent them....' While seventy seemed too large a number to be the subject of prayer, he knew that God would provide according to his will.

One day while walking in the fields overlooking Wuchang with Mr Parrott, talking of the proposal and wondering if such a plan was sensible in the light of the limited resources, Mr Parrott's foot hit something in the grass. Bending down he picked up a string of coins.

359

'See,' he said as he stooped down, 'see what I have found! If we have come to the hills for it, God is well able to give us all the money needed!'

Now there was a definite purpose in the prayers of that small group—seventy extra missionaries for the CIM in China, with the funds to support them.

In the discussions that followed it was agreed that they would ask God to provide the extra manpower within three years. The conference drew to a close with the expectation that God would bring great things to pass within the following three years.

'If only we could meet again,' one said, 'and have a united praise meeting when the last of the seventy has reached China!'

'We will be widely scattered then,' said another…'But why not have the praise meeting now? Why not give thanks for the seventy before we separate?' And that was exactly what happened as all looked to God to answer the prayer of faith.

Another informal conference was held at Zhenjiang between 3–9 December, 1881 with the local missionaries and some newcomers. Again all who gathered, felt the reality of the presence of the Holy Spirit and covenanted that daily they would pray for God to send forth the seventy new missionaries. Some members of other missions were present, which resulted in some criticism implying that Hudson and the CIM were acting foolishly.

Before leaving Zhenjiang a small group met in Hudson's cabin for a time of prayer. Mr Parrott wrote: 'We had prayer in his cabin. Five of us prayed for the Seventy, and Mr. Taylor promised to telegraph home and ask them to receive and send out this number, if we would continue praying….Certainly the Lord is reviving us….'

Then it was off to Ningbo to meet his son, Herbert, who was to teach in the newly founded Chefoo school. Before commencing work, Hudson took him to visit his mother's grave at Zhenjiang and view the site of the Yangzhou riot.

When they returned to Ningbo he prepared an appeal to circulate among the churches in Great Britain. This document was signed by each member of the Mission in China….

> We the undersigned members of the CIM, having had the privilege of personally labouring in many of the provinces of this needy land, and having seen with our own eyes something of its extent, and of the great spiritual needs of the untold millions of its inhabitants, feel pressed in spirit to make a united appeal to the Churches

of the living GOD in Great Britain and Ireland for earnest and persevering prayer for more labourers.

We saw with thankfulness a few years ago the generous sympathy called forth by a knowledge of the terrible famine for bread that perishes in the northern provinces. Some of us personally took part in distributing the practical fruits of this sympathy among the needy and dying. Many lives were saved; many hungry were fed; many naked were clothed; and needy, destitute children were taken and cared for, some of whom are still under Christian instruction.

A more widespread and awful famine for the Bread of Life exists to-day in every province in China. Souls on every hand are perishing for lack of knowledge. A thousand every hour are passing away into death and darkness. We and many others have been sent by GOD and by the Churches to minister the Bread of Life to these perishing ones, but our number collectively is utterly inadequate to the crying needs around us.

Provinces in China compare in area with kingdoms in Europe, and average between ten and twenty millions in population. One province has no missionary. Another has only one, an unmarried man. In each of two other provinces only one missionary and his wife are resident. And none are sufficiently supplied with labourers. Can we leave matters thus, without incurring the sin of blood guiltiness?

We plead, then, with the Churches of GOD at home to unite with us in fervent, effectual prayer, that the LORD of the Harvest may thrust forth more labourers into His harvest, in connection with every Protestant Missionary Society on both sides of the Atlantic.

A careful survey of the spiritual work to which we ourselves are called, as members of the CIM, has led us to feel the importance of adequate and large reinforcements; and many of us are daily pleading with GOD in agreed prayer for forty-two additional men and twenty-eight additional women, called and sent out by Himself to assist us in carrying on and extending the work committed to our charge.

We ask our brothers and sisters in CHRIST at home, to join with us in praying the LORD of the Harvest to thrust out this 'other seventy also'....

But we are concerned that only men and women called by GOD, fully consecrated to Him, and counting every precious thing as dross "for the excellency of the knowledge of CHRIST JESUS our LORD," should come out to join us. And we would add to this appeal a word of caution and encouragement to any who may feel drawn to offer themselves for this work.

Of caution—urging such to count the cost; prayerfully to wait on GOD; and to ask themselves whether they will really trust Him for everything, wherever He may call them to go. Mere romantic feeling must soon die out in the toilsome labour and constant discomforts and trials of inland work, and will not be worth much when severe illness arises, and perhaps the money is all gone. Faith in the living GOD alone gives joy and rest in such circumstances.

Of encouragement—for we ourselves have proved GOD'S faithfulness, and the blessedness of dependence on Him alone. He is supplying, and ever has supplied, all our need...we have fellowship in poverty with Him who for our sakes became poor, shall we not rejoice if the day prove that, like the great missionary apostle, we have been "poor, yet making many rich"? The LORD makes us very happy in His service, and those of us who have children desire nothing better for them, should He tarry, than that they may be called to similar work and to similar joys.

May He, dear Christian friends at home, ever be to you "a living, bright Reality," and enable you to fulfil His calling, and live as witnesses to Him in the power of the Holy Ghost.

While no mention of the prayer request was made in Hudson's reports to the annual Mildmay conference of June, 1882, Lord Radstock who sacrificially supported the work of the CIM spoke out against those lazy Christians in England who had so much, yet ignored the needs of China. He called upon Christians to pray for the work being carried out and remember the physical needs of those preaching Christ in that faraway land.

The years 1882–3 were a trial of faith to Hudson. Giving had not increased, and one year after the decision to pray for the seventy additional missionaries, only nine had arrived.

So depleted were the funds of the Mission that for the first three months of 1882 he remained at Yantai in order to immediately distribute whatever arrived.

In October, 1882 a parcel of mail arrived and was opened by an expectant Hudson. The Mission needed at least £800, but what he found was £96, 9s 5p, to be shared between the seventy stations. He closed the last letter and retired to his room where he fell upon his knees and cried to God in his need and distress. There he rolled his burden upon the Lord.

Having told the others of their desperate need they all approached the throne of grace seeking the blessing of God. In a short time gifts arrived from locals, which met the Mission needs. How they praised God for His faithfulness!

When the same shortage occurred in the remaining months of 1882 Hudson knew it was necessary for him to return to England and 'oil the organization', especially as he later discovered that some money and letters had been sent to China via America.

On the last day of 1882, he told Jennie that three hundred and fifty pounds had been sent from London, when the need was £750. The situation was serious and he concluded with the words: 'Now we shall see what GOD will do!'

And Hudson was lonely. He was often sick, suffering depression that really tested his faith in the goodness of God. On one occasion he wrote to Jennie: 'Sometimes I feel the Lord will say Enough, and call me to the only true rest...Perhaps I may stay here to see the Seventy out and settled, and then return to England for good. Or, I may never return...I must get to Chefoo, I think, and see if I can brace up for a little more work.'

He had received great spiritual blessing from his study of the Song of Solomon which he had used as a basis for talks when he visited Anqing, but his heart longed to see Jennie again—it had been so long since they had been together. His letters home expressed his feelings:

> 'I do live in your love, during this long, long separation....I hope the days of our parting may...be ended, and no more such lengthened separations be our lot....'

In another letter he poured out his heart to her:

> I feel as if my heart would break soon if I don't have *you* yourself. I was almost in mind just to run off by today's P and O, leaving my foreign clothes in Chefoo, and papers and books....Though the tears will come into my eyes every few minutes, I do want to give myself, and you too, darling, for the life of the Chinese and of our fellow labourers....Pray for me, my own heart's love, that neither my faith, nor my patience fail...I have been so pressed and wearied. The strain is very great.

Several days before boarding the ship in early February, he gathered the Chefoo Christians together for a time of prayer, and as he later said, 'we asked Him lovingly to please us, as well as encourage the timid ones, by leading some one of His wealthy stewards to make room for a large blessing for himself and his family, by giving liberally of his substance for this special object.'

When the day came to leave China he knew it was not because of missing Jennie, but because all the work that he had to do was finished.

When he reached Aden a cable was waiting for him—a cable that again showed the faithfulness of his God—a donation of three thousand pounds had been received on 2 February. A year later the same family gave another thousand dollars for a special work in China.

On 23 March, 1883, after a separation of eighteen months he and Jennie were together again, but they were only able to spend one weekend alone.

42

Overworked

Hudson returned to England to be met at the Mission headquarters, by an overworked Benjamin Broomhall and staff.

William Sharp, a solicitor and a new member of the London Council was very concerned that Benjamin was heading for a breakdown. He was responsible for the secretarial work, interviewing prospective Mission candidates, the oversight of publications, the fitting out of those going to China and making the necessary travel arrangements. On top of these duties there was the increasing call upon his time to speak and publicize the work of the CIM.

Hudson saw the need to lessen Benjamin's workload, and while he was also overworked, plans were formulated to bring about changes in the Mission in England and China.

War between France and China had broken out and soon reports filtered through of foreigners becoming the target of Chinese hostility. When some questioned Hudson's wisdom to send an extra seventy men and women to the war-torn land, he replied, 'I have never found in my Bible that the Lord says the Gospel was not to be taken to China when there was war with France.'

Despite the criticism, never before had the Mission enjoyed such popularity in Great Britain. People were enchanted to read of the exploits of their countrymen who walked across China and the stories of the missionaries who faced great hardships taking the gospel to the people.

The result of his visit to England was that by the end of 1884 more than the prayed for seventy had arrived in China; and giving had increased to cover all the Mission expenses. In fact, at the end of 1884, after meeting expenses, the Treasurer announced a credit balance of ten pounds. The Lord had provided exactly what was required!

During his stay in England he received encouraging letters from many including a young person from Cambridge who wrote: 'If you are not dead yet, I want to send you the money I have saved up to help the little boys and girls of China to love Jesus.' Then from his dear friend William Berger came an encouraging letter: 'My heart is still in the glorious work. Most heartily do I join you in praying for seventy more labourers—but do not stop at seventy! Surely we shall see greater things than these, if we are empty of self and only seeking God's glory and the salvation of souls.' Enclosed he found a cheque for three hundred pounds.

He rejoiced to be with his family again, but they were no longer little children but young adults and some of them were ready to sail for China.

He found much of his time taken up visiting his many Mission friends. Lord Radstock and his extended family, William Berger, George Müller, Grattan Guinness and many others entertained their close friend.

There were also the many speaking engagements to make people aware of the great work done by the missionaries.

Before leaving China the final Mission conferences had been greatly blessed by the Holy Spirit. In England, his messages were accompanied with power from on high. Gatherings organised by C. H. Spurgeon, the Bible Society and the Religious Tract Society, the Open Air Missions, the Anti-opium Society and the YMCA, all proved spiritually uplifting .

Hudson called upon his congregations and those who read *China's Millions* to be faithful to God. On one occasion he wrote: 'There are three truths, 1st, That there is a God; 2nd, That He has spoken to us in the Bible; 3rd, That He means what He says. Oh, the joy of trusting Him!…The missionary who realises these truths…knows that he has solid rock under his feet whatever may be his circumstances.'

Many testified to the blessings that accompanied his meetings. The convener of a group of twelve who heard him speak at Gloucester said,

'I can never forget the overwhelming power of that little meeting in my own soul. I was so moved that I had to ask Mr. Taylor to stop; my heart was broken, and I felt, as never before, that I had as yet given up nothing for my Lord....Three (of the twelve) went to China as a result.'

Another incident worth mentioning was at the home of Canon Thwaites in Salisbury. The minister's wife, who was spiritually depressed at that time, found great spiritual refreshment in his words:

> As Mr. Taylor began to speak a great calm and stillness came over me—a fresh revelation of God's coming down to meet human need. The fountains of my innermost being were broken up...I saw a little of what consecration really meant; and as I began to yield myself to God, fresh hope, light and gladness came into my life—streams that have been flowing ever since.

While no appeals were made for financial support, money flowed in— but not only cash! Some people removed jewellery from their clothes, took off their rings or anything they had of value and gave them to the work of the Mission. On one occasion a jeweller's case and all the valuable contents were sent to him. There was no doubting that the Holy Spirit who brought spiritual blessings, also opened the wallets and purses.

Hudson, with others, spent considerable time interviewing the ever growing number of applicants who wanted to serve with the CIM.

Moody and Sankey had been greatly used of God throughout the world, and following their visit to Great Britain in 1882 many converts were searching for some avenue of Christian service. As a result of an invitation from Kynaston Studd, Moody and Sankey visited Cambridge from 5-12 November. The first day of their visit was Sunday, the anniversary of Guy Fawkes 'gunpowder plot'.

Mr Moody approached Cambridge with a degree of trepidation as did the organizers of the meeting. Moody and Sankey were not cultured Englishmen, but their first meeting attracted one thousand seven hundred students. There was a lot of laughter as the students took their seats, some creating a diversion by building a chair pyramid and others igniting fireworks—after all it was Guy Fawkes' Day!

As the visiting evangelists made their way to the stage they were greeted with scornful laughter. Sankey sang some of the great Christian hymns only to be greeted with a sarcastic cry of 'Encore' after each verse. When Mr Moody began to speak, some of the crowd called out, but he continued speaking and at the end of the meeting four hundred students remained behind for a time of prayer.

This meeting played a great part in bringing together the 'Cambridge Seven'; seven young men who offered their services to the CIM.[9]

Major-General Hoste had retired from the Royal Artillery and was living at Brighton. He was a devout Christian who longed to see each of his children converted. When Moody and Sankey visited his hometown, the family went along, except Dixon, who wanted nothing to do with the mission. However when his brother William, home from Oxford, applied brotherly pressure, he relented and attended. The Spirit of God touched his defiant soul with power and under conviction of sin he continued to attend the mission meetings, while his family bowed before the throne of grace imploring God to regenerate his rebellious soul. Dixon later recalled the night of his conversion: 'I shall never, in this life or next, forget how, when under conviction of the sin of my ungodly life, I knelt at the back of the hall in Brighton and placed myself, my whole being, unreservedly at the disposal of the Lord Jesus…thankfully receiving the salvation offered so freely through the sacrifice on Calvary.'

There and then he knew he would give himself to the work of the CIM and made arrangements to meet Hudson, whose advice was to wait a while and mature in his Christian faith before leaving for China. During this time he gave up smoking and chose his future bride. One day while visiting the home of Benjamin Broomhall he saw Benjamin's daughter, Gertrude, who was playing the piano. He thought to himself, 'I shall marry her one day.'

Gertrude sailed for China on 24 September, 1884 and was one of the 'seventy'.

The well-known test cricketer, C. T. Studd was also one of the Cambridge Seven. He was well aware of Christian truth and when he saw his seriously ill brother George, close to death, and caring only for the Lord Jesus and the Bible, he became increasingly aware that what really mattered were spiritual realities and not the things of the world. It was at one of Moody's meetings that he consecrated himself anew to Christ and on his knees prayed the words of the hymn:

> Take my life and let it be
> Consecrated, Lord, to Thee!

The 'Cambridge Seven' were Stanley P. Smith, C. T. Studd, Rev. W. Cassels, Montagu Beauchamp, Arthur Polhill-Turner, Dixon

Hoste and Cecil Polhill-Turner, all young, athletic, in the prime of life and devoted to the service of the Lord Jesus.

Each man willingly sacrificed wealth, fame and a life of ease, to serve the Lord Jesus in China. When England became aware of the sacrificial decisions of those young men, support for the CIM increased dramatically.

The time had come for Hudson to make changes in the administrative structure of the Mission in England. Benjamin Broomhall carried too heavy a load and help was needed. The CIM was growing quickly and consequently he appointed men to share the burden of work. C. Moore was appointed Deputation Secretary; Charles Fishe the Financial Secretary; Cardwell became Benjamin's personal assistant and Robert Landale became editor of *China's Millions*. The work of interviewing women applicants for the Mission was handed over to the Ladies' Auxiliary Council. Benjamin found himself responsible for public relations which proved very time consuming!

Hudson's time in England was drawing to a close as he knew he had to return to China and continue the administrative work of a large and growing missionary organization. His personal secretary, W. Lewis left England on 15 January, and was met by Hudson at Suez, who had left on 20 January, 1885. This meant another separation from Jennie, something he dreaded, but always the service of the Lord and the salvation of souls was the motivating force behind all they did.

Yet to leave England were the 'Cambridge Seven' who faced a round of farewells, the largest being held in London at Exeter Hall on 4 February, 1885. Before this event it was necessary to make arrangements for travel and the outfitting of the men for their work in China.

Mrs Studd was very apprehensive about her C.T. leaving for China as he had been used to a much better standard of living than he would soon face. She also couldn't understand why her son sold many things he once held dear, forwarding the proceeds to the CIM.

Before leaving, C.T. became more conscious of the decadent luxury in which he lived compared to the poor in England. As they moved about, he and his friends were distressed at what they saw. To his mother, C.T. wrote of his shame concerning his way of life: 'so many suits and clothes of all sorts, whilst thousands are starving and perishing of cold, so all must be sold when I come home if they have not been before.'

Mrs Studd was upset when she found out that the money so raised went to the general funds of the Mission, and not to Hudson for personal use. But she continued to write letters of concern about her son: 'I am most thankful that Mr. Taylor's advice as to his wearing proper clothing has been heeded—dear fellow! He is very erratic and needs to be with older and more consistent Christians!'

Then to Jennie she wrote: 'A few lines to ask you to impress on him the necessity of taking what is *necessary to be comfortable*. He seems inclined to take so very *little*, hardly enough to last him, to say nothing about cleanliness in the hot climate....'

Jennie later wrote to Hudson about a further effort by Mrs Studd to ensure her son kept up his social etiquette: 'I am afraid Mrs Studd is going too far in carrying out your suggestions...They told me that a case was going to (Hanzhong) to be unpacked before he arrived that he might find a room ready prepared with curtains...knives and forks, table napkins etc.'

We can only imagine what Charles did with the package when it arrived.

Mrs Smith, also concerned about her son, wrote to Jennie shortly before Stanley departed: 'I am deeply grieved to trouble you, but Stanley...gives no thought to temporal affairs. (Please) write by return of post and tell me what is *absolutely* necessary for (his) outfit as...he fancies he needs nothing and has sold or given away all....'

After their sons had left England, Mrs Studd asked for Jennie or Amelia to come to her palatial home and show them how to get a weekly or fortnightly prayer meeting started.

At last there was the farewell at Exeter Hall, which accommodated a crowd of 3,500 people. There were no special seats put aside for the upper classes and when Lady Beauchamp arrived, she was led inside and found a vacant seat beside her daughter near the organ. Dr Barnardo and some of his friends had to stand for most of the proceedings which lasted for hours.

Each one of the seven spoke, but Stanley Smith, an orator, filled with the Holy Spirit, kept the gathered crowd spellbound as he spoke:

> We are all under obligation to spread the knowledge of the good thing. It is simply this fact, coupled with our having clearly heard the Master's call, that is sending us out to China.
> We do not go to that far field to tell of doctrines merely, but of a living, present, reigning Christ....

We want to come to the Chinaman…and say to him, "Brother, I bring you an almighty Saviour!" And it is our earnest hope and desire that the outcome of this meeting will be that scores and scores of those whom we now see before us will ere long go forth, not to China only, but to every part of the world, to spread the glorious Gospel.

For years in England we have been debtors….And the knowledge of this precious JESUS, who to most of us is everything in the world, is absolutely wanting to thousands and millions of our fellow-men and women today.

What are we going to do? What is the use of great meetings like this if the outcome is not to be something worthy of the name of JESUS? He wants us to take up our Cross and follow Him,—to leave fathers, mothers, brothers, sisters, friends, property, and everything we hold dear to carry the gospel to the perishing….

Oh, to think that Gordon at Khartoum has but to speak a word and millions of money go from England…and in Egypt our noblest and bravest shed their blood…A greater than Gordon appeals to the Church. From the Cross of Calvary the voice of JESUS still cries…'I thirst'.

Ah, that Divine thirst! It has not yet been quenched. It has hardly begun to be quenched.

He thirsts for the Chinese, the African, the Hindu, the South American. Are there none here who would fain quench His thirst? Would you pass by that CHRIST? Behold His agony! You could not do so had you seen Him in the flesh. But now He thirsts with a deeper than bodily thirst. With His great soul He thirsts for the millions of this earth.

David once thirsted for the waters of Bethlehem…and three of his followers broke through the ranks of the enemy and at the risk of their lives brought him that water….

Shall not this Mightier than David have His thirst quenched tonight? Shall not the Divine LORD have His thirst quenched? Shall not the Man of Sorrows have His great heart rejoiced by men and women offering themselves for the work of spreading the glorious Gospel? CHRIST yearns over this earth. *What are we going to do*?…

Does someone ask, 'What is it that is sending you out?' We cannot tell you tonight of visions or dreams; but we can point…to the great needs of the heathen abroad that prevent us from staying in England.

And now a last word. How can one leave such an audience as this? It seems to me as if CHRIST has come right into our midst, and has looked into each face amongst us—men and women, old and young. To each He comes with tender love…and, pointing to the wounds in His pierced side, He asks, '*Lovest thou Me?*'…

'Yes, LORD, Thou knowest that I love Thee.'

What is the test of love?…'Keep My commandments.'

What is the test of friendship? 'Slake My thirst.' 'Ye are My friends if ye do whatsoever I command you.'

And what, Master, do you command? 'Go ye into all the world, and preach the Gospel to every creature.'

The events that night became headline news throughout the English speaking world and many were blessed by what they heard. The 'Cambridge Seven' was a unique event in the history of Christianity in Great Britain and did much to bring the needs of the CIM before the British public.

The day of departure arrived and on 5 February, the seven left for Suez where they caught a boat for Shanghai. They travelled by second class, sharing accommodation which someone described as 'fit only for servants and dogs.'

On board they had an ungodly ship's captain whose behaviour and swearing was upsetting the passengers. D. Hoste took him aside and read to him the Scriptures and together they discussed eternal truths. Other members of the party prayed and joined in. There was much praising of God when the man was converted and gave his life to the Lord Jesus.

On 18 March, 1885 the ship berthed at Shanghai where they were met by a 'Chinaman' they did not at first recognize. It was Hudson who had come to welcome the new recruits to the China Inland Mission.

The seven were warmly welcomed by the Europeans and the Chinese Christians. The local papers reported their arrival and soon they were addressing various groups in the city.

At one such meeting where the gospel was preached with power, the port chaplain, Rev. F. R. Smith came forward at the conclusion and declared that 'if he had died in the night he would have been a lost soul.' He came to understand what it meant to be a Christian and not just a parish minister.

This conversion shocked the European community in Shanghai and many were forced to take stock of their spiritual standing before the Lord.

43

CIM Re-organization

Hudson knew that it was time for work. A mountain of mail had to be answered, in addition to the dealing with difficulties that had arisen within the Mission organization. The headquarters in Shanghai were too small for those needing accommodation, and he soon discovered that the property did not belong to the CIM! The person responsible for renting and caring for the Shanghai office and residence had rented it in his own name and was now leasing rooms and keeping the money for his own use.

Hudson knew a Mission property was needed and so he began to formulate plans that would soon bear fruit.

It was also important to place the Cambridge Seven in areas where they could use their considerable God-given gifts. In Shanghai they proved their great value as they walked the streets preaching of salvation in Christ and the judgment to come.

He divided the group into two parties—one group consisting of C. T. Studd and Arthur and Cecil Polhill-Turner, who were to leave for Hanzhong, escorted by John McCarthy. Montagu Beauchamp was to accompany this group as far as Anqing, where he was to meet Hudson, and they would travel together, just as he had promised Lady Beauchamp.

Along the way they were guests of the foreign settlers who gladly heard them tell their story of Christ's wondrous salvation. Missionaries who heard them speak knew from the messages delivered that the power of the Holy Spirit accompanied what was said.

Much of the journey was by boat on the flooded Yangzi River. While the men enjoyed their new way of life, Chinese language study filled a great deal of their waking hours. Often they walked along the river bank beside the slowly moving boat, taking every opportunity to enjoy a swim. But their boat was the home of rats, and try as they could, the rats continued to keep them company, until they remembered the gift of cheese they were carrying. As an act of kindness they gave the cheese to Dr Wilson and his wife who were travelling in the accompanying boat. The result was that the rats decided the Wilsons' boat was more to their liking.

The other newcomers—Stanley Smith, Dixon Hoste and William Cassels were to travel to Shanxi Province by way of Yantai, Tianjin and Peking. In Shanxi they would complete their language studies and involve themselves in mission work in the area, especially helping Pastor Hsi who was making great inroads into the Chinese communities.

J. Coulthard accompanied them on their journey with great joy, as he had just told Hudson of his love for his daughter, Maria. She was overjoyed with the attention she was receiving and more so when Hudson agreed to their marriage—when she reached the age of twenty-one—three years away.

Again the men had a marked influence upon the missionaries they met along the way; encouraging the Christians to pray more fervently for an outpouring of the Holy Spirit and urging the differing mission groups to work and pray together.

Due to the pressure of work, Hudson sent Montagu Beauchamp with F. Baller to meet the others in Shanxi.

He soon received news of problems with the newcomers. Mr Baller complained that Stanley Smith and Dixon Hoste were injuring their physical health by spending too much time at prayer and fasting.

Word came that Charles Studd and the Polhill brothers had given up the study of Chinese as they believed they had discovered a God-given method of learning the language—they were praying for the gift of speaking in tongues—the tongue being Chinese. This Hudson saw as a work of Satan to interrupt the spread of the gospel. After some months they gave up their short-cut method of learning and settled down to the hard work of studying the language. He knew that it was not just the learning of the new language that mattered, but that in doing so the men learned the culture of the people, which made them feel more at home in that foreign land. Later he said, 'If I could put the Chinese language into your brains by one wave of the hand I would not do it.'

China now was being ruled by Empress Ci Xi, and the court at Peking obeyed her implicitly. The war with France meant that not just the Roman Catholic priests but all missionaries suffered the hatred and scorn of the Chinese who didn't distinguish between the various missionary groups. When the war ended in 1885, priests flooded the land, numbering almost five hundred, while the CIM at the time of the arrival of the Cambridge Seven numbered just one hundred and fifty seven.

Despite some setbacks the work was progressing well. James Broumton, when travelling from Guiyang to Chongqing became ill and was assaulted and robbed several times. Deciding it wise to stay at an inn for the sake of safety, he awoke to discover that everything he owned, except for the underwear in which he stood, had been stolen. He hid in a loft until the local officials came to his rescue and sent him on his way.

An overworked Hudson became ill with his old complaint of dysentery and was forced to relax for a time.

There was welcome news from England. The reputation of the Mission was high and many, including ladies, were offering themselves for service in China. Hudson saw the desperate need for godly women to mix with the Chinese ladies who were largely isolated from the CIM men. Tens of thousands of copies of *China's Millions* had been sold and even Queen Victoria had accepted the gift of a gilt edged edition.

Benjamin Broomhall and others were publicizing the Mission at meetings and by the distribution of Mission literature. During his absence in China, Hudson had contact with Jonathan Goforth from the Canadian Presbyterian Church who wanted to work with the CIM, but Hudson urged him to continue with missionary work through his own church.

And all the time he was missing his dear Jennie, and longed for the day when they would be together again.

Wanting to visit as many mission stations as he could, he began to organize the CIM in such a way that his absences would not create any difficulties. He appointed Mr Dalziel as the Mission business manager in Shanghai. In Wuchang, J. Coulthard was responsible for finances and correspondence with the outlying western and south western provinces, and Mr Parrott accepted the responsibility for Hudson's correspondence of a less personal nature.

Regional deputies were appointed to care for the missionaries in their area. Some objected, claiming that these appointees would become a barrier between themselves and Hudson, while others objected to younger men being appointed over long serving CIM men. However, the calling of regular regional conferences overcame the feeling of being isolated from the decision making process. The regional leaders were then to meet with Hudson on a regular basis.

He also instructed the regional deputies to encourage personal initiative and treat men and women as equal partners in the Mission work. Under no circumstances were the regional deputies to lord it over the Mission members.

Hudson needed someone to act as his personal deputy and with the return of John Stevenson, in December, 1885 he had the right man. Immediately he sent John out to visit the CIM stations that were experiencing difficulties. On this journey he met many of the CIM missionaries.

In April, 1886 Hudson made the formal announcement: 'Mr Stevenson…has undertaken to act as my deputy in districts which I cannot personally visit, and generally in matters requiring attention during my absence from China.'

James Broumton, a man of devout piety, with a total trust in the goodness of God was the ideal man to oversee the financial affairs of the Mission in China. He could work from a Mission centre to ensure a quick and fair distribution of funds as soon as they arrived. This released Hudson to be out and about and not waiting for funds to arrive. A full-time treasurer would also be able to prevent the waste of money which happened on several occasions when two women, who had brought with them kerosene lanterns, had hired coolies to carry heavy drums of kerosene for hundreds of miles. Two other men had left in sedan chairs with sixteen mules loaded with supplies.

Anqing was to become the men's training centre, where they would be supervised by William Cooper and Mr Baller. In Yangzhou the Women's Language School was to be enlarged as Hudson expected an influx of ladies in response to the prayers and appeals for them to serve in the Mission.

He cabled Great Britain for more workers and had in confidence told his close friends and supporters of his plans for women missionaries who would labour in the inland areas of China. To those in the know, he wrote: 'Keep it quiet, until success or otherwise appears.'

The number of CIM workers from overseas was growing, with forty new arrivals during 1885. But financial support had not kept pace with the human resources. Hudson also stressed to Benjamin Broomhall and the London Council the need of extreme care when selecting new missionaries, insisting that they be men and women who walked very closely with God, depending upon Him for the provision of their daily needs. Life would be difficult and men and women of spiritual and physical strength would be the only ones to survive in such harsh conditions.

Towards the end of June, he set out on a pastoral journey, visiting as many Mission stations as he could in the Hangzhou region and beyond. All the time he was searching for areas where missionaries could commence new works.

John McCarthy and Maria Taylor, Hudson's daughter, were also part of the travelling group.

The trip was by boat, but frequently the missionaries left their boats and followed those pulling the boats through the rough waters or over rapids. During one walk Maria fell over a cliff and was fortunate to land on a ledge. Hudson, on another occasion when travelling in a rickshaw, fell out backwards and struck his head on the rough roadway. Sickness was a constant companion with the travellers, but eventually they reached Anqing, where church elders were ordained and discussions took place about the future of the Mission.

Receiving an urgent telegram to come to Yangzhou, Hudson arrived to discover the principal of the training school, seriously ill. After returning to Chefoo with his patient, he set out again for Anqing.

This time there was discussion of the document signed by prospective CIM missionaries concerning their responsibilities when they reached China.

He then moved on to Hangzhou where he was able to spend valuable time with Wang Lae-djün. In this region the church was prospering, although suffering some persecution. His visit greatly encouraged the congregation.

At New Lane he slept in the room that Jennie had once called her own and there met two Chinese Christians who had suffered severe persecution. Dr Zong was one of the faithful men who had been cruelly tortured by those who hated Christianity. Both his ears had been cut off, after which he was lifted from the ground by ropes tied to his wrists and there was tortured and whipped. Fortunately he had been rescued and continued to faithfully teach the way of salvation.

From there it was back to Shanghai to meet John Stevenson who arrived on 24 December 1885 and to face the correspondence which awaited his return. It took him five hours to read it all!

With some relief from duties, accompanied by John McCarthy and Herbert his son, he set out to visit the Jiangxi region. In a second boat they were accompanied by some women. Along the way, he detoured to meet Robert Grierson, and here he had an accident. Robert invited him into his study and after entering the room, Hudson closed the door as he had something to say in private. He was unaware that Grierson, in order to keep his door open, had a cord strung between the inside door knob and the rather large bookshelf. Hudson, in closing the door pulled the bookshelf over and he found himself on the floor under a pile of shelves and books.

Robert Grierson apologised profusely, only to hear Hudson reply, 'There, you see the trouble that comes from interfering with another man's arrangements.'

It was then on to Qü Xian to visit the Douthwaites where Captain Yü had been converted and faithfully preached the gospel. Small groups of Christians held house meetings where the living God was worshipped. Many women had been converted and asked Hudson for a woman missionary.

Travelling through Jiangxi Province, he observed a real need for women missionaries. He had seen the good work done by Maria and Jennie and felt sure any ladies would be treated with respect.

In June 1886 he passed through Poyang Lake and when he reached Xingzi he discovered that Archibald Orr Ewing and a party were soon to arrive in Shanghai. He retraced his steps to welcome the newcomers.

He arrived there on 14 June to discover that the option taken out by the Mission to purchase property at Wusong Road was about to expire. He knew that larger premises were urgently needed at this port of entry and did not want to miss out on what he considered to be an ideal piece of land on which to develop a complex. But time had almost run out to make the purchase. No money was available to conclude the deal and others were waiting to make an offer if the CIM failed to make the deal.

He knew that if it was the Lord's will for the Mission to have the property he would do the seemingly impossible and provide the necessary funds within the few hours left to seal the contract.

Prayer!

Prayer was the answer so he called together the few CIM people and at noon they sought an answer from God. No one outside that room knew what was going on, except the Lord of creation and providence.

Archibald Orr Ewing, a man of considerable means and a friend of John Stevenson, hearing that the CIM wished to purchase the Wusong Road property handed over £1,500, which was sufficient to ensure that the Mission could purchase the property. More money would be needed to complete the deal and build premises, but again Mr Ewing put his hand into his pocket and promised all that was needed.

On 15 June Hudson wrote to Jennie, 'I have today signed the contract for about two acres of building and garden ground in Shanghai—price £2,486.9.2'

This was again a wonderful answer to the prayers of God's servants. Accommodation was required as the Mission was entering a period of expansion under God's blessing, and the number of workers arriving was increasing.

In the middle of March, 1885 the CIM numbered one hundred and sixty three members; in 1895 the number had reached six hundred and twenty one; and in January, 1900 there were eight hundred and eleven working throughout the nation. The Shanghai property would certainly prove its worth!

Archibald Orr Ewing joined the CIM and played an important role in its activities in China until 1911. Following this he served on the London Council until 1930 when he passed into the presence of the Saviour he loved and served.

In England, another property was purchased to accommodate the many who offered their services to the CIM which was experiencing a time of real growth!

With the arrival of Orr Ewing and others, Hudson took the opportunity to again set out on a journey, this time hoping to reach Shanxi. The reason behind the journey was to meet as many CIM labourers as possible and encourage them in their work. All the time he was looking for new areas where the Mission could open stations. Rev. William Cassels, one of the Cambridge Seven was labouring in this large province and was attempting to establish a district of churches following the teaching and organization of the Church of England. Accompanied by his son Herbert, his secretary Mr Lewis, Dr Edwards and Mr Ewing, Hudson set out in June, 1886, the middle of summer. The first part of their trip was by ship for Tianjin and

Taiyuan where he planned to meet as many missionaries as possible at the provincial capital, Taiyuan. This would include the Cambridge Seven.

Once off the boat they had to travel overland, which proved to be hard going as the roads were very rough and riding in springless carts was bone shattering. In other areas flood waters covered the way. Nights were spent in inns wherever possible but often they found themselves trying to sleep on beds of bricks in a dirty room and disturbed by the thousands of bed bugs. The weather was very hot and flies were their constant companions.

Often everyone fell into bed without eating, only to be awakened by Hudson who had prepared a meal for them all. Omelettes were a speciality with him. They were his 'midnight chickens'.

The gospel had been preached in many nearby towns and cities largely due to the work of Frederick Baller whose Chinese was so good that it was said of him, 'When it grows dark, not one in a hundred would suppose he is a foreigner.'

Four of the Cambridge Seven were in the area—Stanley Smith, Dixon Hoste, William Cassels and Montagu Beauchamp. They played an important part in promoting church expansion, building on the work of others.

A copy of Mark's Gospel had been found in Daning, where a Buddhist priest, Zhang Zhiben, had asked the intellectual Qü to read it through and give him a report of his study. Both men were converted through their study of the Gospel and began to burn incense to the Christ and apostles of the book. Finding a New Testament they began to worship the living and true God. When the city officials discovered what was going on they had Zhang beaten, leaving him unconscious, and Qü was whipped in public three times. When Hudson discovered that there were some Christians at Linfen the group made a three day journey to meet them for fellowship. From that meeting a church grew.

William Cassels worked in that area, leaving his friend Montagu labouring with the church at Xi Xian. Cassels had faced opposition because he was a foreigner, although the only marks of this were a pen, a pencil and his English Bible. He lived in a small 'cave house' where he had a couple of square feet to call his own and there he met with those who had professed their faith in Christ and others who showed an interest in Christianity. It was there that he slept and cared for himself.

In 1886, Cecil and Arthur Polhill-Turner ventured into Sichuan preaching the gospel and selling Christian books and Scripture portions. When they and others returned to Hanzhong to attend the May conference organized by John Stevenson the claim was made: 'We had in God's name claimed Sichuan, and thrown down the gauntlet to Satan.'

Reaching Taiyuan on 3 July, Hudson found that smallpox was raging, which necessitated the conference being held over till 5, 6 and 7 July. Instead of the planned activities he gave a series of lectures on the subject, *The all-sufficiency of Christ for personal life and for all the exigencies of service.* At this time Hudson fell quite ill with dysentery and again the time together had to be postponed until 12, 13 and 14 July.

Hudson spoke of the glory of the living, risen Christ and pointed everyone to the written Word which spoke of the living Word. He called the assembly to purity of life and the necessity of the power of the Holy Spirit in all they did. He spoke of the close union that had to exist between the Christian and Christ and the Christian and the sinners he was seeking to save. Addiction to opium could be overcome by the power of the Lord. All of the Saviour's servants needed to be filled with the Spirit so they could persuade the ungodly to turn to Christ.

He urged all present to live a consistent Christian life and to be ready to make every sacrifice for the Lord and His people.

Time and again he returned to his expectation of the imminent, personal return of the Lord Jesus which called for personal holiness and a life lived in that expectation.

It was a true blessing to all who attended and Orr Ewing noted in his diary, 'Joined the Mission, Saturday, July 17, 1886…Its attraction to myself was and is that it is nearest the lines of Scripture of any work I am acquainted with.'

Later Montagu Beauchamp compiled a small book of Hudson's talks which was widely read. But these good times had to end and soon it was time to leave for Hongtong, where it was planned to hold a conference for the Chinese Christians.

Those accompanying Hudson divided into three groups, travelling different paths in order to again preach the gospel and let Christians know of the forthcoming conference to be held at Hongtong, commencing 1 August.

This conference also proved to be a great spiritual blessing for the more than three hundred who attended. Hudson spoke on Christ's words—'My Peace', 'My Joy' and 'My glory'. Following his address the invitation was made for any person to speak. Hundreds heard Pastor Hsi speak of his conversion to Christ. He was followed by many others who rejoiced to speak of God's dealings with them in leading them to faith in the Lord Jesus.

Hudson and the leading Chinese Christians moved on to Hanzhong after a second conference at Linfen. Before leaving Linfen time was spent with Pastor Hsi and the Christians he had won to Jesus. At a meeting where a refuge for opium addicts was opened he prayed for more refuges. Later he told Hudson of the events surrounding the opening of one such place. He had made mention of the great need the people had of Christ, but the problem was lack of finances.

'We have prayed very often for that city,' his wife said at length, 'is it not time to do something there?'

When she was told that money was needed, the question was asked concerning the amount required. The next morning she came and put a package on the table before her husband saying, 'I think that God has answered our prayers about that city.'

When Pastor Hsi opened the package he found all the jewellery that made up her dowry. The jewels were sold and a refuge for the opium addicts opened.

Hearing the story, Hudson asked Mrs Hsi, 'But do you not miss your beautiful things?' To this she replied, 'Miss them! Why I have *Jesus*: is he not enough?'

Before leaving he appointed Pastor Hsi as the one to have pastoral oversight of the churches in the area.

All too soon it was time to move on to Hanzhong, which was near the Sichuan border. With Montagu Beauchamp walking beside his horse, they commenced twenty-four days of harsh roads.

The heat of summer made life uncomfortable and frequently they lost their way. When they came to rivers that could be crossed on foot it was Montagu who carried Hudson across. He at first refused the offer, but at last relented: 'With Mr Taylor on my shoulder and a Chinaman on either side to weigh us down, we were able to cross in safety some strong streams, waist deep.'

Often they travelled during the night to avoid the extreme heat, but Montagu found that at times he fell asleep on his feet. When they slept during the night, the mosquitoes were a constant problem. Thanks to the kindness of Hudson, often Montagu woke to find himself covered by a mosquito net. Sleeping in the open was most uncomfortable, especially when the medicine chest was used as a pillow.

On one occasion the only place they found to rest in was a pig sty. Montagu described the events of that night:

> So we turned the occupant out, borrowed a few forms, took the doors off their hinges to lie on, and rolling ourselves in our plaids prepared to pass the night as comfortably as circumstances would admit. We were only masters of the situation for a short time, however; for the pig came back, charged at the makeshift door, which at once fell in, and settled down to share the apartment with us. After reflection, I concluded that it was too cold to turn out on the chance of ignominious defeat at the hands of the enemy.

The men had difficulty obtaining food, and when they did it was mainly rice and millet, although occasionally they purchased fruit or eggs. Now and again, much to their surprise, a chicken was the main meal.

Once when both men were very hungry and there was no sign of food, Montagu heard Hudson pray, 'We thank Thee, Lord, for this our food.' Montagu then asked where was the food?

Hudson's reply was, 'It cannot be far away. Our Heavenly Father knows we are hungry and will send our breakfast soon; but you will have to wait and say your grace when it comes, while I shall be ready to begin at once!'

Very soon they met a man selling cooked rice, which proved to be a delicious meal.

All along the way both men spent time reading the Scriptures and praying. At night time they read their Bibles by the light of a candle and Montagu noticed that often Hudson prayed lying down—this was because he would spend such long periods in communication with his Heavenly Father, that any other position would soon become painful to him.

Reaching Hanzhong on 7 September and hearing of the riots taking place at Chongqing, they knew it was unwise to go on, so a conference was held there for the local Christians.

Hudson also assisted Dr Wilson by carrying out some surgery.

The final meeting was held in Dr Wilson's courtyard where Hudson spoke on the subject: 'What we give up for Christ we gain, and what we keep back is our real loss.' As he had done many times before he reiterated the need to get the Christian message to every person. He concluded his address with the words: 'Let us make earth a little less homelike, and souls more precious. Jesus is coming again, and so soon! Will He find us really obeying His last command?'

He could have outlined many sacrifices made by members of the CIM in order to take the gospel to the Chinese. One such occasion that deserves mention involved Fanny Stroud. She was caring for the three Riley children upon the death of their mother. When she was asked to accompany Mr Riley and the children to Shanghai, she willingly agreed. Before they reached their destination Riley became very ill and when it was obvious that he needed personal nursing such as only a wife could give, Fanny and he agreed to an immediate marriage.

Fanny nursed him until he died on 19 April, 1886. Hudson, very moved by Fanny's sacrificial action, wrote to Jennie saying, '[Fanny Stroud's marriage] is about the noblest thing I have ever come across in my life. (Of his) recovery the doctor gave her no hope; just to nurse him to the grave and care as a mother for the three children…is what few would have done…She had none of the joys but all the anxieties, toils and sorrows of a wife.'

When Hudson left Hanzhong he rejoiced at the great work being accomplished by Dr Wilson and his faithful supporters.

He had won the support of the local mandarin when he gave medical assistance to his father, who was close to death. What the Chinese doctors could not do, Dr Wilson did and the man survived. As a result the mandarin presented him with a placard praising the doctor for his great skill. This meant acceptance of his medical skills and the gospel he preached.

Before leaving, Hudson let it be known that the newly organized China Council would hold its first meeting at Anqing in November.

When he received word that his close friend, George Müller, now eighty-one years of age, would soon be in Shanghai, he returned to the port. After a joyful time with his Christian colleague he left on a new journey up the Yangzi River, taking with him the newly married Herbert and his wife, as well as Maria and some newly arrived ladies.

After delivering his precious cargo of missionaries to Dagutang, he returned to Anqing to chair a meeting which had far reaching implications for the Mission. This meeting commenced on 13 November, 1886 and about half the regional directors were present. A full week was spent in fasting and prayer as was normally done before such meetings commenced.

The major outcome was what became known as the Manual which was the Principles and Practice of the Mission. Frederick Baller was formally given the job of preparing the course of study for newcomers.

With Robert Landale, he was given the responsibility of establishing the Training Institute at Anqing.

The relationship of the Council to Hudson was defined as an advisory council, not a decision making body.

The responsibilities of the regional superintendents were outlined: 'Such rule always leads the ruler to the Cross, and saves the ruled at the cost of the ruler....Let us all drink into this spirit, then lording on the one hand and bondage on the other will be alike impossible....When the heart is right it loves godly rule, and finds freedom in obedience.'

Then followed instruction about the obligation of members to live as the Chinese did—Chinese dress, language, customs—all in order to win the friendship of the people.

After two weeks of conference Hudson and John Stevenson were given the responsibility of producing the *Book of Arrangements*. It was proposed to send a copy to each regional superintendent and the London Council for comment.

With that matter solved it was time to return to Shanghai.

During the latter months of 1886 the suggestion was made that the Mission could use another one hundred missionaries in the forthcoming year. John Stevenson wrote to Jennie on 16 September, after the visit to the southern section of Shanxi: 'We are greatly encouraged out here, and are asking and receiving definite blessings for this hungry and thirsty land. We are fully expecting at least one hundred fresh labourers to arrive in China in 1887.' Great plans filled the minds of many of the Mission members, but Hudson was wary of the suggestion, thinking some were moving too fast. As Director of the Mission he had to consider the financing of such a proposal, and finances were in short supply.

At the Anqing conference the matter of the one hundred extra missionaries was raised and Hudson found himself once again writing to Jennie: 'We are praying for one hundred new missionaries in 1887. The Lord help in the selection and provide the means.'

At Dagutang, while working on the *Book of Arrangements*, he dictated a letter to his secretary, Mr Lewis: 'We are praying for and expecting a hundred new missionaries to come out in 1887.'

Mr Lewis looked at Hudson as if to say, 'If the Lord should open windows in heaven, then might this thing be.' John Stevenson then sent a message to all Mission members, asking, 'Will you put down your name to pray for the Hundred?' To the Mission supporters in London he cabled: 'Praying for a hundred new missionaries in 1887.'

When a Shanghai missionary heard of the CIM plan for the hundred he said, 'I am delighted to hear that you are praying for large reinforcements. You will not get a hundred, of course, within one year; but you will get many more than if you did not ask for them.'

To this comment Hudson replied, 'We have the joy beforehand; but I feel sure that, if spared, you will share it in welcoming the last of the Hundred to China.'

God did not fail the prayers of his faithful servants!

Hudson was in Shanghai and on 29 December, he wrote to Jennie: 'My darling, my own darling! I have wired tonight. Leaving on January 6th. I (am) almost wild with joy.'

On 6 January, 1887, in the midst of winter, he sailed from Shanghai anxious to be home in order to promote the plans of the Mission. Men and women and finances were necessary and as he believed the plans were in accordance with God's will, he knew he would have joy in seeing them all come to fruition.

44

A Start in America

On his way home Hudson visited William Berger who was living at
Cannes and there, as always, he found his old friend overjoyed at the
prospect of another one hundred missionaries serving with the CIM.
He expressed his concern with the newly published booklet, *Principles
and Practice* which he believed gave the newly established Chinese
Council more authority than the longstanding London Council.
He had always seen the Mission as a family of equals, but to him it
appeared as if 'law' had replaced 'grace'.

Hudson soon discovered that the members of the London Council,
who had spent much time and energy keeping the Mission functioning
smoothly in Great Britain, were not happy with the decisions made
in China. Benjamin Broomhall and his workers had encouraged
financial support for the mission and had selected those who would
serve as missionaries. The London Council felt they should play some
part in decision making; after all, business organizations and other
missionary societies were controlled from their home base.

Hudson was soon to face Council members who were upset with
some of his decisions concerning the discipline of missionaries which
they had approved, especially as several had been dismissed. When
the London Council received complaints about Hudson's actions they
believed he had abused his authority and should have consulted his
London Council before making such important decisions.

Arriving in London on 18 February, 1887, he received a warm welcome home and found he had a free week to use as a short holiday. However, his contact with the members of the Council warned him that all was not well. He wrote to John Stevenson unburdening his concern, but assuring him that he believed all would be sorted out when he had the opportunity to more fully explain what had been done in China: 'The Lord reigns—let us grasp that great truth—a gospel indeed!…Our action (in China) has not met with unmixed approval, but when all is better understood I hope it will be resolved.'

Arrangements had been made for him to begin a round of speaking engagements throughout Great Britain. Great numbers gathered to hear him speak of the work of the CIM and of its plans for the future. Wherever he went, there was correspondence and each day he answered an average of fourteen letters. As well he was involved in interviewing prospective candidates for service with the CIM.

Money was needed to support the prayed for one hundred and this became the subject of prayer with all those who supported the Mission. Five hundred pounds arrived from William Berger, which was just one of the substantial sums given.

When some doubters questioned Hudson's expectation of giving sufficient to support the work of the Mission, he replied:

> The Lord is faithful.…People say, 'Lord, increase our faith.' Did not the Lord rebuke His disciples for that prayer? It is not great faith you need, He said in effect, but faith in a great God. Though your faith were small as a grain of mustard-seed, it would suffice to remove mountains. We need a faith that rests on a great God, and expects Him to keep His own word and to do just as He has promised…Let us see to it that we keep God before our eyes; that we walk in His ways, and seek to please and glorify Him in everything, great and small. Depend upon it, God's work, done in God's way, will never lack God's supplies….'

Giving came from all types of people, even the widow's mite. In those early days of seeking the one hundred and the additional financial support, Benjamin Broomhall received a letter from a poor widow living in Scotland. She was surviving on just a couple of shillings each week, but continued to support the work of the CIM saying that she could go without meat in her diet, but the Chinese could not live without the Christ of the gospel.

The first formal meeting of the London Council took place on 23 March, and strong words were spoken about the newly produced

Principles and Practice. Apologies would come later on, but Hudson was pleased to find the Council supported his prayers for another one hundred Mission workers. So confident was he in the Lord's grace to provide the men and women, he wrote to John Stevenson urging him to prepare for their arrival.

He suggested that the building of the Mission headquarters in Wusong Road, Shanghai begin as soon as possible. In April he was able to send John Stevenson £1,500 which was to be used to raise the land above flood level. In August Archibald Orr Ewing gave another gift for the project, this time being £2,500. Plans were then drawn up for the building, and in 1889 construction commenced.

In England more property was needed and this was soon acquired, in conjunction with a house at Cambridge to be used for Mission candidates who required further education.

In April, Hudson returned to London where he discovered a very unhappy London Council, ready to resign over the issue of the *Principles and Practice* and the small *Book of Arrangements.* Despite the encouraging news from China, the July meeting of the London Council was heartbreaking. He let John Stevenson know that he was 'utterly used up' and 'tempted to wish that my turn had come, but He gives power to the faint.'

Despite the disappointment he was soon on the road again to face the continual round of meetings throughout Great Britain. Again and again he praised God for the strength he was given to present the crowds with the claims of the risen Christ and the work of the CIM.

He spoke at the Keswick convention where his words were received with joy. The church delegates were reminded of their responsibilities to support the work of missions.

But Hudson was tired and as a consequence Lord and Lady Tankerville invited him to holiday at a vacant house on their property near Chillingham Castle.

Soon he was off again and when in Belfast, Jennie wrote expressing her concern about his health: 'Do, as a duty, get all the rest you can... Do rest before it is too late. It will not pay to kill yourself, even to get the one hundred.' On another occasion she wrote, 'Darling, my heart trembles for you. I wish you had declined speaking this evening when you had three engagements for tomorrow.'

Nevertheless, Hudson, empowered by the Holy Spirit, had a message for the people and nothing would prevent him speaking of Christ and China's spiritual need.

The nagging problem of the attitude of the London Council to the decisions he had made in China demanded his attention. He wisely decided to visit each member and discuss the problem. In this way he was able to win them over and gain their support. On 5 August he wrote: 'Things have nearly come around, as to our Home Council, and with a little patience all will be well. God has worked for us, or all would have been broken up....'

With all the volunteers who had been interviewed, the London Mission staff was worn out. However, by November, one hundred and two men and women were on their way to China with more ready to follow. By the end of 1887 the CIM had two hundred and sixty-five foreign missionaries labouring in China and Hudson saw the possibility of another hundred if funds permitted.

He urged John Stevenson to be faithful in prayer when worried about funds:

> One is so glad that God has Himself asked us the question—"Is anything too hard for the Lord?" But...if we get less prayerful about funds, we shall soon get *sorely tried* about funds...but so long as you continue to seek His guidance in every matter and in the midst of the pressure of work take time to be holy and take time to pray for the workers, the LORD will continue to use and to own and bless you.

In Great Britain and North America student groups were formed to support foreign missions. One organization, the 'Student Volunteer Movement', established in 1886 had the motto: 'The Evangelism of the World in this Generation.'

Within a couple of years over two thousand of its members had signed the Movement's declaration, 'I am willing and desirous, God permitting, to become a foreign missionary.'

Robert Wilder, the son of a missionary to India, was instrumental in the formation of the Movement. In the forefront was Henry Frost, who supported the students' movement after he almost lost his life when he was an undergraduate at Princeton University. He was being shown by a friend an old revolver which both believed to be unloaded. When it was accidentally discharged, the bullet passed very close to his head. This close call with death convinced him that God had a special work for him to do. He soon after came into contact with Jonathan Goforth who was preaching about the responsibility of Christians to evangelize the world.

Henry, married, and not being in good health, approached the CIM with a view to acceptance as a missionary, but was told to 'wait upon God for further guidance.'

After much prayer with his wife, he decided that they could best serve the CIM by opening a branch in North America. This idea was not just that of Henry Frost, but when he arrived in Glasgow, he met John Forman who told him that he and his friend Robert Wilder had made it a matter for prayer for some time.

When Henry arrived in England he went to London to meet Hudson and outline his proposal, but Hudson was away on a speaking tour.

However, Benjamin Broomhall opened his home to the American guest, who realized the immense amount of labour needed to run a branch of the Mission. He saw the sincere godliness of the Mission members and became involved in the regular prayer meetings held at the home.

In was on 27 December that he met Hudson, and of this meeting he later wrote: 'I had, then and there, what amounted to a revelation—first of a man and then of his God...From that moment my heart was fully his...and also in a new and deeper sense, his Lord's. [And afterwards] Mr Taylor had seemed to encourage the hope that the Mission would be extended to America.'

Despite the pleasant discussions that followed, Henry left England at the conclusion of 1887, a disappointed man.

Benjamin Broomhall opposed the suggestion as he was sure that a British organization would not prosper in American soil, while Hudson thought it better for the Americans to have their own missionary organization, structured along the lines of the CIM. Later Henry recalled:

> On reaching my lodgings I had one of the most sorrowful experiences of my life. At the threshold of my room, Satan seemed to meet me and envelop me in darkness....I had come over three thousand miles only to receive to my request the answer, No. But this was not the worst of it. I had had positive assurance that the Lord had Himself guided me in my prayer, and had led me to take the long journey and make the request that had been made; but now I felt I could never again be sure whether my prayers were or were not of God, or whether I was or was not being guided of Him.

At that stage, Hudson had enough problems with the London Council but promised that he would visit America when the time came for him to return to China. He would speak at Moody's Northfield Conference if an invitation was extended, as well as at gatherings of students at Niagara-on-the-Lake. When it arrived he gladly accepted.

In the meantime the CIM was expanding under the gracious hand of God. The prayed for one hundred were in China and in 1888 fifty-three new members arrived, with more to follow.

With the extra one hundred on the field the CIM totalled two hundred and sixty-five foreign missionaries, with one hundred and thirty-two Chinese colleagues. Sixty-six Mission churches were scattered throughout the land, as well as eighteen schools and three hospitals. By the end of 1887 another five hundred and fifty-one believers were baptized.

In England, Hudson became more involved with the anti-opium movement than ever before. Benjamin Broomhall was one of the leading figures in the movement, but at the 3rd International Missionary Conference held in England 9–20 June, 1888 Hudson spoke with authority against the sale of opium to the Chinese. He had seen the evils of this trade and urged everyone to stir the British conscience in order to force the politicians to bring the trade to an end. He encouraged all the Conference delegates to warn society of the effects of the opium trade—the disease, poverty, degradation, death, suicide and theft that was the result of men feeding their cruel habit. He spoke of the sale of wives and children by men who needed money to buy more of the drug so freely available.

He told his audience that Pastor Hsi had proved that the gospel was the way to turn addicts from their craving for opium. Years before the Conference, in April, 1882, he had condemned the British for flooding China with opium:

> Nothing is more clear than that the Chinese had both the *right, the power, and the will to stamp out the use of opium in China* at the time they first came into collision with the power of England. We are fully convinced that but for England they would then have accomplished this; and hence we feel that *England is morally responsible* for every ounce of opium now produced in China, as well as that imported from abroad.

Now he continued the same theme, but encouraged all the delegates to reach a conclusion, condemning the politicians for their inaction with regard the flood of opium reaching China. He proposed a motion which deplored the action of the British using the Indian administration to sell opium to China as just another article of trade, and pleaded with the Christians of Great Britain and Ireland to earnestly pray to God, that the trade be brought to an end. The motion aimed to arouse the conscience of the British who in turn would pressure their elected representatives to take action through the House of Commons to bring the degrading trade to an end.

'It is with sin that we have to wage war,' declared Hudson, 'it is against sin that we have to protest...The power of Satan must be seen behind the actions of the government and individuals...But the Son of God was manifested to destroy the devil and his work!' He denounced opium which had effectively made addicts of one hundred and fifty million Chinese in eighty years, while during that same time just thirty two thousand had been won to Christ.

Other conference delegates raised their voices in protest, calling upon ordinary citizens to organize the population to bring pressure to bear on their politicians. Dr Maxwell spoke with force on the subject, supporting Hudson:

> There is the British House of Commons to be reached; and still before that, and most important of all, there is the heart of the Christian Church in England to be touched...Of late years there has crept over Christians in this country a very strange and terrible apathy in dealing with this opium trade...I am sometimes amazed at myself, at the want of feeling concerning the terribleness of this evil among the Chinese...In this hall tonight there is a constituency large enough, if set on fire by the Spirit of God on this subject, to begin to move England from end to end.'

The motion was passed, along with two others dealing with the evils of that age—drink in Africa and licensed vice in India.

Even though the motions were passed the conference committee set them aside as they believed they did not truly represent the feelings of the conference.

Benjamin Broomhall and his supporters were furious at the meeting's decision and decided to use their own influence and capabilities to bring the matter to a head. An organization called 'The Christian Union' was formed, printing its own paper *National Righteousness*, which helped mould the public conscience and played a significant role in forcing the British parliament to act. The paper's motto was words from Proverbs 14:34: 'Righteousness exalts a nation, but sin is a reproach to any people.' Shortly before Benjamin died in 1911, news came that the battle was won.

However, Hudson had some pressing responsibilities. He knew the time had come to return to China and on 23 June, 1888 he boarded the *S.S. Etruria* for North America, accompanied by the fiery evangelist Reginald Radcliffe and his wife, his son Howard and personal secretary S. Frank Whitehouse. Again he and Jennie were separated.

This time he travelled 'intermediate class' and was asked by the ship's captain to conduct worship in the first class saloon.

He was unsure of what lay before him, but was ever conscious of God's providential control of human affairs. Before leaving for America he had received a letter from Annie Macpherson who was in Canada visiting some of the orphans she had worked with in London's East End. She knew the spiritual temperature of North America and was able to write: 'I believe there are more brave and well-educated men waiting for your loved China in the Canadian colleges than in any other part of the globe.'

She had seen the results amongst the students of the work of Moody and other evangelists. Spiritual conferences were held, which resulted in many offering their services for missionary work, and the knowledge of Hudson Taylor's imminent arrival created a stir amongst the student groups. The Northfield Conferences had been blessed by God and his visit was to boost the interest in the work of the CIM.

Early in July, Henry Frost met Hudson and his travelling companions and escorted them all to his father's home, where they settled in to their new surroundings. They were soon to learn that the Americans did things differently to the British.

As was the custom in England, Hudson and his companions left their shoes outside their bedroom door in the expectation that they would be found bright and shiny the next morning. When Henry and his father discovered the shoes, as good hosts they quietly picked them up and polished them to perfection. When Hudson found out that travellers carried their own material to clean their shoes, he purchased a tin of polish and a brush and took over the job of cleaning the Radcliffes' shoes each night. This he did without their knowledge during the time they travelled together.

The men then faced the round of organized meetings and conferences. They were met by Mr Moody who gave them several weeks speaking to students, before facing a conference in New Jersey from 10–12 July,

1888. As usual, the mornings were devoted to spiritual exercises and the afternoons to the exercise of the body.

Radcliffe spoke in his normal, loud voice which was a contrast to Hudson's quiet speaking voice. The Holy Spirit did his gracious work amongst the students and soon there was a request for less physical activities and for more time to be devoted to spiritual matters.

John Forman was later to say of those days that it was Hudson Taylor's lifestyle that created the greatest impression upon his heart. He said, 'One of the greatest blessings of my life came to me *through*, not from, the Rev. J. Hudson Taylor.'

Henry Frost, who accompanied Hudson on most of his preaching tours found tremendous blessings through his Bible readings at the morning family worship, especially his treatment of 'The Song of Solomon'.

Students everywhere heard the call of China's spiritual need and soon many were offering their services to the CIM.

At Northfield the drowning of a student meant those present faced the reality of death and the need to get right with Christ.

Next came a meeting at Niagara-on-the-Lake where Hudson received a letter informing him of a new interdenominational approach to missions. His books had become very popular and many were sold to those with their new God-given interest in mission work.

A second letter contained an invitation to visit Clifton Springs if there was time in his itinerary.

Hudson's topic for the Niagara Conference was the majesty and glory of the Lord Jesus Christ. He spoke of the need of faith in the God who ruled the world and of the need of a total trust in the salvation provided through His one and only Son, the Lord Jesus.

He then accepted an invitation from Mr Moody to visit Chicago between 21–24 July, leaving Reginald Radcliffe and Robert Wilder to address the conference. Both men spoke with great power on the work of missions without drawing any special attention to the work of the CIM.

Robert Wilder in one address spoke of a lady who worked twenty-four hours each day for the Lord. This was by giving twelve hours service each day to the Lord herself, and supporting someone overseas to give the second twelve hours of the day to the Lord. Then he asked: 'We want many from the Niagara Conference to work twenty-four hours a day like this. Christian friends, you who cannot go, why not have your own representatives on the foreign field?'

When Reginald Radcliffe suggested, in response to questions, that fifty pounds would support one overseas worker for one year, the idea quickly caught on.

It had been decided that the offering would be given to the CIM to support any from North America who attached themselves to the Mission. At that time there was only one American working with the CIM and he, Dr Stewart, supported himself. When the collection was counted Henry Frost discovered a sum of five hundred pounds. He was approached by individuals and groups who handed him more money to support Americans associated with the CIM. People had been moved to open their purses and he suddenly discovered that he was the unofficial treasurer of money given to be used with American CIM workers.

When he later met Hudson at the family home in Attica, he had to tell him of God's working:

> I kept my secret, however, until we reached my father's house and Mr Taylor's bedroom. Then fully and joyously, I described to him how after his departure from Niagara the Spirit had swept over the Conference; how the offerings had been given and put into my hands to pass on to him; and how they had been found to amount to a sum sufficient to support eight missionaries in China for a year.
>
> Quietly he listened, and with such a serious look that I confess, for once in my life, I was disappointed in Mr. Taylor. Instead of being glad, he seemed burdened. If I remember rightly, he did just say, "Praise the Lord," or "Thank God", but beyond this there was nothing to indicate that he accepted the news as good news, as I had anticipated. For a few minutes he stood apparently lost in thought, and then said: "I think we had better pray."
>
> Upon this we knelt beside the bed, and he began to ask what the Lord meant by all that had taken place. It was only as he went on pleading for light that I commenced to understand what was in Mr. Taylor's mind. He had realized at once that this was a very marked providence, and that God had probably brought him to America for other purposes than simply to give a few addresses on his way to China. He had enquired from me how the money was to be used, and I had replied that it was designated, by preference, for the support of North American workers. From this he saw that the obligation was laid upon him of appealing for missionaries from North America— a heavy responsibility, in view of all that it involved....
>
> It was becoming clear to him, as to me, that my visit to London and appeal for a branch of the Mission to be established on this continent had been more providential than was at first recognized.

Hudson then wrote to Jennie: 'God is with us. Money for a year's support of several new missionaries is either given or promised, and great issues are likely to result from our visit. There never was more need for prayer than at present. May the Lord guide in all things.'

A couple of days later he wrote to John Stevenson: 'I think we must have an American branch of the Mission. Do not be surprised if I should bring reinforcements with me.'

Now he expected God to provide the manpower to use the financial resources in hand. It was at Moody's conference in Northfield, held from 1–9 August, 1888, that he stepped out in faith and sought volunteers, both men and women, for service with the CIM.

'To have missionaries and no money would be no trouble to me,' Hudson said; 'for the Lord is bound to take care of His own: He does not want me to assume His responsibility. But to have money and no missionaries is very serious indeed. And I do not think it will be kind of you dear friends in America to put this burden upon us, and not to send some from among yourselves to use the money. We have the dollars, but where are the people?'

Volunteers came forward and as meetings continued in America and Canada the selection was made of six men and eight women to accompany him when he left for China. However, there were many more who offered their services and he handed over their wellbeing to Henry Frost who 'would have to do the best (he) could with the rest.'

Of the women to accompany Hudson one, a nurse, named Edith Lucas had support. Mr Moody promised to provide her with her outfit and passage money, while her local church promised to support her while she laboured in China.

The second had a father who said he would fully support his daughter on the mission field for the first year, and longer if the need arose. He considered it his duty to do this and would not have others supporting his daughter as long as he had money to spare.

Then there was Susie Parker whose godly parents rejoiced in her decision to work with the CIM. Her father spoke up and said, 'I have nothing too precious for my Lord Jesus!'

With the giving of more money and the additional volunteers, Henry Frost found his time taken up interviewing and making decisions concerning the ones who would travel to China.

Hudson saw the need of a North American branch of the Mission and longed for the day when Benjamin Broomhall would visit America. Then he also would agree with his decision. In the midst of all the organization and meetings, a gift arrived from Hudson's dear friend William Berger—another five hundred pounds!

The meetings continued and when he was back in Toronto he spoke at the YMCA. The audience was awestruck with the power which accompanied his address. Mr Moody took this as an indication to pass around the plate.

As he had done many times before Hudson said, 'No' to the suggestion. That was not the way the CIM did business. Later it was discovered that a Christian businessman had been prepared to put fifty dollars on the plate that night, but the next morning felt compelled to post the Mission a cheque for five hundred dollars.

Hudson's uttermost trust in the providential working of God was witnessed on many occasions. Once after spending time with some gracious hosts they arrived at the railway station to find that his train had already departed. His host was very concerned that he would not arrive on time for his next speaking engagement. Hudson on the other hand was totally composed.

'My Father manages the trains, and I'll be there,' he said. He found out that another train was leaving which would at some point cross the line of the train on which he had intended travelling. Despite the uncertainty of such a connection being possible he boarded the train and for the first time ever, the train came in time for him to catch the correct train and arrive at his destination in time for his speaking engagement.

On another occasion he didn't have the train fare and his host, who was ready to buy his ticket discovered his need. He asked why he had not mentioned the fact that he was short of money.

'My Father knew,' was Hudson's quiet reply; 'it was not necessary to speak to any of His children about it.'

The woman who told these stories went on to say: 'Many of us who heard of these experiences had learned to bring the greater things of life to our Heavenly Father, but the simple, child-like trust of this godly man taught us to come to our Heavenly Father with the smaller details as well. "Casting all your care (anxiety) upon Him, for He cares for you."'

There were more meetings, but the time had come for farewells. Hudson intended to sail for China in October and suggested a gathering to be held at Attica, the home of the Frost family. He also wanted to use the time to acquaint Henry Frost and others of their responsibilities in doing the work of a *de facto* American Committee of the CIM.

On 25 September the farewell meetings were over and he met with a group of Mission supporters to form a committee which would undertake the selection of suitable Mission workers. They would also be responsible for outfits and travel arrangements.

In a room, Hudson Taylor, Henry Frost and Alfred Sandham had to select a committee. Three names were agreed upon—Dr H. Parsons, William Gooderham and J. Nasmith, and it was also agreed that they should be approached to obtain their agreement to serve on the Council. As the discussions were taking place there was a knock on the door and who should be there but Dr Parsons. He had just agreed to work with Frost and Sandham when there was another knock on the door. To the surprise of everyone, who should enter the room but J. Nasmith.

All present were surprised at the turn of events and more so when a third knock was heard and in came William Gooderham.

Hudson saw the hand of God in the events of that day and was more convinced than ever that it was God's will to constitute an American Council of the Mission, to work in conjunction with the London Council. He was of the opinion that Monday, 24 September, 1888 marked the date of the first meeting of the North American CIM Council. Shortly afterwards another eight members were added to the committee.

Then came the time for departure from Toronto on 26 September. Thirteen people boarded the train and another one joined them along the way, making a party of six men and eight women.

On the train for Montreal, Henry Frost noticed in a college magazine a rather derogatory report concerning Hudson. Having read the offensive article he started to hide it in a pile of papers on the seat when Hudson, who knew about the article, asked Henry to show it to him:

> Hudson Taylor is rather disappointing. I...had in my mind an idea of what (great missionaries) should look like...He being professedly one of the greatest missionaries of modern times must be such as they. But he is not...A stranger would never notice him on the street...except, perhaps, to say that he is a good-natured looking little Englishman. Nor is his voice in the least degree majestic... He displays little oratorical power...He elicits little applause... launches no thunderbolts...Even our own Goforth used to plead more eloquently for China's millions, and apparently with more effect...It is quite possible that were Mr. Taylor, under another

name, to preach as a candidate in our Ontario vacancies, there are
those who would begrudge him his probationer's pay.

Hudson smiled at Henry and replied: 'That is a very just criticism, for
it is all true. I have often thought that God made me little in order that
He might show what a great God He is.'

That night Henry Frost, sleeping in the railway bunk above Hudson
thought: 'It is not hard for a little man to try to be great; but it is
very hard for a great man to try to be little. Mr. Taylor, however...had
entered into that humility which is alone found in the spirit of the
lowly Nazarene.'

On 5 October, Hudson and his fellow-labourers boarded the SS
Batavia.

Arriving at Yokohama he found a pile of correspondence waiting
for him, amongst which he read news that caused him great distress.

45

Some Time in Australia

Herbert Norris, the widely respected principal of the Mission school at Chefoo, had rescued some children from a mad dog which had entered the school yard. The dog had attacked him, causing his death from hydrophobia in September, 1888.

News then followed of the death of Adam Dorward who had made a reputation through his missionary travels in Hunan Province. When he had returned to China to assist with the distribution of famine relief, he declared: 'I feel as if I would be willing to do almost anything that would be honouring to God, and undergo any hardship, if only I could get a footing in Changde, and see men and women turning to God.'

On board the ship a lonely Hudson, faced with a mountain of correspondence to answer, mourned the loss of his dear friends.

In a letter to Jennie he wrote: 'I am almost overwhelmed. "My soul is even as a weaned child." I want to be alone with God and quiet before Him. May He bless you…and all at home. May He make us more holy; more fit for His service *here* as *there*.' He saw these heartaches as the Lord's way to keep him humble and more dependent than ever upon his goodness. He wanted to obey his God more than ever before. Holiness was his great desire!

When he arrived in Shanghai he received more news of sickness and death of Mission members, but he was encouraged by the knowledge that the Lord reigned and never erred. He heard reports of some grumblings in Chefoo by some disgruntled Mission members. He had to deal with that unhappy matter, but first it was necessary to escort the newcomers to their stations. The women were taken to Yangzhou for studies and the men to Anqing.

Meanwhile Hudson rejoiced to find the organization working well under the direction of John Stevenson. But much was happening.

Stanley Smith and his new wife Sophie Reuter had returned to Shanghai, to renew their marriage vows which were then recognized as valid.

John Stevenson's daughter, Mary, was in Shanghai, suffering from a mental illness. As there were no facilities to house these patients, it fell to Dr Hudson to care for poor Mary, accommodating her in a room beside his. Mary often spent hours screaming and tearing her clothing. It usually took several strong people to control her behaviour and Hudson found it almost impossible to cope with the situation. When writing to Jennie he said:

> We are passing through wave after wave of trial. Each day has its full quota. God seems daily to be saying, 'Can you say, "even so, Father" to that?' But he sustains and will sustain the spirit, however much the flesh may fail. Our house has been a hospital; it is now an asylum. All that this means the Lord only knows....The night and day strain are almost unbearable....But I know the Lord's ways are all right, and I would not have them otherwise.'

A CIM missionary couple who had brought their maid with them, dismissed the poor lady in Shanghai. As she was destitute Hudson arranged for her return to England and then had the unpleasant task of rebuking the couple for their heartless behaviour. This was never forgotten nor forgiven by the couple!

In the midst of all the difficulties he found great pleasure planning the buildings for Wusong Road. He spent considerable time drawing up a plan of a building that would give a friendly, homely feeling to all who called. Later the architects drew up accurate plans from which the builders could work.

The newcomers from North America were accepted as full members of the Mission and proved to be a great asset. Life for the women had moments of excitement, such as the riot which broke out at Zhenjiang, just twenty miles from their training school. Hudson read a report of the incident: 'We stayed in the house until the flag was taken and the consul's house burning, and then we were taken…to the steamer… until the morning. (They returned to feed the school children, but then had to withdraw again.) The mob was very great and they threw large stones and pieces of rock at us….' When the mob began setting fire to the mission house, Chinese soldiers drove them away ….'And after Chinese, American and British gunboats anchored offshore…we soon had everything in order again.'

And all the time he missed the company of his dear wife.

News then arrived that most members of the London Council strongly objected to his independent action in the formation of the Council in North America (Toronto). They wanted to know the status of the new body and what was to be the relationship between the two Councils.

From the very beginning, the CIM was controlled in China by Hudson—not London or Toronto—which was different to business organizations that were controlled from their 'home office'. Some members of the London Council were under the impression they had the right to make binding decisions on both Hudson and the Mission.

Hudson knew he had problems when he received a letter from Jennie stating, 'Benj. and the Council are very dissatisfied…It would be far wiser to get them (the North Americans) to run a mission and help all we can. I hope it will be so for I think he is right.'

In the correspondence that passed between China and London, feelings became so sensitive that Benjamin Broomhall said that he would retire from the Mission rather than cause disharmony with Hudson.

In a letter to a member of the London Council, Hudson wrote: 'As to the American question, I shall be glad of your views when you have time to write them, but without a visit to America it is difficult fully to understand the matter.'

In the midst of these difficulties John Stevenson rejoiced that the work of the Mission was moving forward and praised God for the love that existed amongst its members.

One problem that emerged was Hudson's belief that God had directed his steps to North America and to the formation of the Toronto Council. To have done anything else he believed would have been disobedience.

In a letter to Jennie he declared, 'To hesitate would be disobedience in me. I am not praying that he (Benjamin Broomhall) may stay, but that he may "be filled with the knowledge of God's will" and that (our) love may be deepened…This Canadian Council is His will—and others like it He will give us unless I am greatly mistaken.'

He knew that he had to return to England and confront the Council and restore harmony before any permanent damage was done to the Mission's reputation.

Because of the difficulties with the London Council, Henry Frost asked him what he should do with the next group of missionaries who were ready to leave for China.

The immediate reply was that the party should be sent at once so the Lord's work could go forward.

In response to the misunderstandings in the London Council he sent a letter to each member of the mission indicating the problem, and of his intention to return 'home' and bring the issue to a conclusion.

After a meeting with the China Council where the final touches were put to the plans for Wusong Road, Hudson boarded a ship on 12 April, 1889 for Marseilles. On the way he spent much time in fasting and prayer for an outcome that would glorify Christ, and produce a more effective CIM.

At Marseilles he received an encouraging letter from Theodore Howard urging him to do everything possible to retain the services of Benjamin Broomhall, who was the real power behind the work of the Mission in Great Britain. William Sharp simply said that letters had been written using unwise wording, which had been misunderstood, and for the sake of the Mission should be forgotten.

When Hudson visited William Berger at Cannes, William questioned his conviction that he had acted in accordance with God's will. He suggested that Hudson believed his understanding of God's will was infallible, which was dangerous. Concerning the strained relationship between Hudson and Benjamin he said, 'It takes two to make a quarrel. You are to all intents married to Mr B and cannot be divorced.'

Hudson soon realised that the members of the Council saw Benjamin's continued leadership of the Mission in England as essential for its success.

As soon as he reached London, he and Benjamin spent several pleasant days together and found their differences disappearing. At the 18 June Council meeting all difficulties seemed to be gone as both London and Toronto would deal directly with China. Each Council would look after their own finances while all missionaries were full-time members of the CIM. It was also agreed to fine tune the working of the office to relieve Benjamin of a portion of his huge workload.

On 6 July, Hudson sailed for America to encourage the work of the Toronto Council and put it on a more business-like footing. In his pocket he carried a letter of appreciation from the London Council.

As soon as he arrived he was met by Henry Frost and began a hectic round of speaking engagements stopping at eighteen different places. On one visit he met Susie Parker's parents—the ones who had freely given their daughter to missionary service because of their love of Christ. At the time of their meeting they were unaware that she had died. Later, when the sad news arrived, her father said, 'It is still true. Nothing is too precious for my Lord Jesus.' Later Susie's only sister stepped forward to commence a life of missionary service.

Henry Frost was facing a predicament, as his full-time evangelistic service was only possible because of his father's financial support. Due to some bad investments, the family was impoverished which meant Henry was unable to give of his time as he had previously done.

Hudson met with the Toronto Council where the decision was made to centre Mission activities in that city. This meant the establishment of offices to conduct business, which included the selection of suitable men and women to serve in China. He knew that the ideal man to supervise the work was Henry Frost and thus offered him the job—but with no guarantee of financial support. Like all members of the Mission he would depend upon his Lord to provide.

Hudson had been given two hundred and fifty dollars which he handed to Henry for his personal use and left him to make the decision about his future place of residence. It required Henry to move to Toronto, leaving his wife and three children in Attica—unless they agreed to accompany him.

They lived in their palatial home with ornate ceilings and when decisions had to be made concerning their future, Henry's wife went to her room for a time of prayer. Henry wrote of the event which resulted in a united decision to move to Toronto:

> One day as I was in the parlour resting, my wife, unknown to me, was waiting upon God in her own room for guidance. While thus engaged she was led to open her Bible and to read in the book of Haggai; and she had not read long in this portion of Scripture before she had the light for which she had been so earnestly seeking. A moment later I heard her coming to me across the library and hall. She stepped to my side, pointing as she did to the fourth verse

of the first chapter of Haggai. I looked at the words indicated and read as follows: 'Is it a time for you, O ye, to dwell in your ceiled houses and this house to lie waste?'

'It was not necessary that my wife should say anything to explain her meaning; the lesson was self-evident. One look in her face showed me that the Lord had won the victory for her, and one look at the ceiling overhead settled the question finally for myself. From that hour, though it was not an easy thing to do, we were united in our desire to give up our home, in order that we might have part in the building of that spiritual house, the temple of Christ's body, which we knew the Lord was waiting to see completed.'

With a home rented for the Frost family in Toronto, Hudson and Henry spent some time interviewing Mission applicants, as finances were available for the next party of men and women to be despatched. When Hudson was given one thousand dollars to use as he saw fit, he handed the money to Henry, knowing that it would be wisely used for the Mission.

His work in America completed, Hudson boarded a boat to return to England. During his absence William Berger had taken action to put the CIM on a secure business footing, even enacting a Deed of Incorporation which safeguarded the Mission property.

William had decided to establish a fund of four thousand pounds to be used for 'decayed, aged and retired CIM missionaries, and to give £3,000, life interest to us, and then to our children equally divided.' He also introduced efficient work practices in the London office, which promoted a good relationship amongst all the employees.

He also considered who should replace Hudson upon his death. William's business wisdom was put to good use and when the London Council and Benjamin were presented with the proposals, Hudson rejoiced to find all in agreement.

When he received word that John Stevenson was facing opposition by some members of the Mission his advice was to speak to the people involved. Some had made plans for further outreach, so he advised Mr Stevenson to give them their head if they were capable, godly people. If he was unable to solve a problem he advised him to let things stand till he returned, which he trusted would not be far away.

He conducted a series of meetings in England and Scotland which resulted in the formation of the 'Ladies Council', consisting of Jennie, Amelia, Mrs Sharp and Mrs Theodore Howard, with Henrietta Soltau as the secretary and being responsible for running a training school for women selected for service in China.

Then there followed the Auxiliary Council in Glasgow, which was responsible for dealing with Scottish candidates for Mission service.

It was during his visit to Scotland that Hudson travelled by train with J. Elder Cumming who began to praise him for the great honour God had placed upon him in calling him to start the foremost mission work in China. Hudson's reply was to suggest that God had chosen a nobody, a weak person to do the work because then it would be obvious to all that all the glory belonged to God Himself.

The second occasion was on a journey to Glasgow where Mr Cumming, after several hours of travel in quietness, asked Hudson, 'What line of thought will you be taking tonight?'

'I can hardly tell,' was his reply. 'I have not yet had time to think about it.'

'Not time!' exclaimed Mr Cumming. 'Why, what have you been doing but rest ever since we came into this carriage?'

'I do not know about resting,' was the quiet answer; 'but I do know that since we left Edinburgh I have prayed by name for every member of the China Inland Mission.'

About that time Hudson found a text of Scripture causing him some concern. It was the Lord's command to his apostles that they go into all the world and preach to every person the gospel of salvation in Christ. He knew that half his working life was gone and of the two hundred and fifty million Chinese only a very small proportion had heard the gospel story. He was well aware that every generation had to be presented with the message of a Christ crucified and risen again.

He was deeply conscious that there was more to the command, for the apostles were to baptize and teach those who readily accepted the gospel. The task was immense, but what could Hudson do with his small band of willing workers. The answer was not to sit and question Christ's command but to stand up and obey the direction of his Lord and Master. Get on with the work! Do it!

But how?

It was 6 October when he and Jennie were visiting her father at Hastings, on the occasion of the celebration of his birthday. There while walking on the beach and meditating upon his Lord's command the truth burst upon his heart:

> I confess with shame that until that moment the question, What did our Lord really mean by his command, 'Preach the gospel to every creature', had never been raised by me. I had laboured for many years, as have many others, to carry the gospel further afield;

had laid plans for reaching every unreached province and many smaller districts in China, without realizing the plain meaning of our Saviour's words.

There was to be no more talking about the command! He must now obey the Lord's instruction!

First there was the need of concentrated prayer by all Christians for men and women to be raised up to go to China and preach a risen Saviour Christ. A true co-operation between the various missions was necessary in order to prevent duplication of work. The churches needed to accept their responsibility to support those missionaries called to preach the gospel. Finally he saw an immediate need of one thousand missionaries for China.

With one thousand evangelists, each one teaching two hundred and fifty people daily would mean that within a thousand days every person in China would have been presented with Christ's call to repentance and faith. He envisaged preaching Christ to the entire population of China within three years.

He saw the role of his Mission members as seed sowers. Others would have the privilege of reaping a harvest of souls as they followed the first wave of missionaries. This was the basis of an article he wrote for the December issue of *China's Millions*.

Having been asked to deliver the keynote address to the Third General Missionary Conference to be held at Shanghai in May, 1890, he now knew the theme for his talk.

In November, 1889 he received an invitation to visit Sweden to publicise the work of missions, particularly that of the China Inland Mission. On this journey he was accompanied by his son, Howard. Crowds gathered to hear him speak and to his delight he discovered that in England more than fifteen hundred students had attended a Missionary Convention, chaired by C. H. Spurgeon. Of that number one hundred and fifty-two had signed a pledge: 'It is my earnest hope, if God permit, to engage in foreign missionary work.' The name at the top of the list was Taylor, F. Howard, MD, MRCP, FRCS.

Hudson's godly manner created a deep impression upon all who met him. He carried his own baggage even though he was fifty-seven years old and feeling the effects of age and years of hard work. He continued to travel third class on the trains and on one occasion when he was obviously tired from a round of meetings, his son, Howard said, 'You are very tired now. Let me take the second-class ticket.'

Hudson's reply was simply, 'Well, it is the Lord's money, you know; we had better be careful about it.'

On another occasion when the offer was made to meet their travelling expenses he graciously declined saying, 'Well, I have a rich Father, you know. I will ask him about it. But I do not think this thought is quite according to His will. He is sure to provide for me; and I feel that what is gathered by collections ought to be used for the Swedish Mission.'

Several days after his return to England a cheque for fifty pounds arrived in the mail from the Swede to cover the cost of fares. Anything left over was to be used as Hudson determined. He rejoiced in the knowledge that his God was faithful, and in a letter praised his Lord because 'His power is just the same in Sweden as in England.'

He found out that Swedish Christians travelled for many miles to be present at his speaking engagements. People willingly gave liberally to the work of missions. On one occasion an old sailor who didn't have any spare money placed his much loved snuff box on the collection plate which was later sold for twenty crowns. In another situation a lady gave Hudson her beautiful watch, saying that it was for Jesus.

A private audience was arranged for him with Queen Sophia and four of her ladies-in-waiting. The queen sent a royal carriage to bring him to her palace some five miles from Stockholm. Hudson wrote to Jennie of the experience:

> Very shortly after our arrival the Queen entered, and as I moved toward her she came over quite simply and shook hands. She conversed a little about China, and then asked for a Bible reading. Two ladies-in-waiting and two nurses from the Queen's own hospital were present. I took 1 Kings 10:1-13, afterwards showing Her Majesty our map of China, which led to further conversation about the Mission. The Queen ordered coffee and sandwiches to be brought in, and afterwards shook hands very warmly and retired.

Hudson was involved in a three day conference with Swedish Missions in China with the result that those missions became formally associated with the CIM. All missionaries sent to China by the Swedish Missions shared all the facilities and benefits of the CIM.

Back in England he spent much time preparing his address to the forthcoming Shanghai Missionary Conference. The need of one thousand extra missionaries weighed heavily upon his heart and as he meditated upon his subject, he saw the parable of Christ's feeding of the four thousand as an illustration of what Christ could do with little. In a draft copy of his address he wrote:

> I am so glad it was a great multitude, so great that the disciples thought it simply impossible to feed them. Yet the multitude were in real need, and the need too was immediate. It must either be met at once or not at all....Let us notice that in these circumstances the presence of the disciples alone would not have sufficed. They might perhaps have said, 'Poor things!' They might have regretted that they had not more bread with them; but they would have left the multitude hungry. But JESUS was there; and *His presence* secured the carrying out of His compassionate purpose. All were fed, all were filled, all went away satisfied and strengthened; and the disciples were not only reproved and instructed, but were enriched also.

Hudson rejoiced that the same Jesus now sat upon the heavenly throne possessing all power. He would call upon all who heard him speak:

> Oh, let us trust Him fully, and now if never before, now afresh if often before, take Jesus as our Master and Lord, and with unreserved consecration give over to Him ourselves, our possessions, our loved ones, our *all*. He is infinitely worthy; and He will infinitely make up to us all we give to Him. For in return for our little all, He will give us Himself and His great all....There were many commands that appeared impossible to obey, but they were all definite commands: and I think we all need to set ourselves, not to try to obey our Lord as far as we can, but simply *to obey* Him.

Life for Hudson was hectic with the round of engagements, but the time had arrived for him to return to China. He knew he was needed there as John Stevenson had kept him informed of events taking place. He had been troubled with some whose pride had been hurt, others who found difficulties working with the people in their areas and still others who wanted to be independent.

The family who had been rebuked by Hudson for their unfair treatment of their maid had demanded that CIM deputies be determined by election. When this was rejected they had complained to the London Council. Another matter which was causing hurt feelings was the right of the China Council to dismiss unsuitable missionaries. The London Council felt this reflected on the work they had done in the selection of the best possible candidates.

Hudson knew his wisdom and guiding hand was needed to assist John Stevenson, so he made preparations to leave. He was determined to see peace and harmony amongst the members of the CIM before the General Missionary Conference, because disunity was sinful.

He sailed for China on 17 March, 1890 arriving there on 27 April. As was his normal practice, he travelled third class which meant his companions were not the best type. Some were drunkards and most were loud mouthed, rowdy people, but he was no stranger to such fellow travellers. His cabin was in a place on the ship where the air was flooded with the smell of coal and the noise of working engines.

However, he spent his time in prayer, Bible study and preparing his Conference address. He was missing Jennie, but felt guilty for such feelings. In a letter to her he wrote:

> Spiritual blessing…is the one thing I want and need and must have. Given this and I have no fears; without it nothing else will (avail)… May God forgive all that is wrong in me and in our mission… Unwillingness to be separated from you…has brought me under a cloud…but I have left you unwillingly, instead of joyfully…I do want to be whole-hearted in God's service. [And on July 12] My solitary life must continue as far as I can see *indefinitely*!…However heart-breaking it may be. We are His, His slaves.

Upon his arrival in Shanghai he was taken to Wusong Road, and how he rejoiced when he saw his plans had come to fruition. It had been only a month before his return that the first occupants had taken up residence.

He met an Australian minister there, the Rev. C. Parsons who had paid his fare to China and was ready to join the CIM. This was approved and when Hudson received a cable from Australia late in May seeking permission to establish an Australian Council, he replied, 'Sanction Committee.' The following day, 22 May, 1890 the first meeting of the Australian Council took place.

Hudson, longing for God's blessing upon the May Conference, spent much time in prayer pleading for an outpouring of the Holy Spirit. Some sixty Mission members were to be present. He arranged for them to meet at Wusong Road on 1 May for a six day period of fasting and prayer, for the success of the conference, where four hundred and thirty delegates (two hundred and twenty six men and two hundred and four women) would discuss matters of far reaching spiritual significance.

Wusong Road was not built to house such a large number, but with men and women used to roughing it in distant parts of China, sleeping on the floor presented no real problem.

21 May marked his fifty-eighth birthday and some eighty-three CIM members presented him with an illuminated address as well as four hundred and eighty dollars for his own use, which he accepted on the understanding that it would be used to cover the cost of his expected visit to the Australasian colonies.

Sunday, 25 May was set aside for a time of prayer and fasting for the CIM conference which commenced the following day.

At this informal meeting the speakers stressed the necessity of living a life of holiness as the way to please the Lord. Dixon Hoste put it plainly:

> We must get to know God *in secret*—alone in the desert…It seems to me that true spirituality lies in this—utter dependence on God for everything…We shall dread to…do anything in our own wisdom… If a man can only get down before God and get His plan of work for Him, individually, that is what will make him irresistible. It does not matter whether (he) is a strong man or a weak one…'

Again Hudson spoke of his plan of an itinerant evangelistic effort to take Christ to every person in China:

> This work will not be done without crucifixion—without consecration that is prepared at any cost to carry out the Master's commands…*Given that*, I believe it will be done. (But only) the operation of the Holy Ghost (would make it produce results). A man's conversion is, I believe, a regenerative change produced by (Him)—it is not an influence produced by man on the mind of his fellow-man…If the Lord sends Paul to plant, He will certainly send Apollos to water.

The Conference opened with prayer, followed by Hudson's stirring keynote address, where he called for another one thousand missionaries in order that within three years every Chinese would hear the gospel. In his address he was encouraging and gracious in everything he said:

> It would only want twenty-five (evangelists) to be associated with each society, to give us one thousand additional workers…I believe that the Lord would have us appeal for the Thousand…I believe that if we asked them for the CIM He would give them. But I believe that He would have *all* His servants in China share both in the prayer and in the blessing.

An appeal for one thousand men and women within five years to preach the gospel, was made to the Protestant churches. Those with teaching and medical qualifications were urged to apply.

Many other subjects were discussed including the continuing evil of the opium trade and the qualifications needed of the forthcoming missionaries.

Another question that occupied considerable time was Chinese ancestor worship. Was it incompatible with Christianity or was it possible for a converted person to continue such a practice? Most missionaries reported that when the Chinese were converted they gave up what was the practice of idolatry—the worship of their ancestors.

The Conference was a success and it was with light hearts that all the delegates gathered for the formal photograph to be taken. Scaffolding had been erected and rows of people stood on what was thought to be a secure structure with Hudson on the very top. Suddenly the edifice slowly gave way and everyone, without a cry, fell into a heap on the ground. Fortunately no one was badly hurt, although one woman had several ribs and her collarbone broken.

Four days later a second and this time successful attempt was made to have the photograph taken. In a later edition of *China's Millions* a report and photographs appeared for everyone to see. The full Conference report filled eighty closely written pages.

Hudson rejoiced about the fine Christian spirit that had prevailed during the time the missionaries had spent together and wrote to Jennie: 'There is a great spirit of love and unanimity.'

During the conference attention was given to the editing of the *Book of Arrangements*. It was also decided that before important appointments were made, Hudson should consult the members of the China Council. As a result the member who wanted officers elected resigned in protest.

In the Shanghai Mission office, work was divided into two sections— a department for postal work and another for shipping matters.

An invitation to visit Australia was received with joy by Hudson. For ages he had a soft spot for one Australian, Henry Reed, through whom he had been spiritually blessed when he was only twelve years of age. He had moved to Mt Pleasant, near Launceston in Tasmania and had supported the work of the CIM with prayers and money. Following his death, his wife had continued where he had left off and their daughter, Mary, had been amongst the one hundred to work with the CIM.

Many invitations to visit Australia had been received, and having given permission for the establishment of a Mission Council, he felt obliged to go, accompanied by Montagu Beauchamp and his personal secretary, Frank Whitehouse.

413

He also wanted to return to England to sort out some difficulties and help Jennie deal with a rebellious, unconverted Charles, who was having a bad influence upon his brothers and sisters. The children needed their mother, but he also missed Jennie. Having made the decision to visit Australia he asked Jennie to meet him in China when he returned from the colonies.

Jennie agreed, and he sailed for Australia on 19 July, 1890. He refused to travel first class and roughed it in the steerage decks with the tough, rowdy Portuguese sailors.

Reaching Darwin on 12 August he and his companions took the opportunity to preach and spend time with the Methodist minister F. Fitch, who warned him of the anti Chinese attitude of many Australians. He even suggested that it would be difficult to arouse any great interest in the Mission work.

When the party returned to the ship they discovered that the captain had transferred their baggage to first class, explaining that their cabins were needed by the Chinese who would soon board the ship. However, no Chinese arrived.

Reaching Sydney, Hudson and his companions commenced a hectic round of engagements, speaking and interviewing candidates who offered themselves for service in China.

In Melbourne, he met with the three members of the Committee he had earlier sanctioned. The three men were H. Macartney of the Anglican Church, Lockhart Morton a Presbyterian, and the Baptist, Alfred Bird. The fourth member, Charles Parsons, was already in China and a member of the Mission. It was while in Melbourne that Hudson met John Paton, 'The King of the Cannibals' who was well known for his missionary endeavours amongst the cannibals of the New Hebrides.

Following a series of meetings, he moved to the island state of Tasmania where he met Mrs Reed and Mary, who was home from China on recreation leave. She gave him sufficient money to cover the cost of Mary's return fare to China. In Tasmania he again met his friend George Soltau and made a statement that summarized his spiritual philosophy: 'There should be only one circumstance to us in life, and that Circumstance—GOD.'

Money flowed in to assist the work of the CIM and he found himself involved in the selection of volunteers for Mission service. After a visit to Adelaide he returned to Melbourne, ready to leave for China with twelve missionaries—four men and eight women which included

Mary Reed. In discussions with the newly formed Council he laid down the challenge—fifty missionaries in five years and one hundred in ten years from Australia. These numbers were in fact achieved.

Hudson showed his humility and on one occasion when he was introduced as 'our illustrious guest', he rose to his feet and commented, 'Dear friends, I am the little servant of an illustrious Master.'

He had to decline the invitation to visit New Zealand because of the pressure of work waiting for him when he returned to China.

Over three thousand people farewelled him and his party from Melbourne. Because of a shipping strike, and the necessity of the ship to berth at Newcastle to take on coal, he travelled overland to Ipswich to visit John Southey who had written to him. John was somewhat disappointed when he met him as he expected to be confronted by a more impressive figure. Later he commented:

> On reaching home, I mentioned this feeling of disappointment to my wife, adding, however, 'I am sure he is a good man'. But she was of quicker discernment than I, and after a little chat with our guest came and said, 'Look at the light in his face.'
>
> '...In the house he was all that a guest should be, kind, courteous, considerate, gracious. He at once fell into the household routine, being punctual at the meal table, studied to give the minimum of trouble, and was swift to notice and to express thanks for every little service rendered. We could not help noticing the utter lack of self-assertion about him, and his true but unconscious humility. About the Lord and His grace and faithfulness he spoke freely; about himself and his service he said nothing.

From there it was back to Brisbane for some more meetings and then a final farewell on 20 November. The ship called in at Darwin where Hudson again visited Mr Fitch the local pastor. He had his friends remain out of sight while he knocked on the manse door and asked, 'How many cups have you?'

'Why?' Mr Fitch asked. Then Hudson beckoned his friends and everyone made themselves at home for a short time.

On the journey to Shanghai, he took the opportunity to collect plants from the places where the ship berthed. These he planted in the gardens at Wusong Road.

On 13 December, 1890, they arrived at Hong Kong to find that Jennie had been there, but had moved on to Shanghai. Hudson collected some mail which was not all edifying. William Sharp had written, raising issues about his relationship with the London Council and the problem of one aged missionary who was claiming the right to sit on the London Council. The Council sought his advice which was well received: 'He is an old man now. Be kind to him.'

When the Council met he was totally without influence or energy to contribute to its affairs. It turned out that his wife had been the instigator of his letter requesting a seat on the Council.

On 21 December, 1890 Hudson and Jennie were again together, and this was an important reunion for never again were they to be parted this side of death.

46

A Clash of Cultures

Hudson returned to China to face many calls upon his time and energy. The Wusong Road premises received the increasing number of missionaries who would make up the much prayed for one thousand new workers. On 17 February, 1891 while answering the mountain of mail and sorting out difficulties, he saw two young men walking towards the offices. They were from the China Alliance Mission in America and were ready to commence the missionary work to which they were called.

'They must be the Scandinavians,' said Mr Stevenson, the Deputy Director.

Then thinking of the accommodation that would be needed he asked, 'How many are you?'

'We are thirty-five,' came the astonishing reply, 'and there are ten more, or perhaps fifteen, who will be here next week.'

Very soon the additional men and women arrived and during their stay at Wusong Road they provided a tremendous spiritual uplift. Filled with the joy of the Holy Spirit they sang their hymns and joined in the prayer times before setting out to their permanent inland postings.

Not long after this John Stevenson returned to England with Mary, his mentally ill daughter. This left Hudson alone to carry the burden of administration. In June that year he wrote to his friend:

Even you, dear Mr. Howard, can scarcely realize what it is to be out here, to know and love our dear workers, to hear of their sorrows and difficulties, their disappointments and their strifes; learning of sickness, needing arrangements for succour if possible; receiving telegrams asking for direction in peril, or telling it may be of death…not to speak of the *ordinary* responsibilities and the pecuniary claim of the mission now approaching five hundred in number. There is just one way to avoid being overwhelmed—to bring everything as it arises to our Master; and He does help, and He does not misunderstand.'

Funds were in short supply and this proved to be the cause of much heart searching, for Hudson knew that unconfessed sin was a hindrance to blessings. Shortages drove him and his supporters to their knees as they begged God to forgive their sins and supply them with all their monetary needs. While often funds were very low, the Mission was never destitute as the following incident in December, 1891 indicates. Finances were very much needed and Hudson calmly awaited a cable from England containing the funds for that month. When the telegram arrived he bowed his head in prayer and then opened it.

'A hundred and seventy pounds,' he said.

'One thousand seven hundred, perhaps?' asked Mrs Taylor.

'No; a hundred and seventy,' Hudson replied.

Quietness filled the room as those present knew that there was a real need of two thousand pounds. Hudson was calm for he knew from his own experience that he could depend upon the faithfulness of his God and Father.

'Now you will watch,' he said in a confident voice, 'You will watch and see *what God will do.*'

God again proved faithful when some large donations arrived from Australia and other parts of the world. As well, some unexpected giving was received from supporters of the Mission in China. That month each centre received sufficient remittances to cover their expenses and God again proved Himself faithful to his believing, praying people.

Another cause for concern were the people who spread false stories concerning the Mission. The rumour circulated that the China Council had directed all Mission members to avoid associating with members of other missions. Hudson was forced to defend the CIM by issuing a response saying that such an order had never been given.

Then others began to say that in order to become members of the CIM they had to practise baptism by immersion. Again Hudson had to answer the allegation which proved to be a waste of precious time.

When the London Council received accusations against a senior missionary Hudson again was obliged to spend time putting the rumours to rest.

In July, 1891 the *North China Daily News* printed an article which claimed that men and women of the CIM travelled 'huddled together' without chaperones. This of course was untrue but again time was wasted answering the allegations.

When others suggested that the death rate in the CIM was higher than in other missions, Hudson looked at all the statistics and answered, 'We are led to conclude that our Mission is, by God's blessing, one of the healthiest in China.'

Again the old problems of the status of the London Council raised its head. The Council looked upon the five-year-old China Council as a threat to their imagined authority. They believed that the China Council would act as a barrier between London and the missionaries they had selected and funded. They were also suspicious of the appointment of John Stevenson as deputy director.

A true power struggle was taking place and for the success of the Mission it was essential that Hudson retain his leadership as he had a better understanding of the Chinese situation than those living in Great Britain.

Help was needed in China because of the increasing complexity of the Mission work, and as far as Hudson was concerned John Stevenson and the provincial superintendents who made up the China Council were essential to ensure the smooth running of the Mission.

This was how it had always been. In May, 1891 he wrote to John Stevenson: 'Mr Berger is quite right, that the supreme question is that of final leadership and it is equally clear to me that it can only be vested in China.'

To his friend Theodore Howard he wrote, 'We may make mistakes in China and no doubt mistakes have been made in the past; but evils far more serious would result from abandoning what I am convinced are God-given lines for the C.I.M.'

In London the forceful, overbearing lawyer, William Sharp was behind the strong sentiments of the Council. When Hudson wrote explaining that those in China were best suited to make decisions, William Sharp replied, 'Your letter manifests such marked absence of trust…in your Home Council' and the trouble was to be found in Hudson's 'wrong ideas—and your China Council's.'

William Sharp saw the role of the London Council as administrative and even believed that Hudson should leave the Mission. The London Council would run the Mission while Hudson gave his time to preaching the Scriptures and visiting churches to promote the CIM.

The Principles and Practice was tolerated, but the *Book of Arrangements* was a real source of annoyance to the members of the London Council.

The Home Director, Theodore Howard, wrote to Hudson on behalf of all Council members pointing out that his change in administration in China was totally contrary to the established way. He suggested that the Christian public trusted Hudson, but not a China Council, and if a member of the Mission was to be dismissed, the decision should be that of Hudson alone—not the China Council!

They also rejected the 1886 revision of the *Principles and Practice*, on the basis that only a 'small section' of the Mission members were involved in its production. They conveniently overlooked the fact that it was the provincial leaders who had been involved.

The letter concluded with: 'This letter intimates as kindly but as firmly as possible the final (and I may say unanimous) decision of the Council in this matter, and we await your agreement, by wire or otherwise, before proceeding with the revision of the *Book of Arrangements*.'

With the letter in his hand he discussed its contents with Archibald Orr Ewing and Walter Sloan who had arrived in Shanghai. Both men agreed that his position was correct and as a result he wrote a letter to his close friend John Stevenson and a second letter to the London Council. Responding to the London Council's letter Hudson wrote very plainly of the existing situation in China:

> I am greatly distressed and perplexed by it. I feel you do not apprehend the situation nor at all understand the gravity of the position you seek to establish; for I know your love for me personally and your desire to help me, and I know also your deep and abiding interest in this work of God on behalf of which you have spent so much time and thought. I feel that we have reached perhaps the gravest crisis that the Mission has yet passed through, and am very glad that our annual day of united fasting and prayer is so near at hand and will precede the next meeting of our Council here, when your letter must be considered....I dare not for peace's sake

be untrue to my convictions, for if we forfeit the favour of GOD
we have nothing to stand upon. You have not funds to support 500
missionaries; you cannot protect them against insurrection or in
riot; you cannot come out here and administer the affairs of the
Mission; we must walk before God. I am sure you agree with me
in this. For the present the only thing I can see is quietly to wait
upon God. The wire we have just received of £170 to £270 of general
funds [a drop in the bucket] is an instance of how vain it would be
to trust in British resources instead of in the living God; but while
we walk with Him we can rest in His faithfulness. Yours gratefully
and affectionately in Christ, J. H. Taylor.'

Hudson was aware that the *Principles and Practice* and the *Book
of Arrangements* were a source of irritation to the London Council
which considered they had been imposed upon them. He urged John
Stevenson to meet with the Council members individually to discuss
the booklets and show their value.

Despite some encouragements, Hudson was finding the difficulties
very stressful and his health was failing. So depressed was he that
Jennie believed his life was in real danger.

The influx of missionaries resulted in fifteen nations being
represented in the Mission. Then Henry Frost decided to visit China
with some new missionaries, to see the situation for himself and to
spend time with Hudson to make the Mission run more smoothly.
During April, Hudson and Henry held a conference with twenty-
nine of the thirty-one North American missionaries at which, much
to Hudson's delight the decision was made to merge their finances
with the general Mission funds. The thirty-one Americans were also
admitted to full membership of the Mission. Henry Frost then spent
time visiting the areas where the Americans were labouring.

Towards the end of 1891 and into the early days of 1892, great
spiritual blessings were poured out upon the work at Wusong Road.

Geraldine Guinness was in Shanghai and very concerned that very
few were being converted through her witness. She knew she needed
power from on high and after a service on the Sunday before Christmas,
1891, a stranger asked her, 'Are you filled with the Holy Spirit?'

This question so concerned her that she began to pray earnestly
for Holy Spirit power when she preached Christ. Through faith she
believed she received the gift of the Holy Spirit and so prayed that her
Lord would give her some proof of what had taken place in her heart.
The proof she asked for was to see daily conversions at her meetings.

Great rejoicing followed when she saw people being converted as she preached the gospel. At that time, *HMS Caroline* was in port and some of her crew attended the meetings at Wusong Road. The result was that one officer and twenty sailors were converted. In the following months many men and women were won into Christ's kingdom and this thrilled Hudson. As he saw God working his heart was filled with the desire to see all Mission members experiencing the same blessings.

Jennie also rejoiced in what she saw taking place and in a letter home (April, 1892) wrote, 'God is working in our midst, emptying and humbling one and another, and filling with the Holy Spirit. We are having frequent meetings full of liberty and power.'

At a China Council meeting on 16 April, 1892, the session ended in a time of prayer, and the minutes recorded, 'Instead of meeting for conference, the China Council united with the members of the Mission in Shanghai in seeking for themselves, the whole Mission in China and the Home Councils, the filling of the Holy Spirit.'

Prayers for a further filling of the Holy Spirit swept through the Mission compounds with the result that many members had their lives changed and discovered great power in their preaching.

Hudson urged all members to search their hearts and if sin was found, to repent and turn to God in holiness of life. They were all asked to accept by faith the fillings of the Holy Spirit and believe that this had taken place. Then they could get on with the work they were called to do, knowing that God was with them.

China at that time was becoming politically unstable and again foreigners were looked upon with suspicion and distrust as was the growing power of Japan. On 6 May, 1891 a riot against the Roman Catholic mission in Yangzhou took place and in Anqing their orphanage was totally destroyed as they were suspected of harming children.

The anti-foreign feeling spread even to Shanghai where Chinese guards were placed around the Wusong Road Mission premises. When the tension increased it was decided to move the women and children to the Settlement in the city.

Inland some thought it best to move missionaries to safer areas, especially when news arrived of the death of Mr Argent, a Methodist missionary in Hubei province. Again the rumours were spread that children were being used by foreigners for immorality.

Hudson, concerned for the well being of the Mission members, the glory of God and the honour of Christ, wrote a circular letter to all Mission members encouraging them in the dangerous time. He called them all to stand firm and bear a good witness to the truths they had been teaching for many years: 'A holy joy in God is far better protection than a revolver…trust in the living God, who is able to protect…and will do so unless for His own wise purposes He sees His own glory will be more advanced by their suffering.'

He reminded his friends that they were not representatives of any earthly power, but of the kingdom of Christ and suggested that fear was not a good reason to leave their place of service. They were to face the hatred of men with a calmness that would set an example to everyone in their area.

Yes, the time was an opportunity to show the faith they professed and taught in action. He wrote on 17 June, 1891:

> We are continually encouraging our converts to brave persecution and to suffer loss for Christ's sake, and they are apt to think that it is easy for us to speak in this way, seeing that, as far as they can tell, we are well-off and exposed to no danger or loss. When, therefore, we are in danger, they will mark our conduct very closely, and judge for themselves how far we really believe that "Sufficient is His arm alone, and our defence is sure." What a loss it would be if any of them should think that we relied more upon a gunboat or a band of soldiers than upon the living God! Years of teaching would not impress them as our conduct at such times may do. Moreover their sympathy will be drawn out toward us when they see us willing to suffer for the Gospel, as they so often have to do. A time of danger is a grand opportunity for being an object-lesson to the native Christians.

Hudson considered the anti-foreign riots as Satan's attack upon the work of missionaries. In a letter to a woman in Australia he wrote: 'The great enemy of souls has been raging against missions in China. I look on the recent riots as Satan's reply to the Conference appeal for a thousand additional workers. God will have His response however; and while the enemy is mighty, God alone is almighty.'

God's protective hand was about the members of the Mission and no lives were lost. Hudson let the supporters of the Mission in Great Britain know that reports of the riots were exaggerated.

At Dagutang on the Poyang Lake it was suggested that the women leave the Mission premises until the danger had passed. However, the decision was made to remain and the only damage done to the CIM premises was that the hungry soldiers who were on guard, broke into the pantry where they stole some food.

At Wenzhou a riot broke out during darkness and some foreigners took refuge in a foreign battleship anchored nearby. When the ship turned on the searchlights, a modern invention, the rioters thought the end of the world was at hand and quickly retreated. At other times during 1891 and 1892, the rain which fell at the appropriate moment, dampened the rioters' ardour.

The anti-foreign hatred spread far and wide and was tasted by Cecil Polhill, his wife Eleanor and two faithful Chinese Christians, Wang and Zhang. Cecil wanted to take the gospel to the people of Tibet and on 29 July, 1892 they reached Songpan. For several months previously they had preached the gospel without any opposition. A period of drought created the impression that the Christians and their God were to blame. However, the Tibetans and Muslims refused to be involved in the events that took place.

The four missionaries were stripped to the waist and assaulted by the enraged crowd. Then they were escorted outside the city walls and the cry went up, 'Throw them in the river! Stone them! Tie them up in the sun till rain falls!'

Some soldiers came to their rescue, but even in the city official's residence they were not safe. The mob dragged them outside, and they were forced to stand with arms tied behind their backs. When the two Chinese Christians, Wang and Zhang were asked if they would accept a flogging in the place of Cecil and Eleanor they willingly agreed to act as substitutes for their Christian teachers and suffered a whipping with sticks until their backs were red raw. Then they were placed in cangues (a portable set of stocks). Eventually they were allowed to leave, and after several weeks they met some missionaries on holiday and received food and medical help.

Later when talking about the events of that terrible day, Zhang said, 'I couldn't help smiling…when we were being marched through the town with wrists tied—smiling that we were in a very small way like our Master, Jesus Christ.'

Many years later a Chinese Christian told a missionary that he witnessed the whipping and maltreatment of the four Christians, and as a result made the decision that he must follow Christ.

Despite China's problems, Hudson considered the difference of opinion between himself and the London Council was so serious a threat to the continued existence of the Mission that he needed to return to England.

On 10 May, 1892 he and Jennie left Shanghai for the United Kingdom by way of America.

47

A Busy Schedule

Hudson was so exhausted and unwell, that the trip across the Pacific was very trying. He was in need of a complete rest, and when he reached Canada, he spent some time relaxing. When Henry Frost notified Benjamin Broomhall of Hudson's need of rest he received a reply agreeing with the suggestion.

The journey across Canada was done in stages so that he could recuperate before facing speaking engagements in Canada, particularly at the Niagara Conference where his presence and wise counsel was eagerly awaited. He met with the Toronto Council which again proved to be spiritually uplifting.

On 26 July, 1892 he and Jennie arrived in Liverpool—home again to face the problems that weighed heavily upon his heart.

But first he attended the Keswick Conference which was well underway when he arrived. He chaired a conference session dealing with the opium curse, before receiving word of the death of Mrs Robert Howard, the mother of his close friend Theodore. He and Benjamin were invited to conduct the funeral where all members of the London Council were in attendance. This gave them the opportunity to speak informally with each other in an atmosphere of grief.

The first formal Council meeting which took place on 6 September, proved to be a pleasant gathering. All members held Hudson in high esteem and the issue that divided them was not raised.

However, a week later, when the matter of the status of the London Council was raised, Hudson let John Stevenson know that discussions were very pleasing: '…the Council do not now wish to claim the power to adjudicate in dismissals or even to veto, but that in ordinary cases of inefficiency where there is no urgency they might have the statement of the case with a view to either concurrence or suggestion…they will then accept our conclusion…it being understood that there is no appeal from one Council to another.' The London Council wanted to be heard and their view considered by the China Council when making important decisions. They had no wish to act as a Court of Appeal by disgruntled Mission members.

Feelings were still entrenched and some thought Benjamin might resign from his position in the Mission but Hudson had plans for the reorganization of the London administration which would release Benjamin to devote more time to his passionate campaign against the opium trade. Benjamin was also becoming deaf and found the burden of work increasingly difficult. When Hudson asked him what his response would be to sharing his load, he agreed. He would retain his position of General Secretary of the Mission in England and Walter Sloan would be asked to return from China to become his Assistant Secretary.

Hudson then cabled Shanghai, 'Sloan marry at once and come as soon as practicable.'

Then word was received of the impending arrival of Henry Frost and two of his Council members to discuss reorganization of the Toronto Mission.

They arrived in England on 4 January, 1893. Cordial discussions were held between all the council members, even raising old problems, but bringing about a better understanding of the relationship between the two Councils.

Hudson, realizing that the *Book of Arrangements* was a source of friction had it formally put to one side. The objections died when it was explained that the book was only to be used as a useful guide, but was not to be a Mission textbook. The *Principles and Practice*, sent to Shanghai for comment, received the China Council's stamp of approval. There was much godly rejoicing now that peace had been restored.

Somehow, Hudson and Henry Frost were able to convince William Sharp that it was his brilliant idea that Walter Sloan should be appointed Assistant Secretary of the Mission in England. Sloan was well known for his business ability and his Christian character—he truly was the man for the job. Walter and his wife arrived in England on 25 March, 1893.

In June, Hudson formally announced that Henry Frost was Home Director of the Mission in North America.

During his time in England, Hudson travelled extensively promoting mission work and explaining the activities and plans of the CIM. Not only did he travel throughout Great Britain, but he also made several visits to Germany. After this he made new plans to visit Australia and New Zealand. So busy was he that Jennie feared that the stress and strain of the last few years would cause his death.

All the time he was receiving news of events in China and continued to be involved in the discussions to enlarge the Chefoo school. Land had been purchased and plans drawn up for the new buildings and playing fields. These objectives did not come to fruition until the war between Japan and China concluded. At that time Archibald Orr Ewing provided £5,000 for the construction work.

Financial support in Great Britain for the CIM had lessened which caused Hudson great concern and became a matter of much prayer and soul searching. He wanted to root out any unconfessed sin that might be the cause of the poor donations.

On one occasion, in September, 1892, the London Financial Secretary asked him what he should do with the small sum of money that had been given. He asked that the money be held for another day, giving the Council the opportunity to seek the face of God in prayer, begging for further giving. He was reminded however, that any giving received could not be forwarded with the September finances, but would need to be held till the following month.

Hudson sent the cable indicating the funds that could be drawn upon—an amount that would not meet their basic needs. He immediately called everyone together for prayer, imploring God to provide all that was needed. God had never let him down and he was confident that his Lord would again supply what was needed for the month of September.

Late that very afternoon the post arrived with a letter and cheque for five hundred pounds. The letter made the specific request for the money to be immediately forwarded to China.

Meanwhile in China the Council began determining how the first small amount of money should be distributed, but as the need of extra finance was very real, members began pleading with God to somehow provide what was needed.

The following day the arrival of the five hundred pounds was seen as an answer to prayer and the Council members praised God for his goodness.

As John Stevenson had returned to China, Hudson was able to spend a few extra months in England.

Early in 1893 John Stevenson was faced with the arrival in Shanghai of some Americans who had made their way to China without the approval of their council. As they wanted membership in the Mission, John sought references from people in America.

One man, Petrus Rijnhardt was accepted on the basis of a good reference from a pastor in Canada, and after some time at the language school he commenced his missionary work, where he became engaged to Annie Slater. With some more enquiries about Petrus it was discovered he was an imposter. Consequently he was dismissed from the Mission, but Annie could not believe what she heard, and followed him to the United States of America where the dreadful truth was confirmed to her. She had been saved from a fraudulent marriage.

Petrus on the other hand married a doctor and together they returned to China to work independently on the Gansu-Qinghai border.

The CIM was experiencing an influx of newcomers which meant a leap forward was about to commence. Men and women required serious preparation for their future, and one requirement was that all future Mission workers be vaccinated against small-pox.

On 10 November, 1893 Hudson wrote to John Stevenson, 'I propose organizing a thorough campaign for the Mission such as has not yet been attempted.' The new 'forward movement' resulted in an increase in giving, and spirits were high that God would do great things on the Chinese mission field.

As the time had come for him and Jennie to return to China, on 14 February, 1894 they boarded a ship for America, having made formal legal arrangements of what should happen in the event of his death.

Arriving in New York on 23 February, they were met by A. B. Simpson and a group of International Alliance Mission students who were about to leave for Hong Kong and then to work in Guangxi.

During his stay in America Hudson addressed some student conventions and had the opportunity to twice meet Rijnhardt and his pastor where Rijnhardt threatened legal action that would hurt the CIM.

Having made their way across America Hudson, Jennie and Geraldine Guinness boarded a ship at San Francisco for Shanghai. They disembarked on 17 April, 1894 to find an overworked and exhausted John Stevenson.

The Mission had grown greatly since Hudson had appointed John assistant director and it was obvious that he needed help. Instead of two hundred Mission members to care for, in 1894 there were over six hundred workers. While John had men capable of giving assistance, he found the delegation of duties a difficulty.

Hudson set about relieving him of the great burden he carried. William Cooper was appointed Assistant Deputy Director and given the responsibility for all administrative correspondence. Hudson and John were to deal with correspondence marked personal.

Hudson then appointed a Standing Council of John Stevenson, William Cooper, Charles Fishe and James Broumton to assist him when Council members were absent.

Now that the reorganization of the work load at Wusong Road had been effectively carried out, he made the decision to commence a tour of the Shanxi and Shaanxi Provinces where some Mission members were experiencing difficulties. The CIM had been blamed for the thoughtless actions of some members of other missions, and he wanted to resolve these difficulties.

Another problem resulted from the arrival of a large contingent of newcomers at a Mission station. From experience Hudson and others knew they won acceptance by entering new areas one or two at a time. Often it had taken years to win the friendship of the people and this could all be undone by the unwise action of other mission members.

The situation in China was becoming unstable with the threat of war growing. All foreigners were suspect and it was essential that members take great care. In Peking the British Government had appointed a Roman Catholic Consul who was responsible for the issue of passports and Hudson wanted to make sure he was not offended by the actions of any CIM member.

While he looked forward to the renewal of friendships, it was the wrong time of the year to travel. It was May, summertime, and the long journey in the heat was an invitation to stroke, malaria, typhoid and his old enemy—dysentery. Despite the difficulties they faced, he knew the trip was essential: 'If the Lord has further work for us to do,' he wrote, 'He will bring us safely through, and I think He will do so, but should it prove otherwise "we ought to lay down our lives for the brethren".'

Howard Taylor had married Geraldine Guinness and both were concerned with the dangers Hudson and Jennie faced on the journey despite the presence of Joe Coulthard. They made the decision to meet the travellers who planned to address conferences in four cities.

The enlarged party of five travelled by houseboat, followed by wheelbarrow and springless carts in clouds of dust and temperatures of over 100°F.

During the journey Geraldine kept a diary of the hardships encountered.

The entry for 13 June reads: (6 am)

> This is indeed a moment of misery. We are sitting waiting in our carts in this filthy inn-yard, all ready to start—as we have been for an hour—while rain pours steadily down and the carters are obdurate. For several nights…we have slept but little (bed bugs). Outside in the courtyard half a dozen fiery mules were fighting and braying all night long….There being only one room, Mother and I occupied it; Father, Howard and Joe slept in the carts outside.

In most places the travellers were greeted with a smile and this was especially noticed by Geraldine. When she commented on this to her husband, he replied, 'Perhaps that is because we smile at them.'

At times smiles were difficult because of the problems faced. Even staying at an inn often presented problems as it was frequently discovered that a clean cowshed in England would be a luxury compared to the run down state of the places.

At a river crossing, swollen by floods, the party saw one of their carts overturned and swept away.

Travelling by wheelbarrow was rough in the extreme. Again Geraldine explained what such travel was like. The wheelbarrows each had seating for two passengers either side of the wheel on a wooden framework. They each faced the rear of the contraption while the front was packed with food and luggage. A thin mattress was placed on the seat to stop the passengers being shaken to pieces, and over all this was a plaited bamboo matting:

> As soon as we were in, one powerful young barrowman slipped the broad canvas strap across his shoulders, lifted and balanced the barrow—throwing us backward at a sharp incline—and called to another man in front to start away. With a creak, a jolt, and a long, strong pull, the cumbrous machine moved slowly forward. The dust began to rise around us from the feet of the men and the wheel track in the sandy road. With a gasp we clung, as for dear life, to the framework of the barrow, jumbling heavily over ruts and stones. Dry and oil-less, the slowly revolving wheel set up a discordant

wail; large beads of perspiration stood out upon the forehead of the man scarcely a yard away from us, bending so determinedly to his task...'

When the party reached Zhoujiakou in the northern part of Henan they rejoiced to find a flourishing Christian community. They were graciously welcomed by all, but none more so, than old Mr Ch'en. This retired Chinese official loved Hudson for it was he who was responsible for bringing the gospel to him and to many citizens of China. He bowed low before him and repeatedly said, 'But for you, Venerable Sir, we should never have known the love of Jesus.'

He presented Hudson with a large sheet of red paper on which was written:

> I bathe my hands and reverently greet—The Venerable Mr. Taylor, who from the beginning raised up the CIM with its worthy leaders, elders and pastors.
>
> You, Sir, constantly travelling between China and the foreign lands, have suffered much weariness and many labours....It is the glorious, redeeming grace of the Saviour that has blessed us, but it has been, Sir, through your coming amongst us and leading us in the true way; otherwise we had not been able to find the gate whereby to enter the right path....
>
> God grant you, our aged Teacher, to be spared to await the coming of our Lord, when Jesus Christ shall become King of kings and Lord of lords....Among our own household, and indeed throughout the little church in and around Chow-kia-kow, there is no one who does not esteem you highly.
>
> Respectfully wishing peace, The very unworthy member,
> Ch'en named Pearly Wave.
> I bow my head, and respectfully salute.

A sumptuous meal, especially prepared by Ch'en for Hudson and his companions, followed.

When the time came for leaving, Ch'en presented him with a hamper of food for the journey that lay ahead—'spiced meat boiled in oil, spiced carrot kernels, and pickled water-melon.' He had avoided using cayenne pepper when preparing one lot of meat as he knew it upset Hudson's stomach.

Old Ch'en daily prayed for him and the work of the CIM and asked God that he might shorten his days on earth and give them to Hudson so that he might preach the gospel of Christ for a greater length of time.

Now travelling was difficult and dangerous as rain was falling, making the roads a quagmire and the rivers break their banks.

After spending some time in a stinking inn he decided to move on. When their carts reached a spot where they could cross the river, another driver barged in before them. Hudson's drivers were furious until he told them to wait and watch as those rude carters would test the river depth for them. So they waited and watched. All went well until they reached the middle of the river where the current ran swiftly and the water was deep. Everyone watched in amazement as the carts and the mules were rolled over. The passengers and cart drivers were fortunate to live and it was with a prayer of thanksgiving that Hudson ordered his carters to find a ferry where he paid to safely cross the swollen stream.

Despite the rough roads and sub-standard inns they reached Xi'an on 26 June where conferences were held with missionaries from all organizations.

It was here that Hudson's wise counsel was needed to sort out problems that existed between the missionaries. Because of gossip concerning the young women in the Scandinavian party, he agreed that marriage for them was acceptable at any time, and they were exempted from the two year rule that applied to those attached to the Mission.

Towards the middle of July he found himself in the southern part of Shanxi province where he once again met Pastor Hsi.

Difficulties existed there as some Mission members had begun wearing European clothes. Consequently, the Chinese treated them with scorn. He urged everyone to dress and live as did the Chinese. Hudson was of the opinion that those who could not adapt to the ways of the CIM should depart, which some did.

After a time of conference he and his travelling companions spent time with Pastor and Mrs Hsi where they were given a right royal welcome to their host's home. The visitors were escorted to a large farm building where a delicious meal was ready. But there was more than that, for they discovered that the Hsis had prepared bedrooms with the best bedclothing they had seen for quite a long time. Everything had been prepared along the lines of homes in England and they were very surprised to find cakes of 'Pears' soap waiting to be used.

Seeing a surprised Hudson, Pastor Hsi said, 'It is nothing. It is altogether unworthy. Gladly would we have arranged far better for our Venerable Chief Pastor and his family.'

When he tried to thank his hosts for their kindnesses Pastor Hsi replied, 'What, Sir, have you suffered and endured that we might have the gospel! This is my joy and privilege. How could I do less?'

He had painted and furnished a farm building just for the use of Hudson and his companions.

During those days Japan was sending her troops to Korea which was under Chinese control. The forces of China and Japan faced each other and war was soon to break out. Everywhere foreigners found themselves unwelcome in China. It was while staying with Pastor Hsi that the news of the sinking of the Chinese warship Kowshing on 25 July, 1894 was received, which heralded the outbreak of hostilities between China and Japan on 1 August, 1894 in both Korea and China.

As this made travelling even more dangerous for Hudson and his companions he made the decision that they should return to Shanghai before the situation worsened. As well, he was rather ill and needed medical treatment and rest and Jennie's dysentery worsened. After attending the Hoste wedding they boarded a ship on 5 September and soon reached Shanghai safely.

Hudson, following a meeting of the China Council, made the decision that he would return to Shanxi Province alone to encourage and assist wherever possible. Some members needed straight talking because they had departed from the Mission rules. This journey proved very stressful to a worn-out man.

On 25 September, he sailed from Shanghai looking 'very aged and tired.' He knew the dangers he faced and wrote to Walter Sloan in London: 'Now that war has broken out, I am not sure that I ought to leave China....The authorities are diligently trying to protect missionaries...but the greatest danger would arise from rebellion, should the secret societies think the government was so seriously embarrassed as to give them a good chance of success.'

With a Chinese companion, Hudson began the next stage of his journey—inland from Tianjin. In case of an emergency he carried some extra cash, one thousand taels in gold leaf and the same of silver.

Before leaving he wrote to his daughter Amy:

> It may be that in a few days the war may shut the door by which I have entered; and some think...there may be a time of dangerous anarchy before order can be restored...I only know one thing, the LORD reigns and under His reign all things work together for good to them that love God. This will be so if I am alive...to return to you

in peace…But it will equally be so should this note be the last you
receive from me.

Again Hudson found the going tedious. His age was against him and
the way was difficult, but he was encouraged with the zeal of the
Mission members he met. Some who had become a problem, and had
been rebuked on the previous journey had now returned to the fold,
living as was expected of all Mission members.

In Hongtong he met up with the Hostes where he was presented
with a banner which read: 'With one heart serving the Lord.'

Some four hundred Christians gathered for worship which proved
to be one of the high points of his journey.

In mid November (20) he learned that a battalion of two thousand
Chinese soldiers was not far behind him. This meant he had to quickly
move on to Tianjin, where he caught a ship and arrived in Shanghai on
4 December, 1894, still having intact his emergency supply of money.

China was faring so poorly in the war with Japan that it was feared
that Peking might fall to the invaders. As a result a Chinese delegation
was sent to Japan to discuss terms of peace. The Treaty of Shimonoseki
was signed on 17 April, 1895 after the attempted assassination of the
Chinese delegate Li Hongzhang by a Japanese fanatic.

48

1895—A Difficult Year

The Japanese defeat of China shocked the population. Their fleet had surrendered and many groups of dispirited soldiers caused havoc as they returned to their homes.

An influential part of the population called for reform at Peking, while many demanded that the government repudiate the Treaty of Shimonoseki. Foreigners were the object of hatred as many Chinese believed they had played a part in their nation's humiliating defeat. When the call came to attack foreign nationals no one bothered to exclude the missionaries. Even normally quiet Chefoo faced the dangers of uprisings.

During the five years ending in 1895, more than one thousand missionaries had arrived in response to Hudson's call for a thousand men and women to work with the many missionary societies. He was disappointed that the one thousand were not all additional missionaries, but more than half of the new arrivals replaced those who had died or retired.

He knew that China's defeat would result in a push for western technology and possibly an acceptance of the 'foreign' gospel.

However, 1895 proved a difficult year for all missionary societies in China. The social unrest resulted in a new group of martyrs laying down their lives for the Lord Jesus Christ.

Hudson found life demanding because of failing health, and many times was forced to rest. He spent much time moving about between Shanghai and other spots, even travelling overseas for short periods.

In April, he and Jennie set out to visit the Mission settlements along the Yangzi River, but Jennie had to remain at Yangzhou due to a very sore foot.

Hudson continued his journey, but found the going difficult. Often he rested on the boat instead of getting on with the work he had come to do. However, when attempting to solve many difficult situations he said he needed 'the True Solomon's wisdom'. In letters to Jennie he often commented on his health, once saying he was 'fit but feeble'.

With increasing family numbers working in the Mission, the need for schooling became very important.

When Dr Douthwaite in Yantai faced many injured soldiers needing help, he treated both Chinese and Japanese troops. The hospital became in effect neutral territory and this neutrality was respected by the armies. Dr Douthwaite and his hard working companions saved the lives of many men which won the undying respect of everyone, especially General Sun of the Chinese army.

Dr Douthwaite wrote of the events following one battle:

> The Chinese fled towards Chefoo, many of them severely wounded and dying on the way....The poor fellows, bleeding as they were, had no strength to reach a place of refuge....About two hundred poor creatures managed to reach Chefoo in an awful condition, their clothing saturated with blood. One man, I remember, had seven bullets through him; another, with his knee-caps shattered, had walked all the way, forty miles; a third, with a bullet right through his lung, had walked through that bitterly cold weather; while some crawled most of the way on their hands and knees, their feet being frostbitten. Of those that reached Chefoo, we were able to take in a hundred and sixty-three, and care for them with all the kindness possible in our hospital.

Following the war, General Sun, riding his horse, surrounded by his officers and accompanied by a brass band approached the hospital and presented the doctor with a gold inscribed tablet.

Later when the general heard that rocks were needed for the foundation of the school, he had his soldiers do the work. It was the loving kindness of the CIM missionaries in difficult situations that endeared them to the people.

General Sun so respected Dr Douthwaite that when the time came for him to leave he had his troops parade outside the hospital. When the doctor appeared the company of soldiers knelt before him while the general delivered a speech of thanksgiving. A guard of honour then escorted the Doctor and his family to the harbour. Later the Emperor awarded the 'Order of the Double Dragon' to Dr Douthwaite and ten other doctors.

Plans were being made for extensions to the school at Chefoo and Hudson, who was there to recuperate found this work a healing tonic. After the plans were drawn up, a large gift came from Mr Morton in England making it possible for building to commence.

In England Benjamin Broomhall, who had turned sixty-six years, retired to spend his remaining years fighting the anti-opium cause. Walter Sloan then replaced Benjamin in the Mission.

On 8 March, 1895 the Mission offices in England were moved to their new premises at Newington Green, while in China John Stevenson left for Scotland where he was needed by his family. This meant more work for Hudson and William Cooper, both of whom were unwell. Hudson, who turned sixty-three on 21 May felt the strain of the additional work.

During and following the war with Japan many CIM missionaries won a reputation for compassion and love by staying with the people and giving whatever assistance they could, at the risk of their own lives. Such Christlike compassion meant that the Chinese were more receptive to the gospel.

In Gansu Province at Xining, the Ridleys decided to stay with the people despite the very real danger to their lives. The Muslims had rebelled and Chinese and foreigners were being slaughtered. It was the Chinese people who pleaded with them to stay, as their presence gave them a feeling of security. They were parents of a six month old baby which made it a hard decision.

In July the population could see the flames of villages and towns being destroyed by the approaching Muslims. On 24 July the Ridleys had the last opportunity to escape, but they remained at their post instead.

When they were urged by a beggar to visit a Confucian temple to see with their own eyes the pitiful state of the refugees, they were horrified to discover a large number of badly burnt women and children. The horrible smell of burnt, rotting flesh was almost overpowering.

They had no medical skills, but set to work rendering whatever aid they could. When the city officials heard of their good works they also became involved by sending gruel for the suffering people. The Ridleys did their best to stitch up wounds using silk thread and dressing burns using calico—and all their surgery was done without chloroform! When surgery was needed they used either a razor blade or a pocket knife.

Smallpox and diphtheria broke out which killed most of the children. With dead bodies lying in the streets more diseases appeared.

The Ridleys soon became proficient at cutting out bullets and stitching up wounds. Despite the fact that they couldn't cope with every request, the people loved them because of their kindnesses, even changing the name of the Mission house from 'Good News Hall' to 'Save Life Hall'.

Supplies ran low but they simply trusted in the Lord to provide what was needed. They took the words of their Lord seriously: 'Trust in the Lord and do good, so shalt thou dwell in the land, and verily thou shalt be fed.'

Some citizens provided food, medical supplies and money, but the chief city official while visiting the Ridleys discovered that they had to do everything themselves. So he sent four soldiers to assist them in their work. Bags of grain and flour arrived at the Mission and this in answer to prayer, and not to any human request.

And what was Hudson doing during those days? He was unable to get money to the Ridleys and factual news was impossible to send either way. He spent much of his time on his knees, praying for them and the other missionaries facing difficulties. It was not till January, 1896 that the city was recaptured by the Chinese forces, and it was General Sun, the friend of Dr Douthwaite, who guaranteed their protection in the aftermath of the Muslim rebellion.

After a short rest the Ridleys returned to Xining in October, 1896 to help the survivors. When the governor discovered that they were largely without the necessities of life, he supplied them with flour.

When peace was restored in January, 1897 the Ridleys said, 'All the country is now opened up to us—everywhere we go we find a warm welcome…"What, don't you know me?" they asked. "You saved my life in the rebellion!"'

In Sichuan Province the Mission had eleven outposts and it was the Riries at Leshan who saw the Mission premises destroyed. Posters had been put up in the city calling for attacks on the foreigners, but asking the people to leave the CIM alone as they had no weapons with which to protect themselves.

This was respected until some missionaries from other missions sought refuge in their premises. No lives were lost, and Mrs Ririe said, 'We have only lost our homes.'

In Chengdu the three CIM workers were given refuge for three months in the home of the city official.

Where property was destroyed Hudson advised the Mission workers to make no claim for damages. He even said to the Riries who had bravely faced the wrath of the Chinese, 'Christ's commands to us are unmistakable—"Resist not" and "Resent not". If obedience to Christ leads to martyrdom, even, it is none-the-less our privilege and duty.'

In mid July, he and Jennie were both sick at Chefoo. Hudson was suffering severe headaches and required rest. He was concerned for the missionaries and Christians in those places where riots were occurring. When cholera broke out they remained there as a return to Shanghai would endanger the population of that large city.

During his stay, funds became available for the new Mission buildings which greatly encouraged him.

There was a real need for new school premises and much time had been given to prayer for the money needed for the project. Dr Douthwaite received a letter indicating that the much needed £5,000 had been given by Mr Morton, in England.

He also wrote to all Mission members:

> (The people's) pride has been wounded; their respect for their own rulers is lessened; rebellion is in the air, turbulence and unrest are found everywhere…Rioting in (Sichuan) has been followed by riots against Christians (in Wenzhou and its neighbouring city of Bingyae) by the terrible massacre of missionaries in (Fujian)… and by a tendency to revenge on Christians the losses from drought or flood or from other national or local disasters…The Secret Societies may seize the opportunity to try to overthrow the Government altogether, when anarchy with all its horrors might be the result.
>
> [Calling for a day of 'waiting upon God' he continued] The counsel we have given in times past, as far as possible to remain at one's post strengthening the faith of (Chinese) Christians by our own restful trust in the Lord, we still recommend…The (Chinese) know that we possess no firearms, but rely on the living God alone for our protection…It behoves us…not to yield to the spirit of unrest…If filled with the Spirit we shall also be filled with love, joy and peace…Come what may, we are on the winning side.

On 31 July, 1895 near Kucheng some missionaries of the Church Missionary Society had gathered for a conference. Their meeting concluded with the celebration of the Lord's Supper where all repeated, 'Here we offer and present unto Thee, O Lord, ourselves, our souls and bodies, to be a reasonable, holy, and lively sacrifice unto Thee.'

The next morning nine missionaries had been slaughtered and two children and some adults fatally wounded. The house in which they lived had been burned down around them. Never before had Hudson seen God's protective hand lifted as at that time when adults and children faced death at the hands of cruel ungodly people. Missionaries everywhere realized that a great price was to be paid for taking the gospel to the Chinese and they knew that more lives might be sacrificed in order to reach the millions who knew nothing of Christ.

In England when the news of the martyrdom was received many called for retribution, but not so those attending the Keswick Conference. There, when it was announced, 'Not one bitter word was uttered; nothing but sympathy with the bereaved, pity for the misguided murderers, thanksgiving for the holy lives of the martyrs, fervent desires for the evangelism of China.'

Hudson received the news with sadness, but rejoiced that there was no loss of life by members of the CIM. He believed that the future did not look peaceful for the Mission, but he still longed to move into those areas where the gospel was unknown.

In September Jennie and Hudson attended a convention in Kobe.

In October news came from Wenzhou of the death of ten CIM missionaries from cholera. He and Jennie at once left for the city in order to encourage the mission workers, but this trip resulted in a breakdown in his health.

1895 was a difficult year for all mission societies working in China, but there was reason for rejoicing as Hudson said, 'In the midst of our sorrows God has been working, and it is no small joy to record that notwithstanding all hindrances, and in some cases through the very trials reported, many souls have been brought to Christ, so that a larger number of converts have been baptized in 1895 than in any previous year.'

Looking back over the year he declared 1895 to be 'the most trying (year) experienced by (Protestant) missionaries in China.'

He had spent much of his time at Shanghai, with short visits to Chefoo and other centres, but was aware of difficulties between CIM missionaries and those associated with the Mission. He knew he had to return to Great Britain to sort out the matter, because harmony was essential for success.

Before leaving he made a quick trip to India, to speak at the Calcutta Christian Students' convention.

He had been given sufficient money to cover his and Jennie's travelling expenses in the second class ship accommodation, but conscious of the needs of other missionaries travelled third class and sent whatever remained to Shanghai with instructions that the cheque was to be cashed and banked without telling anyone what he had done. This showed the humble, compassionate nature of both him and Jennie—always concerned with the well being of others.

At Darjeeling he also had to meet with Annie Taylor and the Pioneer Mission team who were involved in the evangelization of Tibet. There he was very impressed with the zeal of the missionaries.

It was during his time in India that Pastor Hsi died on 19 February, 1896.

Jennie and he returned to Shanghai in time to meet six new men who were on their way to Sichuan.

After holding a meeting of the China Council, and leaving William Cooper in charge, Hudson and Jennie boarded their ship for home. The trip was uneventful except for a collision with a Chinese boat while still in the Huangpu River, which resulted in the deaths of three hundred Chinese and seven officers.

Hudson and Jennie set foot in London on 17 June, 1896.

49

Another Trip Home

There was an air of expectation in England when people found out that Hudson and Jennie were again returning as then everyone would have firsthand information about the Chinese situation. Hudson had decided not to announce the exact time of his arrival in London at the new Mission headquarters as he knew that they would arrive at the time of the Saturday prayer meeting which he didn't want to interrupt. He also wanted to avoid any big welcome home.

The meeting was still in progress when he and Jennie alighted from their cab and quietly slipped into the back row and sat down. Additional people were in attendance as it was the time of an Evangelical Alliance conference and many delegates were staying at the new Mission premises.

They settled into their rooms at Newington Green for the duration of their stay in Great Britain. (They had privately donated nine hundred pounds towards the cost of the buildings.)

Hudson had missed the annual Mission meeting, but his report was read to all who gathered. He explained that 1895 had been 'in many respects the most remarkable year we have ever experienced,' despite the many setbacks. Statistics indicated that at the conclusion of 1895 the number of Christians attending worship was five thousand, two hundred and eight, and the Mission stations numbered one hundred and thirty five with many smaller bodies linked to the larger centres.

The number of congregations was one hundred and fifty-five and at the end of the year the CIM had six hundred and fourteen members. This number increased to six hundred and seventy-two at the time the report was being presented.

An important appointment before Hudson's return to England was that of William Cassels to the diocese of West China on 18 October, 1895. He was one of the Cambridge Seven and held membership in both the Church Missionary Society and the CIM as a superintendent.

Hudson found that all was working well in the Mission headquarters in London. The new Senior Secretary was the very capable Walter Sloan. As this freed Hudson from most administrative work he spent his time resolving problems on the continent, and visiting church groups that had faithfully supported the Mission.

He met with the London Council and visited John Stevenson, still home on leave.

The difficulty that plagued the Mission was a shortage of funds for general use. The latter part of 1895 and early 1896 saw monthly support dropping to about one thousand pounds which caused some anxiety as the needs of each Mission station could not be fully met. However, everyone associated with the Mission fully trusted in the Lord to provide. The missionaries looked to the wonderful words which were the Mission motto- 'Jehovah Jireh!'—'the Lord will provide'. When funds were low, everyone made do on the lesser amount while prayer was made to the Lord that support might come from those who had sufficient resources to make donations.

When Mr Morton made his big gifts to the Mission they were earmarked for special projects, not least the 'Forward Movement' which weighed heavily upon Hudson's heart.

In England, he commenced a round of engagements which included a visit to the Continent, including Germany. Problems existed because of the marriage of one from the Swedish Mission who was not willing to abide by the CIM marriage rules which applied to all associated with the Mission. Hudson was unwilling to bend the rules for one person, and in discussions, a way out was discovered—the couple could marry and travel to China as independent missionaries. In China they could then become associate members of the Mission.

The trip to Germany involved addressing YMCA conferences in Berlin.

During that time he was invited to speak to a gathering in the drawing room of Mrs Palmer Davies, who before her marriage was

Baroness von Dungern. Those upper class people were anxious to meet the well known man about whom they had heard so much.

The first impression of the Baroness was: 'The stranger who stood in our midst was not of an imposing appearance, and his fair curly hair made him look younger than he really was.'

The Baroness was fearful that some of her friends didn't hold Hudson and the CIM in very high regard, but she had nothing to fear really as she later wrote: 'But how beautifully this heavenly-minded man was able, in the humility of his heart, to conquer all the hidden prejudice against him and his work!'

Hudson explained the working of the Mission—how men and women from a variety of Protestant churches were able to work together preaching the gospel throughout China. He pointed out that Mr Willam Cassels, a member of the CIM was also Bishop of Western China and had membership in two mission societies. He stressed that all those working with the Mission were 'one in Christ', and wherever possible members of a particular church worked together.

He also spoke of his absolute trust in the faithfulness of his Heavenly Father, explaining that because He had not let him down in his youthful days when he prayed to God to provide for the necessities of life, he had gone to China, confident that all his needs would be met. When funds were low, he said he had been able to pray the prayer of faith and money arrived.

He explained that at no time had he or the Mission borrowed money, nor had collections been taken for the work being done in the Lord's name.

As he spoke, standing before his seated audience, the Baroness saw something which she recorded:

> Just then a sunbeam touched his face, so full of joy and peace, bringing a brightness as from above—and I could only think of Stephen, who saw heaven opened and Jesus at the right hand of God. One present bowed his head, covering his eyes with his hand, and I heard him whisper: 'We must all take shame before this man.'
>
> 'Yes,' the white-headed Professor replied to my suggestion, 'you are quite right; we will not trouble our friend any further.'
>
> And rising he crossed the room, put his arm round Mr. Taylor's neck and kissed him.

With the visit to Germany at an end Hudson returned to England for more meetings. He was unwell, again suffering from headaches, neuralgia and tooth ache, which at times required total rest.

He was always involved in the decision making process which meant giving time to sorting out problems that should never have arisen. Anna Jakobsen had announced she was going to marry a native of China and this he believed would create difficulties for the Mission. He feared that parents in Europe would have second thoughts about allowing their daughters to live and work in China—they might marry a Chinese and thus become 'subservient daughters-in-law in unsympathetic families.'

On 10 September, 1896 John Stevenson returned to China to assist William Cooper, but he was still unwell and unable to work effectively with William.

All the time Hudson was praying for gospel success in the western provinces of Sichuan, Hunan and Guangxi. He saw the need of godly, Spirit filled Chinese to take the news of salvation in Christ to the pagan masses in those provinces which had proved so difficult to foreign missionaries.

He rejoiced when he first heard of Mr J. Morton making large gifts to the work of the Mission because they were to him a confirmation that his 'Forward Movement' plans were in accord with the will of God.

Mr Morton was a very wealthy businessman who at first sent books and crates of canned groceries to the Mission workers. As early as June, 1895 he wrote to Hudson saying that he was willing to support the building of schools in the places determined by the CIM. He also was ready to give towards the training of Chinese evangelists, teachers and pastors.

A couple of months later he received word from a Robert Arthington: 'You will receive within a few days a sum of money left by my sister for the China Inland Mission. I should like to see the whole of the aborigines of China embraced in a comprehensive well-arranged plan for evangelization.'

Mr Morton began sending money to each Mission station asking to be told how it had been used. The money was for general Mission work, and was not for the personal use of the missionaries.

He gave a large sum of money which was used to build a new girls' school in Chefoo.

Orr Ewing was financing a boys' school in the same area, and wanting to be involved in the project, Mr Morton gave four hundred pounds. He also gave money for hospital extensions. Then came the suggestion that land should be bought for 'seclusion and relaxation' of tired and ill missionaries. He also offered money to build twelve houses for use by missionaries taking sick leave.

On 11 June, John Stevenson was notified that money was available to purchase all the necessary land in Chefoo to consolidate the Mission properties.

At this time Walter Sloan, who was concerned about Hudson's health wrote that Hudson had reached a state of 'serious collapse from overwork.'

Hudson was well aware of all that was happening in the Mission station and frequently gave wise advice when asked. With money being given for specific projects his 'Forward Movement' plans were soon to become a reality. During 1897 he began to speak and write about the plans he was formulating.

He urged all to pray for an outpouring of the Holy Spirit so that men and women could evangelize the darkest regions of China, preaching the gospel with Holy Spirit power. On one occasion he wrote:

> We missionaries could not take part in such a movement without being greatly refreshed and strengthened; and the fresh anointing would prepare us to arrange among ourselves for the division of the field, and for assisting and guiding the native evangelists whom the Holy Spirit might thrust forward, and the missionary evangelists whom we expect the same Holy Spirit would call from the homelands...We are not immediately appealing for new workers, our first need being to prepare for them in China, and the most important preparation of all a spiritual one.

It was at the May, 1897 CIM annual meeting that Hudson spoke of the Lord's working through the missions in China. He was able to report that church membership had reached eighty thousand, double the number seven years before.

He went on to use the words of one of the martyrs of Kucheng:

> 'What have we to face in China? God and the devil!' She speaks of what a solemn thing it is to be brought face to face with the great enemy of souls, and to know all the time that you are sitting, as it were, over a volcano which, apart from God's restraining power, may burst forth at any moment...God withdrew the restraint, and she and her fellow-workers were honoured with the crown of martyrdom...While we are meeting (here), it may be, some...in some part of China are in extreme danger.

Hudson rejoiced that no CIM life had been lost from violence in China, but now that God's restraining hand had been lifted causing

447

missionaries from other missions to suffer to the extent of dying, he told his audience that he saw no reason why the CIM should be exempt from similar suffering in the future.

Jennie took him to Davos in Switzerland to recuperate and it was while there that he received word that Mr Morton had made out a cheque for the sum of ten thousand pounds for whatever project Hudson decided. The day after writing the cheque Mr Morton died.

This was followed by the news that Mr Morton had left his fortune of over £700,000 to be shared between the China Inland Mission, the Waldensian Church, the Moravian Mission and the Aged Pilgrims Friends Society. While Mr Morton's family challenged the will, the CIM received the sum of £187,500 to be held in trust, with the first payment being made in September, 1898. Payments continued till 1916 when the Mission received another bequest of twenty thousand pounds.

Hudson saw these sums of money as God's provision for the 'Forward Movement', but he was concerned that giving might fall, because people thought the Mission had sufficient money to meet its needs. He also feared opposition by the forces of hell to the 'Forward Movement'.

'We may be quite sure,' he wrote, 'that the spirit of evil will also be active.' Thus he called upon all to pray 'that in every way Satan's power may be curbed.'

Next, advice was received that Jennie's sister, Nellie, had died in China and of the death from dysentery, of the one year old child of Maria Coulthard (nee Taylor) then living in Wenzhou.

When Jennie and Hudson returned to England from Switzerland they received word of the death of Maria.

At Davos, Hudson received a letter from William Sharp indicating that he was needed in China. He urged him to relieve John Stevenson from his position because he was creating tension amongst those responsible for the smooth running of the Mission. He also suggested that he should name his successor to ensure the smooth functioning of the Mission when he passed away.

After a short time home, Hudson made a short visit to his old friend and supporter, William Berger who died the following year, on 9 January, 1899.

He had earlier written to William urging him to, '"Rest in the Lord." Rest, as if nothing more were said. When you need it, rest in body; rest always in spirit. Rest as one "in Him" alone can...Rest in His love, power, strength, riches. Ah, what arms to enfold, what a heart to lean upon!'

Following his visit to France, Hudson, when travelling by boat train from Paris to Boulogne was fortunate not to be injured when the carriage rolled over, but it took time to rescue him from the tangled mess.

With Jennie, Henrietta Soltau and Miss Hanbury, he boarded the ship for New York, leaving on 24 November, 1897. During that journey he spent a lot of time deep in thought and praying for the new project the Mission was about to undertake.

Now they had the finances to make such a project a reality.

He was also mindful of the spiritual well-being of his fellow passengers and took every opportunity to witness to the saving grace of the Lord Jesus Christ.

China was changing. Railways and the telegraph, financed largely by Western nations were stretching across the land. However, there was much suspicion that soon those nations would be draining the nation of her wealth.

In November, 1897 two German Catholic missionaries were murdered in Shandong. Germany took military action against the Chinese, capturing the port of Qingdao and receiving a ninety-nine year lease on the area. This again was seen as a western nation humiliating the motherland, especially when Kaiser Wilhelm declared: 'Hundreds of thousands of Chinese will quiver when they feel the iron fist of Germany heavy on their necks.'

An effort to have the Chinese government legislate for freedom of religion throughout the land failed due to the influence of the Empress Dowager, who held the reins of government tightly in her hands. Of the government members it was said, 'They seemed to have made up their minds that Christians are all a bad lot…'.

50

Political Turmoil in China

Accompanied by Miss Henrietta Soltau and Miss Bessie Hanbury, Hudson and Jenny[10] stepped ashore at Shanghai on 15 January, 1898, but he was unwell and unable to get about. For several months he was confined to his room, but continued to formulate plans for the 'Forward Movement'.

In March, 1898 he wrote to his friends asking for prayer that: '...the Spirit of God may work mightily, preparing the heathen for the gospel and the converts for fuller blessing, likewise raising up from among them, evangelists, called, qualified, and constrained to preach the gospel, as well as live out the Christ-life.'

On another occasion he wrote: 'If there were a widespread outpouring of the Holy Spirit, all these [the unconverted Chinese] might speedily be swept into the fold, and the effect in China of a quarter of a million earnest, active, holy-living Christians would be very great.'

He planned to organize an itinerant evangelistic band of men and women to travel for five years throughout the country, preaching Christ. They would go two by two accompanied by Chinese evangelists and assistants, selling Bible portions and tracts.

He knew that Satan would not remain quiet in the face of such a movement and on his journey back to China wrote: 'If the Spirit of God works mightily we may be quite sure that the spirit of evil will also be active. When the appeal for a thousand new workers went forth from the Missionary Conference of 1890, the enemy at once began a counter-movement, and riots and massacres have from time to time followed as never before.'

Despite continued sickness, he attended all but one of the meetings of his China Council where important decisions were made. It was agreed that all financial support be pooled before distribution. Giving to the General Funds was down, but everyone didn't need a share of that fund as they received private support from their home base. Now all would have an equal share of giving to the Mission work.

Nine associate missions became full members of the CIM which Hudson saw as providing the manpower needed for the 'Forward Movement'.

Henrietta Soltau set about visiting forty-four Mission stations in thirteen months, covering approximately six thousand miles. The Holy Spirit empowered her speaking and wherever she went blessings followed. A visit to the men students at Anqing proved a great spiritual blessing to all who attended her talks. Later Hudson wrote of that visit: 'The Holy Spirit was poured out upon all present, and every one of the missionaries and students received extraordinary spiritual help. Such a Pentecostal season had never been experienced there before. This, surely, is what we need, for ourselves and for our native brethren.'

In June William Sharp raised the issue of a replacement for Hudson when he died. He and others felt that John Stevenson was not the man as he found it hard to work with others and at times was somewhat abrupt in his dealings with Mission members.

However, Hudson had confidence in John, and the fact that he was so well known outside the Mission made him best suited for his position. The Mission had grown and William Cooper was to share the work-load.

He kept to himself the name of the one he would appoint as his successor, despite William Sharp's agitation for Hudson to make known his choice. During 1899 he received correspondence from the London Council making a suggestion: '(we) expect that you will not leave China (for Australia) without...Mr Stevenson retiring altogether from the post (of China Director). In Mr Cooper you have a tried man, loved, trusted and honoured by all his brethren and well qualified for the work. With him should be associated as his second in command a man of somewhat similar gifts, and proven ability, and one perhaps who has had a fuller educational training.' Their suggestion being Dixon Hoste.

While Hudson was travelling to Australia, William Cooper arrived at Shanghai on 21 October to share the burden of work with John Stevenson. (On 8 January, 1900 Hudson announced that William was appointed 'Visiting China Director' in place of his former appointment as Assistant Deputy Director', advising him to visit Chefoo and Shanxi to sort out some difficulties which had the probability of some resignations from the Mission.)

New Year's day of 1898 witnessed the eclipse of the sun which the suspicious Chinese saw as an omen of national calamity.

China was politically and socially very unstable, and the hatred of foreigners was encouraged by Empress Dowager Ci Xi and the Boxers.[11] This anti-foreigner attitude reached a climax when it was realized that the nation was being carved up by foreign powers.

Kiachow had been annexed by the Germans in 1897. The Russians claimed Port Arthur, the English were settled into Weihaiwei and the French had claimed Guangzhouwan. Foreign newspapers were speaking of the partition of China, while the foreign financed railways which criss-crossed the nation caused alarm.

Hudson knew that trouble lay ahead and in July, 1898 he wrote that there seemed 'little hope of averting a complete collapse' of the nation.

The young Emperor Guang Xu was very much in favour of the reform of government and society, and encouraged students to study abroad. He issued a decree on 11 June, 1898, declaring that change was essential. Then followed one hundred days of reform upon reform, ending on 20 September of the same year.

Ci Xi found that her favourites were being replaced by reformers and as there was a swell of ultra conservative opposition she decided to take action to grab total power. Assured of army support on 22 September she overthrew the young Emperor and grabbed the reins of government. Her announcement to the world was that as the Emperor was ill she was obliged to take over.

With anti-Catholic feeling running high many riots broke out resulting in killings and property destruction. Disturbances against Germans and their property were widespread, and soon all foreigners faced serious dangers.

Henry Frost, in November, 1898, wrote an article for *China's Millions* in which he outlined the situation in China:

> Leave God out of the count and fear might well possess and overwhelm us. Bring God into account and there is perfect peace

for us at home and for our beloved missionaries in China…Satan is mighty, but God is almighty. Not one thing can man do that God does not allow to be done, and one outstretching of His glorious arm can subdue every enemy….For thirty-two years of the Mission's history He has preserved life in the face of threatened dangers, so that up to the present time, in spite of robbers, bandits, and rioters, not one person has been called on such accounts to pass through death. And further, suppose He should allow this long record of divine interposition to be broken, would He be less strong to keep in the hour of death than He has been in the days of life? We do not speak lightly; but thinking of God and of His mighty acts, and with the past in view, though faced in thought with martyr fires and rack and sword, we know that God can keep His own, and we believe that He would do so, now, as in the days of old.

Despite the concerted action of Satan's henchmen, people were being converted and the church strengthened in faith. Christians feared God more than man, and their love was centred upon their only Saviour, the Lord Jesus Christ.

Towards the end of 1898 Dr Keller wrote from Chaling:

We have from twenty to forty quiet, attentive hearers at our morning services. Yesterday, Sunday, we held a longer meeting, about sixty being present. We have quite a few callers, and they all drink tea with us without hesitation. Is this not rather unusual? Everything seems peaceful and quiet. Oh, let us praise Him! Reports are brought to us of some harsh talk in a large students' hall near here—threats to kill our landlord and loot his premises, and afterwards make an assault on us. We are in God's hands, and He is almighty….Pray for us.

This dependence upon God's loving care was common to all those men and women who loved God and preached the gospel out of love for their fellow man. Mission members were ready to lay down their lives for their brethren and this number included those Chinese who were part of the vibrant Chinese church.

Hudson felt assured that as God had protected Mission members in the past he would do so in the days that lay ahead, especially the defenceless women who were working alone in inland regions. However, with famine spreading throughout central China and the blame being laid at the feet of the missionaries and their God this was not to be. News of riots and the destruction of various mission properties was reaching Shanghai. Often the anger was directed towards the Roman Catholic church, but most Chinese couldn't distinguish between Roman Catholics and Protestants—they were all foreigners.

Several times when Hudson fell ill he was forced to spend some pleasant times at Chefoo. He walked about the countryside, wrote letters and enjoyed his hobby of photography. He made sure that drinking water was boiled to prevent the spread of disease and arranged for the insulation of the Mission buildings with sawdust covered by sand in the ceiling.

Returning from a trip up the Yangzi River to Jiujiang and Jiangxi he stopped over at Hangzhou which brought to his mind many fond memories.

Much prayer had been made for the Keswick party who were to visit China. Upon their arrival Hudson and Jennir accompanied by Mr and Mrs Inwood of Keswick, set out on 15 November, 1898, for a conference which had been arranged at Chongqing the following year. They planned to meet Mission workers along the way and while at Hankou they received the distressing news of the first murder of a CIM missionary, Mr W. Fleming. Three days later the *North China Daily News* 'Extra' printed a telegram from Chongqing:

'Murder of Missionaries. Mr W. S. Fleming, a China Inland missionary, and a native evangelist were murdered on 4 inst. at Guizhou....' This news reached London on 21 November.

Fleming, a Scot, had been working with the Mission since 1885. While living and working at Panghai, he and two evangelists, both having the name Pan, set out on a two week trip preaching the good news. Along the way they were accosted by robbers who were being urged on by anti-foreigner groups intent on causing trouble. In an effort to protect one of the Chinese evangelists who had been shot, both Mr Fleming and Pan were killed with a cavalry sword.

The local Consul put in an indemnity claim when he heard of Mr Fleming's death, but Hudson sent a request to Mr Sloan in London:

> We hear that the Consul here had kindly thought to help Mr Fleming's parents by claiming for them £2,500...(Could you) use your influence with them not to accept this money as...the effect on the Chinese will be bad;...To the Chinese it will seem as if the parents were quite satisfied to sell their son. It is a pity to encourage the idea that the lives of missionaries can be paid for.

The rejection of indemnity payments was part of the CIM policy and later won the admiration of many Chinese officials.

To John Stevenson he wrote on 22 November,:

> How sad the tidings! Blessed for the martyrs but sad for us, for China, for their friends. And not only sad, but ominous! It seems to show that God is about to test us with a new kind of trial: surely we need to gird afresh "the whole armour of God". Doubtless it means fuller blessing, but through deeper suffering. May we all lean hard on the Strong for strength…and in some way or other the work be deepened and extended, not hindered, by these trials.

The Boxers, who hated foreign citizens were commencing their cruel, callous activities and in December, 1898 a Tongzhou correspondent of a Shanghai newspaper wrote of the actions of a Chinese cavalry group:

> At a slow trot, in companies of fifty; with waving silk banners and fluttering scarlet cloaks and long red-tufted lances quivering in their hands like reeds…so conscious of their strength and their power to crush foreigners, when the word is given, that they look on them more with pitying contempt than with active dislike…
>
> Something unusual is under way; and if the Empress Dowager has undertaken the overturning of the whole Imperial policy towards foreigners, she has taken good care to gather troops enough to ensure the success of her policy, however ruthless. Everywhere, in both city and country, we hear the same tale, that all foreigners are to be killed or driven out, and that our day is close at hand. These remarks are seldom made to us personally…but the ears of native helpers and converts are filled with them.…The feeling of unrest… merely includes the dispassionate though agreeable conviction that our lives are drawing to a close.

At the Chongqing Conference, eighty missionaries gathered for a time of much spiritual blessing. The meetings were conducted from 16 to 21 January, 1899 and during that time an inter-mission committee was established to avoid duplication of effort. Statements were also made condemning the terrible opium trade.

Towards the end of the conference Hudson fell ill with influenza and missed some of the final sessions. In February, his health deteriorated further because of bronchitis and Jenny thought he would die. Fearing such a loss to the Mission she knelt down and prayed a prayer of faith pleading with God for her husband's recovery: 'Lord, we can do nothing! Do what Thou wilt. Undertake for us.'

Hudson knew nothing of Jenny's prayer, but when next she spoke to him he whispered, 'I feel better, dear.' From that day he began to recover.

On 6 April they were back in Shanghai, where on 24 May he farewelled the Inwoods, before setting off for a time of rest at Chefoo.

This proved to be a pleasant time as he was able to use his photographic equipment to the full. He spent hours with the school children watching them playing. Foundation Day was a very enjoyable day as it meant organized games—cricket, tennis and boat racing. During the afternoon he spoke to the young people and together they enjoyed a time of hymn singing.

After tea photographs were taken and a pleasant social time in the school quadrangle followed. Of the night's entertainment Jenny wrote: 'It was a warm, moonlit night, and the lights in the room near the pianos were all that was necessary. One of the teachers, Miss Norris, is a beautiful musician, and with songs and recitations the pleasant day ended.'

On 26 June, it was time to leave Chefoo, as it turned out, for the last time. Before leaving, Jenny wrote to the ladies at the girls' school:

> I do love and value you, and am so glad to know you better! Though we have left, our hearts are still with you, and we would fain have had longer together....I want to send to all of you a good-bye message: it is this: *Determine to prove what faith and love will do.* 'Grip God,' as Mr Inwood says, for one another....Our calling in Jesus Christ is to live supernatural lives, to be 'more than conquerors' day by day. Yield yourselves to God to be more fully indwelt, and to serve only in His strength, and then expect Him to do all that you need, for 'nothing shall be impossible to you...'

Back in Shanghai Hudson faced the round of organizational problems and much time was spent in prayer for Mission members who were facing the wrath of the 'Fists of Righteous Harmony', as the Boxers were known.

It was on 31 August that Dr Frank Keller reached Shanghai after being forced to flee for his life from Chaling in Hunan province. Having escaped with his life, he was ready to demand compensation for his property which had to be abandoned, as well as for his landlord who had lost the dwelling rented to the Mission.

At that time Hudson was resting at Moganshan which was in the mountains, several miles journey from Shanghai. When Dr Keller arrived in a very disturbed state of mind, John Stevenson asked him to refrain from putting his claims before the Consul until first speaking to Hudson.

Hudson was fully aware of Keller's strong convictions and thus spent two days in prayer that the Holy Spirit might bring about a change in his attitude. He was putting into practice his own teaching in such matters: 'What is your spiritual ministry? It is that if you see me to be wrong you are able by prayer, by spiritual power, by tact, by love, forbearance and patience to enlighten my conscience, and thus cause me to gladly turn from my mistaken course to the right one.'

Later Dr Keller recalled his meeting with Hudson:

> Before the interview took place, or Mr. Taylor said a word to me on the subject, my whole position was changed. I saw I had been utterly wrong, and that the CIM principle was right, even in such a peculiar case as mine. He talked about other things, asking my opinion as to the use of certain drugs, and when the dinner-bell rang said that he would like to have further talk with me that afternoon at three o'clock.
>
> I felt guilty over taking up so much of his time, and so, though I had resolved not to open the subject, I decided to tell him frankly of my change of position. At the appointed hour I went to him and said, 'Mr Taylor, I feel I ought to let you know at once that I see things differently, and am prepared to submit the whole matter to you and act as you direct.'

At that Hudson exclaimed, 'Thank God!'

Dr Keller went on to say:

> This experience was a crisis and turning-point in my life. It taught me in a most practical way how even strongly formed purposes can be changed and men's hearts influenced by prayer alone. I have always felt that surrenders made and principles accepted at that time, together with real changes in character that then took place, were God's direct and gracious answer to Mr Taylor's prayers.

Hudson was suffering from dysentery and headaches and needed a time of isolation and rest. News of riots were filtering through but Jenny decided to keep the information from him until he was feeling better. While there it was Jenny who kept the correspondence flowing.

Hudson was then sixty-seven years of age and looking and feeling much older. To his wife and others it was obvious that his active days were drawing to a close.

Hudson however believed his days in China were to be many and purchased a block of land in Moganshan where he and Jenny spent many hours planning the small two bedroom cottage with a sitting room, a kitchen and servant quarters. The spot chosen was in the mountains, some two thousand feet above sea level and overlooking timbered valleys. Another attraction was that it was in a cool part of the region. He had bought the land when it was cheap and of little interest to foreigners, but later it would become a popular resort, especially as it was only a two day journey by boat from Shanghai.

Their plans never came to fruition.

It was on 25 September, 1899, that they made their way to the ship bound for Australia. Hudson still longed to stay in China where he knew his help and encouragement were needed by the members of his Mission who were suffering at the hands of the Boxers, but he was convinced that it was God's will to visit Australia and New Zealand. As well there was a conference to attend in New York.

It was hard to say farewell and little did he know that his working days in China were at an end. With all their luggage safely on board Hudson was missing. He was still at Wusong Road writing his last few letters to missionaries who were being left to suffer the horrific onslaught of the brutal Boxers.

On board, Jenny was writing a final farewell to all of the ladies associated with the Mission. Most looked upon her as a mother and she could not depart without a final, 'Goodbye.' Her letter contained an acknowledgment that this would be her last written to them from China.

It was midnight before he and John Stevenson made their way by rickshaw to the ship, and after farewells, John returned to his home not suspecting the trying times soon to come. Hudson had spoken words of encouragement to the members of the China Council when they met with him for the last time from 11—15 September.

'Pray that we may be kept near to God,' he wrote, 'walking with him, with the eye kept single and the heart pure and simple in these dangerous days…Satan will try to unsettle us and subvert us, and the weak will go to the wall.'

Arrivals during the year meant there were about eight hundred and eleven Mission members working in China.

During the journey to Australia the Boxer rebellion was breaking out with the support of the Ci Xi. With the slogan of 'Uphold the dynasty! Eliminate foreigners!' the slaughter of foreign nationals and Chinese Christians was underway.

But Hudson and his companions were in Australia. He had found the ocean journey refreshing and his photographic activity lifted his spirits. Not only did he take photos, but he had the necessary equipment to develop the pictures he had taken.

During his days in Australia they visited Brisbane, Sydney, Melbourne, Ballarat, Adelaide and Tasmania where he faced a continual round of meetings, conferences and social gatherings. The pace was fast and he felt the stress of addressing twelve gatherings in Melbourne in ten days.

He received correspondence from John Stevenson keeping him informed of the situation in China, but the news was always months old.

On Christmas Day, 1899 Hudson asked, 'How many men have we lost this year and last?' Both he and Jenny were very concerned with the news from China and so, much time was spent in prayer, upholding the missionaries from all societies who were facing the terrors of Satan.

When he received news of the murder of S. Brooks, he feared that he might have to soon return to China, but said, 'I have no light beyond New York.'

When Ci Xi deposed the young Emperor and reigned with total authority, the Boxers had no one to restrain them from their blood-letting and destruction.

After a short visit to New Zealand, Hudson and his party, on 20 March, set off for San Franciso, arriving there on 5 April.

Then it was off to Carnegie Hall, New York, where after a two hour session of prayer he delivered his address to thousands of delegates and visitors including the President of the United States and the Governor of New York state.

The subject of his address was 'The Source of Power' for 'Foreign Mission Work' and his opening words set the tone for what followed: 'Power belongeth unto GOD!'

Years later Henry Frost wrote of Hudson's address:

> I am still meeting men and women who declare that Hudson Taylor's address that morning radically changed their lives....The impressions produced by Mr Taylor were nothing less than phenomenal...There at the front of the platform, (he) stands a moment in silent prayer...As he begins to speak his voice takes

on a kindly, compassionate quality. A hush that can be felt falls on
the vast audience...When Mr Taylor finished, there was almost an
audible sigh of spiritual relief, so many of his hearers realizing that
they understood as never before the will and way of God.'

Another minister present said of Hudson that day, 'Mr Taylor was,
I believe, one of the noblest and greatest leaders whom God has given
to the Church in our times.'

The round of meetings left him stressed and worn out, but it was
with a true joy that he visited Berger House to see the premises, part of
which had been paid for out of Mr Berger's bequest to Hudson.

On 5 May, he and Jenny accompanied by Henry Frost, left for
Boston, to attend some social activities and a conference where he
would share the stage with Dr Pierson.

At the conference while speaking, he suddenly stopped as if unsure
of what he should say. When he repeated himself several times
Dr Pierson realised that all was not well and after gently sitting him
down took over and completed the address.

For Hudson it was time for a complete rest. Howard Taylor and his
wife had previously left North America for England and now it was
time for him and Jenny to follow.

Hudson kept busy by answering correspondence, and made
a contribution to an investigation of the practice of polygamy and
membership in the Christian Church. He wrote, '...that while no
Christian could be allowed to contract a polygamous marriage,
a heathen who had two wives, when converted could not, without
great injustice and scandal, be called to put away either of them, as
this would put an innocent woman in an impossible position, and
render the children illegitimate.'

On 19 June he and Jenny arrived in London and moved on to spend
a weekend with Jenny's father.

That weekend, on 24 June, she wrote in her diary, 'News serious.'

The Taylors met to discuss the treatment Hudson should receive and
it was decided that a holiday in Davos, Switzerland would be best. He
agreed, but longed to be in China to comfort the suffering members of
the Mission. On 6 July he wrote to John Stevenson: 'If my head were
in a condition to do mental work I should certainly have been on my
way back to China before now. We are just preparing to go to Davos
as that seems the quickest way of getting fit for work.'

News was beginning to trickle through of the horrific Boxer
activities, but the real story was not yet fully known.

Hudson and Jenny set off for the home of Mr and Mrs Hofmann who owned a quiet boarding house in the mountain area that Hudson loved so much. They arrived there on 10 July.

Mrs Hofmann, an English lady, was visiting England and while attending a CIM prayer meeting at Newington Green heard of Boxer activity attacking the Foreign consulates in Peking. She immediately returned to Davos as she knew Hudson would be suffering greatly when he heard the awful news.

Jenny however had made the decision to keep the bad news from him, but bit by bit he became aware of the slaughter of Christians, Chinese and foreigners by the Boxers.

He was so distressed by what he heard he said, 'I cannot think; I cannot even pray; but I can trust.'

He felt like Job who in the midst of his suffering expressed his faith in God with the words: 'Though he slay me, yet will I trust in him' (Job 13:15).

Soon he would hear of his friend and colleague, William Cooper who was decapitated at Baoding on 1 July 1900.

51

Dark Days

They were stoned, they were sawn in two, were tempted, were slain with the sword. They wandered about in sheepskins and goatskins, being destitute, afflicted, tormented—of whom the world was not worthy. They wandered in deserts and mountains, in dens and caves of the earth. And all these, having obtained a good testimony through faith, did not receive the promise, God having provided something better for us, that they should not be made perfect apart from us.

Heb. 11:37–40

The words above describe in part what happened to the Christians in China when they faced the Satanic Boxers. It took months for news to reach London from the places where the assaults and murders took place.

The number of European missionaries and Chinese Christians who suffered were many and the stories of most will never be told. When Hudson heard what was happening his tender heart ached until he could stand it no more.

He wept when he heard that Pastor's Hsi's friend and follower, Elder Si, had had a sword plunged through his side, dying months later from the wound.

In Peking the foreign consulates and foreigners generally were ferociously attacked by the Boxers. On 10 June, 1900, the cable link with the outside world was broken, but an urgent appeal had been sent to Tianjin for reinforcements to be urgently sent. The message was simply worded, 'Besieged in British Legation. Situation desperate. MAKE HASTE.' It was sent by a Chinese courier on a piece of cloth sewed into his clothing.

Several days later some Frenchmen rescued some nuns and priests before their cathedral was set ablaze, but when a search was made for Chinese Christians, what was discovered struck fear into the hearts of everyone—'women and children hacked to pieces, men trussed like fowls, with noses and ears cut off and eyes gouged out. Chinese Christians (accompanying the rescuers) ran about in the labyrinth of streets calling upon the Christians to come out from their hiding places...Boxers were even now caught red-handed at their bloody work.'

Rewards were paid for every dead foreigner and those who had been friends of foreigners suffered the same fate as Christian Chinese.

On 24 June, the secret decree of Ci Xi, the Empress Dowager was circulated: 'Slay all foreigners wherever you find them; even though prepared to leave your province they must be slain.'

Several high ranking ministers in the Chinese government were horrified when they saw the decree and managed to substitute in some cables the word 'protect' in place of 'kill.' Later, for their treachery to Ci Xi, they were executed.

During the siege, one Chinese officer, Yong Lu refused to fire his big guns into the British Legation because he knew that 'the persons of envoys are always held inviolate within the territories of any civilized state. He then said, 'This attack on the Legation is worse than an outrage, it is a piece of stupidity which will be remembered against China for all time.'

All foreigners who could reach the British compound did and for several months played their part in keeping the Chinese forces at bay. When eight weeks later the relief columns arrived, they, in retaliation, slaughtered both innocent and guilty Chinese, with a ferocity equal to that of the Boxers. The Russian troops lead the others in their action against the citizens.

As the reports filtered through to Hudson he was overcome with distress. When he and Jenny had the opportunity they wrote to John Stevenson to encourage him and all those who were in contact with Shanghai.

In Baoding the actions of the Boxers were particularly violent and many missionaries and Chinese Christians died for their faith. When

Horace Pitkin knew his end was near he wrote a note to his wife and had a Chinese Christian escape to eventually deliver the message: 'Tell little Horace that his father's last wish was that when he is twenty-five years of age he should come to China as a missionary.' Horace fulfilled his father's dying wish!

On 1 July, William Cooper was beheaded, but the news of his death did not reach Hudson until 29 October.

When Walter Sloan heard of his death he commented of William: 'One of the very few blameless lives that I have ever come into contact with.'

As Mary Morrill and Annie Gould bravely went to their death Mary spoke of Christ to the Boxers as they carried out their wretched work. Thirteen years later at a mission meeting in Peking, Major Feng stepped forward to confess his faith in Christ. He was one of the Boxers, present on the day when Mary had tenderly spoken of salvation in Christ before her death.

Major Feng encouraged the missionaries to take Christ to his fellow countrymen. He took every opportunity to preach to the soldiers under his command, with the result that many of his officers became Christians.

In Baoding, a Mr Simcox, holding his two little sons by their hands, was incinerated in their home, the Boxers lighting the fire.

In Taiyuan when John Robinson and T. Piggott were being taken to execution they continued to preach the gospel to their captors and any who would listen. One listener commented: 'You're going to be killed for preaching, yet you go on doing so.'

The following describes the scene as some met their death on 9 July, 1900:

> The whole number of men, women and children were then stripped to the waist like common criminals, and were made to wait in this degrading condition until the Governor came out to inspect them. [He asked their nationality, laughed scornfully at their answer, and at once gave the order for their decapitation.]
>
> 'The first to be led forth was Pastor Farthing. His wife clung to him, but he gently put her aside, and going in front of the soldiers, himself knelt down without saying a word, and his head was struck off by one blow of the executioner's sword....' When the men were finished, the ladies were taken. Mrs Farthing had hold of the hands of her children who clung to her, but the soldiers parted them, and with one blow beheaded their mother. The executioner beheaded

all the children and did it skilfully, needing only one blow; but the soldiers were clumsy, and some of the ladies suffered several cuts before death. Mrs Lovitt was wearing her spectacles and held the hand of her little boy even when she was killed. She spoke to the people saying, "...We came to China to bring you the good news of salvation by Jesus Christ; we have done you no harm, only good; why do you treat us so?" A soldier took off her spectacles before beheading her, which needed two blows....Pastor Piggott and his party were led from the district gaol....He was still handcuffed; so was Mr Robinson. He preached to the people till the very last, when he was beheaded with one blow. Mr Robinson suffered death very calmly. Mrs Piggott held the hand of her son, even when she was beheaded, and he was killed immediately after her. The lady and two girls [Mary Duval and the Atwater girls] were killed also, quickly. In all on that one day forty-five foreign people were beheaded— thirty-three Protestants and twelve Roman Catholics. A number of native Christians were also killed....All were surprised at the firmness and quietness of the foreigners; none cried or made any noise, except two or three of the children.

In many cases the children saw their parents slaughtered before they were killed, while on other occasions parents watched as their beloved offspring were murdered. They then followed.

At Qü Xian, on 22 July, Etta Ward and her baby, drinking from the breast, were thrust through with a sword killing both. Then Etta was beheaded. Others suffered the same fate that day.

In some places Chinese officials did what they could to prevent the excesses of the Boxers and saved the lives of the foreigners. One wise senior Chinese official commented, 'While you are the ones to suffer now, the tables will be turned, and China's turn of suffering will come within a very few months.' His words were prophetic!

When Hudson received the distressing news he could do little more than weep and pray.

Then arrived the last letters written by Miss Searell and Miss Whitchurch—written the day before they were killed.

'Oh, think what it must have been,' he broke in on the sad recital, 'to exchange that murderous mob for the rapture of His presence, *His* bosom, *His* smile! They do not regret it now. A crown that fadeth not away. "They shall walk with me in white, for they are worthy."'

Hudson and Jenny longed to be with their suffering friends in China to comfort them, to weep with them, but such was impossible: 'I might not be able to do much,' Hudson said, 'but I feel they *love* me.

If they could come to me in their sorrows and I could only weep with them, it might be a comfort to some.'

He was suffering great stress, but his faith in the goodness of God was strong, as his world in China was falling apart.

He often said: 'Before I had children of my own I used to think God will not forget me; but when I became a father I learned something more—God *cannot* forget me.'

In China John Stevenson was holding up under the extreme pressure that rested upon his shoulders, but Hudson knew it was time to give him permanent help. Dixon Hoste was assisting him and suspecting that Cooper was dead, he pinned his hopes upon replacing him with Dixon in the near future.

In China, the missionaries were planning how they could return to their people. One, Matilda Way, wrote of the Christians at Linfen:

> Nearly all have a large cross on their forehead, inflicted by the Boxers....I rejoice to think of the glorious harvest yet to come. I heard that the Taigu Christians had met for worship, and the Boxers had come and killed them all but two....My first twelve months in China have been full of a wonderful experience....I am hoping to have a rest, and return to my work in Shanxi.

Another mother, who was dying from her injuries, quietly said to her husband: 'I wish I could have lived, I wish I could have gone back there, to tell the dear people more about Jesus.'

Such was the attitude of most missionaries!

As heartbreaking news continued to come in, Hudson made a decision which he forwarded to John Stevenson. He was to receive no new missionaries until the situation in China was settled. Those working inland should remain where they were as travel was very dangerous. He urged John to forward all the available money to missionaries as he knew the banking system was breaking down, even suggesting the use of the Morton legacy to anyone who needed a time of rest.

Towards the end of July he cabled China urging all women working in the inland areas to make their way to the safe areas on the coast. He also suggested that the Chefoo school be transferred to Japan for the duration of the hostilities.

Early in August, following the receipt of worse news from China, Jenny wrote to Marcus Wood concerning Hudson's state of mind: '(He) felt as if he must get out or he would go crazy, so Amy (their daughter) and he went up a mountain.' And to John Stevenson she wrote, 'We are suffering with you all so much that I don't think we could feel more.'

On 6 August Howard and Geraldine Taylor came to be with their ageing and distressed parents for several weeks. And as the news continued to arrive Hudson's health deteriorated to the point where he could barely move about and his pulse rate fell from eighty beats a minute to forty.

Knowing that the time had come to give the overworked John Stevenson help he sent him a cable on 6 August, appointing Dixon Hoste 'to act as General Director...during my incapacity...so that the responsibility may be shared.'

Dixon received the news with surprise and after prayer cabled Hudson declining the position, but he indicated that John Stevenson had asked him to stay and share the heavy load he was carrying. Dixon was happy to do so and when Orr Ewing heard of the appointment he wrote to Hudson saying, 'I fear if some such steps as this were not taken, soon the love and harmony in the Mission would have been seriously affected; numbers have spoken to me of the very unsatisfactory way in which their matters have been dealt with.'

John Stevenson now had to accept as his senior the younger man and this was made doubly hard as he found it difficult working in a partnership. Very soon however, he was thanking God for the wise advice and general help Dixon was giving him.

While Hudson was very unwell he still exercised wise oversight of the Mission.

In Shanghai, Dixon contracted typhoid and developed clots in the veins. His life was in danger, but the prayers of the faithful and the medical care he received, resulted in his recovery. On 15 December he wrote to John Stevenson of his decision: 'I feel I ought to accept the appointment; if, however, you do not see your way to agreeing...I shall feel free from responsibility.'

John Stevenson was happy with the decision and in March, 1901 he notified all Mission members of the appointment.

Hudson spent considerable time writing to those who had suffered so much, both missionaries and their parents. He had written letters of comfort, but the replies so often were letters of encouragement, praying for his recovery.

Towards the end of 1900 when he received a letter from Shanghai, signed by three hundred members of the Mission he replied: 'As we have read over your signatures one by one we have thanked God for sparing you to us in China. The sad circumstances through which we have all suffered have been permitted by God for His glory and our good, and when He has tried us and our native brethren He will doubtless reopen the work at present closed, under more favourable circumstances than before.

We thank God for the grace given to those who have suffered. It is a wonderful honour He has put upon us as a mission to be trusted with so great a trial, and to have among us so many counted worthy of a martyr's crown. Some who have been spared have perhaps suffered more than some of those taken, and our Lord will not forget. How much it has meant to us to be so far from you in the hour of trial we cannot express, but the throne of grace has been as near to us here as it would have been in China....May we all individually learn the lessons God would teach, and be prepared by His Spirit for any further service to which He may call us while waiting for the coming of the Lord.'

With the new year, 1901, the Mission work started to return to normal and Hudson's health showed improvement. He was visiting friends, including the ageing Mrs Berger and at sixty-eight years, he began to hope that once again he would visit China.

He started to move about, visiting London where he met some of the survivors from Shanxi and Henan. During his stay, Lord Northampton invited him to become Vice President of the Bible Society, which he graciously accepted. He and Jenny also visited Jenny's eighty-four year old father.

This was followed by a visit to Germany and then Geneva where Walter Sloan and Henry Frost met him to discuss Mission affairs.

From there it was back to Switzerland to enjoy the walking, climbing and photography. But on 15 August he had a fall which aggravated his old spinal injury and limited his movements for some time. When he told Jenny of that fall he said, 'I must have had a stroke.'

Problems arose with Stanley Smith who had begun to believe that everyone would be saved and denied the doctrine concerning the punishment of the ungodly in eternal hell. This issue, which occupied much of Hudson's time ended when Stanley was asked to resign from the Mission.

When peace was restored in China, the matter of the payment of indemnities for the damage done by the Boxers was raised. There was a clamour by so many for payment that the CIM found it necessary to make a definite statement concerning their attitude towards the receipt of compensation.

Hudson had early in 1900 outlined the policy of the Mission: 'CLAIM FOR NOTHING, but to accept, where offered, compensation for destroyed Mission premises and property, as I feel we hold these on trust for God's work.

'For private property, we must leave each missionary free to accept or decline, *through the Mission only*.

'For injury or loss of life, to refuse all compensation. The Mission, likewise, should be responsible for the orphan children of Missionaries. For native Christians...I think we should do what God enables us to help them, and to care for bereaved relatives.'

Soon after Hudson indicated to everyone that 'as a Mission we will not accept any money compensation....It therefore seems better to me now that we should trust in God to enable us to rehabilitate our stations when the time comes to reopen them. Though it will mean many thousands of pounds to restore all that was destroyed, He is able to provide.'

The Governor of Shanxi was amazed when he found that the CIM would accept no indemnities as that was very unusual. The result was that the Governor, on 11 October, 1901 issued a proclamation to be erected wherever the CIM had suffered. In the proclamation the name of Jesus was made very prominent by having it raised above the other words. It read:

> The Mission, in rebuilding these Churches with its own funds, aims in so doing to fulfil the command of the SAVIOUR OF THE WORLD, that all men should love their neighbours as themselves, and is unwilling to lay any heavy pecuniary burden on the traders or on the poor. I, the Governor, find...that the chief work of the Christian religion is...to exhort men to live virtuously. From the time of their entrance into China, Christian missionaries have given medicine gratuitously to the sick and distributed money in times of famine....They regard other men as they do themselves, and make no difference between this country and that. Yet we Chinese...have treated them not with generous kindness, but with injustice and contempt, for which we ought to be ashamed....How strangely singular it is that we Chinese, followers of the Confucian religion, should not appreciate right actions, which recall the words and the discourses of Confucius, where he says, 'Men should respond with kindness to another's kind actions.'

I charge you all, gentry, scholars, army, and people, those of you who are fathers to exhort your sons, and those who are elder sons, to exhort your younger brothers, to bear in mind the example of Pastor Hoste, who is able to forbear and forgive as taught by JESUS to do, and, at the same time, to exemplify the words of Confucius... Let us never again see the fierce contention of last year...to enforce this on all persons, soldiers or people, is the aim of this special proclamation, which let all take knowledge of and obey.

As well as the proclamation which went a long way to restore good relations between the missionaries and the people, the Governor gave a large sum of money to assist suffering Christians.

By the end of 1900 the CIM missionaries were back at their posts or on leave before returning. How true are the words of Tertullian: 'The blood of the martyrs is the seed of the church.'

In January and February, 1902 Hudson's health had improved greatly and he was getting about with a degree of ease. However, a visit to England left him feeling exhausted and feeble.

When they returned to Geneva he looked frail. When he turned seventy he was still the General Director of the Mission, but he and others realized that his days of active service were fast drawing to an end.

Thus Dixon Hoste's position was confirmed and Walter Sloan was appointed Assistant Home Director with Theodore Howard.

Hudson and Jenny rented some rooms in the Pension La Paisible in Chevalleyres, Vevey, Switzerland, across the lake from Geneva from which they had a splendid view from their balcony. Their rooms were comfortable and meals were provided. This was to be their home for two pleasant years. Early in their time at the Pension, Jenny wrote: 'My beloved husband is very frail. I am thankful he can be so quiet here and comfortable. We are looking forward to seeing Mr Hoste.'

Then came news from China of a cholera epidemic at Chefoo which resulted in the deaths of some very close friends. His sister Amelia's grandson also died from what was thought to be ptomaine poisoning. Hudson and Jenny were distressed with the news, but again their faith did not waver.

He then wrote to John Stevenson urging him to direct all missionaries to eat and drink only cooked foods which showed that he was keeping up with his medical reading. It was in 1903 that he completed the reading of his Bible for the fortieth time.

A series of meetings with Dixon Hoste and later with Henry Frost and Robert Wilder covered all aspects of Mission work, and the company did him the world of good.

Realizing that he was free from all Mission responsibilities Hudson said, 'Now I have *no one*—no one but God.' He found it difficult doing *nothing* for Christ, but letters had to be written, people were to be visited, there was his much loved photography, as well as some trips with Jenny. But more than ever he had more time to spend with his God.

The news from China was encouraging. Many Chinese were being converted and the work of the gospel was progressing at a rapid pace by men and women filled with the Holy Spirit. In Hongtong a chapel had been built with seating for one thousand and in Yüwu, a conference had attracted some eight hundred Christians.

He then found that Jenny was not so well, and often when he was ready to go walking she remained at home, saying she needed to catch up on her letter writing. In July, 1903 he cabled his son Howard and his wife Geraldine to let them know that she was ill.

Jenny had an abdominal tumour which was confirmed by a visiting American, Dr Howard Kelly. He carried out his examination using chloroform and his report was that a further operation was *not necessary*. Because of his words Hudson and Jenny were unaware of the seriousness of the cancer, and the family decided to leave it that way. They continued with their normal life, enjoying the remaining days together.

However, there was no celebration of the anniversary of two important dates in Hudson's life—the 19 September, 1903 marked the fiftieth year of his sailing from Liverpool on the *Dumfries*, and 1 March, 1904 which was the anniversary of his arrival in Shanghai for the very first time. During those long years more than one thousand, three hundred men and women had joined the CIM and gone to China to proclaim the love which God had for sinners.

Jenny's well-being was all that really mattered!

Howard fully expected a drawn out painful death, but she was largely free of distress until the very last.

She gave much time to correspondence and to her joy the last payment of her Australian legacy arrived before her death. This money she and Hudson distributed amongst the mission societies they had for a lifetime supported. The Church Missionary Society received a gift as well as the Rev. John Wilkinson who worked amongst the Jewish people.

In March, 1904 Jenny commented on her health saying, 'Well, I have got thin and weak, and have more or less of discomfort at times. I vary a good deal, but am so thankful to be able to keep about....My beloved husband keeps very frail....We match one another very well—both so thankful for a quiet life without strain. We have many pleasures and such kind friends.'

Back in Chevalleyres Jenny enjoyed the garden and flowers, but spent much time worshipping the God she had for so long served. She loved her chair on the verandah and began to spend more time in it than ever before.

On 7 June she commented that it was good to have Howard with them because, 'It relieves the strain on my dear husband about me as nothing else could. I do very fairly, night and day, except for the weakness which makes it difficult to get across the floor now. The Lord has "our times" in His hand, and it is well.'

Then on 24 June she wrote: 'My strength seems ebbing fast away. I trust I may not linger on in a quite helpless condition; but however it is, it will be all right.'

By the end of June, she was unable to dress herself and their son Charles and granddaughter Amy came over to help nurse her.

In the middle of July Jenny wrote that she was confined to bed, but enjoyed the company of others. She went on: 'I could not be better cared for or happier. It is just a peaceful, quiet time, though in weakness and sometimes pain. I have been praying, often, "Let GOD arise"; it seems to be all that is needed anywhere.

'I am nearly home—what will it be to be there! It is all goodness and mercy, and will be to the end. The Lord is taking me slowly and gently, which is such a mercy for dear father's sake.'

It was several hours before her death on 30 July, 1904 that she began to have breathing difficulties, but continued to say for Hudson's benefit, 'No pain, no pain.' But as her breathing became more laboured he became distressed. She beckoned to him and whispered in his ear, 'Ask Him to take me quickly.'

Later Hudson confessed that this was one of the most difficult prayers he was ever asked to pray. He asked the Lord to 'take her from me to Himself.' Of those moments he later said: 'Never did I feel more gratitude than when my prayer...was answered within five minutes.'

The last words Jenny spoke to her husband were words of victory: 'My grace is sufficient—He will not fail.' She closed her eyes as she breathed her last and was escorted by the angels of God into the presence of the Lord Jesus who loved her and had given Himself for her.

Jenny had chosen the spot where she wanted to be buried and her body was laid to rest near the church tower of La Chiesaz at St Legier, a beautiful spot looking across Lake Geneva.

Hudson's niece, Mary Broomhall, stayed on at Pension and with her care his health recovered. Many times he visited Jenny's grave to tend the flowers which he planted.

With the company of many good friends and the letters of condolence he received concerning Jenny's death, he was cheered and his health began to improve. The peace of God flooded his heart and he began to plan a final visit to China.

52

Peace, Perfect Peace (1905)

With improving health and the assurance that his doctor son, Howard and wife Geraldine could accompany him, the decision was made for Hudson to visit China and meet the Christians who had survived the terrible months of the social and political upheaval.

Leaving England on 15 February, 1905 he arrived in Shanghai on 17 April having visited North America where he again met many people closely associated with the Mission. He then sailed across the Pacific Ocean to China, by way of Japan.

Reaching the outskirts of Shanghai stirred the old man's heart. As the boat drew near the dock he saw many old familiar sights and could smell the atmosphere of the city he had left behind many years before.

As the boat pulled into the dock he was welcomed by his many close friends. Dixon Hoste was there as Hudson had planned his arrival to be in Shanghai before Dixon left for overseas. Also waiting was John Stevenson, the one who had borne the heavy responsibilities during the Boxer rebellion days. In the crowd of well-wishers was his dear friend from Ningbo days, James Meadows.

His arrival at Wusong Road thrilled his heart for there so many people had gathered to give him a resounding welcome. The old warrior was returning to the scene of so many memories and victories under the hand of God. The China Council was meeting at that time and he found it a wonderful blessing to again sit with the spiritual giants who were responsible for the affairs of the Mission.

He thoroughly enjoyed the reunion and many photographs were taken of him surrounded by crowds of friends. His room was filled with beautiful flowers and letters and cards of welcome and thanks, for his valuable contribution in bringing the gospel to China.

He noticed many changes since he had left Shanghai. The city had been modernised and many of the Mission members now wore European clothing because in some of the coastal cities the European population was very large and for a European to dress in Chinese clothing would make him the man out of character.

Soon his journey commenced and it was off to a spot that was always precious to him—Zhenjiang; for it was there that Maria and their children had been buried. Indeed, many times he had expressed the wish that he could be buried beside Maria, to await the glorious resurrection, but it now seemed that such a wish could never be fulfilled.

He also visited Yangzhou, the scene of the 1868 riot which he still vividly remembered.

It was at Zhenjiang that he had the opportunity to speak to some young missionaries who were soon to move to the inland posts:

> You do not know what lies before you. I give you one word of advice: Walk with the Lord! Count on Him, enjoy Him...He will not disappoint you....Forty years I have made it the chief business of my life to cultivate a personal acquaintance with the Lord Jesus Christ....No (trifling) with self-indulgence or sin—and there is no reason why the Holy Spirit should not be outpoured.
>
> It is a great privilege to meet many of you here. I have met many here in days gone by. My dear wife died by me here....In spirit our loved ones may be nearer to us than we think; and HE is near, nearer than we think. The Lord Jesus will never leave nor forsake us....Do, dear friends, be true to Him and His Word.

To one young missionary he spoke before he left for Hankou: 'You may be tired and lonely often, but the Lord knows just how much each cup costs. Look to Him; He will never disappoint you.'

Hudson's days in Hankou were wonderful. There he met his old friend Griffith John who was seventy-four years old, just one year older than himself. Together they reminisced about old times and the goodness of God they had experienced every day of their lives. Together they sang beautiful hymns that magnified the grace of God and glorified the Saviour who loved them and gave Himself for them. On 29 April, seventy-eight year old William Martin arrived and the three old spiritual warriors had their photographs taken together.

The time came for Hudson to move on to Hunan, and along the way he was welcomed by many who knew him personally or had simply heard of the great Hudson Taylor. He travelled by train and this was such a comfortable trip compared to what he had experienced many years before. What once took two weeks of dangerous, rough travelling could now be done by a comfortable train journey in twenty-four hours. Often he sat at a window to wave to the people, or stand on the platform to receive their greetings. The train owners allowed him to sleep on the train which saved him a walk to the inn. On another occasion when visiting some Christians, he was obliged to spend the night at an inn and went to bed early as he was exhausted.

About midnight when everyone was asleep a voice was heard calling outside a window. When Mr Joyce looked, he discovered it was a member of his congregation. The man had heard of Hudson's presence and after work had walked from his village to meet the 'Venerable Chief Pastor'.

When Mr Joyce explained that Hudson was sound asleep and shouldn't be woken the man understood. He pushed a little bundle of paper through the window as Mr Joyce asked, 'Why, what is this?'

'Oh, nothing,' the poor man replied. 'It is only my poor little intention. It is my duty to provide for the Venerable Pastor while he is near our village.'

Having given his gift of money he disappeared into the night. Everyone was disappointed they had not been woken up to meet and thank the man, but on Sunday he came to the service and Hudson was able to thank him personally for his kind gift.

Hudson kept moving along and everywhere received a gracious welcome by the many who loved the one who had done so much to ensure the gospel was spread throughout China.

Travelling from place to place was tiring, but he enjoyed meeting the many Christians who loved him dearly. On one occasion he was welcomed with a scarlet satin banner on which was written in golden letters: 'Benefactor of Inland China...O Greatly Beloved!'

As he moved about the country his spirits were buoyed. Tired? Yes. But enjoying every meeting he attended. Chinese Christians came from far and wide to meet the great man. Some called out when they saw a copy of *Punch* in the basket of food that was provided for him,

'See, what an example to us! The venerable teacher must be at least a hundred and there he is still storing his mind with wisdom.'

Then it was back to Hankou with an extra companion—Jane af Sandeberg whom he had known when she was just a child.

On 26 May in Hankou he met his old friends once more. His dear friend Griffith John said, 'I never felt more attached to him than I did...before he started for Changsha. I was longing to see him again on his way to Shanghai and home.'

The time arrived to move on to a spot he had never before visited—Changsha. The ship on which they were to travel cheaply ran aground and the party was transferred to saloon class on the largest steamer travelling the route. As he had noticed some sweet moments between Jane and Geraldine's brother, Whitfield, who was a doctor, he invited them to come along for the ride. Two days later and still on the ship, they were engaged!

It was on 2 June that he stepped from the ship onto the soil of Hunan province for the first time where he found a flourishing congregation and was surprised to learn that one hundred and eleven missionaries from thirteen missions preached the gospel of salvation to the Chinese.

He enjoyed the sights of Changsha, particularly when he stood on the city wall and looked over the countryside. He also saw the land which had been offered to Dr Frank Keller for a new hospital.

The weather was hot and humid and he was not sleeping very well, but when invited to speak at a church gathering in the morning he was overjoyed. The days that followed were pure joy for the white-haired old man.

When it was time to leave, he refused because the boat sailed on Sunday. He would not travel on the Lord's Day, unless in exceptional circumstances!

On the Saturday evening he attended a luncheon in his honour, attended by the missionaries living in Changsha, as well as the custom house employees. Hudson appeared in a suit of Shandong silk looking his best.

A record of the events at the gathering illustrate the gracious character of the man who was being honoured:

> It was cool and pleasant in the little garden on to which the sitting-room opened, and tea was served on the lawn, surrounded by trees and flowers. Father went out and sat in the midst of the guests for an hour or more, evidently enjoying the quiet, happy time, and interested in the photographs that were being taken.

After all had left, Howard persuaded him to go upstairs....It was still evening, and while they were talking Father rose and crossed the room to fetch two fans. One of these he handed to Dr. Barrie, who exclaimed: 'Oh, why did you not let me bring them?'

'I wanted to get you one,' was the reply, in a tone which deeply touched his companion.

Speaking of the privilege of bringing everything to God in prayer, Dr Barrie said that he was sometimes hindered by the feeling that many things were too small, really, to pray about.

Father's answer was that he did not know anything about it—about such a distinction, probably. He added: 'There is nothing small, and there is nothing great: only God is great, and we should trust Him fully.'

Hudson felt tired and said he would not go down to the evening meal, but intended to rest a little. Howard came along with some supper for his father and while he went back to get something which he had forgotten Geraldine stood out on the open roof to catch a glimpse of the city in the evening light. She was talking when she noticed Hudson take a breath. She thought he was going to sneeze, but simply noticed that he took another noticeable breath.

Realizing that all was not normal and that he was unconscious at least, she called out to her husband.

Dr Keller and Howard were quickly on the scene and saw him take his last breath. 'He gave no cry and said no word. He was not choking or distressed for breath. He did not look at me or seem conscious of anything,' Geraldine wrote.

The Daily Light reading for that evening was headed by the most appropriate verse: 'And Enoch walked with God...and God took him' (Gen. 5:24). As Howard stood beside his father's dead body he thought of the words: 'My father, my father! the chariots of Israel and the horsemen thereof!'

Geraldine continued: 'And, oh, the look of rest and calm that came over the dear face was wonderful! The weight of years seemed to pass away in a few moments. The weary lines vanished. He looked like a child quietly sleeping, and the very room seemed full of unutterable peace.'

It was on 3 June, 1905 that Hudson Taylor was received into glory.

The local Chinese Christians insisted that they provide his coffin at their own expense, while those who loved him so dearly remained for a time in the room.

Again we read the words that Geraldine penned:

All the house was still, hallowed by a serenity and sweetness that hardly seemed of earth. Though he was gone, a wonderful love and tenderness seemed still to draw us to his side. Oh, the comfort of seeing him so utterly rested. Dear, dear Father, all the weariness over, all the journeyings ended—safe home, safe home at last!'

A trickle of visitors who loved the dear old man made their way to that special room. One loving woman whispered in triumph as she left the room: 'Thousands and myriads of angels have welcomed him!'

A young Chinese evangelist and his wife, who had expected to meet Hudson the next day, came to his room when they heard of his death. They had asked if they might gaze upon his loving face. Both stood quietly by his bedside and the evangelist asked, 'Do you think I might touch his hand?'

The young man gently took Hudson's hand and lovingly stroked it as he talked to his body as if he were still alive:

Dear and Venerable Pastor we truly love you. We have come today to see you. We longed to look into your face. We too are your little children. You opened for us the road, the road to heaven. You loved us and prayed for us long years. We came to-day to look upon your face.

You look so happy, so peaceful! You are smiling. Your face is quiet and pleased. You cannot speak to us tonight. We do not want to bring you back: but we will follow you. We shall come to you Dear and Venerable Pastor. You will welcome us by and by.

With the coffin prepared and Hudson's body gently laid to rest in it, the local Christians asked if he would be buried in Changsha, but Howard explained that his father had always expressed the wish, if it was possible, to be buried beside the body of Maria and his children at Zhenjiang.

The ship's captain flew the flag at half mast out of respect for Hudson and his mighty work for the church in China.

John Stevenson and Dixon Hoste came to Zhenjiang and it was Dixon who conducted the burial service. This was a service of victory in the Lord. Sorrow? Yes, but not as those who have no hope.

And as word of Hudson's death spread, memorial services were held in Shanghai, London, and many other parts of the world. However, of all that was said and done, Howard and Geraldine said: 'But the voices that linger longest are those he would have loved best—the voices of the Chinese children singing sweet hymns of praise as they laid their little offerings of flowers upon his resting place.'

Many tributes were spoken in honour of Hudson Taylor, and his friend Griffith John wrote words so true : 'Faith and prayer gave Hudson Taylor power with God....Firmness and love procured him a moral sway over the hearts of men.'

A newspaper columnist wrote: 'He had but one aim—to preach CHRIST to China by any means that came to hand....There was nothing so real to him as the individual soul, and GOD in CHRIST for its salvation.'

The words that John Bunyan put into the mouth of Mr Valiant for Truth are words that could well apply to Hudson Taylor at his death:

> Then he said, 'I am going to my Father's and tho' with great difficulties I am got hither, yet now I do not repent me of all the trouble I have been at to arrive where I am. My sword I give to him who shall succeed me in my pilgrimage, and my courage and skill to him that can get it. My marks and scars I carry with me, to be a witness for me that I have fought his battles, who now will be my rewarder'...
>
> As he went he said, 'Death, where is thy sting?'...'Grave, where is thy victory?'
>
> So he passed over, and all the trumpets sounded for him on the other side.'

"IT IS NOT DEATH TO DIE!"[12]

The story of Hudson Taylor is ended, but not the work which under God he had commenced. On that great day when we all stand before the throne of our Lord and King, Jesus Christ, it will then be revealed all that God did through that gentle man.

Endnotes

1. This act of humility involved kneeling and tapping the forehead a set number of times on the ground.
2. See Chapter 4 for outline of this incident.
3. The queue was the plaited 'pigtail'.
4. What is commonly known as a 'pig-tail' by foreigners.
5. Broomhall, A. J., Hudson Taylor and China's Open Century, Vol. 4, Hodder and Stoughton and Overseas Missionary Fellowship, London, 1984; p. 416 gives the text of the agreement.
6. William Rudland commenced the practice for which CIM missionaries became well known—the use of the wheelbarrow as a cheap means of travel.
7. Broomhall, A. J., Hudson Taylor and China's Open Century, Vol. 5, Hodder and Stoughton and Overseas Missionary Fellowship, London, 1985, p. 285.
8. Guinness, M. Geraldine, The Story of the China Inland Mission, Morgan and Scott, London, 1900, pp. 282–86.
9. For the story of the 'Cambridge Seven', see—Pollock, J. C., The Cambridge Seven, Inter-varsity Fellowship, London, p. 962.
10. It was about this time that Hudson began using a different spelling of his wife's name.
11. The Boxers were a grouping of secret organizations and the more violent members of society, formed to promote boxing and gymnastics. They believed themselves to be invincible to bullet and sword.
12. Bunyan, J., Pilgrims Progress, Banner of Truth, Great Britain, 1977, p.376.

Photographs and Maps

Bibliography

Benge, Janet and Geoff, *Hudson Taylor. Deep in the Heart of China*, YWAM Publishing, USA, 1998.

Broomhall, A. J., *Hudson Taylor & China's Open Century*, Hodder and Stoughton and The Overseas Missionary Fellowship, London. (7 volumes).

Volume 1: *Barbarians at the Gates*, 1981

Volume 2: *Over the Treaty Wall*, 1982.

Volume 3: *If I Had a Thousand Lives*, 1982.

Volume 4: *Survivors' Pact*, 1984.

Volume 5: *Refiner's Fire*, 1985.

Volume 6: *Assault on the Nile*, 1988.

Volume 7: *It is not Death to Die*, 1989.

Broomhall, Marshall, *By Love Compelled: The Call of the China Inland Mission*, Hodder and Stoughton, London, 1937.

Guinness, M. Geraldine, *The Story of the China Inland Mission*, Volumes 1, Morgan & Scott, London, 1897.

Guinness, M. Geraldine, *The Story of the China Inland Mission*, Volumes 2, Morgan & Scott, London, 1890.

Lyall, Leslie T., *A Passion for the Impossible: The China Inland Mission*: *1865–1965*, Hodder and Stoughton, Great Britain, 1965.

Pollock, J. C., *Hudson Taylor and Maria, Pioneers in China*, Christian Focus Publications, Great Britain, several printings.

Pollock, J. C., *The Cambridge Seven: A Call to Christian Service*, Inter-Varsity Fellowship, London, 1962.

Robson, W., *Griffith John: Founder of the Hankow Mission Central China*, S.W. Partridge & Co., London. (No publication date given.)

Ryle, J. C., *The Christian Leaders of the Last Century*, T. Nelson and Sons, Edinburgh and New York, 1899.

Steer, Roger, *J Hudson Taylor. A Man in Christ*, Overseas Missionary Fellowship (IHQ) Ltd., 1990 reprint.

Taylor, Dr. and Mrs Howard, *Hudson Taylor and the China Inland Mission. The Growth of a Work of God*, Overseas Missionary Fellowship International, 1996.

Taylor, Dr. and Mrs Howard, *Hudson Taylor in the Early Years. The Growth of a Soul*, Overseas Missionary Fellowship International

Persons Index

487

Subject Index

HUDSON TAYLOR & MARIA

A MATCH MADE IN HEAVEN
John Pollock

Hudson Taylor And Maria:

A match made in heaven

John Pollock

The story of Hudson Taylor is one of adventure and excitement - of improbable answers to prayer, opposition from the establishment and triumphs of faith. Even more interesting is the story of the relationship at the heart of it all - the story of Hudson and Maria Taylor.

There are few love stories as enchanting as that of Hudson Taylor the pioneering missionary, and Maria Dyer. Their relationship and short marriage flourished in the bitterest of circumstances because their lives were firmly rooted in their devotion to God, as well as each other.

They were a perfect match, (though not perfect people), a couple who show us how to share our lives at the deepest level.

John Pollock draws his material extensively from original letters and papers. What unfolds is a picture of courage and adventure in Imperial China, a lost world of pigtails, Mandarins and dragon-roofed temples. It also shows how Maria played a crucial role in shaping the ministry of a Yorkshire lad who, against oriental and western opposition, changed the way that missionaries work

John Pollock, an award-winning biographer has a flair for telling a dramatic story. He has used this talent to write many biographies including D.L. Moody and Major General Sir Henry Havelock.

ISBN 978-1-85792-223-3

PASTOR HSI

A STRUGGLE FOR CHINESE CHRISTIANITY
Geraldine Taylor

Pastor Hsi:

A Struggle for Chinese Christianity

Geraldine Taylor

Here is an amazing story about a man whose life made such a great impact for God. The Bible is filled with stories of God's work in the lives of ordinary men and women who did extraordinary things for the Lord. These stories were written not only to give us the truth but also to inspire us to trust the Lord. Pastor Hsi experienced danger, adventure, persecution and great power to heal the sick. But what marked his life the most was not the great things he did for God but his deep and profound awareness of his dependence upon God. This book will challenge you to follow the example of this man. He saw the sovereign in-breaking of God, time and time again yet did not allow it to puff him into pride or arrogance.

His simple childlike faith led him to take the New Testament at face value: he put into practise whatever he read. He fasted, he prayed, he laid hands on the sick and cast out demons.

The reality of these experiences should compel us to search our hearts again and ask if we are availing ourselves of the authority that has been given to us. If you dare to be changed read on!

The record of his devotional life, his times of prayer and fasting, his remarkable energy and force of character, his courage and determination in the face of danger and persecution is challenging and inspiring.

John J Murray, Evangelical Times

We are indebted to Overseas Missionary Fellowship for making this book available again to us. I believe the book will be a great inspiration to many believers, and will be a channel through which God will call many into missionary service.If you dare to be changed, read on!

Floyd McClung Jr,
International Director, Youth With a Mission, 1985-1992.

ISBN 978-1-85792-159-5

Three of
China's Mighty Men

Subtitle. *leaders of the Chinese church under persecution*

Subjects. Wang Ming-Dao
Watchman Nee
David Yang

Author......... *Leslie Lyall*

Three of China's Mighty Men:

Leaders of Chinese Church under persecution

Leslie Lyall

There are many heroes in the Chinese church. Today, humanly speaking, it should not exist - having been stamped out by the pressure of authorities prior to, and during, the Communist era. Yet today the church is larger than ever - and still growing.

Some of this phenomenon can be attributed to the quality of leadership in the Church. People suffered for their faith, often in brutal and cruel ways, yet God maintained their faith in remarkable ways.

Whilst there were many leaders of equally courageous stature in the church, three men have stood out in the 20th century. Wang Ming-Dao, Nee Duo-Sheng (Watchman Nee) and Yang Shao-Tang (David Yang)

Leslie Lyall knew all three as a friend, and worked with two of them. He brings out their different personalities, analyses the effect they had on the church and compares their views in some key areas. All three worked outside the 'official' church, all three knew and respected each other.

Their stories are inspiring, terrifying, solemn and joyous. They are an encouragement to us all.

ISBN 978-1-85792-493-0

A Christian's Pocket Guide to

the Chinese

A Christian's Pocket Guide
to the Chinese

From Mao to McDonalds: a nation transformed.

If you go to the Wangfujing shopping centre in Beijing then you will find it bustling with shoppers and lines with expensive stores. Taking a break from the throng you can stop for a coffee at Starbucks or have a snack at McDonalds. These are all signs of an increasing 'westernisation' in China but behind the scenes there is also a spiritual transformation taking place.

This book is designed to help you if you have regular interaction with people from China. Firstly, it gives you a brief outline of the major changes that have taken place in recent history so that you can understand their cultural background.

Secondly, it looks at Chinese students in more detail. Why are they in your schools and universities? Where in China do they come from and what difference does that make? What has changed in their attitude to study? What is their lifestyle likely to be like? What will they think of you?

Thirdly, it looks at how best to befriend Chinese people and make them welcome in your country and Fourthly, how best to engage them in discussion (including a valuable FAQ section with answers and further resources to go to) and Fifthly, how to speak on spiritual topics.

There is also an appendix with suggested further reading.

If you meet Chinese people at work, socially or in education you will find this an invaluable tool. It is also useful for those travelling to China for work or leisure.

ISBN 978-1-84550-315-4

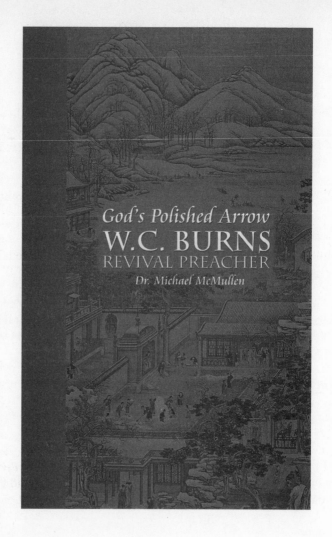

God's Polished Arrow
W.C. BURNS
REVIVAL PREACHER
Dr. Michael McMullen

God's Polished Arrow:

WC Burns; Revival Preacher

Michael McMullen

William Chalmers Burns was surrounded by revival. Not only was he used by God in Scotland, Continental Europe and North America, but he was also a pioneer missionary in China (Where he persuaded a young man called Hudson Taylor to dress in Chinese clothes). In his journals are recorded a first hand account of revival and the life of a spiritual man with an adventurous spirit - a man whose favourite books as a boy were 'The Pilgrim's Progress' and 'The Life of Sir William Wallace' (Braveheart).

'Burns was only twenty-four when he preached in Dundee for the saintly Robert Murray McCheyne and we know him best for that great flood of revival. However, Dr. Michael McMullen warmly presents the whole of this godly man's revival preaching and missionary zeal, with portions of his compelling journal, and letters and sermons never before published. God's Polished Arrow is about the sacrifices and massive affect of an eminently holy man.'

Jim Elliff,
Midwestern Center for Biblical Revival, Kansas City, Missouri

'Sometimes while reading stirring biography I wonder why I read anything else. The life of W.C. Burns falls into this category. Like David Livingstone, John Paton, and Burn's colleague in China – Hudson Taylor, he was a flint-faced pioneer. Few men have seen more of the Lord's evident blessing on their preaching than Burns. Fewer still have seen such dramatic results both in their own homeland and among previously unreached peoples. I am delighted to see Michael McMullen providing the church with a fresh reminder of what God has done – and can do – through men like W.C. Burns.'

Dr. Don Whitney, Associate Professor of Biblical Spirituality,
Southern Baptist Theological Seminary, Louisville, Kentucky

Dr. Michael McMullen is Professor of Church His.tory at Midwestern Baptist Seminary, Kansas City.

ISBN 978-1-85792-395-7

• Hudson Taylor •

AN ADVENTURE BEGINS

Catherine Mackenzie

Hudson Taylor:

An Adventure Begins

Catherine MacKenzie

Hudson Taylor was a sickly child. He was often ill and had very poor eyesight. But God chose him to evangelise the Chinese. So at the age of 21 Hudson Taylor left the United Kingdom to sail half way round the world to China. Why did he do this? He did it to tell the Chinese people about the good news of Jesus Christ and to give them a message of hope.

This story covers Hudson's childhood and traumatic teenage years as well as his life as well-known pioneer missionary. We see him in facing sickness, poverty, heartache and death and we see him trusting in God throughout.

When in China he became like the Chinese in his dress and manner, which ostracised him from the other missionaries. He did eventually find love but difficulties did not end there as Hudson and his wife Maria saw some of their own children die and then eventually Maria herself died.

This is a story of Romance and family ties but also of the amazing things that God can do through one person who is entirely given over to the cause of Christ.

Includes thinking further topics.

ISBN 978-1-85792-423-7

Christian Focus Publications

publishes books for all ages

Our mission statement –

STAYING FAITHFUL

In dependence upon God we seek to help make His infallible Word, the Bible, relevant. Our aim is to ensure that the Lord Jesus Christ is presented as the only hope to obtain forgiveness of sin, live a useful life and look forward to heaven with Him.

REACHING OUT

Christ's last command requires us to reach out to our world with His gospel. We seek to help fulfil that by publishing books that point people towards Jesus and help them develop a Christ-like maturity. We aim to equip all levels of readers for life, work, ministry and mission.

Books in our adult range are published in three imprints.

Christian Focus contains popular works including biographies, commentaries, basic doctrine and Christian living. Our children's books are also published in this imprint.

Mentor focuses on books written at a level suitable for Bible College and seminary students, pastors, and other serious readers. The imprint includes commentaries, doctrinal studies, examination of current issues and church history.

Christian Heritage contains classic writings from the past.

Christian Focus Publications Ltd
Geanies House, Fearn,
Ross-shire, IV20 1TW, Scotland, United Kingdom
info@christianfocus.com

Our titles are available from quality bookstores and
www.christianfocus.com